Claire Beaugrand is Gulf Research Fellow at the Institute of Arab and Islamic Studies, University of Exeter. She previously worked as a Gulf Senior analyst with the International Crisis Group and as a researcher at the Institut français du Proche Orient (Ifpo). She holds a PhD in International Relations from the London School of Economics (LSE).

STATELESS IN THE GULF

Migration, Nationality and Society in Kuwait

CLAIRE BEAUGRAND

I.B. TAURIS

LONDON • NEW YORK • OXFORD • NEW DELHI • SYDNEY

I.B. TAURIS
Bloomsbury Publishing Plc
50 Bedford Square, London, WC1B 3DP, UK
1385 Broadway, New York, NY 10018, USA

BLOOMSBURY, I.B. TAURIS and the I.B. Tauris logo are
trademarks of Bloomsbury Publishing Plc

First published in Great Britain 2018
Paperback edition printed 2019

A catalogue record for this book is available from the British Library.

A catalog record for this book is available from the Library of Congress.

ISBN: HB: 978-1-7807-6566-2
PB: 978-1-7883-1802-0
eISBN: 978-1-7867-2323-9
ePDF: 978-1-7867-3323-8

Series: Library of Modern Middle East Studies, volume 143

Typeset in Stone Serif by OKS Prepress Services, Chennai, India

To find out more about our authors and books visit
www.bloomsbury.com and sign up for our newsletters

To Professor Fred Halliday
To K.H.

CONTENTS

LIST OF ILLUSTRATIONS

PHOTOGRAPHS

LIST OF ABBREVIATIONS

AI	Amnesty International
AOU	Arab Open University
CCPR	International Covenant on Civil and Political Rights
CEDAW	Convention on the Elimination of All Forms of Discrimination against Women
CGH	Comoro Gulf Holding
CRC	Convention on the Rights of the Child
CSB	Central Statistical Bureau
GCC	Gulf Cooperation Council
GUST	Gulf University for Science and Technology
HRW	Human Rights Watch
ICRC	International Committee of the Red Cross
INGO	International Non-Governmental Organisation
IO	International Organisation
KADWV	Kuwaiti Association to Defend War Victims
KBA	Kuwait Bar Association
KD	Kuwaiti Dinar (KD 1 = £2 for quick calculation)
KOC	Kuwait Oil Company
KSHR	Kuwait Society for Human Rights
KU	Kuwait University
KUNA	Kuwait News Agency
LIGH	Low Income Group Housing
OHCHR	Office of the High Commissioner for Human Rights
PAHW	Public Authority for Housing Welfare

POW   Prisoner of War
UDHR   Universal Declaration of Human Rights
UNHCR   United Nations High Commissioner for Refugees

NOTE ON TRANSLITERATION

This book uses a simplified system of transliteration. It is inspired by the *International Journal of Middle Eastern Studies* and the *Encyclopaedia of Islam*.

When authors have published in English or interviewees provided me with their business cards, I have reproduced the English transliteration as it was. Exceptionally, Comorian names follow the French transliteration system.

Names of famous places (Najd), persons (Al-Saud) or current first names (Abd al-Aziz), as well as nouns naturalised into the English language (sheikhs) have not been subjected to sophisticated transliteration but have been kept consistent throughout the book.

All translations are mine.

ARABIC TRANSLITERATION TABLE

Consonants

ء	' (except at the beginning of words)
ا	a
ب	b
ت	t
ث	th
ج	j
ح	h (without diacritics)
خ	kh
د	d
ذ	dh
ر	r
ز	z
س	s
ش	sh
ص	s (without diacritics)
ض	d (without diacritics)
ط	t (without diacritics)
ظ	z (without diacritics)
ع	'
غ	gh
ف	f
ق	q
ك	k

ل	l
م	m
ن	n
ه	h
و	w
ي	y
ة	a (in construct state: at)

Short Vowels: a, u, i
Long Vowels: ى a, و u, ي i (without diacritics)
Doubled: ّي iyy, ّو uww
Diphthongs: َو aw, َي ay or ai

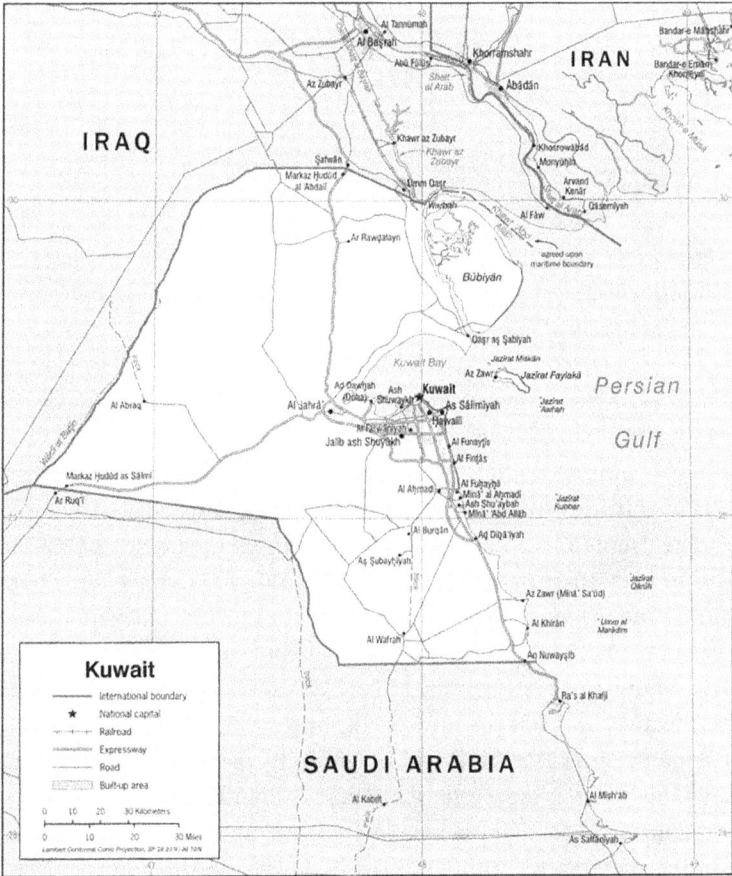

Map of Kuwait
Source: Wikimedia commons (not transliterated as per the Note on Transliteration)

FOREWORD

Alanoud Al Sharekh
Kuwaiti scholar, Research Associate at the London Middle East Institute at
SOAS University of London.

A few years ago I was asked to assist a British NGO in verifying the identity of a Kuwaiti *bidun* who was claiming asylum in the UK. I was asked to provide linguistic expertise on whether the asylum-seeker's accent was truly 'Kuwaiti', an assignment I declined.

This 'verifying of Kuwaitiness' is played out on a daily manner in the country these *bidun* – stateless individuals who have been born and reside in Kuwait and claim to be citizens of it, but who do not have the qualifying documents to prove themselves so – left behind. The argument can be made for its relevance from a security perspective, and not just in the UK. In Kuwait, many of those who work on the nationalisation issue within the government have cited ongoing security concerns with many claimants from the *bidun* community. For civil societies who have adopted the cause, the flipside of these security concerns is the permanent damage these insinuations do to the *bidun* people and the anti-*bidun* propaganda they generate. Increasingly, young activists from outside the *bidun* community [editor's note: soon followed by its members] have taken up the human rights aspect of the struggle and disregarded the 'authenticity' argument. Some of the loudest voices calling for an end to this nationality discrimination are inner district (*hadar*) youths, despite the fact that many of their political representatives have traditionally maintained the stance that nationality should be the privilege of 'real Kuwaitis'.

This brings us to the thorny question of nationality and socio-economic/ethnic identities. The story of the *bidun* population in Kuwait is one of rentier state benefits, a national identity based on ethnic cronyism, and the collapse of a functioning naturalisation system. As rentier state politics held sway over the post-independence nation state building, the granting of citizenship became more of a ruling class privilege than an induction into the role of citizen. Kuwait's peculiar classification system of nationality – first, second, stateless – has given credence to the idea that this is a class issue. In her analysis of this aspect of the struggle for nationality, Claire suggests that the *bidun*'s Bedouin origins, as nomads who were on the periphery of the modern state project, is another factor that hindered them in seeking citizenship. Her systematic breakdown of the historical and socio-political factors that contributed to the creation of these 'un-people' draws attention to the origin of the idea that they might be 'children of a lesser god' quality – a posture that the original *biduns*, the 'peripheral Bedouins' still adopt today.

There have been demographic changes to the make-up of Kuwait's national population that have resulted in an electoral base made up of over 60 per cent of tribal Kuwaitis, from mostly Bedouin origins. Some of them have elected pro-*bidun* MPs, who are accused of seeking out naturalisation for those who are related to them, or whose votes will benefit them in coming elections, and excluding *biduns* from other tribes or other networks. Some pro-*bidun* MPs have even gone as far as to fake claims that certain individuals from the *bidun* are members of their own respective tribes to increase their voter base, only to have these claims refuted and rejected through security checks, which has complicated the *bidun* issue further, and in ways that do not necessarily serve to draw further sympathy to the humanitarian aspects of the cause.

This resurgence of tribalism and Kuwaiti 'authenticity' has meant that xenophobia is on the rise even amongst the *bidun* themselves, and their resentment of others being granted citizenship is palpable. In November 2014, at a Women's Cultural and Social

Society conference on the status of national women married to non-nationals, a young *bidun* man from the 'Anaza tribe berated one of the female Kuwaiti 'Anaza attendees for marrying outside her nationality. He argued that he and those like him were more deserving of Kuwaiti nationality than the children of 'foreign men'. Ironically, the bitterness and frustration he felt were shared by the Kuwaiti women at that event more than he realised, as many of them are married to *bidun* men. Although the children of widowed or divorced Kuwaiti women married to non-nationals are legally eligible to apply for Kuwaiti citizenship, they are mostly unable to get nationality even when these conditions can be applied. This is symptomatic of the gap between existing nationality laws and their application in Kuwait and the impotence of those denied citizenship, especially with no distinct naturalisation processes or legal recourse open to them.

Lastly, the suffering of *bidun* populations is played out in similar ways in neighbouring countries. The need to rethink nationality processes is a regional issue and not an isolated Kuwaiti case. In the United Arab Emirates (UAE), stateless people were offered permanent residence if they gave up their claim to UAE citizenship and accepted Comoros citizenship instead. Qatar's constitution specifies that no more than 50 new nationalities are issued each year, which makes it nearly impossible to naturalise non-nationals, who far outnumber the Qataris as residents. Saudi Arabia has a stateless population that is much larger than Kuwait's and that has remained largely suppressed as a matter of national discussion, with the exception of sporadic coverage in some local papers. Citizenship and the mechanisms granting nationality are equally flawed in the region, and Kuwait is only exceptional in the transparency of the problem and the fierceness of the advocates who lobby for the rights of the *bidun* whose voices are silent, or silenced, elsewhere. The measures that were put in place to preserve 'national identity' and the original inhabitants of the Gulf countries may have made sense in light of the first influx of foreign workers coming into the region following the discovery of oil, but today that preservation mentality has become counter-intuitive.

Like the millions of stateless migrants seeking refuge across the globe, Arab workers from Syria and Yemen now find themselves stranded in the Gulf with no countries to which they can return: a geopolitical mess that has no fast resolution in sight. If no real naturalisation solutions are introduced for the region, they and others like them will face a similar destiny to the *bidun* who have put up with generational humiliations in their wait to become acknowledged Kuwaitis, a wait many endure for a 'dignified life' of free housing, guaranteed employment in government agencies and a quasi-democratic constitution, a nationality gamble that may or may not bear fruit after years of explicit discrimination and injustice.

ACKNOWLEDGEMENTS

This book is based on the results of a doctoral dissertation defended in January 2011, but significantly revisited and updated in the light of the post-2011 upheavals in Kuwait. *Biduns* staged their first-ever protest on 18 February 2011, less than a month after my thesis defence – a protest that marked a meaningful rupture in the political consciousness of people known for their submissive patience in the face of oppressive circumstances. Throughout this intellectual journey, I incurred many debts of gratitude.

My first thoughts go to Professor Fred Halliday, my original supervisor at the London School of Economics (LSE), who passed away on 26 April 2010, as I was still his supervisee. Early on, as I was only a master's student at the LSE, he encouraged me to strengthen my linguistic skills, which led me to study Arabic in Kuwait in 2002–3. From him I learnt to use languages, to reach out to sources and academic literature, but most importantly to reach out to people. Fred's supervision was a source of inspiration and he is present in his teachings. It is an honour to dedicate this work to him.

I would like to express my sincere gratitude to Professor Madawi Al-Rasheed, at King's College, London, and Professor Fawaz Gerges at the LSE, who took over my supervision very smoothly. Professor Al-Rasheed had faith in my topic; her anthropological expertise, which was reflected in her precision in handling fieldwork data, and her guidance in the final steps towards completion considerably benefited my research. I also would like to thank Professor Gerges for setting the highest standards in academic writing. It was a rare privilege to work with them. My thanks to Professor John Sidel and my examiners, Professors Charles Tripp and James Mayall who commented on the doctoral thesis. To all who helped me go through the painful experience of losing someone who was far more than a supervisor to me, I am very indebted.

Laurence Louër, Fatiha Dazi-Héni and Ghanim Al-Najjar encouraged me to pursue my research on the *biduns* when the project was only in its infancy. They have been a great source of inspiration.

Studying the Kuwaiti society is fascinating; but living in Kuwait on a modest budget is not easy. My fieldwork research was funded by the three-year fellowship of the CEFAS, the French Research Centre for Archaeology & Social Sciences, formerly based in Sana'a, Yemen and re-opened in Kuwait in 2015. I am grateful to friends in Kuwait who kindly hosted me and made me feel at home. I wish to thank also my Kuwaiti and Gulf friends who, through discussions and shared experiences, gave me some keys to understand the depths of their complex societies. The European Research Council funded programme, entitled 'When Authoritarianism Fails in the Arab World' (WAFAW) and headed by Dr. François Burgat funded my last fieldwork in April 2014 and provided me with a very fruitful intellectual framework. Since I met François Burgat and Laurent Bonnefoy in Yemen in 2001, their encouragements and faith in my work and abilities have been invaluable and crucial in giving me courage and determination.

My most sincere thanks go to all my interviewees, all those who helped me obtain interviews, used their networks to suggest contacts and sources and showed me remote and hidden places. I incurred among them the most irredeemable debts. I cannot say much more than that their contributions are the living substance and the priceless value of this research.

As for the written sources, I would like to thank all the team of the Information Centre at the *Al-Qabas* newspaper in Kuwait and particularly its director, Hamza Olayan. I spent weeks and months in an intellectually stimulating environment, with a quiet place to look into the archives during the day and benefiting from the passing of journalists from the entire Middle East region and Kuwaiti intellectuals when evening came.

My work has been considerably enriched through conversations and discussions with academics and researchers, but also through shared projects and conferences: Kristian Coates-Ulrichsen, Pascal Ménoret, Amélie Le Renard and Roman Stadnicki, Farah Al-Nakib, Reem Alissa, Neil Partrick, Atossa Abrahimian, Kristin Diwan, Karen Young and Filippo Dionigi, Roel Meijer and Nils Butenschøn, Engin Isin, Hélène Thiollet and Audrey Macklin. Special mention should be made of the benefits in exchanging views with Rivka Azoulay on Kuwaiti politics. Mona Kareem, whom I met when I first embarked on this project and whose rare intellectual skills flourished even quicker than this research matured, has been a constant source of inspiration and feedback. Errors are my own responsibility.

My friends — Nicolas Barotte, Denis McAuley, Peter Harling — all brought me fresh ways to look at or research the Middle East, my husband — a new way to enjoy life.

I wish to thank also my cartographer and friend, Florence Troin from the University of Tours, Sylvaine Giraud at the CEFAS for the family tree and Pat Fitzgerald for the brilliant work of copy-editing — for which ERC-WAFAW financial support was crucial. This book would not of course be published without the remarkable patience and support of my editor, Sophie Rudland, to whom I am also grateful for providing two very useful and constructive anonymous reviews.

Finally, I express my profound gratitude to my late grandmother, to my parents and my sister, who tirelessly supported me not only throughout this authoring experience but also through all the others, past and future.

PREFACE

The man seated next to me on the Qatar Airways flight from Kuwait to Doha claims he is a Bedouin. He has held as many as three passports, Kuwaiti, Saudi and Qatari. Until the Iraqi invasion of Kuwait in August 1990, he used to live in Ahmadi, the oil city in the south of Kuwait where the employees of the Kuwait Oil Company (KOC) have been accommodated since the first barrel of oil was exported in 1946. He now resides in Dammam, where Saudi oil was discovered; he lives on his state pension, after retiring early and leaving a menial job that seemed to me pretty ill-defined.

While sharing my research on the sensitive topic of the *biduns* (the disenfranchised part of the population that the State of Kuwait considers illegal but that human rights defenders regard as stateless) he enthused about the topic: he had known them well in Ahmadi, he said in a toothless smile, sitting cross-legged on his plane seat. They were part of his youth memories, part of the life on the Gulf State's margins.

I first heard of the *biduns* in 2002. I had decided to go and study Arabic in Kuwait and was discouraged from doing so by a London-based Iraqi acquaintance: 'Don't go to Kuwait, they are mean, they have *biduns*.' At the time, the word made no sense and the advice did not deter me.

During my stay at the University of Kuwait, where I studied Arabic for a year in 2002–3, the question was never raised. For sure, *bidun* students were not admitted in public higher education; the Arabian girls from the Gulf Cooperation Council (GCC)'s countries, with whom I shared accommodation in the university's womens' dormitory, had no reason to mention it either. Yet, even when I got to know the society in Kuwait better, from the intimacy of luxury Kuwaiti homes to the different styles of expatriates' or foreigners' quarters, the presence of the *biduns* remained stubbornly hidden as a societal taboo. The *biduns* were to be found somewhere in the far off periphery of the main town, or just invisible, occupying the interstices of the society itself. As I frequented literary circles, for instance, I was completely unaware that one of the writers attending the gatherings was a *bidun*. I was to discover it much later; his daughter, the little girl he introduced me to, a talented poet, would become a famous critical *bidun* voice, Mona Kareem.

I remembered the word in a rather unexpected situation and started to grasp its concrete implications a few months after my return to the United Kingdom in 2003. On a train from Kent to London, the Arabic-language book I was reading caught the attention of a fellow passenger, intrigued that I could understand it at all. As I shared my experience of learning Arabic in the small Gulf emirate, between discovery and seclusion among the female students from the Gulf countries, he recalled the country with fondness and bitterness. 'I am not quite Kuwaiti, almost one but not a full-fledged one,' he said, eventually adding, like a confession: 'No, indeed, I am a *bidun*.' Engaged in a process of claiming asylum in the United Kingdom, he would join the ranks of other refugees coming from war-torn or most destitute countries. However, he came from a peaceful, if semi-authoritarian, country boasting among the highest GDP/capita in the world around US$ 40,000 GDP/capita in 2004, according to the World Bank figures. As such, he would have a difficult case to make to justify the fear of persecution and the subsequent impossibility of going back to his country, as defined by the UN convention and protocol relating to the status of refugees.

Biduns, an Arabic expression for *bidun jinsiyya* or, literally, 'without nationality' are people who think they have or had legitimate grounds to apply for Kuwaiti nationality, while the State of Kuwait rejects this claim, treating them as illegal residents. This results in their being *de facto* stateless, as no other state will regard them as their citizens. Gulf countries are more famous for the tremendous wealth they obtain from hydrocarbons than for their refugee communities. Yet in the London suburb of Harrow, where the Kuwaiti Community Association provides assistance and advice to fellow stateless people in the asylum seeking process, 'Kuwaitis' share an office with the Somalis – who barely have a state to which to claim affiliation. How can people, ethnically and culturally extremely close to Kuwaitis – or having become so in their will to integrate – seek asylum in the United Kingdom because of their discriminated status? How can we understand the construction of the Kuwaiti national identity if, other than the sole emphasis on ethnicity, shared language or culture, we do not take into consideration the idea of class or economic standard?

At a time when transnational movements, based on religious ideology but also superimposed on centuries-old patterns of communication and tribal solidarity, put the solidity of national identities to test in Iraq and the Levant, this book enquires into the historical circumstances under which modern national identity, in particular in Kuwait, was constructed and manufactured over the previous half-century. It analyses how the economic oil revolution, tribe-based social interaction and international security threats interplayed to reshuffle the lines of personal and collective affiliation and create the situation we know now, where nationality serves as the fundamental and intangible principle of social organisation in the Gulf countries.

CHAPTER 1

From Invisibility to Stigma: Who are the *Biduns*?

Open secrets: discussable but not publishable[1]

The *biduns*, short for *bidun jinsiyya*, literally 'without nationality' in Arabic, and better translated as 'paperless people', form a group of people who claim entitlement to the Kuwaiti nationality based on the absence of other state affiliation, while the State of Kuwait considers them 'illegal residents' on its territory. Nowadays, the group is part and parcel of the sociology of Kuwaiti society. This contention between individuals and a state could remain secondary to the politics of the country if the group were not numerically significant. The number of cases in dispute represents a huge 10 per cent of the Kuwaiti national population.

The *biduns* occupy the interstices of the complex and multilayered Kuwaiti society as a ghost population. They are invisible on official lists of national states. They are also invisible to all but insiders in Kuwait as they resemble middle-class Kuwaitis, who would have accepted private jobs. So invisible are they that outsiders such as Egyptian migrants take them for Kuwaiti nationals and mistake the petty jobs they are accepting for a mark of humility of the generous people of Kuwait, while, ironically, these very menial jobs will unerringly betray them in the eyes of the nationals because, as they put it, 'no Kuwaiti will ever occupy such a position'. The *biduns* speak the same kind of dialect[2] as Kuwaitis, with occasional tribal overtones.[3] Most wear the same attire, gown and headgear, the *dishdasha*, '*iqal* and *ghutra*,[4] although this is a distinguishing privilege of Kuwaitis. They mingle with Kuwaitis of comparable social backgrounds, follow Kuwaiti politics and recall Kuwait's history of urban development, naturalisations and demographic changes. Yet they are not Kuwaitis. They are long-term residents of the emirate who came to Kuwait from neighbouring regions between the 1950s and 1980s to seize opportunities offered by the oil economy, but who have failed until now to be granted citizenship,[5] while having no other national community in the region to which they are able or willing to claim affiliation. The absence of legal clarification of the first cases, who genuinely never held a passport nor had ever recognised any state affiliation, created an incentive for foreign nationals from neighbouring countries to get rid of their identification papers in order to blend into the category, allowing them to benefit from more privileges than foreigners. The *biduns* are thus administratively foreigners but from an ethnic and cultural stock shared by nationals.

The origin of the *biduns* comes from the fact that the provisions of the 1959 Nationality Law[6] left people behind. According to the law, original Kuwaitis were those who could prove continuous residence in the emirate since 1920 – a symbolic date marking the battle of Jahra during which the Ikhwan, tribal recruits fighting non-Wahhabite infidels, who came from Najd, were repelled and a defence wall was built around the port-city. Those who could prove this continuous residence in front of the committees of nationality that operated between 1960 and 1965 stemmed mostly from the city-port of Kuwait or what the Kuwaiti sociology refers to as *hadar*. Those present in the emirate since 1945 (Arabs) or 1930 (non-Arabs) were granted nationality by naturalisation, although deprived of political rights. Naturalisation applied to foreigners but mostly to Bedouins[7] (*badu* in Arabic), who settled comparatively later than the *hadar* townspeople.

According to the official narrative, the *biduns* are latecomers who arrived in the country after the completion of the process of nationality granting in 1965. The *biduns* claim, however, that while present on the desert outskirts they failed to register with the competent committees of nationality because they were unaware of either the process or the idea of nationality altogether. Because they held some other forms of documentation attesting to their application for nationality and state services or proving their link to the country, they lived in the hope of an eventual happy solution.

Since 1986, when the highest state authorities reclassified this heteroclite group as 'illegal residents', the government has claimed that the *biduns* come from surrounding countries, attracted by oil wealth, and that they destroyed proof of their origins to fit into a genuine category whose nationality status was then in dispute – thereby acknowledging the loopholes or disputes that existed during the initial registration process and the heterogeneity of the category. This label of 'illegal' was dictated by the new strategy decided on by the State of Kuwait to get rid of this category of people without legal status which attracted new migrants from Iraq. As a matter of fact, in the midst of the first Gulf War, the group's number was growing. The underpinning rationale was to pressurise people claiming to be *biduns* through the stripping of socio-economic rights in order to make them disclose their presumed original 'passport'. From then on, the 'illegal residents' were barred from all the state-provided services they had enjoyed up to then due to their undecided status, be it employment, access to public health and schooling or legal documents of identification. This policy clearly targeted Iraqis who were coming from a country at war and who hid on the Kuwaiti margins.[8] Non-signatory to the 1951 convention relating to the Status of Refugees, Kuwait has had no policy of welcoming any asylum seekers or refugees, so that the persons fleeing conflict arrived via illegal channels. This measure grouped all the different cases of *biduns* together under a unifying label that dressed the idiosyncratic ad hoc *bidun* phenomenon in the robes of the international legality conferred to sovereign states by the international system. The 1990 Iraqi invasion provided a traumatic opportunity to further assert the alienness of the *biduns*, who were collectively portrayed as Iraqi traitors to the nation and siding with the enemy.

Although the label of 'illegal residents' seems to conflate the *biduns* with other foreigners in breach of the 1959 law on Aliens Residence, the former are distinct from just any overstaying Indian or Jordanian who would be unlikely to think of claiming entitlement to Kuwaiti nationality. First, since the early 1990s, special institutional bodies within the Ministry of the Interior deal with *bidun* files. Secondly, the history of the *biduns* is closely intertwined with that of the nascent state and part of its population. Although arguably the category entails a lot of different cases, *biduns* represent 'near foreigners' and mostly claim to come from a tribal background and in particular to belong to what is known in Kuwait as 'Northern tribes'. Northern tribes are the tribes roaming the deserts of Hamad, Hajara and the Syrian Jazira, whose territory straddled the State of Kuwait and Iraq, as opposed to Southern tribes, whose territory stretched towards the south, in the desert of Najd and Qasim in what is now Saudi Arabia. Between 1967 and 1981, the extra-legal naturalisation of tribesmen from the Southern tribes by members of the royal family willing to strengthen their voters' base nurtured the hopes of other tribesmen to be granted original Kuwaiti nationality. This was counting without the tensions that had poisoned relations between Kuwait and Iraq since the latter claimed sovereignty over the former on its independence in 1961. Third, the *biduns* have occupied a peculiar position, despised by nationals, in the nascent Kuwaiti state apparatus: they provided low-level recruits of the defence forces precisely because of the ascribed characteristics of tribesmen known for their loyalty, obedience towards their commanders and their pride in combat.

After a decade of silent repression, during the 1990s, when the state policy of rights stripping was devised to make *biduns* 'reveal their original nationality' – or seek just any other nationality, including a falsified one – *bidun* proximity in Kuwaiti society eventually led to some nationals taking up their fight in the second half of the 2000s. In February 2011, *biduns* demonstrated and started to take up their own cause, articulating a new range of arguments, emphasising their actual presence over the historical one of their ancestors, embracing their cultural differences over their forebears' insistence on emulating 'real' Kuwaitis. Yet this narrative, on exercising rights in the place one inhabits, seems at odds with other tendencies that affect nationality.

Since 2008, Kuwait and the United Arab Emirates (UAE) have been engaged in the process of purchasing nationality from the Comoros Islands and possibly other undisclosed African states to solve the decade-long presence on their territory of *biduns* without granting them access to what they see as a high-value nationality. While at the time of writing Kuwait is still reluctant, the UAE went ahead with the scheme of 'economic nationality'.[9] Both states want to avoid opening the door to naturalisation by any means – a solution that would seem obvious in immigration states and that is premised on the link between territorial residence and citizen belonging. However shocking, the chosen logic is, to borrow Noora Lori's words, a 'market solution',[10] and reflects an evolution of the concept of citizenship, based on an increased need for mobility for the global wealthier and an imperative of policing the moving poor, that both disengage territory from citizenship.

Biduns, the Gulf States, global migration and the deterritorialisation of citizenship

Addressing the question of identity via those excluded, non-citizens but also non-aliens, tells us a great deal about global migration, the concepts of nationality and citizenship, belonging and their relation to territory. The evolution of the policies implemented towards the *biduns* illustrates a broader international phenomenon with regard to the territorial understanding of citizenship. The context is one of global mobility where the sole nationality does not determine the actual possession and enactment of rights but where migration, residency status, and ethnic belonging also have an impact on the rights enjoyed in different environments. Undocumented people with nationality but no residence rights live side-by-side with First World inhabitants of large cities like London, Paris or New York;[11] jet-setting individuals purchase several nationalities in order to evade fiscal obligations or escape visa constraints,[12] mixed or mobile couples have dual nationality, depending on the diasporic policies of the states to which they relate. More than ever, people want or need to belong to places they were not assigned to by accident of birth, whether for economic, personal or political reasons, and live in places where they do not exercise their full citizenship rights or exercise a hybrid form of citizenship, partly linked to their origin country, partly to their receiving country, and acquired by virtue of residence rather than birth. The debate around granting foreigners voting rights in local elections, especially in the European Union's member states, is a case in point.

The evolution of the *bidun* issue illustrates the ebb and flow of the brief historical period that ran throughout the twentieth century and that was characterised by the territorialisation of citizenship.[13] Emerging from the necessity to regulate emigration from Europe to North American emigration countries, the principle of the exclusivity of territorial citizenship was posited in the Convention on Certain Questions Relating to the Conflict of Nationality Laws of 12 April 1930, referred to as the Hague Convention. In its preamble it established that 'it is in the general interest of the international community to secure that all its members should recognise that every person should have a nationality and should have one nationality only'.[14] This juridical framework for the principle of territorialised citizenship remained mostly untouched until the last two decades of the twentieth century. The post-colonial and post-Cold War world has generally been no different from Europe in the first half of the twentieth century, with its endeavours to build homogeneous nations that took the form either of aiming to assimilate naturalised citizens into civic nations or of population transfer in ethnic ones, and in particular in Turkey and the Balkans.

Since their inception, the states of the Arabian Peninsula have barely upheld the principle associating state territory and exclusive and homogeneous citizenries. The oil-based economy and system of rent redistribution that form the basis of the social contract have prevented them from pretending to be willing to integrate aliens who came to build the country, paid by the hydrocarbon windfalls. However, new practices and ideas have emerged that question the assumptions of a citizenship that it is territorial and exclusive of any other form of citizenship, as a form of bond to a bounded and homogenous state, and put the Gulf model of multilayered urban societies right back at the centre of the debate on deterritorialised nationality, belonging, differentiation and purchase of rights.

Three new practices can be observed, all linked to the evolution of global migration. First, the number of states tolerating expatriate dual citizenship has increased in 50 years from one third to two thirds at the global level, especially since the 1990s.[15] A migrant-sending state like Mexico that originally sought to exercise control over its diaspora by penalising the acquisition of foreign citizenship through the loss of Mexican citizenship has, since 1998, recognised dual citizenship. It even promotes the re-acquisition of Mexican citizenship for those naturalised in the US, arguing that 'mexicanidad' (the quality of being Mexican or Mexicanness) could in any case be maintained. Several other major migrant-sending countries like the Philippines or India have also changed their policy towards their diaspora and developed new statuses and institutions to take charge of their nationals abroad.[16] This institutionalisation of diasporic citizenship clearly dissociates the link between citizenship and territory, as states maintain links with their population living in a foreign country. Based on an ethnic definition of nationals abroad, it reinforces the essentialised definition of the nation, redrawing borders of belonging beyond territorial boundaries. In the Gulf countries, this translates into the fact that sending countries take greater care of their nationals employed in the oil-rich states, defending and negotiating their working rights. They even compensate for the deficiencies of host states: in August 2016, the Indian Minister of Foreign Affairs ordered the provision of humanitarian help to 100,000 Indians stranded in Kuwait and Saudi Arabia because they had not been paid by a defaulting employer.

Secondly, in immigration countries the model of integration or assimilation as a way to thwart the perceived threat of aliens inside their borders has also ceded ground to new modes of governing the increased fluidity of migration. Sealed borders and exclusive citizenship are no longer options to ensure population control and security. States rather establish profiling schemes to assess risks of illegal migration, trafficking, international crime or terrorism as they relate to different communities. Citizenship matters, but it becomes only one criterion among others to assess the risk posed by mobile individuals. The use by the Organisation of the Islamic State of citizens of targeted European countries shows the limits of sole citizenship as a benchmark of loyalty and a sign of belonging.

Finally, a third trend, which is a subset of the profiling-based approach of governance, pushes the logic of deterritorialised citizenship even further. I call it 'the commodification of nationality', referring to the practice of acquiring citizenship through economic investments for high net worth individuals (HNWI). Although this represents only a very small minority of the population, citizenship is conceived as a reward in exchange for a contribution to a given state. These contributions range from investments (in most cases) to sporting ability, entrepreneurial or artistic skills. National football teams, not just the Qatari handball team, are full of naturalised talented sportsmen. The new passport industry that markets nationality like merchandise has thus completely severed the link that equated citizenship with belonging to a place, turning it into a completely tradable commodity. From St Kitts and Nevis, Antigua and Barbuda, Grenada, the Commonwealth of Dominica, Malta, Bulgaria, Cyprus and Austria, nationality documents are for sale from $200,000 (Dominican citizenship) to millions of Euros (Austria or Malta, giving access to the precious Schengen area).

Latecomers to the international system, the Gulf States offer cases in which the conception of citizenship is certainly exclusive but has never been premised on a territorial homogeneous state. In a way, the states did not experience the phase of citizenship territorialisation. Before modern states were established in the Arabian Peninsula and nationality laws passed upon independences, affiliation to a sovereign went to local emirs as a part of a group identity. Individual identification played a role only when events involved the interface with the British Empire. Ottoman subjects from Arabia were, for instance, requested to apply for a passport in order to visit British-controlled Iran.[17] The Gulf States passed straight from a system of group-based allegiance to a sovereign, a sheikh or a tribal chief, to a nationality-based hierarchical society with little or no pretence on the part of the rentier state of population homogenising on an ethnic, let alone civic, basis. Or rather, they mixed the two approaches.

The conception of citizenship has remained linked to some form of allegiance (*tabi'iyya* in Arabic) in the Gulf monarchies. Saudi Arabia is the prime illustration: one is Saudi by virtue of following the House of Saud, whose name the country bears, rather than by virtue of any link to the land of Arabia – in which case one would be an Arabian. Dual nationality (*izdiwaj al jinsiyya*) is forbidden in all the Gulf Cooperation Council (GCC) states and campaigns occur against suspected dual nationals, usually targeting tribesmen who have a reputation of having collected passports of states whose borders cut across their tribal territories.

The development path of the six oil monarchies resulted in the mass migration of labourers at early stages of the state's independence. Colonial history accounts for the introduction of qualified oil personnel from the rest of the British Empire, and in particular the Indian subcontinent. Spontaneous migrations from the rest of the Arab world also brought large numbers of migrants to oil-rich sibling countries, especially Kuwait, the first country – the Kingdom of Saudi Arabia excepted – to be granted independence from the British in 1961. From the outset, the population was divided along nationality lines with no real vision, plan or intent to homogenise it territorially. In the British Empire, nationality was a particularly confused and hybrid matter, defined ad hoc and on a case-by-case basis;[18] various statuses coexisted in the Gulf States, with sheikhs' subjects, British protected persons and, later, nationals of newly independent states. The colonial and local rulers did control the population residing in a given emirate by sorting out issues of different ethnic or national communities. The colonial legacy and the foreign labour-based economic development combined to explain why the territorial referent has never been the main criterion for inclusion or exclusion from citizenship in the GCC countries, those countries preferring instead ethnocultural markers of identity, irrespective of the place of residence. New states focused somehow on the homogenisation of their ethnically defined nationals only, and part of this homogenisation took the shape of a selective entitlement to social welfare. In addition, the states laid heavy stress on cultural symbols that distinguished the limited local citizenry from the rest of the residents.

Gulf societies nowadays are known for their population's composition, where, apart from Saudi Arabia, foreigners represent the majority, even approaching 90 per cent (in Qatar and the UAE). The diversity of foreigners is sometimes naively mistaken for an emerging form of cosmopolitanism that transcends national boundaries. On the contrary, governance of the multicultural population is based on the control of communities hierarchised along national lines, all subject to strong state surveillance. Gulf states exert particular control on national communities whose allegiance and loyalty to a foreign state (Iran, Iraq, Syria, Yemen) or to a political faction (Lebanese Hezbollah) are considered a security threat; they also are at the forefront of new modalities of surveillance involving individual data collection (biometrics) and supplementing the citizenship criteria. In 2016, Kuwait generalised the compulsory collection of DNA information to all citizens, residents and travellers to the country, as a way to govern and securitise the population on its territory that has been, from the outset, diverse and heterogeneous.

Gulf States have found themselves at odds with the normative language of the international community that has tended to territorialise citizenship: during the second half of the twentieth century the official narrative was that foreign labour was to be temporary and ultimately replaced by nationals. The term 'immigrant' was banned from the political lexicon, pointing at the absence of political will for integration or naturalisation and the use of 'expatriate' (*wafidun*) was recommended to refer to foreigners (*ajanib*). In this context, many think that the uncertain status of the *biduns*, who are ethnically and culturally impossible to differentiate from Kuwaitis, was not properly solved to artificially inflate demographics.

In the 1990s, through the labelling of *biduns* as 'illegal migrants', the two types of migration – those from the near-periphery as opposed to the foreign manpower imported for the purpose of economic development – have been amalgamated. This measure placed Kuwait on a par with other liberal democracies that silently tolerated *de facto* statelessness or the absence of formal state protection as a residual phenomenon of migratory flows – an issue hotly debated in the literature on migration in liberal democracies[19] and that happens when migrants overstay or when a request for asylum is rejected. It also erased any kind of political agency and, by the same token, tended to differentiate the Kuwaiti situation from cases of statelessness resulting from active political decisions of rights deprivation, when the regime is held responsible and condemned.[20]

The stalemate in the decade-long conflict that has set the Kuwaiti state in opposition to its *bidun* population claiming nationality entitlement illustrates the confusion in the understanding of transnationalism,[21] which needs to be better historicised. In this conflict, the line of argument taken by the Kuwaiti authorities is borrowed from recent discourse pertaining to the regulation of global migration. Yet this official narrative clashes with an alternative one held by *bidun* individuals, based on a different reading of history. *Biduns* claim their entitlement to first degree Kuwaiti nationality on the basis of a different understanding of sovereignty and territoriality, when political power was associated with the control of inland tribes, together with the trade routes they commanded and far-flung military resources they could mobilise so that their age-old roaming patterns and seasonal *musabila* (Bedouins' seasonal visits to town markets for the sale and purchase of goods) is as good a proof as any of their presence in the North Arabian region. Moreover, their enrolment in great numbers in the country's armed forces is not so much on the basis of their readiness to serve a quite remote and abstract Kuwaiti nation as on the basis of a shared cultural understanding with the surrounding tribes of the notion of loyalty (*wala'*).[22] With the passing of time, however, the national army has come to be understood as the defender of the Kuwaiti nation to such an extent that the nationalist *topos* of people who 'died for the nation' is probably the most powerful argument when it comes to raising sympathy for the cause among Kuwaitis nowadays.

With the evolution of international politics and the new dominant narratives of increased mass migration, deterritorialised nationality in wealthy countries and what Stephen Castles calls the 'rediscovery of temporary migrant workers' programmes in democratic states',[23] nationality-based discrimination and a proclaimed rejection of integration is becoming the norm. The previously unquestioned prominence of the European model, which drew the line between nationals – inside – and foreigners – outside – by means of physical borders is being challenged in certain circumstances.

The Gulf states with large non-citizen populations inside their frontiers, [have drawn] the line by other means, which ... prefigure[s] what we all

face as part of globalization ... The rule with modern states seem
to be that the greater the degree of economic and political
interconnectedness, the greater the stress on exclusivity, often
expressed in essentialized terms of 'culture'.[24]

As shown above, the latest developments in citizenship practices
and conception resulted in dissociating nationality, residence, civil
rights, citizenship and territory. This disconnection fits far better
the situation of the Gulf countries, with their complex mix of
nationalities, different kinds of expatriates, long residents, highly
qualified Indians, Iranians or Levantine Arabs or temporary low level
labour forces. Three conceptions that generated a form of unease have
become more acceptable, explaining the unashamed option to get rid
of the *biduns* issue.

First, although still taboo, as shown by the sensitive nature of
demographic data and their government-controlled release in Qatar
and the UAE, the idea that the national population can be in a
minority on a state's territory is now widely accepted. Qatar and the
UAE have abandoned the pretence of reversing the trend to solve
their 'demographic imbalance'. Secondly, diasporic policies of state
transnationalising their control over and rekindling links with
overseas citizens, in particular in labour-sending countries like India
or the Philippines, have made the idea that national communities in
Gulf States ought to be taken care of by their state of origin more
acceptable. Finally, consumerist schemes of citizenship for sale, at
odds with the UN-endorsed conception of nationality constituted
into a human right, has worked so well that some jet-set
individuals in the Gulf thought to apply it to the lowest, stateless,
part of the society. The *bidun* issue illustrates the situation of an oil-
rentier state, Kuwait, in the midst of three processes – state building,
the evolution of practices and conceptions of citizenship, as well as
that of the normative standards in terms of nationality and
statelessness and the relaxing of the association between territory
and citizenship.

This book explores the grey area between nationals and foreigners,
insiders and outsiders, and the different shades of citizens and aliens.
To do so, it calls the idea of margins.

An approach through the margins: building a counter-narrative
In his book *Marges de la philosophie*, Jacques Derrida reflects on the concept of margins. He notes that the margin is first and foremost the limit (*peras, limes, Grenze*). Using the metaphor of a book, it posits the margin as the 'blank, virgin, empty space', 'homogenous and negative, leaving what is outside, with no mark, no opposition, no determination'.[25] The margin is thus the tool through which the self is defined. In the case of the philosophical discourse that interests Derrida, by mastering its own margins the philosophy is able to keep up the pretence of a homogenous discourse characterised by uniqueness. Likewise, the margins define the national self, presented as homogenous and unique. Secondly, the margins, for Derrida, ought to be yet another text: 'the [philosophical] written text overrun its own margin and makes its own meaning crack'.[26] From this perspective, the margins are also a place of critical vision.[27]

In what follows, my approach takes the world of margins, the frontier between inclusion and exclusion as its *privileged field of investigation* in order to analyse how the understanding of law, nationality and rights evolve and how legal and political lines are delineated and do shift.

Investigation through the margins further breaks the official narrative of homogeneous societies pacified under the wise leadership of their fatherly rulers. At a closer look, oppositions exist between nationals and foreigners but also among privileged and disenfranchised nationals. The presence of the *biduns* reveals an explosive taboo present in all the Gulf States: it is not so much the unequal wealth distribution as the sheer presence of destitution and poverty affecting the 'sons of the country'. In a sense, it would signify the failure to accomplish the paternalist vision on which the social contract is based.[28] The Kuwaiti way to thank a person for his/her invitation – *ma qasart*[29] – literally means 'you did not skimp on means (to receive me)'. Being regarded as a miser is one of the greatest disgraces. The Kuwaiti margins thus offer a renewed vision of the social reality of the emirate, multifaceted, multilayered and riddled with struggles.

The rest of this book seeks to present a counter-narrative to the Kuwaiti state narrative that has consistently vilified the *biduns* and used its access to media to defame and criminalise them but, even more, has deprived them of economic tools, estranging them in a society where economic status accounts for the major part of what nationality is. Counter-narratives are understood here in the sense defined by Madawi Al-Rasheed and Robert Vitalis[30] as 'self-conscious and compelling revisionist accounts of life' in the emirate. This study engages on 'analytical *terra incognita*'; as such it does not seek to establish a single truth but to open up a dialogue with all those, especially among the *biduns* and the Bedouins, who endeavour to produce narratives that differ from the conventional wisdom written by the state. In *Stories of Democracy*, Mary Ann Tétreault[31] discusses the Kuwaiti myths as illustrating the nationalist construction of identity. This book expands Tétreault's work by debunking the democratic myths that form the foundation of Kuwaiti nationhood and are based on the very exclusion of *biduns*. It gives voice to the stories of the excluded, who are trying to contest these national myths and to re-imagine and rewrite an alternative Kuwaiti past in which they fit better: it is against these myths that part of the *bidun* claims are made. My research recounts the other side of the *Stories*, the histories of the margins that are as real for the *biduns*: it investigates the shantytowns' peripheries where the line between citizens and non-citizens is not clear; it records the feeling of anti-Bedouin prejudice and look at how the foundational myths are challenged by those based on presence.

The approach from the margins is doubly heuristic. First, historically, the work shows that away from the port-city, where the state is being put in place, the delineation between citizens and aliens took place concretely in the desert periphery, on the Bedouin margins. According to Kuwaiti national mythology, the town dwellers and their acquaintances constituted the self-evident and clear-cut national core of Kuwait in 1920, year of an Ikhwan attack on the city launched from Najd. Those present at the time of the battle were retrospectively defined as original Kuwaitis in what resembles a claim to autochtony. Those who were not but could prove their continuous presence since 1945 for Arabs and 1930 for non-Arabs were given a second degree type of nationality by naturalisation. This included the Bedouins who were traditionally outside the walls of the port-city and had some commercial relations to it. These simple rules seemed to be fairly clear. Yet, among the Bedouins they were not, and questions of entitlement and qualifying criteria remained obscure. This was all the more the case as, for political reasons, the government naturalised (with a first degree nationality) newly arriving Bedouins from Southern tribes from the late 1960s onwards.

My historical researches suggest that the actual delineation between nationals and foreigners took place differently from the official picture, where Kuwaitiness seems defined by objective and tangible criteria of territorial belonging. The basis on which nationality was granted became unclear and the question of who is Kuwaiti and who is not emerged years later, in the blurred context of the Bedouin margins, upon which the embryonic state has had little grip. The fracture line between Kuwaiti Bedouins and non-Kuwaiti Bedouins started to develop as the abstract notion of 'nationality' turned into a concrete reality endowed with a material dimension and differentiated between those who would get state-funded housing, access to state employment and services and those who would not.

The opposition between aliens and nationals appeared at the decisive moment when the question of the integration of the Bedouin classes into the citizen body, economy and urban landscape powerfully imposed itself in the 1960s. With the collapse of the Bedouin pastoral economy linked to the internationalisation of the oil-based Kuwaiti economy, the Bedouins shifted from a sociocultural category to a destitute class. I use the Marxist concept of 'class'[32] deliberately here as it reflects the fact that they had nothing but their labour force to face the socio-economic transition. While they kept a strong cultural and symbolic capital as heirs to long and memorised lineages, their economic worth dropped to virtually nothing. For the nascent State of Kuwait, solving the question of the integration of lower classes overlapped with that of the delineation between nationals and aliens.

To sum up, the definition of the aliens occurred at two different levels: in the centre through the immigration policies and the importing of foreign labour necessary to the development of the country. People born far away – Palestinians, Yemenis or Indians, for example – clearly featured as the archetype of 'the other'. On the Bedouin margins, a process of 'othering' occurred among newcomers from the desert. The two hierarchies that were being put in place did not overlap and were governed by different types of legal provision. The integration of lower classes into the state and citizenry only concerned particular parts of Bedouin society.

Semi-settled at first, with continued links to the desert until the 1960s, the Bedouins were soon trapped in the rigid logic of salaried employment and settled in distant working-class slums. The growth of bureaucracy coupled with massive migration from the desert gave birth to a world of margins, between Bedouin tents and outright shanties, referred to as illegal settlements, which grew in isolation from the political centre where nationality matters were decided. Throughout the 1970s, the public authorities engaged in a losing battle against the spreading of informal settlements, proposing quick-fix solutions to Bedouin housing. Different state institutions operating in the desert periphery pursued contradictory policies of data gathering. This is how the engineering of administrative knowledge played a role in blurring the lines of citizenship entitlements. Population census authorities would register as 'nationals' persons whom the Committee for Illegal Dwellings in charge of resettling the shanties' inhabitants in nationality-based housing schemes would not. Despite the state's unquestionable willingness to eradicate the phenomenon in the late 1970s, slums sprang up again in the following years, further away, mixing displaced dwellers of razed shanty areas and newly-arrived shepherds and migrants in barracks that had little to do with traditional Bedouin tents.

The history of the *biduns* cannot be written without placing it back into the broader framework of the desert, constructed as a place of lawlessness and illegality – which is somehow the reality to which the official designation of the *biduns* as 'illegal residents' refers. This history results from the economic domination of the core in the desert territory and the oil it entails, its exploitation as well as the centre's relative neglect of the most remote inhabitants. The intricacy of the *bidun* issue and its sensitivity as the most inextricable and divisive political issue in Kuwait nowadays cannot be understood without retracing the history of the desert margins. Part of this history is vanishing and some is lost to the country's memory for ever: 1960s shanties have been bulldozed and the first housing specifically designed for the Bedouin's accommodation has been demolished, leaving few places of remembrance for those who claim belonging.

Secondly, the approach through the margins locates this work on a little-known country within the academic debates occurring in the field of citizenship studies. This research is based on the belief that once the positivist, legalistic approach to citizenship as a formal, legal category is posited, its boundaries cannot but be shifted through pressures coming from the margins. This book depicts the long process through which people left outside of formal existence and outside of any body politic – be it voluntarily or involuntarily – came to articulate organised grievances and claim a common identity. Focusing on the margins enables us to analyse not only the 2011 *bidun* mobilisation but also its slow genesis throughout the 2000s, when most of the fieldwork was carried out, in the light of the theoretical framework used for other struggles for rights and regularisation fought by undocumented immigrants, *sans-papiers*, clandestine workers and illegal persons in Western contexts.[33] Once the *biduns* are classified as 'illegal residents' on the Kuwaiti territory, they gradually fall out of the scope of the law. They do not properly fall into invisibility because the phenomenon had never been anything but a hidden one, confined to the distant suburbs of the city. Yet their situation then resembles that of other undocumented migrants: they are treated neither as subjects of the law nor as objects for deportation – since, to the best of my knowledge, no *bidun* has ever been deported, although some who had fled to Iraq, notably during the occupation and liberation of the country between August 1990 and February 1991, have not been allowed back. They are treated as people without presence, without existence, and '"processed" as inexistent beings'.[34]

From then on, questions posed in the different context of undocumented migrants arise: how and why do people, presented as the most destitute and vulnerable, turn to collective action and mobilise to exit their condition? As demonstrated by Siméant, 'mobilisations "of" undocumented migrants [or in the case of France that she studies, the undocumented immigrants, called *sans-papiers*] precisely, are never *uniquely* mobilisations of undocumented immigrants. They are as much the deed of populations that we could qualify as "supporters" of the movement'.[35] What is meant here is that there is no clear-cut distinction between insiders who would have an interest, as right-deprived individuals, in taking part in the movement, and 'outsiders' acting as moral or selfless supporters of the cause; there are definitely different social actors, who act for various motives and play in different registers. Part of this book will thus be devoted to the ambiguous relationship between the *biduns* and their Kuwaiti supporters. The intimate link with a segment of supporters from the Bedouin periphery reveals the embeddedness of part of the *biduns*' category within the society of nationals and, by the same token, the fact that the fracture line between nationals and aliens cuts through the thick of the family fabric. At the same time, the benevolent attitude of Kuwaiti nationals is also resented as a paternalistic and self-interested approach. I posit in what follows in the rest of the book that the very results of the Kuwaiti-led actions contributed to the questioning of the unequal relation or the relation of domination that exists between nationals and *biduns*. The Kuwaiti supporters helped decompartmentalise the claims to nationality or rights that every *bidun* nurtured on an individual basis, as a variable of their proximity to Kuwaiti citizens or loyalty and service to the state. In a sense, it created the possibility of a common identity and organised claim by cutting the vertical bond between each *bidun* and their interface with the state (be it a ministry or a family member holding nationality) and enabling an horizontal front between *biduns* themselves.

Lastly, the approach through the margins seeks to capture the forms of agency deployed by the *biduns*. In a way, this research fits into critical citizenship studies, which advocate a shift in the theoretical approach to citizenship that could accommodate the practices carried out by non-existent beings who, by virtue of their acts, constitute themselves into legal or political subjects.[36]

Although *biduns* have so far failed to reach their goal of naturalisation or obtain legality, through which they would be fully subjects of law, their actions, be they survival strategies or later mobilisations, deserve academic attention, not because *biduns* are political actors, since they are not entitled to vote, but marginally, as actors in the public debate.

What is striking is that the current debate is still overwhelmingly dominated by the dichotomies between nationals and foreigners already loaded with fixed meaning, as if 'nationality', defined from the top, has never been the object of struggle, at least at its margins. Yet, 'the meaning that we give to words, far from being neutral, often carries the vision of the winners, the point of view of those who managed to impose their vision'.[37]

This book shows how the meaning that we give to 'nationality' or national identity has been the object of struggles. The population of *biduns* was indeed constructed as a new category in the sociology of Kuwait; it was also turned into a public issue.

Who are the biduns? The construction of a new sociological category in Kuwait

Kuwait, originally the name of a port-city, is a small state of 17,820 km² located on the northern edge of the Arabian Peninsula, south of the mouth of the Shatt al Arab river. Its arid climate, with hot and long summers when the average daily temperature reaches above 40C, and colder winters, recording temperatures below zero, made it inhospitable to human habitation; yet its favourable location on the Kuwait Bay and its natural deep-water port enabled it to become an important commercial centre on the trade routes going through the Persian Gulf in the eighteenth century. Historians of Kuwait usually date the arrival of the ancestors of the present Al-Sabah dynasty to the early eighteenth century, when part of the 'Anaza tribe, the Bani 'Utub, settled on the coast.[38] From then on the history of Kuwait is linked to trade routes that stretched far away, beyond the needs of the market created by the tiny city. Commerce was composed of both seafaring and caravan trade.[39] On the one hand, the Kuwaiti boats or booms – Kuwait earned a considerable reputation for shipbuilding – captured the sea trade between Basra,

India and the Red Sea. On the other hand, Kuwait also became an important station for trade caravans to the south of Iraq, Syria and middle and eastern Arabia, witnessing great economic and trade prosperity.[40] Different populations moved to and settled in the open port-city, depending on the ill fortune of other ports or regions, as was the case, for instance, during the Persian siege of Basra (1775–9) or during the conflict between the Wahhabis and the Bani Khalid, rulers of Eastern Arabia until 1795.

The West's interest in Kuwait coincided with what is often seen as the beginning of its 'modern' history. This is when part of the current sociological divides started to take shape and crystallise. 1896 marked the ascension to the throne of Mubarak al Kabir, following the assassination of two of his brothers. Until that date, Kuwait had remained largely outside of the Ottoman sphere of influence – or that of others chiefdoms. Fearing that his opponents who had fled to Basra might seek the help of the Ottomans, Mubarak turned to the British for help. This decision eventually brought Kuwait under British protection in 1899. By allowing the latter a certain amount of money annually the agreement between the British and Sheikh Mubarak contributed to separating the ruling family (*al usra al hakima*) from the rest of the merchant class (*tujjar*), which resulted in the emergence of a political opposition in the 1920s and 1930s, led by the merchants, in spite of their former political and economic alliance with the Al-Sabah. This trend affected the sociology of Kuwait for a long time as, compared to other merchant classes in other Gulf countries, this class of merchants has maintained an important bargaining power.[41]

Until the discovery of oil in 1938, the economic prosperity of Kuwait largely depended on its access to outside markets and trade routes. At the beginning of World War I, supply lines to the Turks and their allies in Syria and the Arabian Peninsula passed through Kuwait: as a result, the British imposed a naval blockade, hoping to pressurise Sheikh Salim Al-Sabah, who was too sympathetic to the Ottomans for their taste. Likewise, in 1921, following a disagreement over the levy of taxes,[42] Abd al-Aziz Al Saud imposed a trade blockade on Kuwait that lasted until World War II. These economic sanctions impoverished the Kuwaiti population, whether nomadic or sedentary. Moreover, in addition to these blockades, two technological innovations further deteriorated the economic situation: the British protection treaty opened the Kuwait port to British steamers, which greatly affected the shipbuilding business and sea transportation by sailing ships. Secondly, cultured pearls from Japan ruined the pearling business, also hit by the Great Depression, which had rendered pearls a luxury. Before the discovery of oil, the sociological divide between the merchants and the ruling family was further aggravated by the fact that the Al-Sabah did not suffer as much as the merchants from the economic crisis as they had invested in a palm plantation in Basra – dates being a basic staple commodity that continued to be in high demand throughout the economic hardship.[43]

Parallel to the semi-capitalist mercantile system of merchants and caravans was that of Bedouin tribes (*badu*), who formed a third socioeconomic category. Bedouin noble tribes constituted 'independent camel breeding societies whose social status, power and prestige depended on their great camel herds'.[44] The tribes also wielded a great deal of military strength because of which, in the absence of territorial states, they occupied huge desert territories and controlled all caravan trade. Regarding themselves as free camel herders and raiders, they scorned other trades and valued products less by their exchange value than their use value. Finally, families of less prestigious pedigree did not belong to noble lineages but also lived in the desert, as sheepherders.

Pre-oil Kuwait' economy was characterised by the combination, certainly not separation as sometimes retrospectively constructed, of the two different systems of merchants and tribes. The exploitation and export of oil from 1946 nevertheless changed the deal. As the truck replaced the camel as the primary means of transport,[45] the number of full-time pastoralists declined and the number of sheep increased, feeding the burgeoning urban markets. Although the pre-oil systems of desert territory and caravan trade control disappeared along with the pre-oil type of seafaring, sociological categories survived after oil revenues started to accrue to the state and new modes and relations of production were established. In a new social contract, the economic aristocracy or merchant families allied with the ruling family, the direct recipient of the oil revenues, to control the new economic resource: the merchants traded their political support against considerable economic advantages in the form of trade monopolies, priority access to public tenders, guaranteed provision of subsidised energy and cheap labour.[46] The Bedouins were largely left out of this integration into the global economy, oscillating between their noble origin and their actual standing as indigent 'gypsies'.[47]

The present sociology of the Kuwaiti Emirate, partially inherited from the past, is divided between *hadar* or urban dwellers and *badu* or Bedouins, i.e. tribesmen, referring to the conceptual opposition between *hadara* (settlement or civilisation) and *badawa* (life of the countryside).

The *hadar* has come to include all the settled people of the pre-oil era, Sunnis and Shiites, whether merchants or not (craftsmen, workers, slaves ...).[48] Within the *hadar*, the Sunni merchant families, who trace their origins back to pre-oil Kuwait (i.e. prior to 1938) and even before 1920, represent an elite group: they participated in the initial power sharing with the royals, who became heads of state and government.[49] While the 1962 constitution creating a parliament enabled them to defend their interests and privileged economic position, the merchants gradually faded from the political arena. A second *hadar* group is comprised of those who strongly pushed for control of the power of the Al-Sabah, led the Arab Nationalist Movement in the 1950s onwards and succeeded in negotiating the adoption of a constitution in 1962. They represented a rising middle-class intelligentsia, still influential nowadays among what is known as the liberal ranks. The Shiites, albeit mostly *hadar*, socialise in distinct community-based institutions: historically key allies of the ruling family in its confrontation with Sunni merchant opposition, they went into opposition with the rise in the 1970s of Shiite political Islam, before siding again with the royal family from 2008 onwards in the face of the growing sectarianism affecting the country and the region.[50] Although enfranchised, the *hadar* have long struggled to keep alive these mechanisms of power sharing, against the autocratic tendencies of the royal family.[51] They fought to obtain full citizenship in terms of political and civil rights and constitute themselves into fully-fledged 'citizens' rather than mere 'subjects',[52] including women.[53]

The *badu* are latecomers to the body politic, although they now represent 60 per cent of the Kuwaiti population: while many of them were naturalised between 1965 and 1981 to form a loyal support base for the royal family in the face of *hadar* opposition, they are no longer reliable and acquiescent supporters of the regime. As of the end of the 1990s, a new generation of educated tribesmen started to raise its voice to defend the interests of its mostly civil servants and mostly tribal followers. Throughout the 2000s, yet another different generation of tribesmen, born in the 1970s and 1980s, has come to the fore in politics, denouncing the corruption of the economic and political elite. Many of them participated in the storming of Parliament in November 2011 and in the dignity marches or anti-regime protests, along with *hadar* youth, both Shiite and Sunni. The rising low- and middle-class tribal Kuwaitis largely consisting of salaried citizen-employees has turned into a significant political force in Parliament. Along with the numerical prominence of the *badu*, their tangible rise, not only in politics but also in a few other positions otherwise reserved for *hadar*, has created some class tensions expressed in identity terms between the *hadar* and the Bedouins (*badu*).

Under present circumstances, when all are living a settled life, the historical-cultural origin of the *hadar/badu* distinction does not help to grasp its revival and persistence.[54] The ongoing *hadar* criticism of the *badu* is much more 'an expression of anti-immigration feelings'.[55] In Kuwait, as in other countries, the welfare state system engenders processes of ethnicisation and the rise of ethnopolitics, whereby entitlement is based on some form of recognisable ethnic belonging. This process of ethnicisation mainly took place between the 1950s and the 1980s, when state-building strategies gave differentiated access to citizenship and housing schemes. This contributed to fix *hadar* and *badu* as 'not only socially distinct but also geographically bounded groups',[56] as integration mechanisms and social mobility within the national body were lacking. While the *hadar*'s housing and role remained central, the *badu* were relegated to the periphery of the city, both politically and geographically, and at the bottom of the Kuwaiti leaders' concerns. As a result, 'the lived realities of these incoherent policies' explain 'how the *badu* shifted from being the rulers' main loyalty base in the early oil decades to becoming their primary opposition today'.[57]

This research on the *biduns* concentrates on this latter part of Kuwait, the realm of the 'Bedouin margins', where things have been ordered top-down, imposed upon people with no or little means to utter their opinion. It belongs to a new generation of research that seeks to enter into the study of Gulf societies through the eyes of those excluded. The dichotomy between aliens and citizens is, of course, the most prominent one in Gulf societies, as those excluded are the foreigners *par excellence*. The structural presence of the migration population in a nationality-based hierarchical society, which Anh Nga Longva[58] compares to a colonial 'plural society' where people only have social interactions in the market place for commercial transaction, functions as a contra-distinction for the nationals. Yet this foundational segregation obscures other processes of exclusion that are even more taboo to Gulf rulers because they affect their citizen body. The nationals, however small their number, have often been seen as a monolithic or homogeneous bloc, more difficult to break into – apart from the case of the Shiite communities, which have attracted so much scholarly attention,[59] or the case of women.[60] Investigations of the margins among nationals themselves are difficult to undertake as these margins are often made up of unorganised groups who resort to scattered acts of discreet but profound subversion.[61] For instance, young male Saudi relegated to the outskirts of the capital of the petro-kingdom as the city sprawled have turned the practice of *tafhit* (joyriding or drifting) into a subculture expressing political, economic and social frustrations, which is a form of resistance in its own right.[62] Not only do joyriders challenge law and order but they also 'poke fun at and play with the two roots of the Saudi legitimacy: real estate and consumer-goods distribution'.[63] Likewise, the presence of the *biduns* is a testimony to the term Farah Al-Nakib coined as 'incoherent policies' towards them and a form of resistance to the solidified, rigid and closed defined national identity.

The *hadar* depiction of *badu* as desert populations who settled in urban areas comparatively later than they did, or worse, after the exploitation of oil in order to benefit from its windfalls, illustrates a first level in the time-tested process of delegitimising people on the basis of their origin – a phenomenon widely observed in other welfare states in Europe. Yet the Bedouin category itself is not monolithic: it also refers to a complex social universe of chronologically differentiated stories of integration within the Kuwaiti polity, with tribes from Saudi Arabia being naturalised for political purposes. Those among the Bedouins who arrived last, and indeed too late, through various unofficial channels before, or at the same time as, the administrative system of foreign migration control using Western technology to record migrations have been quietly kept outside any prospect of integration and form the subject of this book.

The existence of *biduns* draws our attention to two parallel phenomena at work in the constitution of Kuwaiti national identity. On the one hand, international migration from Asia and other Middle Eastern countries was based on a pre-existing national affiliation and sense of belonging, which precluded any feeling of entitlement to Gulf nationality. The case of the Palestinians in Kuwait illustrates the fact that migrants who came with a constituted national identity or nationalist consciousness did not claim nationality: the Palestinians were never included among the *biduns*. On the contrary, in the official censuses they were lumped together with those who possessed a nationality and considered as 'Arabs belonging to Arab states',[64] whatever their initial status and their *de jure* statelessness.[65] The migrants incontestably represented foreigners, noncitizens excluded from the welfare state privileges and national identity.

Yet, the second, often overlooked, type of migration concerns movement across borders at the periphery of the country and raises a core question as to the delineation of privilege holders. This type of migration triggered by the discrepancies between national incomes among GCC countries (referring here particularly to Saudi Arabia) constitutes one of the causes of the prejudice against *badu*.[66] It is also where to locate the prejudices against *bidun*, seen as greedy, profiteers and spongers, in the difference in revenues with neighbouring countries, even though in the confines of the desert all the Bedouins excluded from the economic prosperity shared the same miserable standard of living. The process of othering thus did not affect the migrants who came from further away as much as those who crossed the border from the near-periphery, whether they were Arabs or not.

Variations in denominations and the manufacturing of aliens

The denomination of *bidun* is itself problematic.[67] The numerous changes of denomination reflect various attempts by those in power to engineer and order an existing complex social reality of differentiated integration to fit into rigid rationalised and 'legible' administrative categories[68] congruent with international laws and their normative underpinnings.

The word *bidun* is a vernacular term that appeared in the 1970s to refer to a person with no nationality but also implicitly, *biduns* insist, from Kuwaiti stock, though from the desert. At first, the category was subsumed under the common sociological expressions 'sons of the desert' or 'dwellers of the Kuwait desert' (*abna' al badiya* or *badiyat al Kuwait*) and indistinct from them. The members of tribes represented *de facto* a special legal category with regard to the Kuwaiti migration system: they were exempted from the requirements of the Law 17 of 1959 on the Residence of Aliens[69] that imposed the requirement for a visa and a residence permit on foreigners entering the country. Unlike foreigners, they could travel freely and move across the borders at will.

The 1959 Law 15 on Nationality had tangible effects when, in 1965, the committees that decided on matters concerning the granting of nationality completed their work. From then on, a new legal category emerged but in the negative, its main characteristic first being 'non-Kuwaiti' (*ghayr Kuwaiti*), that is, not eligible to the entitlements linked to nationality. For the Bedouins, this mainly meant at the time being excluded from the government housing facilities. In the 1980s, some other terms, such as 'of undetermined nationality' (*ghayr muhaddidu al jinsiyya*) or 'of unknown identity' (*majhul al huwwiyya*) appeared, alongside 'non-Kuwaiti.' Yet these categories made little juridical sense and were still defined negatively by what their members did not possess – the Kuwaiti nationality or some other attribute that had been determined. Further distinctions were drawn according to the type of written identification document that individuals possessed. In his doctoral thesis written in 1989, Mohammed Al-Fahed, for instance, used the expression 'non-Kuwaiti birth certificate holders':

> Kuwait, being a small country, fervently attempted to contain its social parameters by politically differentiation [sic] almost from its onset native Kuwaitis from others who were later absorbed into the community in the capacity of either non-Kuwaiti birth certificate holders or foreigners.[70]

Confusion definitely surrounded the positive characteristics attached to this category of 'non-Kuwaitis' as distinct from 'foreigners'. Al-Fahed, who clearly identified it as a third category, wrote: 'most [of the policemen] are birth certificate holders, which is a secondary-type citizenship'.[71] This 'secondary-type' of citizenship refers to a set of tacit benefits linked to employment, including housing rental and access to education for 'non-Kuwaiti' children, but not to nationality.

These advantages relied less on a legal basis than on an informal patronage link with the oil company, and later on, most importantly the state-employer and its growing institutions and ministries. 'Patronage' here is defined, in the sense developed by Noiriel, as a mode of domination by which the enterprise, here the civil service (including armed forces), uses pre-existing understanding of social relationships to its own benefit.[72] In our case, the link between the *biduns* and the state is based on tribal 'dispositions' towards loyalty, abiding by traditional hierarchical arrangements and showing little interest in material conditions as long as personal honour is safeguarded – dispositions that were bent and adapted to the needs of the new oil industry and public sector work. The patronage relation is a form of soft transition from a type of pastoral/commercial activity to one requiring regular presence and submission to a new 'master', whose soft character can be explained by the structural lack of (indigenous) personnel that prevents enrolment for work being effected by force. As a result, the relationship is marked by the fact that the action of the state employer is considered natural or legitimate by the tribesmen employees, as the former's authority is anchored in inherited modes of domination that prevail in the tribal societies. This explains the absence of direct contestation, never reaching the level of political grievances.

This peculiar link between *biduns* and the state was dissolved at the end of the 1980s when *biduns* were re-aligned with the labour-salary relations that characterise other foreigners. *Biduns* lost advantages that had been based on their employment relation to the state rather than their legal relation.

Following the 1991 liberation of Kuwait, the *biduns* were officially relabelled 'illegal migrants', or *muqimun bi surat ghayr qanuniyya*, residing in the emirate in contravention to the Law 17 of 1959 on the Residence of Aliens since 1986 when their exemption from the requirements, in terms of compulsory visa and residency permits, prescribed by the Law 17 was nullified. Though finding themselves in a similar situation with regard to the letter of Law 17, the *biduns* have little in common with other labour migrants overstaying for some years. The latter came through a system of recorded work permits that registers a country of origin to which they can be deported,[73] and since 1975, through the sponsorship system, making the presence of any foreign worker dependent on a work contract linking them to a Kuwaiti national or institution.

Since then, the government has referred to the *biduns* as 'illegal residents' and insisted on this denomination. The name of the category remains the object of struggle: while the majority of *biduns* reject the label, there is a debate between pro-*bidun* activists around the question of their status and their recognition as 'stateless people' (*'adimun al jinsiyya*). Some Kuwaiti human rights activists fight for their recognition as 'stateless people', which would force international obligations on the State of Kuwait. Although, Kuwait like the other GCC countries and any other states where situations of protracted statelessness are to be found,[74] has failed to sign either the 1954 Convention relating to the Status of Stateless People or the 1961 Convention on the Reduction of Statelessness,[75] a number of other covenants and conventions have opened the door to the UN Commission for Human Rights for international scrutiny in Kuwait.[76] *Bidun*-run movements consider themselves as Kuwaiti, at least in cultural terms and insist on being called 'Kuwaiti *biduns*'; they distrust an internationally-recognised status that could acknowledge the possibility that they are not intimately linked to the Kuwaiti emirate and that casts doubt on their Kuwaitiness.

Though acknowledging the shortcomings of this elusive category, I have opted for the term *bidun* for two main reasons: it is under this generic name that the evolving 50-year-old phenomenon of this in-between legal situation has come to be known. It has even been re-used in other GCC countries where indigenous or long-term residents were excluded from the body politic.[77] Secondly, and most importantly, it is the name used by the actors themselves. While the government insists on calling them 'illegal residents' and refuses to acknowledge any other denomination, deviating from its legal interpretation, the rest of the society has kept on using a name that has become part of the common lexicon. *Bidun* was originally a non-identity, an administrative identity attributed to people as a result of state policies: in spite of some broadly attested characteristics such as their overwhelming presence in the military, the *biduns'* situations present a great variety in legal or socio-economic terms, networks and rights enjoyed. This explains why it took so long for the group to forge a common identity: some have Kuwaiti relatives; some boast years of service for the Kuwaiti state; some claim that they refused a second degree of citizenship; all hold various documents of identification. When I first started my fieldwork, *bidun* was seen as a derogatory term.[78] Yet despite the variety of cases that made nearly every *bidun* hope that the solution would come from their patron or employer, and deliberate divide and rule strategies, years of discriminatory policies have contributed to fashioning the group into an almost consistent one. Kuwaiti activist movements have contributed to decompartmentalising the *biduns*, and some new youth *bidun* activists now claim that they are fighting on behalf of the entire group.

This book enquires not so much into the composition of the *bidun* category but into the process of social categorisation. Parallel with the process of segregation based on the international system of migration organised along nationality lines there has been a process of manufacturing *others*, on the basis of tribal belonging and class but also as a result of international factors.

The rentier state theory has proved useful to explain the stability of Gulf authoritarian regimes and make sense of the exclusive nature of their citizenry.[79] Defined by Beblawi and Luciani[80] as states deriving their revenues from external resources rather than taxation, rentier states buy their citizens' acquiescence through the provision of cradle-to-grave welfare services, highly subsidised energy, water, housing and employment in the public sector. In this context, the redistribution of oil revenues endowed nationality with 'a real economic worth'.[81] This redistributive system creates a double Malthusian incentive to limit the size of the citizenry.

First, on the part of the citizens, the insiders associate the inclusion of newcomers in the polity with a real or perceived reduction of their socio-economic benefits. As noted by Longva,[82] this is not peculiar to either the rentier or the Gulf State. It is a common nationalist reflex even in less generous production states where migrants are blamed for 'stealing jobs' and 'taking advantage of state allowances' at the expense of nationals, especially at times of economic recession. Secondly, since welfare provision, the main mechanism through which political dissent is controlled, is a burden on the state's budget, the rentier states have an interest in keeping the citizenry at a manageable size.

Kuwait is nevertheless a special case with regard to nationality matters because of its peculiar history and the immediate claim on the country by Iraq upon its independence in 1961, which ended up endowing it with a constitution and then a parliament.[83] The Kuwaiti parliamentary experience had complex effects on the control over citizenry. On the one hand, it reinforced the tendency of the enfranchised citizens to vote according to their interest, and this interest implies not to share the economic pie with excluded groups. Moreover, when citizens in control of politics have a say in the enfranchisement of other groups, their view tends also to be restrictive, as was exemplified by the MPs' opposition to the government's bill to grant women political rights (until it was passed on 16 May 2005).

On the other hand, the Kuwaiti parliamentary Constitution of 1962 played a role in the politicisation of citizenship and naturalisation: the royal family saw in democratic elections a risk to the extent of its power being reduced. It sought to mitigate the risk by keeping control over political participation – either enlarging or restricting the size of the citizen base. This strategy is further complicated by the need, by competing sheikh contenders for the position of crown prince, to secure support in Parliament, according to article 4 of the constitution.[84] Between 1967 and 1981, the regime sought to broaden its support base by enfranchising Saudi tribes in an extra-legal way (granting them first-degree nationality with political rights).

This is currently seen as the cause of the political deadlock in Kuwait, since the middle class of state employees coming from the enfranchised tribes is now demanding a greater share of the state income. Part of the *hadar* response has been to delegitimise these claims by pointing to the original dual nationality (*izdiwaj al jinsiyya*), hence the disloyalty of their authors. Over the summer of 2014, in a rare decree of denaturalisation and a clear sign to restive tribes, the government stripped not only prominent opposition figures of their citizenship for undermining state security but also Bedouins from the Saudi transnational tribes of Mutran and Shammar suspected of forgery in the naturalisation process (*tazwir al tajnis*). This precedent of loyal tribal constituencies turned into opposition is another factor explaining the obstacles to the naturalisation of the *biduns*, and all the more so as the *biduns* have come to see the tribal opposition as their most natural ally.

Beside the domestic factors, this research also highlights the role played by the international context in manufacturing aliens in Kuwait. Invisible at first in the public space, the *biduns* have been referred to using the lexicon of tribes (Northern tribes), then sect, as 'Shiites', in the 1980s and later 'Iraqis' (1990s), following the trauma of the Iraqi invasion. Throughout time, the category has been presented as embodying the outermost enemy or, in other words, the perceived main security risk. Yet, to be sure, none of the three big Gulf States – Iran, Iraq or Saudi Arabia – ever sought to use their nomads[85] or citizens to influence or justify any irredentist claim on Kuwait.[86]

The international factor has played a double role of invisibilising the *biduns* as much as stigmatising them. A latecomer to the international stage, constrained by difficulties in being recognised by Iraq and the USSR, Kuwait has been trying to send signs of legitimacy to the international community on which its recognition and survival depended.

It did so when, in the face of the Iraqi external threat, it adopted a constitution.[87] It also sent a signal to the international community by hiding its demographic imbalance, underplaying the fact that, due to ultra-restricted citizenry, the national population was a minority in the country. Counted as nationals in the official population census, transnational Bedouins masked the tiny proportion of Kuwaitis in their own country, an original embarrassment also exemplified in the tenacious discourse on the temporary character of its migrant majority until the national population takes over – that is dictated by the norms set by the 'nationalist' ideology.

International crises, nevertheless, marked important steps in the construction of a discourse of stigmatisation and a gradual shift in the opposition of 'us' vs 'them'. The exclusion of aliens, through the claiming of an autochthonous superiority over others, has a history that stretches into antiquity. What interests us is the form that the us/them schism takes. The decisive moment here took place when the opposition between nationals and foreigners replaced the difference between Northern and Southern tribes.

The international factor undeniably played a role in shaping a political discourse justifying discrimination and stigmatisation on the basis of the presumed Shiite sect and then ascribed nationality. The situation of the *biduns* may have continued to be an invisible domestic matter, as is still more or less the case in certain Gulf States,[88] had Kuwait not faced major international crises, in particular with its northern Iraqi neighbour.

The eight-year first Gulf War waged at the door of Kuwait, who sided with Iraq, caught the emirate up in the regional turmoil with its many refugees, but also because of infiltration.[89] Compounded with the economic crisis triggered by the drop in oil prices, these security concerns led Kuwait to exercise a tighter control on the populations and territory denominated as its own. The regime sought to redress the implications of decades of loose border control when borders were conceived as 'horizons' rather than 'fences', that led new migrants and refugees to exploit the legal loophole of the undefined *bidun* status. While the official policy of pressurising the *biduns* almost certainly worked to force out some imposters and deter other Iraqis and Saudis from trying to claim the category and its privileges, after some time it forced, in effect, the entire *bidun* population to drop its claims on Kuwaiti citizenship, by a systematic deprivation of rights and delegitimising of its narratives.

The 1990 invasion of Kuwait constituted the second step in the process of stigmatising the *biduns*: since most of the foot soldiers and lower grades of the army consisted of *biduns*, the category as a whole was portrayed as largely responsible for the humiliating defeat. It took less than three hours for the Iraqi troops to cross the northern border and reach Kuwait City. Moreover, since the *biduns* had come, at various times, mostly from transnational northern tribes, they were officially labelled as illegal residents and unofficially referred to as Iraqis not only in the wider public debate but also in the administrative procedures, with *biduns* identity papers pre-completed with the phrase 'from Iraqi origin'. Considering the trauma that the Iraqi invasion constituted for the Kuwaitis, conflating *biduns* with Iraqis contributed to their dramatic estrangement from the rest of the society. The presence of *biduns* became the 'problem of *biduns*' (*qadiyya al bidun*).

The elusive question of figures

As a matter of fact, the category of *biduns* has been evolving over time, from an unsettled legal category to a separate administrative one in between aliens and nationals. Likewise, the numbers have fluctuated with some naturalisations in the 1970s and departures of *biduns* who left the country to seek asylum in the West as early as the 1980s,[90] while at the same time, refugees and migrants from other countries slipped in the category, as denounced by the Kuwaiti authorities.

From the outset, the collection of reliable data and figures is a difficult task for two mutually reinforcing reasons. The first has to do with the nature of the subject investigated, namely unrecorded migration. As the name suggests, the mere fact that the entries are defined as unrecorded contradicts the idea of an easy count. This is certainly not peculiar to Kuwait or the region; we do not need to go very far to find controversy over the reliability of government figures regarding illegal immigration, and the extent to which its estimates are politically biased and their disclosure deliberately hampered.

It is a recurrent debate in British politics too,[91] and the subject of investigation in migration studies.

Secondly, if not peculiar to the region, this lack of reliable data on a subject with such potential for political manipulation is nevertheless all the more difficult to get around in Kuwait where absences of Parliament impaired accountability. Questions on the reliability of such figures are compounded, at least in the first post-independence decades, by widespread illiteracy, the lack of administrative structure or its dysfunctioning and the social and cultural norms of the region, whose people are unfamiliar with data collection on private matters.[92]

TABLE 1.1   NUMBER AND PROPORTION OF *BIDUNS* IN KUWAIT'S POPULATION, 1957–2013

	Biduns	Kuwaitis	Total	% Kuwaitis in total	% *Biduns* in Kuwaitis	% *Biduns* in total
1957	113,622		206,473	55		
1961	161,909		321,621	50		
1965	51,266	168,793	467,339	36	30	11
1970	347,396		738,662	47	–	–
1975	164,333	307,755	994,837	30	53	16
1980	178,918	386,695	1,357,952	28	46	13
1985	210,815	470,473	1,697,301	27	44	12
1989*	250,651	545,738	2,040,961	27	46	12
	121,421				18	7
1995	*135,000*	653,616	1,575,570	41	*20*	*8*
	*275,000***				*42*	*17*
2000	119,000	831,631	2,189,668	37	14	5
2005	–	860,324	2,193,651	39	–	–
2010	105,702	1,056,900	2,672,926	39	10	4
	*212,421****				20	8
2014	–	1,191,234	3,767,415	31	–	–

Estimates are in italic.

    *   Until the statistical year 1989, the number of *biduns* was included in the total number of Kuwaiti citizens in official population statistics. After 1989, *biduns* numbers are estimates[93] or drawn from the official booklet, *Central System to Resolve Illegal Residents' Status*.[94]

    **   The three figures provided in 1995 correspond to: 1) the number of *biduns* registered with the Central Committee; 2) Human Rights Watch (HRW) report's estimates of *biduns* still in Kuwait calculated on the basis of the 1993 number given to the National Assembly by the Minister of Interior using the

TABLE 1.1 *CONTINUED*

growth rate of 3.79 per cent. The report mentions that the experts' estimates are 180,000, that is 27 per cent of the Kuwaiti population; 3) the official estimate of the Central System based on the number of *biduns* before the invasion, and calculated with natural growth rate. As for HRW, it estimates that with the same growth rate of 3.79 per cent, and based on pre-invasion numbers, the total number of *biduns* (including those outside Kuwait) would be 315,948 (48 per cent of the native population).

*** The second number in 2010 corresponds to the same calculation as 3) above.

Sources: Until 1989: Central Statistical Bureau, Ministry of Planning, State of Kuwait, *Annual Statistical Abstract* in 25 years, 1990, Table 4, p. 22;[95] Nasra M. Shah, 'Kuwait revised labor laws: implications for national and foreign workers', *Asian and Pacific Migration Journal* 20/3–4 (2011), pp. 339–63, p. 340.

After 1989 (Kuwaitis and total data): Central Statistical Bureau, Ministry of Planning, State of Kuwait, *Annual Statistical Abstract*, 2000, 2010 and 2014.[96]

For the year 1989 (all figures) and for *biduns'* estimates (after 1989), HRW report, 1995[97] and the Central System to Resolve Illegal Residents' Status.[98]

The question of the figures requires further explanation as there exist some landmarks in the chronology when the number has been ascertained. Until the statistical year 1989, the annual statistical abstracts, the authoritative statistics issued yearly by the Ministry of Planning Central Statistical Bureau (CSB),[99] counted the *biduns* as Kuwaiti nationals. In 1989, three years after the 1986 decree classifying *biduns* as illegal residents, the CSB retrospectively issued new statistics covering the years from 1965 to 1985, subtracting the *biduns* from the number of citizens and adding them to the non-Kuwaiti population. The date of 1965 corresponds to the end of the nationality committees attributing Kuwaiti nationality according to the 1959 Nationality Law. The difference between the pre- and post-1989 censuses gives us the estimated number of *biduns* until mid-1989.

The numbers given by the CSB are corroborated by those provided by the Ministry of the Interior in response to several parliamentary questions that emerged after the re-instalment of parliamentary life in 1981 – at a time when the *bidun* number was still included in the total number of Kuwaitis.[100] The Minister of the Interior quoted an estimate of 200,000 in response to MPs queries in 1984 and 1985.[101] Moreover, several times in 1983 and 1984 the Ministry of the Interior, headed by Sheikh Nawaf al-Ahmad, released the figures of 72,259 heads of households who registered for naturalisation during the legal period in which to do so, between 21 December 1980 and 21 December 1981.[102]

A remark ought to be made here: the figures refer to a population that did not knowingly enter the country in an illegal manner but whose names were clearly registered as applicants to Kuwaiti nationality.

The invasion of Kuwait represents a second important step in the calculation of *bidun* numbers. After 1989 the number of *biduns* being added to the category of 'Arabs' in the official statistics is inferred, using a natural growth rate ranging between 3.5 per cent and 3.79 per cent (that of the native population).[103] The invasion led to a drastic drop in numbers as many people fled through the only open border to Iraq and were not allowed back after the liberation of the country. From an estimated peak of 260,000 *biduns* before the invasion,[104] the number was estimated at 122,000 who remained in 1995, after the Iraqi invasion. The fate of the 140,000 *biduns* who went to Iraq is undocumented.

After liberation, the government became less forthcoming with estimates of the number of *biduns* still living in Kuwait. The figures were obtained through the data provided further to parliamentary questions[105] (and growth rate-based calculations) and via the figures provided, in retrospect, by the Central System to Resolve Illegal Residents' Status. Created in 2010, this institution succeeded two others mandated with following the *biduns* files: yet contrary to those two, the Central System has a Department of Public Relations and Media in charge of releasing facts and data. Presumably, the core aim of the figures released by the Central System is to illustrate the gradual decrease in the number of *biduns* as a result of their recovering their original nationality. This is why the data released present different envisioned scenarios as a sort of control variable against which to assess progress made in reducing the number of *biduns*. This enabled the Central System to highlight the fact that in 1995 154,000 *biduns* did not return to Kuwait as a sign that they stayed in their original country. Secondly, from 1995 till 2010, the discrepancy between the figure based on the growth rate calculation and the actual number of registered cases amounts to 106,769 'who did not come back'. This last expression is unclear, it certainly includes the 64,915 who 'since liberation showed their original nationality or corrected their status'[106] – among whom some took up falsified nationality which, upon expiration of their identification papers, does not ultimately resolve their situation. However, it also means that some *biduns* may not have registered with the newly established institution.

As a result, the official numbers of *biduns* since liberation given above should be seen at best as conservative estimates and, as such, further discussed. The US Department of State *Human Rights Report* of 2013 stated:

> Although the exact number of Bidoon residents was unknown, in November the minister of interior reported to the National Assembly that there were more than 111,000 Bidoon in the country. The UNHCR estimated that the total Bidoon population was between 93,000 and 120,000, while NGOs such as Refugees International estimated the total to be as high as 140,000.[107]

Likewise, according to Human Rights Watch, 'some Bidun activists say that the real number of Bidun in Kuwait is closer to 240,000, reflecting the government's failure to update its statistics'.[108] This latest figure has emerged recently among *bidun* activists based on the facts that, in addition to the above-mentioned failure to register with the Central System or the resort to fake nationality, many children of *biduns*, lacking proper birth certificates, do not appear in the statistics.

As for the composition of the category – itself evolving over time, it is impossible to describe it with any kind of certainty: the sole agencies authorised to release data on the *biduns*, the Central System, the Ministry of the Interior and the Ministry of Planning, have provided no information as for the gender ratio, sectarian or (presumed) origin of the *biduns*. The tenacious rumour about the *biduns* has been that they are Shiite in majority but no figure was ever released to support this claim. What is sure though is that the *biduns* stem from tribes mixed from a sectarian point of view. The Central System nevertheless releases the nationality of the *biduns* who recovered another nationality since 1986. The overwhelming majority of Saudis is striking, although no conclusion can be ascertained as for whether this reflects the composition of the *bidun* category.

TABLE 1.2   NATIONALITIES RECOVERED BY *BIDUNS* SINCE 1986

Nationalities	Numbers	%
Saudi	59,079	67.3
Iraqi	11,998	13.7
Syrian	7,899	9
Iranian	1,896	2.2
Jordanian	550	0.6
Yemeni	480	0.5
Other	5,896	6.7
Total	87,798	100

Source: Central System to Resolve Illegal Residents' Status, *Illegal Residents: Facts and Data (2013)*.

METHODOLOGY

Researching such a taboo, politicised and elusive topic has not been an easy process. This research is based on two types of source gathered during two different periods of field investigations, before (in 2006–8) and after the 2011 Arab uprising that affected Kuwait through its own dynamics (in 2014). Fieldwork data were collected between November 2006 and May 2008, and completed by a second trip carried out during a fortnight at the end of April 2014.

The first type of source is a historical, written one, and consists of press archives held at the Information Centre of *Al-Qabas* newspaper in Keifan, which has kept thematic files of articles drawn from the entire press spectrum.[109] Three press archive files are devoted to the broad topic of nationality issues (law, naturalisation and revoking) and the question of the *biduns*.[110] The articles consulted can be said to reflect a certain plurality of views at the time; this is a reasonable assumption since the newspapers were owned by members of the urban elite, but with different stances towards the government's politics in general and in particular on the question of Bedouins and naturalisation. For instance, rumours linked the ownership of *Al-Siyasa* to Jabir al-Ali Al-Sabah, the then information minister, who was seeking to position himself as crown prince, and did so by wooing tribal support and nationalising some of the southern tribes.[111] This variety of viewpoints decreased in periods when the freedom of the press was restricted (namely the 1976–81 and 1986–92 dissolutions of Parliament) and in the post-liberation period when the issue of the *biduns* became particularly taboo. The documents have thus been analysed keeping in mind that they represented the point of view of the government, announcing its various measures (opening registration periods, for instance, for nationality applicants), on the one hand, as well as that of the urban elite, debating nationality matters in Parliament. Although conveying a one-sided perspective, these documents tell a great deal about the evolution of the lexicon, the uncertainty regarding the exact legal meaning of the denominations used by the authorities, the first reports of claims of being 'without (*bidun*) nationality' in May 1979 until the reference of *bidun jinisyya* as a group or category by the then Undersecretary for the Nationality, Passport and Residency Affairs in September 1981. Read critically, the press, albeit under control, reflects the complexity of the debate surrounding nationality, reflecting also the kind of expectations emanating from the society.

The research is also based on material acquired through qualitative interviews with members and supporters of the *biduns*. A general unease surrounded the issue of the *biduns* and rendered the fieldwork difficult: Kuwaitis, whatever stance they might take on the issue, have long shared a concern for the country's international reputation, although this may have receded in 2011 with the new generation involved in human rights. The majority of nationals agreed that the *bidun* issue should remain an inter-Kuwaiti affair: any investigation into the file was generally felt as an attempt to 'put the country into disrepute' or 'tarnish its reputation'. Kuwaitis tend to see migration policies as acts of generosity by which the global poor can benefit from the emirate's wealth. A major donor to aid and relief UN agencies, the country is loath to accept interference in the issue. The concern for international reputation is an extremely powerful leitmotiv for suppressing or downplaying such an issue.[112]

In 2006 there was no organised group focusing on the *biduns* and operating among them that could serve as an entry point into the community. My first fieldwork research concentrated on getting access to *biduns* themselves. This endeavour was greatly helped by the concomitant work of Kuwaitis, the ones referred to by Siméant as 'support persons'. A significant part of my interviews was then conducted among Kuwaiti intellectual and activist circles, in particular those involved in the first ever activities seeking to give *bidun* a voice and offer a counternarrative to the official one on a clear cut dual vision of citizens and aliens. Secondly, I was interested in the life narratives of the *biduns* themselves in order to explore their own relation to Kuwait, its social hierarchies and their understanding of citizenship, but even more of the process that led to their discrimination and exclusion and finally their strategy of coping in the margins. This has been the most difficult and challenging part of the field research, as *biduns* were mostly reluctant to meet with foreigners, a reaction explained either by mistrust or the fear of retaliation that could be exerted by the Kuwaiti authorities, losing them their already meagre chance of naturalisation.[113] I also drew on my observations, as interviewees often adapted their statements according to what they think you expect from them. In particular, they tended to adopt a discourse of discriminated victims suited for researchers working for human rights organisations rather than for academics. Through sustained interaction, I found out about memories and places erased as a sign of premodern destitution and lost to the national identity narrative, which I investigated further in the press archives.

During my second fieldwork trip in April 2014, access to *bidun* informants was incomparably easier, as was the access to the area of *bidun* housing – which might no longer be the case at the time of writing. First of all, in 2008 *bidun*-run organisations had been created in the wake of the activities of Kuwaiti-run initiatives; secondly, a new generation of organisations (both *bidun* and Kuwaiti) had emerged from the February 2011 *bidun* mobilisation. New charismatic figures appeared and allayed the fear of interacting with foreigners, even boasting about doing so (even though the government still intimidated *biduns* who would be too forthcoming with foreign reporters and researchers).

Finally the question of the validity of the *biduns'* life stories remains. Although Kuwaiti officials warned that one should not 'believe in what *biduns* say', I have had no way or intention of verifying or assessing the validity of *biduns'* testimonies. I was more interested in analysing the issue from a constructivist point of view, emphasising what people perceived as real, thought they knew or could know, that is the realm of *representations*. I understand that the passing of sometimes three generations causes the genuine phenomena of memory distortion, and possibly the burying or misportraying family stories of migration and settlement. Yet the presence of the third generation of *biduns* and the resilience of their claims to belong attest to the efficacy of the weapons of these powerless people that flourishes in the shadow of marginality and illegality, and to the fact that this tenacious category is part and parcel of the emirate's history.

SEQUENCE OF CHAPTERS

Chapter 2 sets the broad historical background by explaining the pre-national understanding of the relations between polity, sovereignty and territoriality before the discovery of oil actually linked political power to circumscribed territory and delimited population, and the effects of the chronologically differentiated adoption of the state system on the North Arabian region. Chapter 3 discusses the construction of the Kuwaiti social pact by looking first at its institutionalisation in the Nationality Law of 1959. More than the actual content of the law, it delves into the practices and processes that conferred the new nationality and shows that it resulted from an *entre-soi* mechanism disconnected from the ever-growing periphery over which the state has had little control. The presence of the *biduns* goes back to the divisions that were created among Bedouins who obtained housing and nationality and those who did not. The historic misunderstanding that would eventually open the door to the illegals that the state is claiming to fight lies in the confusion between applying for nationality, seen as an act of registration, and actually obtaining it. In a sense loyalty was nurtured by expectations made possible by delaying tactics on the part of the state. Chapter 4 deals with the process of 'manufacturing aliens', through the association with the Iraqi enemy, but also through a process of economic downgrading in a country where national hierarchies have gradually come to equate with economic levels and types of occupations. From the perspective of the *biduns*, it looks at the strategies of resilience. Chapter 5 deals with the emerging mobilisation around the issue and how it evolves almost into a 'cause'. First, it analyses the internationalisation of the issue, after the 1991 liberation, through its inscription in the agenda of human rights advocacy networks and, from then on, describes the mobilisations of Kuwaiti nationals fighting for the cause, their motives and the complex relationship they created with *biduns* placed in the position of victims. It also analyses the arguments, held by the opponents to the *biduns'* integration, on the protection of welfare and other privileges attached to citizenship in much the same way as any other welfare states – except with more money involved. Finally, Chapter 6, as an epilogue, uses and discusses the theoretical frame of *sans-papiers'* or undocumented migrants' mobilisations to understand the *bidun* protest movement that erupted in February 2011.

CHAPTER 2

The Transnational Foundations of the Kuwaiti Emirate

'Ce n'est pas à "l'école du desert" qu'ils avaient pu apprendre à wilsonner.'
Life experience in the desert would not have taught them [the Bedouins] how to 'Wilson' – think along the lines of US President Woodrow Wilson.[1]

The historical backdrop against which the issue of the *biduns* emerged corresponds to a time when the discovery of oil had not yet linked political power to circumscribed territories and delimited populations. Different populations settled in the Bay of Kuwait at various times, which explains the current social hierarchy based on the perceived longevity of implantation.

Until independence, the Kuwaiti city, made up of a variety of communities like a mosaic, constituted a small world, which, despite different waves of migration, has survived relatively unchanged. The port interacted with the surrounding villages of semi-settled pastoralists and agriculturalists in a way that was more integrated than the retrospective *hadar* nationalist view of a 'maritime Kuwait' is willing to acknowledge. The founding myth that portrays the city-dwellers from within the mud wall as the founding fathers of the modern state is a biased political vision.[2] For sure, the merchants going as far as India and Africa and dealing with Europe and America's pearl amateurs had greater exposure to the outside world. Yet this vision somehow obscures the role of the hinterland. Underplaying the role of the desert tribes in controlling trade routes can be explained by the fact that, until recently, they were perceived to be loyal allies of the ruling family. George Joffé, in a survey of the three types of sovereignties in the Gulf region, distinguishes between one type based on territorial Western-developed international law (Iran), another based on Islamic constitutional theory (Saudi Arabia) and a third based on the ability to control the tribes of the hinterland (small Arab emirates).[3] Accordingly, the political power and legitimacy of the Gulf rulers was derived as much from their control of the majority urban coastal populations as from their command over the nomadic tribes of the interior – though their number was much less. While the urban population was controlled through a paternalistic system of absolute authority combined with consultation through a *majlis* or council, the command of tribes was different: on the one hand it involved maintaining their loyalty with the promise of booty, large subsidies and the provision of refuge in case of raids,[4] and on the other, it involved the collection of taxes[5] on commercial transactions from the tribes whose territory ran across that which the ruler claimed as being under his authority. Compared to other incomes, the revenues from the tribes would have been insignificant, yet they still played a disproportionate role in terms of power legitimation and the strength and prestige of the ruler.[6]

> [The ruler's] rise or decline in coastal politics could usually be measured by his ability to enforce his authority over the tribal chieftains in the area he claimed as his territory. Conversely, the extent of a ruler's territory was governed by the extent to which the tribes roaming the area would support him in time of need.[7]

In the post-independence period, tribal networks continued to play an important role in the legitimation of the regime. Their integration into the Kuwaiti polity depended not only on the closeness of their relations with the Kuwaiti sheikhs but also on the relations of their sheikhs and the Al-Sabah with the new national centres of power in Baghdad and Riyadh.

The chronologically differentiated adoption of the state-system in the North Arabian region resulted in setting population in movement. The desire of new territorial states to control and sedentarise took different ideological forms, from coercive administration to more lenient incorporation. This cultural factor affected the choices of location for settlements, adding a dimension to the pull-push phenomenon, which explains the movement of populations across national borders in terms of employment opportunities and the discrepancies between the national incomes and bordering regions of the (later to be) Gulf Cooperation Council (GCC) countries as well as between the GCC, Iraq and Iran.[8] It is in these intra-regional population movements, which occurred at the same time as labour import migrations but via different, solidarity-based channels, that the *biduns* are to be found. They are the 'near-foreigners' or 'non-Kuwaitis'[9] who shared the history of the once borderless area, forming a consistent economic and security entity. They are distinguishable from the rest of the migrants, Arab or non-Arab, who are culturally different from Northern Arabians. In the face of these social identities, emerging national geographies mattered little, since a Bedouin whose nomadic family originated from Palmyra would fall in the 'non-Kuwaiti' category while a Damascene teacher would undoubtedly belong to the alien labour force. On a deeper level, the distinction reflected different political and cultural orientations, and the resort to one or the other served different goals: the educated government employee from the Levant embodied the will for modernisation and development, while the Bedouin of the Hamad Desert[10] was a remnant of a different mode of patriarchal government and the past times of lineage pride and destitution, whose loyalty would be appropriate in other occupations such as guarding oil facilities or policing the city.

POLITY AND TERRITORY IN HISTORICAL PERSPECTIVE

Communities in old Kuwait City, semi-sedentarised villagers and desert tribes

Part of the difficulty in grasping the transnational aspect of the *bidun* issue comes from the fact that the transnational foundations of the tiny emirate are themselves often overlooked. 'Any academic work on Kuwait should go deep into these social layers', assures Dr. Faris al-Waqian,[11] political scientist at Kuwait University (KU) referring to the great variety of backgrounds, tribes and social statuses. 'People of

Kuwait all come from Saudi Arabia, Iraq, Iran', further adds Sheikha Fawzia al-Salman Al-Sabah,[12] a lawyer member of the royal family involved in the legal defence of *bidun* cases.

First, although settled for more than two centuries and cut off from their proper base of tribespeople from the 'Utub branch of the 'Anaza, the Al-Sabah have always emphasised their tribal background and identity and their origins at the heart of the Arabian Peninsula as a sign of nobility.[13]

At the top of the social hierarchy are the tribes from Najd, as well as those who can claim a form of autochthony, that is having been in Kuwait since as long as the Al-Sabah in the eighteenth century. Whether their families arrived at the same time as the Al-Sabah or later, over the centuries Kuwaitis of Najdi descent are still considered to share the latter's noble (*sharif*) origins. For example, the reputed al-Nafisi family comes from Najd, as Abdullah Ahmad was the first commercial representative of Ibn Saud, sultan of Najd.[14] His noble character also came from his activities as a trader in pearls and later horses. Belonging to the Kuwaiti elite requires the entrepreneurial spirit. Some recall how their forefathers, pushed out of Najd by starvation, settled in the amenable port and demonstrated their entrepreneurial skills by importing cotton fabrics and selling metal utensils etc., becoming *tujjar* (merchants). This is the case of the Ghanim, the Shaya' and the Nusf. The wealthiest acquired berths and boats and sometimes a fleet in Qibla, as did the Khurafi, the Saqr or the Mulla. The Saqr, for instance, were involved in the trade of dates from their plantations in Basra, the Mulla specialised in the tobacco trade, which flourished while the rigorist religious interpretation in the territories under Ibn Saud forbade it.[15]

Kuwaitis also refer to some families as the Zubara', that is, coming from Zubayr, near Basra, mostly in the first half of the twentieth century: this is also regarded as noble origin since the inhabitants of Zubayr, following the Hanbalite school of Sunni jurisprudence like all the Kuwaitis from Najd, considered themselves as originating from this region and close to the religious beliefs of Ibn Abd al-Wahhab.[16]

Being able to claim a settled lineage in Kuwait since as long as there has been a royal family is another undeniable sign of respectability: this is the case for some Shiite families, like the

Ma'rafi or Bahbahani, whose presence in Kuwait is said to date back to the eighteenth century. They used to live in Sharq and their relationship with the royal family is close: when the Sunni merchant class endeavoured to share power with the Al-Sabah in 1921 and 1938, excluding their Shiite counterparts from the initiative, the latter allied with the Al-Sabah, playing the role of a political counterweight.

On the Sunni side, the community was also composed of workers from the Sunni parts of Iran (the Balushs), some distinguished lineages of the Hijaz and also Sunni families from Iraq, although, as a designation of origin, the term Iraq was not used. Rather, the Kuwaiti vocabulary is more precise, referring instead to the Basrawis. The families who migrated from the north are clearly a minority and include the Naqib and the Rifa'i, as well as the Sa'dun, the Sunni ruling lineage of the Muntafiq tribe whose tribesmen converted in majority to Shi'ism.

On the Shiite side, the micro-local sociology also distinguishes between the *'ajam* or Shiite of Persian origin (i.e. family Jawhar), the Hasawis (i.e. family al-Baghli) and the Baharna, the indigenous Arabs from Bahrain. The Baharna usually came later than the others, when one looks at elite families, the migration of workers having been steady whether before or after the discovery of oil. Well-known for their physical ability, *'ajam* used to occupy craft or strenuous jobs like water-carriers or *kandari*, an occupation that later gave its name to some of the families (including Persian Sunni families).

The crowd of craftspeople, clothmakers and owners of coffee and grocery shops constituted a lower class of the inner city. This class also included sailors (*bahara*), and at its social pinnacle, though financially constantly in debt, were the pearl divers. Whether the interpretation is retrospective or not, any activity having to do with the commerce of pearls is today socially very highly valued. Finally, slaves of African origin mixed with this urban population. These subtleties of origin recalled by all the Kuwaiti families might appear at first as sociological refinements, yet they are very much present in today's Kuwait: every family remembers its *nasab* or genealogy as a justification of its social status, even though as *hadar* they have maintained no stronger relation to their locality of origin than the determination of their religious school.[17]

The relations between the city-port and the desert were complex. In pre-oil Kuwait, the Al-Sabah's rule did not limit itself to town dwellers: it also covered semi-sedentarised and nomadic tribesmen. Though the town of Kuwait had a specific maritime dimension, the form of the Al-Sabah political authority fulfilled the core characteristics of a sheikhdom, as described by Khoury and Kostiner:

> [It] is a power-sharing partnership involving pastoral nomads on the margins of cultivation, semisedentarized (especially agriculturalist) tribesmen, occasionally urban dwellers, and a ruler or chief domiciled in a town or in the countryside. In the chiefdom, the nomads and semidesentarized tribesmen are expected to refrain from the disruptions and to contribute military forces for protection and expansion.
>
> In return, town dwellers are expected to provide these rural forces with access to marketing and organized religion. The chief's function is to supervise the partnership.[18]

In the Kuwaiti lexicon, the semi-sedentarised tribesmen are referred to as *'arib dar* – a class in between *hadar* and *badu*.[19] Their primary characteristic is that they inhabit the villages (*al qura*) like Jahra or Fahahil: they are close to the *hadar* because they practice pearl diving, fishing, the *musabila* (meaning that they sell and purchase goods at the town market) and simple agricultural activities. Their language, though, notes Hamad Muhammad al- Sa'ydan, is closer to that of the *badu*.[20] Like the *badu* they are pure Arabs but they differ from them because of the semi-settlement with which other *badu* were not comfortable. This class is seldom mentioned today and has tended to disappear from public debate, which could be explained by the fact that the *'arib dar* were looked down on by the nomadic tribes or settled members of these nomadic/noble tribes. As a result, the expression came to be considered derogatory and I have never heard anybody claim their origin in these terms. Rather, nowadays it designates tribes with weak identity that were successful through luck because the Al-Sabah bought the land they occupied in the early 1950s, without it being necessarily theirs.

The majority of the *'arib dar* are formed by the landless tribes of the 'Awazim and the Rashayida living on the 'Ajman's and Mutran or Mutair's tribal territory respectively (see Map 2.1).[21] These semi-nomadic tribes followed the rains in search of grazing or cultivable lands, traded their sheep and the products of their agriculture with downtown Kuwaitis for supplies and, most importantly, settled in and around Kuwait during the dry season when they took part in fishing and pearl-diving to sustain themselves. The 'Awazim were known for catching fish on the southern coast of Kuwait town as far as Hawalli and Salmiyya. On the eve of World War II most of them were sedentary.[22] This explains why the Al-Sabah gave them land, the value of which skyrocketed with the later expansion of urbanisation. The Rashayida occupied the plain called the Dabdaba, around 150 km west of the city, where they grazed their animals, hunted and collected (white) truffles. The rest of the *'arib dar* comprises the 'Adawin, Hawajir, Sb'an (Sbay'i), and the Suhul – the Suhul specialised as ironmongers and black smiths.

The domestic mode of production of semi-nomadic tribes became integrated within a larger labour structure articulating both the sedentary and the semi-nomadic groups, which did not happen with the noble tribes, which as producers of camel and horse products

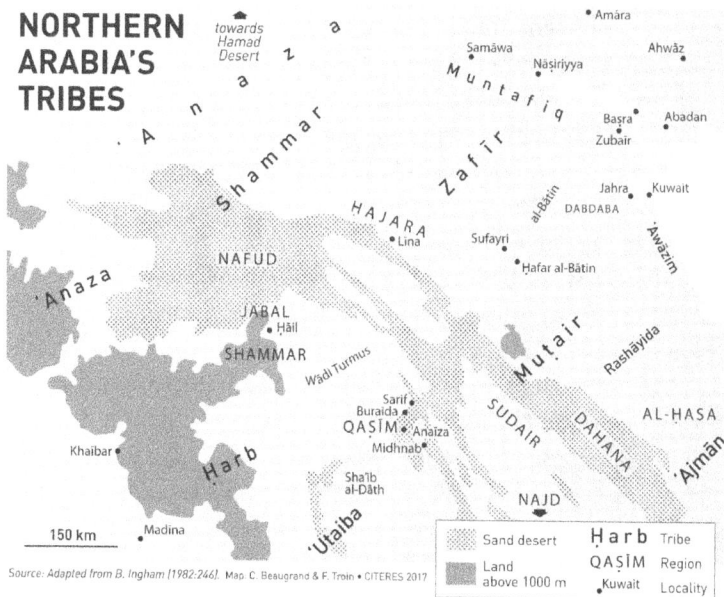

MAP 2.1   Northern Arabia's tribes

were more independent.[23] This differentiated integration proved crucial at the time of granting nationality – a period during which the previous social hierarchy was completely overturned. This attempt at sociological classification does not describe a systematic connection between the tribe's affiliation, sedentarisation or activity. Some members of the noble tribes usually defined as pastoral nomads, like the 'Ajman, Dawasir or Mutair,[24] had settled in town and given their names to certain districts; some had joined the ranks of the *'arib dar*; others had also adopted agricultural activities among the palm trees of the oases. Jahra was said to be the summer quarters of the 'Ajman, but was also a village of settlers. Likewise, the Fudul – said to be affiliated with the Bani Khalid – and their Dabbus tribal ruling lineage were established in the fertile coastal villages of Fahahil, Fintas and its little sister Finitis.

The noble tribes of the region were divided into southern tribes, comprised of the Sunni 'Ajman, Dawasir and Mutair, closer to the Kuwaiti city-port, and northern tribes, referring to the Zafir, the 'Anaza and the Shammar. The last-named two are usually referred to as tribal 'confederations' (so wide was their extent) and ought to be seen on a different scale. The 'Anazi affiliation was acknowledged from the Levant (and what is now the borderland between Jordan and Saudi Arabia) to the west of Iraq, where the lineage of the paramount sheikh, the Ibn Hadhal, was to be found.[25] Likewise, the Shammar's name is claimed by both the tribes around Ha'il and those established in the Jazira, between the Tigris and the Euphrates, north of Baghdad and led by the Jarba lineage.[26]

Affiliation with these tribes was and still is extremely prestigious. The Zafir formed a tribe, traditionally headed by a member of the Ibn Suwayt lineage, through the fusion of several tribal cores, which also explains their large extent. Finally, a major difference between northern and southern tribes (except the Fudul) is that the northern tribes were exposed in the nineteenth century to the movement of conversion to Shi'ism that spread in Iraq.[27] As a result the northern tribes include both Sunni and Shiite members.

Though the horse breeding of the tribal elites had flourished with the export of thoroughbreds to colonial India, their tribal might was not financial but geo-strategic. Financial power was the main feature of the prominent urban merchants who, richer than the Al-Sabah, were their creditors, as many Kuwaitis from those families like to remind us, emphasising that 'my grandfather used to lend them money'[28]. By contrast, tribes with no material revenues were important *regional* actors because their alliances/defection would determine the outcome of battles and as a consequence fix the fluctuating area of the sheikhs' influence. As a consequence, the tribal confederations came into contact with Kuwait when the geo-strategy of the times required it and only at a distance from the town.

The separation of desert tribes and townspeople as it is depicted by the Kuwaiti nationalist discourse ought thus to be slightly qualified. No port exists without a hinterland, and the desert tribes of the Arabian interior, no matter how low their purchasing power – and it was low indeed – controlled this hinterland and its trade routes. Three facts are worth mentioning to demonstrate a greater integration between the two segments of the population than is usually acknowledged. First, many of the pearl divers were not permanent residents of Kuwait but Bedouins who would combine the pearling season in the summer with their winter herding, fighting or semi-agricultural activities. As already mentioned, many of the *'arib dar* were specialists in this combination. According to the historian Salwa Alghanim the extra income drawn from their several activities enabled a few Bedouins to organise themselves into cooperatives independent from the dominant pearling merchants.[29] Their tradition of reciting poetry exalting bravery, steadfastness in hardship and solidarity would even have influenced the pearl divers' folk culture.[30] Yet pearl divers may have come from further away than the immediate outskirts of the town. The monthly record of *The Geographic Journal* of 1912 that reports on the expedition of the Danish geographer Raunkiær to the Arabian Peninsula noted that the adventurer travelled from Riyadh to the eastern coast in a caravan that largely consisted of 150 pearl fishers bound for Bahrain, Kuwait's pearl diving rival.[31]

Secondly, the symbiosis between townspeople and tribes was manifested not only in the role of the tribes as consumers but also as haulers to the larger markets of Central Arabia. Kuwait's desert lies through the geological depression of the Batin, at the end of many

caravan routes from Najd and Jabal Shammar but also in the north on
the route to Zubayr and Basra. The imported goods for onward sales
included cloth, rice, sugar, spices and tobacco, while in addition to a
few products from the desert tribes (wool, hides, clarified butter),
Kuwaiti merchants would export dates from South Iraq, and from the
1890s onwards thrived on the covert trade in arms destined for
the interior.

Finally, and at a different level, tribal politics were indeed the *high
politics* of the pre-oil epoch. Al-Rasheed sums up this point when she
analyses the military activities tied to tribal politics: 'Raids were the
means which made possible the establishment of political and
economic hegemony ... when these raids were carried out by
established power groups, they became entangled with centralisation
of political leadership, dynastic ambitions and territorial
expansion.'[32] As a consequence, striking military or indeed political
deals with tribal leaders was the exclusive prerogative of the ruling
sheikhs and lineages of the different trading centres. The British and
Ottoman empires, whether they wanted it or not, would have
leverage on foreign affairs understood as inter-imperial affairs, but
international politics seen from the horizons of the local sheikhs for
the main part escaped them. Likewise it is unheard of that any
particular *hadar* trader would ever have reached a long-lasting
alliance with any *sharif* or noble tribe to assert military-based power.

This pattern of power distribution explains why the issue of the
biduns, who claim affiliation to large tribes, in particular Shammar,
'Anaza, Zafir and Fudul, has largely become a bone of contention
between the ruling family and their main *hadar* opponents. The
sheikhs with familial ties with tribes used this connection to create
political support by naturalising them. Today the Sunni notables,
with Nasserist leanings in the 1950 and 1960s, readily put the blame
on the Al-Sabah sheikhs as being responsible for attracting distant
tribes to the country. The issue of stateless people in Kuwait not only
pits a disenfranchised minority and its supporters against the state
but also the two most powerful components of the Kuwaiti society,
the rulers and the *hadar*.[33] Tribal relations were not only the high
politics of the time and the preserve of the sheikhs, excluding the
townspeople and their merchant elite, they could also be used against

them, as the dissolution of the 1938 Legislative Council illustrated. This explains why the issue of the *biduns* would later raise little sympathy from the town dwellers who would then be allies of the ruling family.

What follows looks at the patterns of tribal alliances and subsequent security systems set up by the Kuwaiti ruling family, starting with Mubarak Al-Sabah, the last sheikh involved in expanding Kuwait's influence in Central Arabia. By highlighting the legacy of the pre-modern security system, this historical perspective lays the analytical foundations to explain why the Kuwaiti armed forces were developed by integrating mostly 'near-foreigners'.

High politics before-oil: tribes and security

When Mubarak, known as Mubarak al Kabir or Mubarak the Great, seized power in 1896 through the murder of two of his brothers, Arabia was under the domination of the Al-Rashid of Jabal Shammar. Yet, contrary to the Al-Rashid, who stemmed from and were supported by their own tribe, the Shammar, Mubarak had to rely mostly on the support of tribal allies to fulfil his aspiration of playing a leading role in the affairs of Central Arabia.

Nonetheless, it would be wrong to see him as a town ruler, forging alliances with the desert tribes of 'Ajman and Mutair in the same way he agreed treaties from his town palace with the great powers of the time, the Ottoman and British empires. This picture of an urban ruler is propagated by Dickson, the political agent in Kuwait from 1929 to 1936, who interpreted Mubarak's fratricide as revenge for being sent away from the town as Amir al badiya, the charge consisting in controlling the desert territory and policing the tribes.[34] The reality is certainly less dramatic or lyrical: family coups or the overthrowing of rulers by their relatives were not uncommon in the Arabian Peninsula and the Gulf sheikhdoms for centuries. Likewise, the title of Amir al badiya, although perilous, is not known for being associated with banishment or punishment. As a result, Mubarak had probably assumed the role of maintaining order in the desert around Kuwait and along the caravan routes from Najd, Basra and Hasa on behalf of the Al-Sabah family for years and his seizure of power did not make him an urban dweller either.

Mubarak's links with the desert tribes ran deep: first, he was himself an experienced desert warrior and leader. He had been involved in desert warfare and Ottoman military campaigns, as he had led the Kuwaiti contingents during the reconquest of al-Hasa in 1871 and the campaign against the Sheikh Jasim of Qatar in 1895. As a result he had built strong alliances among the Rashayida and the 'Ajman tribes, from which he gathered the small group of followers who helped him murder his brothers.

A second significant link was the marriage bonds he made with ruling lineages. Born himself to Lu'lu'a Muhammad al-Thaqib, daughter of the ruler of Zubayr, Mubarak took as one of his wives the daughter of the paramount sheikh of the 'Ajman, Daydan bin Huthlayn.[35] This pattern of intermarriage with the 'Ajman was to be continued by his descendants after Mubarak's death in 1915 and had some influence on the future of naturalisation.[36] It is also reported that in order to reconcile the 'Ajman, to whom he was related, and the Mutair, Mubarak married a daughter of the sheikh of the Mutair in June 1899.[37]

At the core of the tribal support gathered by Mubarak were the Rashayida and 'Awazim, living in the close periphery of Kuwait, as well as important elements of the Mutair and almost all the 'Ajman,[38] who were not traditionally part of Kuwait. In addition to these four tribal clusters, Mubarak forged a strategic alliance in the summer of 1899 with Sheikh Sa'dun of the Muntafiq, based in the region of the southern Euphrates. This northern alliance was of core importance in Mubarak's struggle against the hegemony of the Amir of Ha'il and his loyal Shammar tribe: together with Sheikh Sa'dun, he was able to deprive the Rashid of their supplies to Najd and Jabal Shammar by raiding and cutting off the roads linking them to Basra and Zubayr, Kuwait and northern Hasa, at least twice, in October 1900 and June 1901.

Mubarak is often portrayed as the founder of modern Kuwait. Through a secret agreement with the British he bound his heirs to the succession of the throne, which would later be enshrined in the 1962 Constitution and still forms the basis of the succession within the Al-Sabah today.[39] One of his main legacies was the building of Kuwait's legitimacy on the political map of the time: this spared his emirate

from the fate of the emirate of Arabistan, led by his close friend
Sheikh Khaz'al (r. 1897–1925), who, abandoned by the British, saw
his fiefdom incorporated by force and ruse into the state of Reza
Pahlavi in 1925.

Along with his ability to enforce his authority over the tribal
chieftains in the area he claimed as his territory, Mubarak asserted his
legitimacy, which reinforced his role as an essential interlocutor to
the British.[40] Ironically, it is his most bitter defeat at Sarif, in face of
the Shammari forces led by Abd al-Aziz Mut'ab Al-Rashid, in March
1901 that best illustrates his political ambitions in Arabia. The
location of the battle and its distance from Kuwait port are quite
telling in terms of the territorial ebb and flow: Sarif is situated at the
very heart of Qasim (see Map 2.1). For this expedition, Mubarak was
joined by Sheikh Sa'dun, leading the Muntafiq and Zafir's forces, and
also had the support of Abd al-Rahman Al-Saud, together with the
'Ajman and other Najdi tribes loyal to him.

A closer look at the composition of this expedition helps to
understand the background, in terms of security and social prestige,
against which the citizenry and military would be formed in Kuwait
once a non-fluctuating or international law based territorial
sovereignty was imposed on the region in the 1920s.

Among the tribal supporters of Mubarak were the 'Awazim,
Rashayida, 'Ajman, Bani Khalid and Mutair, to which should be
added the tribes of southern Hasa, the Murra and Bani Hajar.[41] The
second element in the Mubarak expedition was made up of the levies
from *ahl al Kuwait* or people from Kuwait.[42] These would be drawn
from the urban and pearl-fishing populations, but were considered to
be of mediocre military ability.

The subordinate position of the urban maritime community, in
spite of its crucial financial role, is illustrated by Mubarak's last
expedition, assembled against Sheikh Sa'dun in 1910. This episode
exemplified both the fact that power was exercised first and foremost
by the control of tribes and, secondly, the material limits of his
power. Mubarak gathered forces in retaliation against the raids on
Kuwaiti tribesmen and merchants by Sheikh Sa'dun and a tribal
leader of a subsection of the Zafir, both of whom Mubarak considered
a serious and direct threat to his sovereignty. Leaving the raids

unpunished would open the door to attacks by any large force of Bedouins, which could eventually be headed by one of the competing power groups of the region. In preparing his attack, Mubarak disregarded the agenda of activities of the town dwellers by declaring a ban on the season's diving.

The defection of three pearl traders, who left with their fleet and crew to Bahrain, eventually subdued him. If the merchant substructure had developed so successfully that the real power was clearly embedded in the financial-commercial class, the power of the value system still remained in the ruling family and its tribal allies, at least until the flowing of oil revenues and the delineation of boundaries.

On the desert front, with signs of the growing independence of Ibn Saud, rallying the Najdi tribes around him, and the defection of Sheikh Sa'dun in 1907, Mubarak abstained from direct forceful intervention, preferring to wage his wars in Central Arabia by proxy and to offer financial support to Ibn Saud. The provision of money and arms to the tribes in exchange for men to promote his schemes and keep danger away from Kuwait proved quite costly. Yet even in the absence of raids, Mubarak maintained his power and prestige, as a point of contact between Ibn Saud and the Ottomans or the British as well as an arbiter in tribal quarrels between the 'Ajman and Murra, as in 1906.

Compared to desert diplomacy, which was exclusively a matter of sheikhs and for the centralised power a question of asserting legitimacy, the security of the city was considered lower politics. Yet it was still ensured by the rulers themselves, although notables made attempts to organise some surveillance and policing tasks into a matter of public interest rather than a private concern in the hands of the various members of the royal family. Here again, the role of the Bedouins was essential.

At the beginning of the twentieth century the main forces of coercion in Kuwait were private: the *fidawiyya* – roughly translated as 'those ready to sacrifice themselves' for their master or 'devotees' (also called *khuwiyya*, literally fraternity, but pointing to the obligation to protect a master like one's own kin) – who were private retinues hired by the different sheikhs of the ruling family.

These private guards earned the name 'Armed Bedouins' as they were armed with guns and recruited exclusively among the Bedouins as opposed to the city dwellers. Among these retainers there were former slaves, identified by their dark skin. Later, in the late 1950s, Mueller, an American engineer employed on the building of Shuwaikh port facilities described the entrance of the Public Security building, the first and for a long time the main official building on the Sahat al Safa, the main public square in Kuwait:

> Il n'y a que des bédouins et des Noirs qui soient accroupis ici dans leurs vastes habits drapés, et il n'est pas pensable de les supprimer du protocole; leur soumission est légendaire et ils encourraient la peine de mort s'il arrivait quoi que ce soit au Cheikh [Abdullah Mubarak].[43]
>
> [Only Bedouins and Blacks squat here in their large cloaks; it would be completely unthinkable to remove them from the protocol; their submission to the Sheikh [Abdullah Mubarak] is legendary and they would face the death sentence should anything happen to him]

These retinues were hired on the basis of their personal acquaintance with the sheikh without any specific task to perform, but they would follow their master wherever he went and obey his commands. For instance, the gatekeepers of the city wall (*sur*), erected in 1920, before the battle of Jahra, under Salim al-Mubarak, were taken from the Emir's private retinues.

The *fidawiyya* also played a role in the war of the nearby desert, including, later on, the patrolling of the petroleum wells. The Sheikh himself would send his guards to complement (or duplicate) the private patrols provided by the oil company. In the early twentieth century, three members of the royal family were known for commanding groups of armed Bedouins in desert operations, showing that the task counted as a distinctive sign, a privilege.[44] In 1928, the battle of Riqa'i, northwest of Jahra was the last desert battle fought against Saudi Ikhwan, involving sheikhs from the Al-Sabah family and Bedouin followers.[45] The desert war leaders of the Al-Sabah would later form the backbone of the command of the new state's nascent armed forces. This explains why the Kuwaiti army tended to be a matter of both the royals and the tribes.

The Emir Ahmad al-Jabir al-Mubarak was said to have 50 bodyguards, called *khuddam* – literally, 'servants' – in addition to a private armed force (trained by the British and Palestinians) of 1,000 followers, who would not only protect his person, the city and the oil installations, but bring another 1,000 of their tribal kinfolk on demand in case of need.[46] These tribesmen, the *fidawiyya*, received financial and other assistance in return for not migrating to pasturage and thus remaining nearby as available reserves. A number of *khuddam*, the personal bodyguards, were detached for use in the service of the town lieutenant or administrator while others were, when necessary, sent out to investigate quarrels or other troubles among the Bedouins. There was no permanent desert control system. Such emissaries, when sent out, travelled in armed lorries, which had been given to the ruler by an oil concessionaire.[47] The Bedouin private guards depended entirely on the Al-Sabah sheikhs for their subsistence: living in tents in designated areas, the sheikh they served would provide them with dates, rice and a new suit of clothes, summer and winter. After 1945 the sheikhs started to pay them a salary, whose amount varied according to the sheikh himself. The Bedouins in return demonstrated an impeccable devotion and loyalty towards their sheikh-benefactor.

Parallel with these private forces with undefined policing functions, another system of maintaining order developed in the form of the 'city and market guards'. Under Mubarak, around 20 Balush guards were responsible for the control of the various souks in Kuwait, and were armed with sticks. The head of the city and market guards, who replaced the Balush chief, became almost synonymous with the role, so devoted was he over a quarter of a century to his nights and days patrolling. Sheikh Sabah al Du'ij took up the name of 'Sabah al Suq'. In spite of his misleading name, Sabah al Du'ij was not from the royal family. The position of head of the market guards was not the privilege of the Al-Sabah, but was, as a matter of rule, delegated to commoners. A consistent surveillance of the town markets emerged with the Balush guards. Their presence in Kuwait in a *firij*, or quarter, under their name, can be linked to the influence of the British under Mubarak; its management fell under the purview of townspeople.

When the municipality was established in 1930, the 12-member municipal council took over the responsibility of organising the town and market policing and soon started to cooperate with Sabah al Suq and his guards. It gradually replaced the ad hoc system with rules defining the functions of the market guards[48] and the responsibilities of their chief.[49] It set up fines and organised the recruitment, geographical dispatch (also creating the coastguards) and pay of the guards.[50] Eight years later, in 1938, when the Legislative Council (*majlis tashri'i*) was established to introduce reforms leading towards more participation in political decisions and the establishment of a civil administration, to counter what was perceived as a 'backward' sheikhly rule as opposed to the progressive one in Iraq, six out of its 14 members were members of one of the previous municipal councils.[51] The dissolution of the two 1938 *majalis* had two major consequences: it confirmed the alliance between the ruling family and the *badu*, but this time in an open confrontation with the *hadar*. Secondly, it laid the basis of the modern organisation of the Kuwaiti armed forces.

The first June 1938 council was dissolved without violence with promises of a new election. This resulted from a demonstration of force by semi-nomadic Bedouins from the south coast of Kuwait who answered Ahmad al-Jabir's call for arms and entered the city.[52] In contrast, the dissolution of the second council (December 1938 to March 1939), which had refused to agree to the change of its role from executive to advisory by the Emir Ahmad al-Jabir, led to physical coercion exerted by the *fidawiyya* and their Bedouin allies. It resulted in one execution and the imprisonment of five men. The episode of violence was triggered by the exhortations of Muhammad al-Munayyis to continue supporting the dissolved council until the support of the Iraqi army arrived. It is vividly depicted in the memoirs of Ahmad al-Khatib, who recalls the hanging of Muhammad al-Munayyis on a cross as the worst unleashing of savagery he had ever seen.[53] Most importantly, al-Khatib described the perpetrators as 'men of foreign appearance, shirtless, with thick hair like women'.[54] He also linked this childhood memory to a later discovery he made in the British archives, according to which King Abd al-Aziz Al-Saud had, upon British instructions, sent 600 tribesmen to help the Amir of Kuwait in his fight against the Legislative Council, among which 300 were from the 'Ajman and

Stateless in the Gulf

300 from the Mutair – though the latter were turned down by Ahmad al-Jabir because they belonged to the enemy tribe that had attacked Kuwait at Jahra. Whatever the role of Ibn Saud, what is clear here is the early resort to transnational or distant tribes with whom the sheikhs of Kuwait had had previous alliances in what I have called the high politics of the region, to support them in their power conflict with the notables. The use by the ruling family of the human reservoir provided by transnational tribes in order to bolster its loyalty basis constitutes a common pattern of Kuwait's military structure and more generally Kuwaiti politics. Secondly, al-Khatib's recollections show that this reputation for brutality and blind obedience contributed to the early stigma attached to the Bedouins in the eyes of the town dwellers at a time when the economic foundations of the tribal system were collapsing.

The second important legacy of the Legislative Council is its attempt to organise the Kuwaiti armed forces. Until 1938, the order of the past was localised and transient, 'consisting of multiple overlapping hierarchies that were maintained in multiple, overlapping ways: neighbourhoods organised around mosques, family elders watching youngsters, merchants monitoring markets, ship captains monitoring divers'.[55] Moreover, the Emir managed crises by sending his personal guards to restore order – after which they returned to the services of the Emir.

Article 2 of the inaugural law, which delineated the functions of the Legislative Council elected in June 1938, claimed authority to establish a law of public security. As a result, the Legislative Council formally set up different departments, in charge of town surveillance, traffic, public morality and the newly created police of the ports and borders. It issued laws that recognised and organised the police through uniform, training and stations. After the dissolution of the 1938 *majlis* the police fell under the authority of the ruling family, not the legislature.

From then until 1962, the police were under the direct authority of the ruling family. Even though the police force technically became a government organisation in 1962, it was still influenced by the ruling family, as the Ministry of the Interior has always been headed by a member of the ruling family in the role of Minister of Interior.[56]

The Public Security Force then included both the army and what was to become the national police. It was headed by Sheikh Ali Khalifa Al-Sabah, who had previously led desert operations, until his death in 1942. During this period, the Public Security Force grew in importance and became more specialised into the Public Security Force and Border Forces, with a proper army gradually being created. In 1953, the Border Forces became the basis for the new army and split from the Kuwait Public Security Force, which then formed the police department and later the Ministry of the Interior.[57] Sheikh Abdullah Mubarak,[58] last son of Mubarak the Great, founder of the first Aviation Club in 1953 and General Commander of the armed forces became the head of the Kuwaiti Army.[59] 'By the late 1950s, more than 2000 men had enlisted within the formation of the Kuwaiti Army.'[60]

Abdullah al-Mubarak became an extremely powerful figure during the whole of the 1950s. The testimony offered by Mueller, the American engineer working on the port-building project, gives an interesting insight into the way his power was perceived:

> Koweït est un grand village où tout le monde se connaît, où chacun sait tout des autres et où il est difficile de dissimuler quelque chose. Abdullatif Thuwayni, bras droit du Cheik Mubarak et chef de la Sûreté Publique est très exactement au courant de ce que nous faisons, tous, dans quels milieux nous évoluons et quels sont nos amis.[61]
>
> [Kuwait is a big village where everybody knows everybody; everybody knows everything and makes it difficult to hide anything. Abdullatif Thuwayni, right arm of the Sheikh Mubarak, head of the Public Security knows with precision what we are doing, each of us, what are our social circles and who our acquaintances.][62]

In 1959 Abdullah Mubarak was chosen to head the Department of Public Security, which merged both security apparatus as a result of a major internal political crisis between the government and the opposition.[63] As the last son of Mubarak the Great, he was an extremely serious and senior contender to the throne; a great figure of Arab nationalism (and maybe too much so to the taste of the British).[64] Abdullah Mubarak retired from the political scene in 1961 in unclear circumstances and settled in Lebanon.

After independence in 1962, two separate ministries, one for defence and another for internal matters (the Minister of the Interior), were established. From 1964, and after a political crisis in parliament, which led to a major cabinet reshuffle, the two ministries, although independent from each other, were headed by just one minister, Sheikh Saad Abdullah al-Salim al-Mubarak, until he became Prime Minister in 1978.

The remainder of this chapter looks at the policy of surrounding countries towards their tribal and nomad population. Although it recognises Kuwait as one the most attractive centres to provide employment from the 1950s on, the interpretation of historical data proposed here departs somewhat from the 'Gold Rush' version, the state narrative, according to which an undifferentiated and implicitly greedy crowd flocked to Kuwait in search of better living conditions and to benefit from the generous Kuwaiti welfare system. On the contrary, it analyses in detail the *push* and *pull* mechanisms, identifying regime ideology as a core factor to be added to this primarily economic model.

NATIONAL INTEGRATION AND TRANSNATIONAL MIGRATIONS IN NORTHERN ARABIA

Although it is based almost by definition on fragmentary sources, in what follows I try to piece together a picture of the impact of the political, economic and social changes in the less controlled areas of the Syrian Desert on the living conditions and values of certain categories of the population, to such an extent that it responded and adapted with an exit strategy as a means of resistance and survival. I argue that the tribespeople who came to settle in Kuwait had previous 'transnational' links with the sub-region through migration patterns or sister tribes which, among other things, explains their belief in the legitimacy of their claims and made their migration possible in the first place. Secondly, though concomitant and sharing the common feature of escaping rural impoverishment, this trans-border choice of settlement should be distinguished from the domestic rural-to-urban migrations that took place in Iraq and Syria, as it signifies a rejection of the national integration projects and a refusal on the part of the tribespeople to rethink their existing political identities and values and imagine themselves in national terms. The broad-brush history depicted here ultimately shows that beyond the undeniable material factor, there is an ideational motive, i.e. resistance to being drawn into the field of distinctively national politics.

Nomadism and nascent states

As it made its first appearance in northeastern Arabia, and before the territorial states were defined with anything approaching precision, the national factor set off mechanisms of state building and regime support consolidation. Whether in the case of Ibn Saud turning his domain into a fully-fledged eponymous state or of the French and British mandates, tribes identified as the basic components of the social fabric of the region along with the urban milieu were perceived as a key element in the aggregation of support around the nascent states.

First, Ibn Saud, with his knowledge and use of tribal politics, instrumentalised the Najdi tribes turning them into Ikhwan, to his advantage to serve his purpose of territorial maximisation; in the frontier areas, the tribes' occupation of traditional lands was acknowledged, valued and its preservation encouraged; Abd al-Aziz sought to obtain tribal allegiance through the payment of *zakat*, a form of religious payment, and the control of their trade as it would provide him with grounds on which to base his further territorial claims – with the hidden hope, as of the 1940s, that any new territorial gains, in addition to increased power and prestige, might also bring oil fields.

The British-brokered border arrangements between Kuwait, Najd and Iraq decided at the Muhammara conference (5 May 1922)[65] are very telling about the Saudi policy towards tribes. Article 1 of the Muhammara agreement reads as follows: 'The clans of al Muntafik, al-Dhufair and al-'Amarat shall return to Iraq and the Shammar of Najd to Najd.'[66]

The agreement also forbade any border transgression by any of the clans, let alone any aggression, yet secured the pilgrim route and freedom of trade and tribal movements; the 'Uqair Protocols famously gave two-thirds of the 1913 Anglo-Ottoman-defined Kuwaiti territory to Najd.[67] It established two neutral zones between Najd and Kuwait and Najd and Iraq where grazing resources and watering places and wells were to be shared by the bordering tribes. These protocols are important for the understanding of what would later become the issue of the *biduns*.

First and foremost, one difficulty was the profound divide between the state founders and their broader tribal society, as exemplified by the consequences of the border agreements. If, in a moment of grace, Abd al-Aziz Al-Saud managed to conflate the two visions (state expansion and tribal logic) by means of religion, then disappointment at the imposition of the alien concept of boundaries brought the differences back to the surface. This was particularly the case for the Ikhwan, whose continuous raiding led them to eventually revolt; more benignly, they continued roaming the desert and stuck to their habit of switching allegiance long after the border delineation. As for the first manifestation of this growing divide, it is evidenced by the flight to Iraq of splinter groups from the Ikhwan tribes, who wanted to escape economic taxation from the centralising Najdi state and joined the Shammar refugees in raiding Najd and the pro-Saudi Zafir of Hamud Ibn Suwayt. Moreover, after the signing of the Bahra and Hadda Agreements in November 1925, fixing once and for all the boundaries between the Sultanate of Najd and its dependencies, on the one hand, and Iraq and Trans-Jordan respectively on the other, and making the border crossing conditional on the obtaining of a government permit in concert with the other government,[68] the allied tribes addressed Ibn Saud in these words:

> The entire badiya [desert] is ours, we people of Najd. We therefore register our protest about your unjust decision to contain us within borders in the badiya. You then responded that border demarcation does not mean giving up the possession of land, but is only a way of settling disputes which may arise in the badiya. You told us that we were free to graze in the badiya.[69]

Borrowing the words of Kurpershoek, who studied Arabian tribal poetry, 'in Arabia, the power of the spoken word, used subversively or in a counter-revolutionary way, is infinitely greater than the written word'.[70] In this case, the power of the pervasive genealogical discourse on the Najdi origins and Najdi unity, at first uttered by Ibn Saud and later by the most immoderate Ikhwan, prevailed over the written word of the international treaties.

That period left a second legacy: it formally initiated moves from North to South that laid the first milestones for later movements, once tribes found themselves in the grip of the new nationalist regimes or encountered adverse natural conditions. Two events ought to be mentioned here, as they can be regarded as paving the way for later settlements based on tribal gathering.

Part of the Zafir led by Hamud Ibn Suwayt, though located on Iraqi territory and, according to the 'Uqair agreements belonging to Iraq, had paid the *zakat* to Ibn Saud in 1922 and as a result were the target of rebellious Ikhwan. When Hamud died in 1925 they were still Iraqi subjects, yet his successor 'Ajimi Ibn Suwayt decided two years later to secede to Najd and relocate near Hafr al Batin in al Sufayri, while his followers continued grazing their livestock in Iraqi territory and in the Neutral Zone.[71] Indeed, contrary to the romanticised argument commonly advanced – by Raswan and Ashkenazi[72] – according to which tribes retreated southward to the Arabian Peninsula to preserve their traditional way of life, it seems that in this case it was less a question of freedom of circulation, as the borders were quite relaxed for the nomadic movements, than a clear political calculation on the part of Ibn Suwayt, dissatisfied with the Iraqi government's security provision and its firmer grip in terms of tax collection.[73]

It was indeed part and parcel of Abd al-Aziz Al-Saud 1920s expansionist policy in the peninsula not only to gain allegiance from nomadic tribes but also to grant nationality to those dissatisfied with or disenfranchised from the national policies of neighbouring countries that could increase his regional influence. This is illustrated by the granting of papers of Najdi nationality to the people of the desert town of Zubayr, southwest of Basra, who feared the conscription bill that Baghdad was intending to issue, in 1928.[74] It is no novelty that attempts to impose conscription as one tool as well as a symbol of national integration were universally fiercely opposed. In the national era, resistance to conscription undoubtedly benefited from the proximity of an international border. The people of Zubayr were certainly not the only ones to use their international links to brace themselves for the encounter with the expanding central state: the Shiite population around Muhammara took out Persian passports.[75] In spite of calls by 'members of the commercial elite … [for] mass emigration to an area of vacant land within Kuwait',[76] the population of Zubayr, on the basis of their strong Najdi identity manifested in their following the Hanbali school of Islamic jurisprudence and their tribal myth of Najdi descent, did not cross the border: they symbolically opted out of the nation building. While the exact number of people from Zubayr who eventually took out Najdi nationality is not known, registration was quite popular, although it could only be granted by the agent of Ibn Saud in Kuwait or a prominent Basra merchant of Najdi origin. However anecdotal this episode, it is significant from at least two points of view. First, it shows an early deterritorialised conception of nationality understood as a claim for protection based on a mix of ethnicity, pragmatism and ideology. This conception is illustrated by the opposite move of leading Kuwaiti families who owned date gardens in the Basra region taking up Iraqi nationality in the 1930s to affirm both their property rights and their Arab nationalist credentials.[77] Secondly, it hints at the role assigned to the smaller emirate of Kuwait, drawn in spite of itself into the game of its more powerful neighbour.

What was the situation of Kuwait in this large picture? The presence of Abdullah al-Nafisi, the agent of Abd al-Aziz in the city of Kuwait, points to Ibn Saud's conception of the extent of the sovereignty exerted by his smaller port-town neighbour: as an unofficial ambassador entrusted with looking at the interests of Saudi subjects, al-Nafisi's position tacitly, though reluctantly, recognised the independence of Kuwait. Yet this acknowledgement of sovereignty was seriously limited, since in the eyes of Ibn Saud, the wide spaces outside the towns, the domain of the Bedouins, belonged to him and stretched right up to the frontier of the settlement, that is, to the very limits of urban Kuwait. This conception was translated into practical action through the Saudi blockade of tribal trade with Kuwait – a response to Sheikh Ahmad's refusal to allow the Saudis to establish a customs post in Kuwait to levy taxes on trade with Najd. Some sections of the surrounding tribes helped him in this enterprise, notably, in 1931, the branch of the Zafir headed by Ibn Suwayt that had stayed in Iraq (when another member of the Ibn Suwayt family had left for Najd) because it was unwilling to pay the *zakat* to Ibn Saud.[78] This idea of the desert as a hostile environment subject to foreign influence and manipulation was deeply anchored in the minds of the Kuwaiti townspeople by the time of the definition of nationality. This can only have been reinforced by the instrumentalisation of nomads by the nascent Iraqi border administration. Following the rise in custom taxes in Iraq in 1932, Iraqi customs officers did somehow go beyond their task of cracking down on the smuggling of goods from tax-lenient Kuwait and exacted more than they should have from some Bedouins performing their usual *musabila* to the city-port.[79]

Here appears the fundamental twist that gave rise to the issue of *bidun* in the region: the essential dissociation between the understanding of territory and international boundaries through the prism of their economic value – that is the prospect of discovering oil[80] – and the deterritorialised meaning of nationality. Particularly in the case of smaller emirates under British protection, this deterritorialised conception is rooted in the historical claims made by Ibn Saud, even though these claims were largely untenable in the long term as they were part and parcel of an expansionist strategy that eventually failed, since Ibn Saud never made it to the sea. In the words of Zahlan, referring to an annex to a letter sent by Ibn Saud to Sheikh Abdullah of Qatar, the former explained that:

> He had already explained to the British representatives that the people of these shaikhdoms were his subjects, and that they had been the subjects of his father and grandfather before him, but he deferred to their own wish to be under British protection. There could be no question in his mind however, of the rulers of these places having claims to anything but the towns; the desert and allegiance of the tribes roaming that desert had always been under his sovereignty and under those of his ancestors.[81]

The disconnection between the actual territory and the idea of the community was rendered possible by the phenomenon of nomadism that prevailed in the region until the late 1960s, the Bedouins being 'ceux que la terre n'a pas encore accrochés' [those not yet bound to the land][82] but also strengthened by the profound mistrust in their shifting loyalties – a mistrust that, decades after their sedentarisation, is still pervasive and kept alive in Kuwaitis' minds.[83]

Though with far less proficiency and a great deal of romanticised misconception, the French and British mandate powers also sought to instrumentalise the tribal system in order to assert the authority of the new state they were building. They also strived to spread the state apparatus to the population, as they believed that the tribal sheikhs were in control of a cohesive force and thus able to assume the role of potent intermediaries. One way to secure support, following the precedent set by the Ottomans, albeit with a different rationale, was to grant land and subsidies. In countries with agricultural potential like Iraq and Syria, but also Iran, entry into the national era was accompanied by a particular concern for territory, translated into land reforms. As land reforms were very much favoured by the landowning classes, since it would clarify, recognise and affirm their property rights, these measures helped to build support around the nascent state by linking the interests of a class with the existence and consolidation of the centre. Yet the successive military coups, whether in Syria or in Iraq after the 1958 revolution, that toppled the monarchy, eventually leading to the establishment of the Ba'ath, renewed the basis of regime support, with the traditional tribal aristocracy and what remained of its following falling into at least ideological disgrace.

A cultural approach to transnational migrations

The contrast between conservative Gulf monarchies and their republican neighbours has rightly constituted a structuring feature of the analysis of the region, having a far-reaching impact on its international relations. At the infra-state level, the regime's different ideological hue had implications for the population coming to grips with the socio-economic changes, and the nationalist or national-integrationist projects reshuffled the existing social hierarchy. Those least fit to join the nationalist vision yet still powerful and transnationally well connected enough to resist it – that is, the former top of the hierarchy, nomadic camel-herding tribes – made a fully informed choice to migrate to the neighbouring traditional regimes, which they believed to be more tribe-friendly. This belief was encouraged early in the twentieth century when, during his negotiations with Iraq in the 1920s, Ibn Saud declared that the ideal eastern border of his domain was the Euphrates;[84] yet without losing its momentum, the trend continued after King Abd al-Aziz's expansionist dream, based on sovereignty over the nomads, had vanished in the face of the implacable international understanding of territorial sovereignty.[85]

Anthropological works investigating the tribes in the 1950s converge to note that nomadism, even though in decline, continued far into the second half of the twentieth century in Northern Arabia, even until the 1970s. In the current context of a settled population in the region and marginal pastoralism, it is easy to forget this near past, as nomadic tribes appear backward not only to academics but first and foremost to the state builders and rulers of the new independent states, who saw their presence and their encampments that had turned into shanty towns, as a source of embarrassment. The nationalist-primordialist tendency of new states to erase the conditions of their origins in asserting their credibility as if they have always been on the world map is indeed a widespread phenomenon well-known to nationalism studies, and yet this does not prevent it from remaining an obstacle to the understanding of the dynamics of those very states and societies.

The delineation of international boundaries, though necessarily constraining, had little impact on the tribespeople's decision to stick to pastoralism or settle. In the cases where the tribe was not segmented or dispersed into different countries, like the subsection of the Rwala whose settlement was studied by Al-Radihan, the tribe kept its nomadic lifestyle but refrained from moving northward to graze animals in what had become foreign (Jordanian) land, having at the same time benefited from more grazing space due to the exodus of a great number of Rwala to Syria.[86] Al-Radihan's informants mention group unity as being of the utmost significance to them.

In the case of tribes situated astride international boundaries, grazing movements continued as well, formally acknowledged by the existence of the neutral zones between Iraq and Saudi Arabia, and Saudi Arabia and Kuwait, and practically rendered possible by the porosity of the borders in the 1950s and 1960s. It is a consistent contention in national-centred literature that border disputes occurred because of the Bedouin movements between countries in search of pasture, and that inter-tribal territorial squabbles resulted from the imposition of a virtual border in the Syrian Desert, which divided the various branches of the tribes or impeded their ancestral migration patterns. However, beyond the lingering remnants of old raiding habits, the rivalries between branches of tribes and the fluctuating alliances, notably but not exclusively with and against Ibn Saud, the full significance and implications of the international border were not understood until far later, when the first effects of the differentiated policies of economic development or national integration began to be felt in the desert.

Al-Radihan's monograph on the causes of sedentarisation high-lights important points:[87] the overriding factor in the tribes' decision to settle in 1956 was the drought that affected the whole North Arabian Peninsula during the decade. Second to this largely contingent ecological factor, with its obviously dramatic economic consequences, two other motives are mentioned: the decline of pastoral economy following the country's oil exports and the state intervention to induce tribes to settle. The scale of the drought in terms of duration and damage was unprecedented: from the Syrian Desert (especially in 1958–61) to the Qasim region of north central Najd in the 1960s[88] the stories are the same – ruined pasturelands and decimated animal populations causing the poverty-stricken Bedouins to settle temporarily, as the traditional strategy of moving elsewhere was rendered impossible by international boundaries and land privatisation. The Bedouins' acceptance of jobs with the oil company, in checkpoints and pump stations along the new northern pipeline in the middle of grazing lands or in the Eastern Province oilfields, cannot be understood without reference to the impact of the drought and the loss of the main Bedouin capital, their livestock.[89] One of the reasons they accepted settling was because they saw this solution as temporary: working in the pump stations, around which they set up their tents, allowed them to maintain a minimal level of herding and to lead a semi-sedentarised life. Those who received government funds to sedentarise hoped they would accumulate enough capital to buy camels and return to nomadism after the drought. The camel had lost its value as a means of transportation and thus as an asset – first comparative to sheep, which could be transported by truck, and then in absolute terms, and the camel trade was completely marginalised by the size of the oil revenues. These factors are the well-known economic mechanisms of the pull-push model of migration, according to which socio-economic pressure is the prime motive explaining human migrations. My intention here is certainly not to challenge the primacy of the economic factor – that is the complete demise of the Bedouin economy through the intrusion of foreign market forces in the region – but to qualify it by adding to the picture ideational factors, in terms of the state's proclaimed identity and the community's beliefs, to account for the decision to leave and the choice of place to go. This is what can be called a 'revolution of the national'.

Two kinds of regime indeed emerge as regards their approach to the still independent, mostly nomadic, tribes and their relation to the new states. The main dividing line is the espousal or not of a nationalist-integrationist ideology, which underpins the republican/monarchical divide. The emotional aspect that Europeans, since the French Revolution, had attached to the divide between the republic, embodying the popular sovereignty, and the divinely legitimised monarchies is completely absent in the region. These categories are ill suited to the history of the region. What appears, though, is that in the successor states to the European mandates there have been attempts at making the national, the territorial and the political congruent, through a developmentalist approach, falling just short of the high-modernist ideology defined by Scott.[90] On the other side, the traditionally labelled regimes of the Peninsula[91] were not really versed in nationalist ideology, which they soon equated with Arab nationalism as a threat to their independent rule: they opted for a deliberately non-integrationist policy, a social 'laissez-faire, laissez-passer' completely exclusive of any involvement in domestic politics. In a nutshell, the former proclaimed their aim of *nation* state building, involving increasing integration between state, politics and society,[92] while the latter opted more quietly for a *single* state building.

This has implications for the incorporation of tribes. For the tribal aristocracy of the southern desert margins who, unlike the Jarba, had not produced leaders able to operate outside the context of tribal and intercommunal politics or command political power in national affairs to stir group mobilisation, the proximity of the international border and the neighbouring conservative regimes took on a particular significance. Even though the most famous camel-herding tribes remained nomadic for the longest, it would be naive to assume that in spite of the policies of the mandates that had artificially maintained the role of the sheikhs after undermining their legitimate foundations in security and transport provision, they did not feel they were the losers in the socio-economic revolution that was taking place. Yet the national integration processes, far from buffering their decline, destroyed the traditional group cohesion and hierarchy. As early as 1923, Glubb reported how Ibn Hadhal, the sheikh of the 'Amara branch of 'Anaza, regretted that 'the government was undercutting the roots of the old society, by strengthening the lower classes and by sacrificing the noble'.[93] The noble tribes indeed opposed the levelling and melting into the community of equals (at least non-ruling, non-owning) that nation building assumes, and the gradual blurring of the pre-national social hierarchy:

> by the 1950s it seemed as if the creation of new tribes with new shaikhs was in favour ... since internecine fighting had been forced to end, the possibility of proclaiming an equal and independent status for smaller tribal groups had advantages ... [like the al-Ghannaniim people petitioning for an independent pipe from the canal on the basis that] they [were] not a lineage (*fukhuth*) but a tribe (*ashira*) and so should have a right to their own water supply.[94]

Escaping the national logic for mobile tribes had long-lasting consequences.

CONCLUSION

To sum up, this chapter has provided the historical perspective to help to understand the long-lasting consequences, manifested in the *bidun* issue, that were triggered by the dramatic changes in power relations following the revolution of the 'national'. It reached two main conclusions with regard to: first, the impact of integration into the international system on power legitimation, and secondly, the impact on domestic power relations, and in particular the relations between the rulers the *hadar* and the *badu*.

First, under Mubarak the Great, the legitimacy of the rulers was based on their ability to control a fluctuating territory, outside the cities, via the roaming tribes. Financial dealings with the merchants belonged, in contemporary vocabulary, to low politics, since tribes could be mobilised to counter recalcitrant merchants, as the crackdown on the 1938 Legislative Council demonstrated. With the evolution of the understanding of sovereignty increasingly linked to a fixed, bounded territory and the settled population, the role of tribes gradually changed too. They no longer played any part in securing a territorial sovereignty guaranteed by the recognition of the international community; their contribution to supporting the regime's legitimacy was gradually lost to the urban polity, due to the norms of popular sovereignty and the state's representation of its national people.

The conception of 'national' politics became, for the sheikhs, a matter of personal and sizeable following within the limits of the bounded, even urban, territory. As a result the human reservoir offered by the tribes was mobilised: contrary to the *hadar*, the tribes were not politicised, and their networks were larger. Moreover, the tribes and the sheikhs shared a common *Weltanschauung*, as most of the senior members of the ruling family in Kuwait had more 'on-the-job' education to govern than a formal one.[95] This mobilisation would gradually reach the tribespeople present in the areas of pre-national interaction. It is this utilisation of sociological networks across national boundaries that I refer to as transnational actors. I cannot but refer to them as such once the notion of the modern territorial state appears. By contrast with the widespread perception of their recruitment among Kuwaitis nowadays, the reason behind this integration into the security apparatus was as much the need to bolster the numbers of loyal, though possibly idle, supporters as it was the importance of warfare in tribal values or the dexterity of tribesmen at manipulating weapons.

Secondly, this historical overview has laid the foundation for understanding the attitude of the merchants, who let the ruling family get embroiled in the question of the relation with what they consider as its tribal allies. For them, the resort to transnational or far off tribes, with whom the sheikhs of Kuwait had previously allied themselves in the pre-modern high politics of the region, represented an ill-fated attempt on the part of the Al-Sabah to gain support against their reformist ambitions. The next chapter analyses the utilisation of the tribal resources with transnational links to assert the legitimacy of the regime and the state until the middle of the 1980s.

This chapter has also explained why some of the tribes found themselves completely at the mercy of the sheikhs. Before a new set of values based on education and economic logic spread to the region, the system of cultural beliefs valued noble genealogies over material wealth, high politics of territorial expansion, prestigious tribal alliances and the building of legitimacy over the low politics of the urban polity and its power sharing ambition and financial might, which were tapped for military campaigns. This system survived the complete destruction of the geo-political and economic foundations on which it was based, after the extent of power politics in Kuwait was scaled down from Arabia to the state of Kuwait. In spite of the oil-induced economic revolution and the end of the actual role of tribes whose territory cross boundaries in politics, the members of prestigious tribes still thought of themselves as belonging to the genealogy-based aristocracy of the region. Yet in concrete terms, the common *Weltanschauung* gradually turned to the advantage of the ruling family and part of the *badu* turned, in spite of their noble origins, to what could be called in Marxist terms, had Kuwait been an industrial country, the *lumpenproletariat*, that is the lowest economic stratum of the society with all its Brechtian attributes of insalubrity[96] and life in slums and squatters.[97]

CHAPTER 3

From Shanty Bedouins to Illegal Residents

Minister of Interior to the National Assembly: the [Kuwaiti] nationality of brothers is not considered a legal basis on which to grant nationality.[1]

Against the background of the transformation of pre-national power relations and the complete socio-economic reconversion imposed at the regional level, this chapter looks at the nature of the social pact institutionalised in the Nationality Law of 1959. This social pact forms the basis of an aristocracy, where ancient deeds justify present privileges and result in behaviour of 'elite *distinction*', rather than an 'ethnocracy', strictly speaking.[2] If the contradistinction on the basis of ethnicity evoked by Longva worked perfectly vis-à-vis the foreign workers, it does not help us to grasp the discrimination within the same ethnic group that generated the category of the *biduns*. The process of inclusion was not based on a legal principle of nationality brought in the 1959 law from the West via Egyptian legal experts but, rather, it depended on networks of proximity, which were limited.

In the face of a structural lack of a national population to form the core of the modern state, the 'near foreigners', left behind or resisting the national integration projects in the neighbouring states, played a role in guaranteeing the regime's stability. The Al-Sabah had to adapt quickly to a constitutional parliamentary system designed by Egyptian lawyers in consultation with the *hadar*-educated elites, which *de facto* turned their familial rule into a democratic state.

These democratic credentials were of utmost importance in the face of the 1961 Iraqi claim on Kuwait.[3] Bedouin human resources were also used for the state to gain acceptability and legitimacy on the international stage. In that respect, the constitution of national armed forces was essential not only for policing but also symbolically for facilitating greater integration in the community of Arab states.

THE KUWAITI SOCIAL PACT: CONCEPTION AND PRACTICE OF NATIONALITY

Kuwait has had two laws defining nationality: the first was issued in 1948 while the second, still in effect but amended several times, dates back to 14 December 1959.[4] The Law on Nationality, issued by Emiri Decree No. 15 of 1959, defines Kuwaiti citizens *bi ta'sis* (by origin), *asli* (original) or *madat ula* (article 1), i.e first-class Kuwaitis endowed with political rights, as are those and their descendants (article 2) who can prove continuous residence in the emirate since 1920.

Nationality *bi tajannus* – that is to say by naturalisation – could be acquired, according to the initial article 4, by those of good character, proficient in Arabic and having a legal source of livelihood who could prove their lawful residence in Kuwait for eight (for Arabs)[5] or 15 (for non Arabs) years.[6] At first, the number of naturalisations was limited to 50 a year.

Article 5 also gave authority by Emiri decree to naturalise:

- any person who has offered exceptional services to Kuwait
- an Arab person who was resident in Kuwait before 1945 and has maintained residence there until the promulgation of the decree of naturalisation
- a non-Arab person who was resident in Kuwait before 1930 and has maintained residence there until the promulgation of the decree of naturalisation.

These last two paragraphs were modified and replaced by a single paragraph 3 of article 5, according to which any person who was resident in Kuwait before 1965 and has maintained residence until the promulgation of the decree of naturalisation can be considered for naturalisation. The holders of this second degree of nationality, beneficiaries of the socio-economic advantages, would enjoy their political rights after a 'probation' period (article 6).[7]

Much has been written about the symbolic date of 1920, the year that marks the quashing of the Saudi threat embodied in the attacks of Ikhwan troops led by the Mutairi Faisal al-Duwish.[8] This was achieved at the 'battle of Jahra' (10 October 1920) and through the building (from May to June) of the third defence wall that enclosed the historic city of Kuwait, and was later to be replaced by the first ring road. As a result, the Ikhwan never reached the town. Longva notes:

> Much of the mutual identification among town-dwellers, therefore, derived from the need to protect themselves against common dangers. One such danger ... occurred in 1920 ... For two months, the population of Kuwait worked round the clock to build a wall to protect their town ... The wall and the collective efforts that went into its erection remained the symbol of Kuwaiti unity against external threats. The battle of Jahra in 1920 created a special bond between the town- dwellers who had taken part in it and invested them with an unshakable claim to membership of the Kuwaiti community. This event, it is often said, saw the birth of an explicit Kuwaiti 'national awareness'.[9]

These 'citizenship myths', however, were diffused in a way that 'remembered and recounted [events] as singularly *hadhari* accomplishments', notes Tétreault.[10] She goes on to highlight the cracks in this myth of unity:

> Today, Kuwaiti hadhar speak with pride about the defence of Kuwait town by their ancestors but are unashamed to say that they have never been to Jahra' ... Tribal Kuwaitis whose ancestors had been settled inhabitants of Jahra' since before the Ikhwan wars are especially resentful at recently settled badu among first-category citizens when so many of their own numbers have been denied this status.[11]

The national foundational myths of Kuwait, with symbols of the Kuwaiti *dhow* or the city wall (*sur*), belong to the *hadar's* history and appear clearly as part of an elite enterprise still vivid in Kuwait nowadays. Advocating an ethno-symbolic approach to nation building that would take into account the genealogical cultural sense of lineage identity and the conditioning role of the past, Sula al-Naqeeb writes, reflecting the common Kuwaiti nationalist discourse:

> Therefore, the state in 1959, when the first citizenship law was established, recognized the wall as an expression of a cohesive collective identity of a people, and the state used the year 1920 as a point of departure in implementing the citizenship law. In other words, the state recognized the building of the Sour as the starting point of Kuwait's personal historic *ethnie* whereby a community of people, or even tribes in this instance, with a shared cultural and economic vision came together in solidarity. The Sour is also a symbol of the community's intention with regards to their relationship with a specific territory.[12]

Today this 'relationship with a specific territory' is challenged by the people of Jahra, who bore the brunt of the clashes with Iraqi invading forces on 2 August 1990, while the *hadar* mocked them for having fled in the face of the enemy – when most of the Kuwaitis were in fact abroad on holiday during the very warm summer time. Likewise the 'shared economic vision' is today under pressure to be renegotiated by the deputies of *badu* background in Parliament. Since 2008, two issues have dominated the parliamentary agenda: the transparency in the handling of public tenders, which led to the cancellation of several development projects,[13] and the request to bail out citizens' debts.[14] In Parliament, public markets attribution is seen as prioritising benefiting the merchants' enterprises while writing off consumption debts is regarded as just redistribution for middle-class people in the face of the bail out of banks,[15] viewed as protecting the investments of the wealthiest.

The existence of the 1948 Nationality Law clearly illustrates the contingency of this national identity. The original documents of the 1948 Law, kept in the Public Record Office in London, identified Kuwaiti subjects as ruling family members, those permanently residing in Kuwait since 1899, the children of Kuwaiti men and the children of Arab or Muslim fathers also born in Kuwait. Naturalisation was possible after ten years of residence in Kuwait with employment and proficiency in Arabic, and also by special order for those offering valuable services.[16] The polity, based on a narrower urban base but with the wider inclusion of those entitled *jure soli*, would have looked very different from the one we know now.

At the time, since the exploitation of oil had barely begun, the inclusion of *jure soli* envisioned by the Emir Ahmad al-Jabir and drafted by his trusted secretary 'Izzat Ja'far, was certainly designed to allow a progressive sedentarisation of tribespeople and naturalisation of Arab foreign expertise – like Ja'far himself, a Lebanese, Egyptian national.[17]

What had changed 11 years later? The strategic importance of Kuwaiti oil exports put the country at the heart of British concerns. The overthrowing of King Farouk by Nasser and his Free Officers in 1952 later led to the emergence of a very powerful Arab Nationalist opposition, also present in Kuwait and led by Dr. Ahmad al-Khatib, who returned from the American University of Beirut in 1955.[18] The new ruler Abdullah al-Salim also had to face Nasserist opposition in his own camp in the form of his uncle, Abdullah Mubarak, head of Public Security. The republican and military coups multiplied, reaching Iraq; Egyptian prestige in the region, at its zenith following the 1956 Suez attack, had a great impact on the Sunni Kuwaiti elite. These factors dramatically changed the conditions for defining the citizenry, whose control was key for the regime's survival. The 1959 Nationality Law thus dropped the inclusion of *jure soli* and restricted naturalisations and political rights, so as to keep the number of citizens and voters limited. The Nasserists were deprived of potential supporters in the electoral game, which they were to embed in the 1962 Constitution. As for the royal family, it was also hampered in its endeavour to increase the following it had drawn from the nearby tribes with which it had traditionally dealt. Yet these limitations proved too restrictive for both the purposes of state building and regime stability.

Thus it is the concrete threat to his rule, as much as the awakening of the new sheikh to the existing community feeling within the wall/ *sur*, that presided over the drafting of the new Nationality Law. The application of the law fell into the hands of the *hadar*, together with the shared oil revenues, whose lavish redistribution Sheikh Abdullah al-Salim initiated. In this sense, Kuwait illustrates Halliday's statement:

> For the modernists history does not explain what peoples or movements do in the present. What they do in the present is dictated by present concerns, and the past is the source from which legitimation, justification and inspiring example can all be drawn.[19]

Dependency and rentier state theories have shown that the expansion of the state was at the expense of independent social institutions and that oil money not only exempted the rulers from the demands for democratic participation but also led to the depoliticising of social groups by buying them out.

The buying out of nationals, through advanced welfare services, employment programmes and targeted hand-outs, has been effective in isolating citizens from 'new coming' foreigners,[20] yet not quite so effective in dissuading the regional insiders of the system, who were excluded from an ill-defined citizenry, from feeling they would eventually belong to the community of nationals. It is the integration of this under-researched part of the Kuwaiti population that the remainder of the chapter examines. Seen as loyal to the sheikhs, they were treated with mistrust and hostility by the Sunni Arab nationalist elite. Dr. al-Khatib recalled that the Ministries of the Interior and Defence were staffed with recruits loyal to the royal family rather than the state, and officers were asked during their recruitment if they read *Al-Tali'a* or had shed a tear when Nasser died.[21]

AN HYPER-TERRITORIALISED DEFINITION

The Nationality Law currently in force in Kuwait is the odd product of the sudden oil windfall and the question of its redistribution on the one hand, and on the other, the alien legal expertise from Egypt – itself inspired by French civil law. It is also an odd mixture of an original 'snapshot *jus soli* principle' understood in a strict literal sense, with a subsequent narrow *jus sanguinis* application where nationality is only transmitted by the genitor. As a result, the nationals were defined as the settled population.

The characteristics and underlying principles of the Kuwaiti citizenry are sometimes misrepresented. Citizenry is based on an urban rather than national understanding of the territory: Kuwaitis by origin are defined as those who could prove by testimony their uninterrupted presence in the territory of the emirate since 1920,[22] yet this refers to the town itself since the 'national' territory was, ironically, not yet bounded. The would-be international borders of Kuwait with its northern and southern neighbours were not to be defined for another two years, in the 1922 Protocol of 'Uqair, according to which Sheikh Ahmad al-Jabir lost two thirds of his territory to Ibn Saud.[23] It would be another 46 years before they were definitely fixed, with the disappearance in 1966 of the Neutral Zone shared with Saudi Arabia that allowed nomadic movements to continue.

Those who settled between 1921 and 1959 in this rather inconsistently defined 'Kuwait' were classified as second-class citizens who enjoyed all but political rights. To the second-class Kuwaitis one should add those who were naturalised by the application of the 1959 Law's various clauses of naturalisation. However, the great majority of the naturalisations that occurred after the registration period came to an end in 1965 were actually carried out in a discretionary way, under article 5, for *khidmat jalila* or special services rendered to the state. First-class political rights may have been granted, in spite of a 1966 amendment to the Nationality Law (article 6) that forbade it and subjected those naturalised under article 5 to the same 'probation' period as those naturalised according to other articles.

Interestingly, the original process of delineating community boundaries was not racist or sectarian or classist, but hyper-territorialised and hyper-localised. It was based on the social networks of the town dwellers. The dominant minority that initially found itself in the position of insiders and beneficiaries of Kuwaiti citizenship was a hybrid mix bound by neighbourhood relations. Unsurprisingly, it included the royal family, which was in effect turned into the state itself, as well as the economic aristocracy involved in maritime and inland trade, whether Najdi, Hasawi, Basrawi, Zubayri or Persian.

It also included manumitted slaves of African origin[24] and the economically poorer layers of the pre-oil society. The poorer strata encompassed the pearl divers and other crew members, especially since pearl diving, albeit not money-earning, was socially respected, but also the artisans of less-regarded crafts or toilsome occupations like *kandaris* (water carriers), carpenters, or even frowned-upon activities (butchers, ironsmiths), whatever their religious persuasion. Finally, in addition to the town dwellers, defined as people living within the protection of the 1920 wall, inhabitants of peripheral

OLD KUWAIT CITY
BEFORE 1957

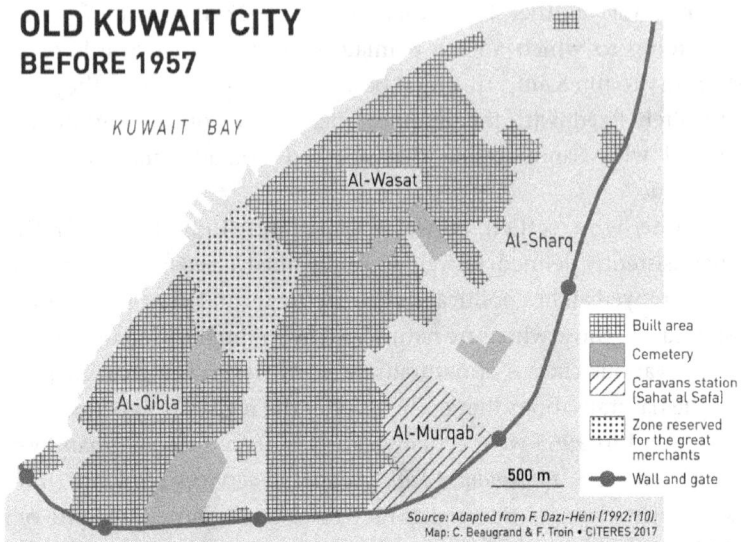

KUWAIT BAY

Al-Wasat

Al-Sharq

Al-Qibla

Al-Murqab

500 m

Built area

Cemetery

Caravans station
(Sahat al Safa)

Zone reserved
for the great
merchants

Wall and gate

Source: Adapted from F. Dazi-Héni (1992:110).
Map: C. Beaugrand & F. Troin • CITERES 2017

MAP 3.1   Old Kuwait City (before 1957)

settlements like Salmiyya, Fahahil, Fintas or the oasis of Jahra, which was populated by semi-settled tribes of shepherds ('Awazim in Salmiyya, Dabbus in Fahahil, and other *'arib dar* or semi-settled tribes), were close enough to the limited network of settled Kuwaitis to qualify for citizenship. Their frequent visits to the town markets to sell vegetables, fish and animal and woollen products had rendered them more familiar to the urban population than the Bedouin caravan haulers of the Sahat al Safa (the caravans station in al-Murqab).

The Committees of Nationality (1959–65) based their decisions on the 'who's who' of pre-oil Kuwait, organised into *firij* or micro-level neighbourhoods.[25] On 18 April 1978, the newspaper *Al-Siyasa* significantly published a statement from the Ministry of the Interior, in which the ministry justified its decisions regarding the appeal against nationality granting in the following terms: 'The Members of the Committees looking into the nationality applications have a thorough familiarity with and a perfect knowledge of the Kuwaitis and their families.'

This mental mapping of people according to their pre-oil residence remains significant nowadays. It is eloquently illustrated by the publication of the book on Kuwaiti families sorted by their original location within the wall or nearby villages, *Al 'awa'il al kuwaitiyya fil ahia' wa al qura al qadima*.[26] The use of the word *'a'ila* – the family that did not necessarily keep links with their pre-Kuwaiti past – is meant to be differentiated from that of *qabila*, reserved for the Bedouins, whether settled, semi-settled or nomadic, who have kept links with their larger solidarity network.

There were four Committees of Nationality and a higher committee;[27] three committees were in the old city, in Sharq, Qibla and Murqab, and the fourth one was located possibly in the south near the Saudi border, designated to register the 'Ajman.[28] When the work of the nationality committees ended in 1965, an unknown number of people were still living in the desert, with no information about either the existence or the significance of the ongoing process of registration for nationality. The prevailing forms of identification at the time were membership in a tribe (for Arabs), place of origin (for Persians) or professional activity.[29]

The work of the committees took place in the context of repeated attempts by the Kuwaiti merchants to enhance the efficiency of the nascent administration through sharing administrative tasks with the royal family. This led to the creation in 1954 of the High Executive Committee, composed of three young sheikhs and three non-royal members, with authority to reorganise the government administration. The nationality committees had little if any administrative experience and possessed almost no documentary records to prove settlement before 1920. As a result, they resorted to subjective methods, including oral evidence given by witnesses, family names and reputation. Nationality was commonly granted on the basis of belonging to a neighbourhood or *firij*. For others, the credibility of the evidence depended solely on its ability to convince the committee.

The task of the nationality committees was made more difficult by the fact that thousands of Bedouins applied for Kuwaiti nationality on the ground that they currently and had for a long time, lived within the territorial limits of Kuwait but not within a city or town. Similarity of culture, traditions, appearance, dialect and costume existing between the Bedouins of the Arabian Desert, which extends between Kuwait, Saudi Arabia, Iraq, Syria and Jordan, made it more difficult still for the committee to distinguish between dwellers of the Kuwaiti desert and others. Proof of belonging to a tribe settled within the territory of Kuwait was furnished through a statement from the leader of the tribe, that the individual person was a member of the tribe.[30]

A *bidun* recalls:

> My father brought seven witnesses from senior Kuwaitis to the Nationality Committee in order to prove his residence in Kuwait before 1920 but the file has not been decided upon until now. The Committee was left to its own device to eventually decide whether an individual was Kuwaiti or not.[31]

But there was no coherent criterion for accepting or refusing any application. Since there was, and still is, no judicial review of decisions of the nationality committees, the final outcome of their work has resulted in the creation of a large number of people who insist that they are Kuwaiti nationals notwithstanding decisions of the committees to the contrary.[32]

Nationality had become a matter of personal networks. For those involved in politics, sheikhs or influential families, it was also a matter of personal following, and strengthening their power base. Clans in Kuwait were also involved in the process, as one *bidun* informant, who lived in Maqwa'a, just northwest of Fahahil, and whose mother was from the Fudul, narrates:

> In the 1960s, Fahahil was controlled by the Dabbus family who belong to the Fudul tribe. They helped the Ajman tribe to obtain Kuwaiti nationality, which they did not do for their own brothers because they were at feud with them at that period. The Ajman tribe soon outnumbered the Fudul and the latter [eventually] lost their position to the Ajman in the National Assembly.[33]

The 'sense of pragmatism' and 'economic necessity' characterising tribes becomes extremely tangible when it comes to dealing with state administration. In a discussion about the 'Awazim, I was told by an 'Anazi *bidun* that the advantage (he saw it as a problem) of small tribes is that, since they are not divided by rivalries, when they want to increase their numbers, any member who gets nationality can register all his cousins under his name so that they become Kuwaiti without having to register.[34] While no 'Azmi counts among the *biduns*, the members of what is one of the widest-spread tribes of

North Arabia acquired a bad reputation, as some *'ajam* were said to add the last name 'Anazi to their own to obtain nationality.[35]

This collective understanding of entitlements suggested that rather than the concept of citizenship, the notion of social pact is better suited to the Kuwaiti context of sociologically tribal societies. And 'social pact' here means more than membership of the citizenry, possibly including access to politics. Borrowing Heydemann's term, it is used to refer to 'an institutionalized bargain among collective actors [...] encompassing a set of norms or shared expectations about the appropriate organization of a political economy in general'.[36] These norms shape perceptions concerning whose interests need to be taken into account in making economic and social policy, which actors have a legitimate claim on state resources, which institutional forms are accepted as legitimate mechanisms for organised interest representation, what kind of demands state actors can legitimately make on interest groups, what mechanisms are available to both state and social actors to resolve conflicts and what kind of policy instruments state actors can legitimately deploy to achieve their aims.

The notion of social pact is analytically far more illuminating than the one of citizenship, whose shortcomings have already been denounced by Altorki. She noted that the understanding of citizenship, defined in the language of rights and obligations as 'processes and practices by which contract-making individuals defend their interests in society', carries individualistic assumptions that do not suit the Arabian Peninsula context.[37] The plasticity of the social pact as outlined above, with its concepts of collective actors, bargaining and prioritising policies in the interests of one or other of the groups, is far more appropriate to the Kuwaiti polity.

Yet the notion of 'kin' forming the basis of the group does *not* denote a set of static and clearly definable tribal groups. It is a fluid concept over space and time and dependent on changing socio-economic and political conditions as well as a variety of other factors, in particular self-perceptions and the perceptions of others, especially in relation to the dominant group or to the state. It follows from this that at the outset of the 1960s, the pastoralist and semi-pastoralist tribal groups, confronted with the collapse of their tribal economy, perceived their kin as particularly extended in order to carry weight in the social contract but also to assure a living. This resulted in the collective understanding of nationality or naturalisation and led to puzzles, frequent in the *bidun* circles in Kuwait, whereby brothers (*shaqiq*) possessed different types of nationality. Some, left with second-class nationality while their brother acquired first-class, rejected it as an offense.

The consequence of this 'urban snapshot' conception of citizenship is, first, that it fails to embrace the whole territory of the internationally recognised state, let alone acknowledge the reality of nomadism; but secondly, and most importantly, it evolved into a sclerotic, static vision of Kuwaiti citizenry as soon as the welfare benefits started to rise and foreign labour started to flood into the country. This sclerotic vision assumes that the national population will grow only through the birth rate of Kuwaitis, whose fertility rate was also promoted.

A STATIC VISION OF THE POLITY

The legal provisions regarding the conditions of naturalisation have not always been consistently applied.[38] According to Rania Maktabi,[39] 'between 100,000 and 200,000 Saudi and Iraqi Bedouins, known for their loyalty to the Sabbahs, were granted Kuwaiti citizenship in the 1970s in order to strengthen the pro-government electorate'. Although naturalised, they benefited immediately from their voting rights, so as to influence the results of the elections.

The Nationality Law was amended several times. The conditions of naturalisations have also been made gradually more stringent. New conditions were added by amendment: the applicant must keep his/ her residence in the country (1960); he/she must be Muslim by birth or by a conversion, dating back a minimum of five years (Law 1/1982). Most importantly, the number of naturalisations by virtue of article 4 was limited to 50 persons a year in 1960, and then to a yearly number decided by the Council of Ministers as of Law 100/1980.

As a consequence, most of the naturalisations have been carried out by virtue of three other articles: article 5 regulating 'extraordinary' forms of naturalisation, including paragraph 1 for special services (*khidmat jalila*); to a lesser extent, article 7, governing the right of a foreign wife to acquire Kuwaiti nationality when her husband was naturalised, as well as that of the children of the naturalised father;[40] and article 8, concerning the naturalisation of foreign women married to Kuwaitis *asli* (or original Kuwaitis).

The notion of 'exceptional or special services' proved to be extremely flexible. It has been used to date to naturalise prestigious personalities like artists, and increasingly football players, but also sheikhs of historic tribes. Lists of Kuwaiti showbiz personalities who acquired the Kuwaiti nationality circulate on the internet, with the famous case of Dawud Hussein, of Pakistani origin and a Bolivian passport holder, who acquired Kuwaiti nationality in 2007.[41] Likewise, in 2007, 12 members of the al-Hadhal family, paramount sheikhs of the 'Anaza, based in Iraq, were granted Kuwaiti nationality.[42]

Yet, at least until 2000 and with the exception of a 1972 amendment to article 5 of the 1959 Law specifically directed at the case of *biduns*, all the above-described legal dispositions did not seem to have been designed for, nor did they apply to, the case of the *biduns*.

Paragraph 3 of the 1972 amended article 5 authorised the granting of nationality to stateless children born in Kuwait, provided that they maintained their normal residence in Kuwait until they reached the age of the legal majority and completed secondary education in Kuwaiti schools. This amendment was repealed by decree in 1980 in the absence of Parliament, which had been dissolved four years earlier. The number of cases naturalised by virtue of the amendment has remained secret until now; Human Rights Watch[43] suggests it was 294 *biduns*. In any case it is unlikely that it was a large number, just as paragraph 2 of the same article 5, regarding the children of divorced or widowed Kuwaiti mothers, was applied in scarce numbers. Seeing the complexity and the frequent changes made to the letter of the law, most Kuwaitis and *biduns* alike considered the naturalisation gate to be closed, and all the more so as the final word on nationality remains, in any case, in the hands of the ruler.

Largely outside the remit of the Nationality Law, the *biduns* were not subject to the dispositions of Law 17 on the Residence of Aliens of 1959 either, designed as it was to manage migrants' stay in the country.

Article 25 of the 1959 Law 17 on the Residence of Aliens lists the cases that are exempted from the law requirements, mentioned in its paragraph (h),[44] the *afrad al 'asha'ir* or tribal members entering

Kuwait by land from places where they used to do so for the purpose of performing their ordinary business. By leaving its borders open to seasonal migrations, the young state of Kuwait initially played a significant role in facilitating the survival of the nomadic tradition. It also created an incentive for them to settle in the emirate in the face of the economic revolution that made this survival impossible. Moreover, when the tide of sedentarisation affected the desert tribes in the 1960s, the Kuwaiti state allowed them to stay on its territory without formally granting them the status of citizens.

After the registration period to gain access to nationality expired in 1965, the situation became more complex when the Kuwaiti administration issued compulsory birth certificates.

> The requirements for the issue of such certificates in the early 1960s were so lenient that virtually any person residing in Kuwait was able to obtain a certificate in effect, merely upon his assertion of birth in Kuwait, the assertion being corroborated by a witness. These certificates are now the primary documents large numbers of stateless persons rely on as evidence of their birth in Kuwait.[45]

These birth certificates were understood as a third degree of nationality. Sheikha Fawzia, a prominent lawyer specialising in cases of *biduns*, underlined that for registration in the 1965 census, the population – and *a fortiori* the *biduns* – needed only their birth certificates.[46] Yet they were discarded later as invalid proof on the basis of which to register a file and claim nationality, according to a former *bidun*, naturalised in the early 2000s.

The doctoral thesis on Kuwait's police forces submitted by Mohammed Al-Fahed at the University of Exeter in 1989 bears witness to the ambiguity of the status. Al-Fahed wrote: 'once again, it is reiterated that rank and file policemen and watchmen who volunteer for the job must be citizens. Yet most are birth certificate holders, which is a secondary-type citizenship'.[47] He developed the socio-economic differentiations further:

> Lower ranks of the Kuwaiti police force are filled by non-Kuwaitis who are not only perceived by the community as second-class citizens, but are in fact, socio- ethnically deprived because they are only birth certificate holders. Therefore, they have no legitimate claim or right to any political, social or economic privilege as guaranteed to those who

possess full native Kuwaiti status. This heightens uneasy tensions, which inherently exist between the police and the community.[48]

Al-Fahed also gave the *raison d'être* of the whole hierarchy between native Kuwaitis and 'others who were later absorbed into the community in the capacity of either non-Kuwaiti birth certificate holders or foreigners' as being 'a practical and acceptable method of differentiating groups within the society to prevent those who might later attempt to lay claim to Kuwait by usurping some share of political power from being able to do so'.[49] He identified as the most critical issue in the Kuwaiti police the discrepancy between the law establishing the police and its application, specifically in terms of recruitment, hiring, promotional practices and educational opportunities,[50] which implied the two-tier functioning of the police and the existence of *biduns*.

This most critical issue did not pertain only to the police; it was the crucial issue faced by the Kuwaiti rulers in maintaining the security of the state and the stability of their regime in such a difficult context. The context was difficult for them for the following reasons: first, the Kuwaiti Arab nationalists, forming the majority of the Kuwaiti intellectual elite at the time, were questioning the legitimacy of their rule. Secondly, the national population alone was not enough to build the modern state that they required to sustain their authority and needed to be supplemented by outside human resources. However, the tiny size of the citizenry could not be enlarged to dilute the opposition of the Arab nationalists. Finally, while the Egyptian influence was mainly channelled through the Kuwaiti Arab nationalists, their Iraqi rivals threatened not only the regime but the existence of the state altogether.

FROM SHANTY TOWN TO POPULAR HOUSING: WHEN ILLEGALITY FIRST OCCURS

After having highlighted the legal confusion around the status of a part of the population residing in Kuwait, this section seeks to shed light on the historical conditions that presided over the emergence of the *bidun* phenomenon. In Kuwait, shanties populated by Bedouins flocking from the desert were sprawling. The Kuwaiti government faced difficulties in addressing the phenomenon and differentiating between the different cases of *biduns*. *Biduns* recall places, habitats and Bedouin settlements that no longer exist. The history of Bedouin shanties, which have now disappeared, represents the unwritten history of post-oil Kuwait, the flip side of the modernity coin, the state's struggle to keep pace with the growth of shanty towns on the periphery of the main urban centres of Kuwait City, Jahra and the oil city of Ahmadi, where the petroleum company was based.

Farah Al-Nakib shows how urban policies have contributed to shaping Kuwaiti social identities and eventually entrenched the *badu/hadar* dichotomy. *Badu* housing at the periphery of the main city centre, in self-contained areas with relatively poorer state services led, she argues, to the social construction of the category of *badu* as a 'backward' underclass in Kuwait with lesser opportunities.[51] Likewise, the history of the *biduns* is part and parcel of the urbanisation process, and more precisely of the sprawling informal housing in Kuwait, referred to as *'ashish* (sing: *'asha*) or wooden huts. The existence of shanty towns corresponds to the particular period of economic development that generates mass exodus towards urban centres, and raises the crucial question of integration and the exclusion/isolation of newcomers via housing policies.[52] Kuwait's housing policies towards newly arriving Bedouins contributed to their geographical and social marginalisation, which in turn, undermined their claim of belonging to Kuwait.

Although the *hadar* population of Kuwait had been coming throughout its history from the Arabian Peninsula, the shanty Bedouins who came in the 1950s to live in informal housing formed a separate community, with its own social characteristics. The exact period of the Bedouin arrival to the periphery of Kuwait urban centres, as well as their number, is not known – as there was no census until February 1957.[53] Al-Moosa, who wrote a doctoral thesis on the shanty towns in Kuwait in 1976, nevertheless distinguished between the Bedouins who came in the 1930s and settled in permanent dwellings in Kuwait City or the other urban centres,[54] abandoning their desert customs altogether to adopt urban ways of life, and those who came in the 1950s and clung to their tribal and grazing habits, settling only temporarily near the oil fields, changing from tents to shanties, and finding employment with the oil companies.

Harold Dickson, a former British political agent in Kuwait who then worked for the Kuwait Oil Company, noted a mass influx of Bedouins between 1952 and 1953, when the population jumped from what he estimated to be 160,000 to 250,000 – although the figures ought to be taken with critical distance. The influx makes sense at a time when Kuwait opened its borders to immigration without restriction. The oil boom nurtured ambitious ideas about social and economic development hindered by a too small indigenous population.

Informal housing, known locally as the *'ashish*, appeared in Kuwait in the 1930s. They spread in earnest at the end of the 1950s after the discovery of oil.[55] Bedouins began to change their traditional accommodation, from tent to shanty, when the Kuwait Oil Company (KOC), the first industrial institution and main job provider, established houses for its labourers, among whom were newly-arrived Bedouins, and offered facilities and services for the settlements in Maqwa'a, Subaihiya and Fahahil. The Bedouins, uncomfortable in the new houses, preferred to live in their traditional black tents on the perimeter of the built-up area. The oil company dealt with their preferences by offering them 20 per cent of their wages as an accommodation allowance, instead of providing them with concrete housing. Bedouins occupied most of the unskilled jobs, especially guard jobs, in the oil companies, which allowed them at the early stages to quit periodically their labouring during the season when the pastures were flourishing.

The discovery of oil is one of the main elements that attracted Bedouins and led them to settle and accept jobs matching their limited qualifications with the Kuwait Oil Company (KOC). The KOC thus played a role in enticing the tribes to settle in shanties. Shanties were recorded in Maqwa'a as early as 1936.[56] Ten years later, the 'colonial company town' of Ahmadi was built:[57] it presented a socio-spatial segregation in the hierarchical allotment of houses and lot sizes, which varied in the north, mid, and south sections of the town. While the northern part, with its spacious houses and lots, was destined for the senior expatriate staff (British and American) and the mid section, endowed with smaller lots, hosted junior Indian and Pakistani staff, the south section, with its undersized orthogonal row housing, was reserved for labour.[58] This labour was made up of Arabs and Iranians. In 1947, faced with the urgent need to accommodate its employees, the company could only provide Nissen huts to more than 500 staff,[59] while 115 artisans[60] were housed in local mud brick houses and the 1,000-person strong labour force in *sarifas* – that is, shelters made from reeds and straw matting. Two years later, at the end of 1949, the number of unskilled KOC labourers was 6,672, that is 56 per cent of the 14,260 total personnel; the company had no intention of providing housing for local Arab labour, so that the latter had no choice but to settle informally in an area between Maqwa'a and Ahmadi. Because the growing 'slum areas', reaching even as far as the entrance to the site, was an eyesore to the company officials, they decided to move the 'fringe population' to a 'new camp near Fahaheel, called Badawiyyah'.[61] In 1954 1,000 families, 700 of whom were KOC employees, moved their shanty houses to the new camp in order that their presence was physically and visually out of sight. In 1956, the Suez crisis triggered a virulent anti-colonial rhetoric that targeted the KOC, especially with regard to its policy in Badawiyyah and its discrimination against and neglect of services for Arab unskilled labour. *Al-Fajr* denounced the fact that 'Ahmadi's Arab Village, which the KOC claimed provided housing for Arab workers, was instead housing Indian and Pakistani employees while the Arab workers lived in 'hovels'.[62] As of 1956, KOC public relations campaign highlighted improvements in the accommodation of Kuwaiti employees. The question remains open as to whether the KOC differentiated among the Arab labour between those who had proof of Kuwaiti citizenship and those who did not.

The oldest shanties that appeared in Maqwa'a and Jahra in the 1950s grew steadily in the 1960s until the 1970s. A decision of the Council of Ministers prohibited any new shanties in the country in 1965, which did not stop the phenomenon. By then, Sayhad al 'Awazim had become the largest shanty area, because it was the place where the occupants of shanties demolished by the municipalities in 1972–3 were resettled. Other shanties mushroomed in a very short time anywhere near the sources of livelihood, either on the fringe of

SHANTY AREAS AT DIFFERENT STAGES

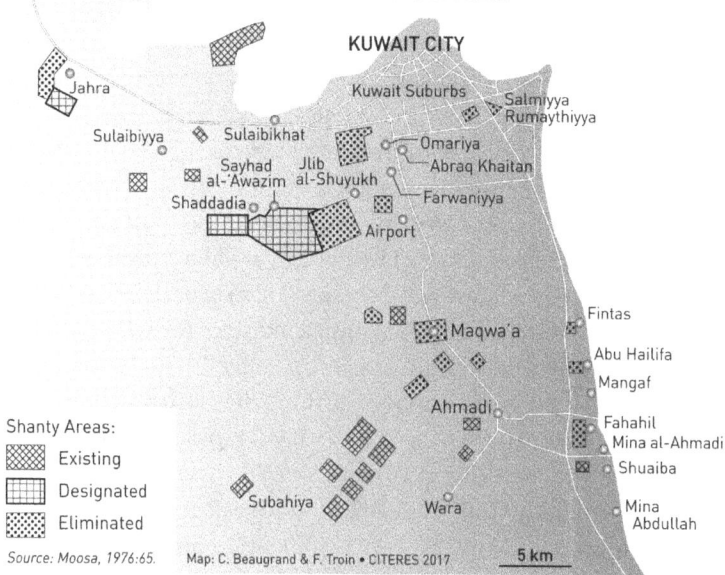

KUWAIT CITY

Jahra

Kuwait Suburbs
Salmiyya
Rumaythiyya

Sulaibiyya   Sulaibikhat
Omariya
Sayhad   Jlib
al-'Awazim   al-Shuyukh
Abraq Khaitan
Shaddadia
Farwaniyya
Airport

Maqwa'a

Fintas
Abu Hailifa
Mangaf

Ahmadi
Fahahil
Mina al-Ahmadi
Shuaiba

Shanty Areas:

▨ Existing

▦ Designated

▨ Eliminated

Subahiya   Wara

Mina
Abdullah

Source: Moosa, 1976:65.   Map: C. Beaugrand & F. Troin • CITERES 2017   5 km

MAP 3.2   Shanty areas at different stages

urban areas,[63] or near oil fields or where grass or water was available. In 1972, the press was reporting in eight different areas affected by informal housing,[64] while the 1975 census counted 18 shanty towns. According to Al-Moosa's sample, 60.5 per cent of the shanty dwellers were Bedouins who had moved from the desert.[65]

The Committee for Illegal Dwellings was established in 1974 specifically to deal with the issue of housing built without licence. It was made up of representatives of the ministries concerned with the question. It supervised the Department Concerned with Illegal Dwellings (*idarat al buyut ghayr murkhasa*), created in February 1975 with the mandate to implement the Master Plan,[66] and in particular its recommendation to restrict all shanty residents to designated shanty areas that were fenced and endowed with health services (Jahra, Sayhad al 'Awazim and Shadadiyya). According to the resettlement plan, each family moved to the designated area, was allocated a 25 m² plot on which to erect their dwelling, and was placed according to its tribal group in blocks of 80 plots each.

To register in the designated area with the Department Concerned with Illegal Dwellings, each member of the family had to present a birth certificate, a health card and a ration book for the whole family, and was issued an identification card, renewable monthly.

Many conversations with second-generation *bidun* informants have indeed brought up the memories of these lost informal habitats that no longer exist, but that marked the history of urbanisation in Kuwait. The most commonly cited places are Shadadiyya as well as Maqwa'a. For instance, a *bidun* from the 'Anaza tribe depicted the mix of Bedouins that were living in Maqwa'a, north of the oil installations in Ahmadi, when he was a child in the early 1970s, especially his Dawasir[67] neighbours. Another (from the Rubai' tribe) even mentioned a place called al Rabiya, near Farwaniyya, which was nicknamed *Nasariyya* after the Iraqi town.[68]

The history of informal settlement in Kuwait is one of the state's failures to keep up with the pace of migration and housing needs. 'The city of Kuwait was passing through [a phase] of rapid urban (*hadari*) development between 1950–1970, and we can infer that the development of urban areas in Kuwait had an big impact on the spreading of *'ashish'*.[69]

As for the figures for inhabitants, it appears that what the press reported was below reality: a 1958 article of *Al-Fajr* stated that the Kuwaiti municipality counted 4,626 *'asha* (or wooden huts) hosting 13,990 people, including 3,277 Kuwaitis, living in squalid conditions – that is, with no water nor electricity.[70] The figures, based on official censuses, are shown in Table 3.1.[71]

During these years, Kuwait's housing policy consisted of trying to rein in the sprawling of shanties, and while doing so, giving priority to Kuwaitis, with reference to access to housing.

Kuwaitis were (and still are) eligible for government housing schemes, in particular Low Income Group Housing (LIGH, *buyut dhuwi al dakhal al mahdud*). Set up in 1954, this scheme offered houses, distributed throughout residential urban areas in Kuwait,[72] to all low-income Kuwaitis (*hadar* or not) on a long-term hire purchase without interest basis. The average plot for a LIGH was 400 m².[73] All applications were dealt with in order of application, but between

TABLE 3.1   SHANTY POPULATION, 1957-75

Census	Total population	Kuwaiti population[74]	Shanty population	Kuwaiti shanty dwellers
1957	206,473	113,622	57,745	
1961	321,621	161,909	43,320	
1965	467,339	220,059	78,329	57,278
1970	738,662	347,396	96,205	
1975	991,392	470,123	131,257	104,703 (Bedouin)

Source: Abdurasoul A. Al-Moosa, 'Bedouin shanty settlements in Kuwait: a study in social geography', unpublished PhD thesis, SOAS, University of London, 1976, p. 96.

1962 and 1973 Bedouin families had been granted only 21.6 per cent of the total successful applications of Kuwait families.[75]

A second type of housing scheme existed specifically for the Bedouins, the popular housing built between 1972 and 1983. It was first named 'Badu housing', later changed to 'Badiya housing' and was finally referred to as *masakin sha'abiyya* or *buyut sha'abiyya* (popular housing). The Credit and Saving Bank was responsible for the scheme, decided in 1970. As a new way to proceed, it called for international tenders to cover its implementation from the design phase to the finance, execution and maintenance. Yet 'financial considerations were unduly allowed to outweigh the wider interests of the scheme', according to Al-Moosa, who regrets that no proper studies for the planning of the design of the settlement and houses, nor social and economic studies on Bedouin, were prepared.[76] The result was a very ill-conceived housing area, built on the cheap.

The popular housing plot was 150 m², as compared to the 400 m² of the LIGH.[77] It consisted of two to three rooms, a kitchen, a bathroom and a roofed space, all located around a courtyard. The materials used were cement blocks, the walls were ready-made units, with the doors of the rooms and the front door made of iron. While Bedouins had organized their *'asha* in the shanties around an open space, with a separated *diwaniyya* or guest room, animal pen, garage for their car and a latrine outside with sufficient space left with the other *'asha*, they had to move to houses organised along parallel roads dividing housing units. Moreover, the facilities (sports centre, recreation areas, main roads, green areas) that were initially planned were never built. Out of the initial schemes, only the dwellings themselves were built, without any attention to the need for such facilities as roads, schools, health centres, religious institutions, water and electricity supplies, in spite of all the facilities being shown on the plans for the scheme.[78]

The scheme soon turned into a fiasco. The first occupants were dissatisfied and disappointed with the dwellings. Although prohibited by the Ministry of Housing, they made alterations to heighten walls or add animal pens. They suffered from the lack of *diwaniyya* (the Kuwaiti traditional salon or *majlis* for men) or garage, the lack of privacy. The government had alterations destroyed at the expense of the occupants, who became convinced that government policy in moving them from shanties to popular housing was not based on the wish to improve their amenities but on the wish to restrict them to the new areas. This feeling was reinforced by the fact that the new housing was located in areas at least 10 kilometres (km) (six miles) from the nearest residential areas. Owing to the commuting time needed to get to work, the occupants of popular housing had very little opportunity to interact with other people in Kuwait.

The allocation of the scheme's dwellings had been distributed equally between the Ministry of Housing (created in 1975) and the Ministry of the Interior and Defence. Those allocated to the Ministry of the Interior and Defence went to its military personnel, although some of them had not yet been granted Kuwaiti nationality. As the scheme was a failure, Kuwaiti Bedouins refused to stay and applied to move from popular housing to LIGH,[79] and the popular housing ended up going to non-Kuwaiti Bedouins, who, as employees of the Ministry of the Interior and Defence, considered themselves owners while the Ministry of Housing considered them as tenants.

Despite the failure of the first scheme to reach its aim of accommodating Kuwaitis, the government of Kuwait went ahead with a second Scheme at the end of the 1970s.[80] The 1978 study published in *Al-Ra'i al 'Amm*[81] mentioned that the government planned to build 9,696 units of Popular Housing, before December 1979 in Jahra and Sulaibiyya.[82]

In total, about 80,000 persons were to be relocated in the newly built popular housing. The stated goal of building these housing units was to replace the *'asha* (wooden huts) and eradicate the phenomenon of *'ashish*. The three designated shanty areas of Jahra, Sayhad al 'Awazim and Shadadiyya, made up of 6,000 *'asha*, were to be demolished, and any new *asha* built in Kuwait would be considered contravening the law. Two committees composed of the government General Secretariat, representatives of the Ministry of the Interior and Defence, the Ministry of Housing and the Department Concerned with Illegal Dwellings allocated the housing units.[83] It is on the basis of their employment that policemen (Tayma, Jahra) and military (Sulaibiyya) were allocated a 200 m^2 house made of concrete and corrugated tin, where most of the *biduns* live now. Out of the 16,000 *'asha* with demolition orders to be carried out by March 1979, only 9,000 families were resettled: priority was thus given to those who held Kuwaiti nationality and those who qualified for the LIGH. In an article dated 10 September 1978, featuring an interview with the head of the Department Concerned with Illegal Dwellings, the newspaper *Al-Siyasa* called for the private sector and other institutions to help with the building of popular housing for employees who had been working in Kuwait for 25 to 30 years.[84] In any case, it seems that few Kuwaiti citizens settled in the two new popular housing complexes that received shanty people.

Despite the efforts to get the *'ashish* under control, the phenomenon did not disappear. As the designated areas of Jahra, Sayhad al 'Awazim and Shadadiyya were demolished by the end of 1979,[85] *'ashish* sprawled in other locations, further away from the urban centres. They were reported in the north Subayya but also in the south in Jali'a, close to the Kuwait navy base, in the desert, south of Jahra and Sulaibiyya. In a report in Subayya, north of Jahra, *Al-Qabas* interviewed some *'ashish* dwellers: after the demolition of their shanty dwellings in the designated areas, the cost of which they had to bear, they said they had to move further away.[86] They represented the 7,000 *'asha* that were not resettled at the time when the designated areas were cleared, as the popular housing only housed 9,000 and priority was given to the staff of the Ministry of Defence and Interior or employees of other ministries. Those not eligible for the schemes built new *'ashish* without licensing from the municipality, as used to be required in the designated shanty areas.

In a separate development, some *'ashish* were licensed by the municipality for employees of the Kuwait fishing company. Likewise, the agricultural authority also licensed some shacks for sheep herding or horse breeding.[87] Those shacks were referred to as *jakhur/jawakhir* and owned by Kuwaitis who got the licence.[88] Yet owners tended to rent them not to shepherds but to foreigners who came from neighbouring countries with entire families, unable to afford other types of accommodation in the city.[89] During these years, the uncontrolled growth of informal housing started to become associated with a security threat.[90] In 1984, the press raised the issue that it was difficult to assess the numbers of people living in *'ashish* who claimed they had no nationality. In 1985, the occupiers of some *jawakhir* were clearly identified as infiltrators (*mutasalillun*), having crossed the border illegally; the unlawful habitation became associated with lawlessness (illegal border crossing, illegal alcohol traffic, and licensed animal herding barracks turned into refugee dwellings).[91]

By 2010 the majority of *biduns* were said to be living in Tayma, Sulaibiyya and Ahmadi, the oil city 36 km south of Kuwait. The personal *bidun* stories are interwoven in the history of the Kuwaiti urban margins.

One *bidun* recalls: 'My dad was first in the drilling team in the desert, then he worked as a fire-fighter in the oil city; in the capacity of which he got a reward for fire extinguishing in 1964.'[92] Fieldwork interviews showed, nevertheless, that as a rule, in the *bidun* genealogy, the first generation would work in the oil sector but then move to more stable employment in the ministries of defence or interior, without staying in KOC housing. This was the case for the above-quoted *bidun*: 'My grand father, was born in 1935 in Kuwait and had a house in Ahmadi but my father settled in Tayma as a member of police forces, for which he has been serving 42 years.' Other testimonies agree:

> My father worked four to five years in the oil sector. He was a worker with the Company of Ahmadi. He had a salary there. In 1957, he became an employee of the Ministry of the Interior. He was working at the police station of Fahahil. My maternal uncle is Kuwaiti but my mother is *bidun* from the same tribe. ['Anazi from the Hamad]

My father started to work in the Oil Company in 1957. Then he worked for a governmental ministry, the Ministry of Municipality and died in 1986. ['Anazi]

My father joined the navy in 1974. In 1990, he was dismissed without pension. Before, he worked in the oil company in Ahmadi: the oil company used to pay a daily salary, while the Army [armed forces] gave a monthly salary. My paternal uncle, as for him, entered the police in 1977 where he still is as he was reinstated after the liberation. [Zafiri][93]

Contrary to the popular housing schemes that, although initially designed for Kuwaitis, were deemed too uncomfortable and eventually ended up being occupied by non-Kuwaitis who were not eligible for state housing, the KOC housing does not seem to have met the same fate. It is unclear how *biduns* eventually occupied houses within the oil city. The company meant to gradually replace expatriates, and from 1958 implemented gradual policies of nationalisation of the workforce at the mid and senior levels. In the 1960s and 1970s, Ahmadi had become a model for urban modernisation, and its planned residential neighbourhood units were intended for Kuwaitis, KOC keeping ultimate responsibility as a landlord. Although there may have been exceptions for outstanding workers, the presence of non-Kuwaitis and *biduns* in south Ahmadi corresponds to the period after 1975, when the oil city began to deteriorate and its appeal for nationals to erode. Until then, living in Ahmadi was desired because of its different and superior architectural quality and urban services in comparison with Kuwait City. With the development of Kuwait City and its suburbs, these glorious days became a memory. Modifications to the built environment, illegal expansions such as the addition of rooms or *diwaniyyat* (as was seen in popular housing) and the spreading of subletting all affected the town's architectural form, contributing to its urban downgrading.[94] Anti-social behaviour also appeared, with reckless driving inside the town, graffiti and vandalism. While the shift was identified as starting in 1975 with the management change following the company's nationalisation, the final nail in the coffin of Ahmadi's past glory was the Iraqi occupation of Kuwait, which purposely destroyed 2,100 out of the 3,600 existing houses.

Possibly a legacy of the *'ashish* that had spread out near Ahmadi, informal settlements still existed in Umm al Hayman when the Iraqis invaded Kuwait in 1990, and *biduns* were living there. As the Iraqi army forced them to flee the informal settlement, some of them sought refuge in the south Ahmadi houses that had been abandoned by their occupiers. In 1993, the Kuwaiti government demolished the district of Umm al Hayman and its inhabitants were forced to relocate[95] – according to a US cable, to the *bidun* areas of Tayma and Sulaibiyya.[96] In place of the informal settlement[97] the government built residential units for Kuwaiti nationals, as it also did for the new Na'im area in Jahra, where the first scheme of popular houses was located. In September 1997, the Public Authority for Housing Welfare (PAHW) opened applications for 3,800 units comprising house and plot of 400 m^2 to Kuwaitis who had registered their housing demand with it up to 31 August 1987. Likewise, 490 plots and 460 houses were open for applications in Na'im (Jahra).[98] Umm al Hayman was renamed Ali Sabah al Salim, in a gesture to erase the memory of the place. Around the same time, on 30 July 1997, the KOC tried to evict the *biduns* from south Ahmadi, to no avail.[99] One *bidun* from Ahmadi recalls that in 1996 the *biduns* protested for the first time in their lives when they were asked to return the houses.[100] At the time of fieldwork in 2014, these housing units looked mostly unoccupied. According to a *bidun* whose father lived in south Ahmadi, 'they are now demolishing the houses once the occupier dies'.[101] In between, in 1998 the idea of redevelopment of the city of Ahmadi was launched and then endorsed by the Emir Sabah al-Ahmad in September 2006, followed by the establishment of the Ahmadi Township Redevelopment Team (ATRT), in charge of the city's new master plan.

Looking at the development of housing schemes, and in particular of Bedouin housing, helps understand the misunderstanding regarding nationality. Bedouins who came to Kuwait were primarily looking for jobs. They were also hoping to obtain housing, bearing in mind that Kuwait is a country with very high temperatures in the summer but is also cold in the winter.

Hitherto Bedouin had not found boundaries relevant to them, as they had thought of themselves more in terms of Arab Bedouins, having all Arab land as their homeland. But with the political division of the Arabian Peninsula, and the closer association of groups of Bedouins with particular states, some Bedouins had begun to adopt the nationality of the country in which they were settling. In Kuwait, Bedouins having Kuwaiti nationality were at an advantage when seeking employment, and obtaining dwellings or state welfare generally, which encouraged others to claim it too.

It is extremely difficult to calculate the number of Kuwaitis among the shanty dwellers; it is in the discrepancy in Bedouin statistics that the origin of the *bidun* phenomenon is to be found. In 1969, Colin Buchanan and Partners estimated that 81 per cent of the shanty dwellers were Kuwaitis.[102] The same figure was quoted in a press article, on 17 March 1978, probably based on this source.[103] According to Al-Moosa,[104] Buchanan's figure includes all the Bedouins who claimed nationality as opposed to those to whom it had actually been granted. His own survey in 1974 found that only 14.4 per cent of the shanty people had Kuwaiti citizenship while 78.3 per cent claimed they had it, since they had *applied* for it. He dismisses the claim that 70,000 had been granted nationality on the basis that the stated number of housing application based on the same period (1965–70) did not reach more than 33,774.[105]

A discrepancy occurred between two different statistical public institutions: the state census statistics classified inhabitants of shanty areas as Kuwaitis even if they had not been *granted* nationality but believed they were merely waiting for the government to give them an official recognition or document. On the contrary, the Central Statistic Department working for the Committee Concerned with Illegal Dwellings considered Kuwaitis to be only those who had proof of Kuwaiti citizenship. As a result, the percentage of Kuwaiti nationals among the Bedouin shanty dwellers diverges (see Table 3.2).

A number of Bedouins claimed that they were Kuwaitis, without ensuring that they actually possessed the nationality. They appeared in the census figures as Kuwaitis. Yet this claim was insufficient to allow them to benefit from the state services reserved for citizens.

TABLE 3.2 PERCENTAGE OF KUWAITI NATIONALS AMONG THE BEDOUIN SHANTY DWELLERS

	State census		Committee Concerned with Illegal Dwellings		Difference (a) – (b) those who thought they are Kuwaitis but were not (percentage of the total)	Total
	Kuwaiti (a)	Non-Kuwaiti	Kuwaiti (b)	Non-Kuwaiti		
Jahra	14,368 96.8%	474 3.2%	148 1.2%	14,694 98.8%	14,220 (95.8%)	14,842
Sayhad al 'Awazim	39,635 94.8%	2,160 5.2%	4,848 11.6%	36,947 88.4%	34,787 (83.2%)	41,795
Shadadiyya	22,582 88.9%	2,810 11.1%	1,208 4.7%	24,184 95.3%	21,374 (84.1%)	25,392
Maqwa'a	7,540 87.5%	1,076 12.5%	646 7.5%	7,970 92.5%	6,894 (80%)	8,616
Ashairej	1,054 9.2%	10,430 90.8%	46 0.4%	11,438 99.6%	1,008 (8.8%)	11,484
Doha	11,865 94.3%	718 5.7%	47 0.4%	12,536 99.6%	11,818 (93.9%)	12,583
Other areas	7,659 45.6%	8,784 54.4%	3,298 19.9%	13,147 80.1%	4,361 (26.3%)	16,545
Total	104,703 79.8%	26,452 20.2%	10,241 7.8%	121,016 92.2%	94,462 (71.9%)	131,257

Source: Abdulrasoul A. Al-Moosa, 'Bedouin shanty settlements in Kuwait: a study in social geography', unpublished PhD thesis, SOAS, University of London, 1976, p. 98; provided by Planning Board 1975.

TURNING THE AL-SABAH'S RULE INTO A CONSTITUTIONAL STATE

Creating a national army

The question of the Bedouins' integration overlapped with the issue of state building under the constraint of limited national population. Both crystallised around the question of building armed forces. The irredentist claims formulated by Abd al-Karim Qasim as soon as Kuwait proclaimed independence in 1961 marked a turning point in the foundation of the armed forces. On the one hand, Kuwait invoked article 4 of the friendship agreement with Britain, requesting British military assistance. This is the basis on which the British flew troops to the newly independent country under the code name 'Operation Vantage'. On the other hand, the new state, freshly released from colonial rule, sought support from other Arab states that would only grant it if the British withdrew their own forces from Kuwaiti territory. From then on, Kuwait gave assurances about belonging to the Arab nationalist camp. The Kuwaiti government took major steps to develop its armed forces and participated in the Arab–Israeli wars of June 1967 and October 1973 as well as the War of Attrition between 1968–72. The Kuwaiti contingents in the Arab–Israeli wars were extremely important in the foreign policy of Kuwait, to show that the state, although created and sustained by the British, was supporting the Arab cause. It was all the more important that the USSR vetoed Kuwait's admission to the United Nations until 1963, after the fall of Qasim.[106]

As a few *biduns* were said to be among the soldiers who passed away during the operations outside of the country, these operations are given special attention in what follows.

Kuwait dispatched troops in the 1967 war.[107] On 5 June 1967, the Emir Sabah al-Salim issued a decree declaring the country in a state of defensive war against the Zionist entity occupying Palestine. He had ordered Kuwaiti troops to be transported via Kuwait Airways in the shortest possible time, their equipment to be airborne by military transport aircraft, while the rest would follow by land. Kuwaiti troops were the only Arab troops to fight in the Rafah area, on the Egyptian front.[108] In November 1967, the British Minister of State at the Foreign and Commonwealth Office, Goronwy Roberts congratulated

Saad Abdullah, the Kuwaiti Minister of Defence, saying he heard the Kuwaiti 'had acquitted themselves very well last June'.[109] According to an *Al-Watan* article, the Yarmouk Brigade (the Kuwaiti military unit disptached on the Egyptian front) may have represented one third of the three brigades that constituted the Kuwaiti army at the time.[110]

The Kuwaiti Yarmouk Brigade stayed in Egypt for seven years, until 6 October 1974. It participated in the War of Attrition. According to a brigadier from the Yarmouk Brigade, Sa'adi Falah al-Shammari, Kuwait left a battalion, renewed every three months, in between the Farsan island (Ismailia) and the Crocodile Lake. The Kuwaiti troops were building shelters, fortifications and lines of communications under the command of the Second Field Army. In April and June 1970, Israeli shelling from the other side of the Suez Canal took the life of 22 soldiers of the Yarmouk Brigade's battalion, so that it was relocated to Fayed, near the Great Bitter Lake.[111] The fifth infantry battalion took part in the October war in 1973, and lost 18 of its soldiers, together with their commander, Major Khalid Abdullah al-Jiran.

Kuwait also contributed to the troops on the Syrian front. Partrick writes that 'Kuwait had been one of eight non-frontline Arab countries that sent troops [during the October war] – in Kuwait's case adding to its existing troop presence in Egypt with a contingent on the Syrian side of the occupied Golan Heights'.[112] After the outbreak of the 1973 war, on 15 October 1973, the Minister of Defence, Sheikh Saad Abdullah, decided to create a new force, the Jahra Legion force (*quwwat al Jahra' al mujahfala*) to fight on the Syrian front.[113] Composed of 3,000 men and several battalions,[114] the first deployment occurred by air the same day and, together with the forces dispatched by land, integrated the Syrian forces 15 days later. The Jahra force first protected Damascus, near Sayda Zeynab, before joining the Syrian Third Division on the Golan Heights, and officially left Syria on 25 September 1974.

Until 1991, the category of *biduns* played an important role in staffing army and police forces. Two laws laid down the organisational principles of the Kuwaiti army:[115] the law issued on 16 January 1963 and amended by that of 15 June 1969 on the 'Organization of the Ministry of Defence' specifies the full responsibility of the armed forces under the Ministry of Defence. Secondly, Law

32/1967, issued on 12 July 1967, organises the functioning of the army (up to the time of writing). According to Al-Najjar,[116] the law 'allows for other nationalities to become officers in the army, with the exception of the *biduns*'. It was not until 1993 that an amendment to article 29 of the army law (Law 21/1993 of 14 August 1993) restricted access to the army to non-Kuwaitis, but only those who hold a nationality (excluding those with an 'unknown' one such as *biduns* had). At the time, *biduns* with undefined nationality were encouraged to take on another nationality, which they would do so as to keep their employment. The question of the recruitment is a prominent one.

Law 13/1976 (16 March 1976) provides for the organisation of military service. According to al-Khatib,[117] former leader of the Arab Nationalist Movement, the Parliamentary Defence Committee submitted a law proposal in order to render military service compulsory as early as 1964, but the Al-Sabah wanted to keep control of the recruitment process in the armed forces and ignored it until 1975, election year. This is plausible since the army rests traditionally on bonds of loyalty between the sheikhs and their recruits. The law was passed after the newly elected Jasim al-Qitami,[118] former head of the police during the 1956 Suez crisis, resurrected the draft. The law began to be implemented in March 1978. Yet as early as 1979, the second group of conscripts took to the streets demonstrating against the bad practices of the army training division and the ignorance of the government bureaucracy,[119] so that the law was amended in 1980.[120]

With regard to the police (including coast- and border guards), Law 23/1968 (21 May 1968) provides for its organisation, while duties and responsibilities of the Ministry of the Interior are to be found in the law issued on 7 January 1979. Article 26 of the 1968 law permitted non-Kuwaitis to be employed in a technical capacity or as experts on a temporary basis, yet citizenship was required for all other military positions, whether officers, soldiers or policemen, as well as for training in schools and academies. The approval of the Minister of the Interior and Defence, Sheikh Saad Abdullah al-Salim Al-Sabah, who occupied the post from 1965 to 1978, when he became crown prince was needed for non-Kuwaiti volunteers to fill the positions of watchmen, policemen or the rank and file of the armed forces (article 26).[121] Nevertheless, the law of 1968 did not forbid the recruitment of stateless people. As a result, a large number of Bedouins were hired in the police forces with what was perceived at the time as 'limited citizenship', as Al-Fahed called it.[122] The dubious solution to the recruitment problem of the police forces did not stir public debate and did not reach the press. Article 15 of the law relative to the organisation of military forces prohibited any recruit from disclosing information about his job, keeping official documents, writing in newspapers or publishing his opinion in any form without prior permission. Prohibition also affected their involvement in any business or any paid job for another employer (See Table 3.3).

Although no official statistics exist, it is estimated that until 1990, approximately 80 per cent of the regular army personnel were *biduns* who never reached the rank of officer. If the same proportion is assumed for the police forces, in the mid-1980s as many as 24,000 *biduns* may have served in the armed forces of Kuwait.

Among the *biduns* Longva distinguishes between nomads and mercenaries. She puts forward cultural and political explanations for the exclusion of the first category, explaining that the nomads simply did not register with the authorities when the 1959 Nationality Law came into force, which resulted from 'a combination of failure to understand the importance of the newly introduced concept of citizenship and an attempt to hold on as long as they could to their pattern of cyclical migration'.[123] Unlike the nomads, who had never had any citizenship previously, the mercenaries were nationals from surrounding countries, mainly Iraq, Syria and Jordan, who came to occupy the lower ranks of the armed forces, for want of recruits among nationals. Although the distinction is analytically absolutely correct, there was a close link between the two categories belonging to the same cultural stock and related by tribal bonds.

Rashid Hamad Al-Anezi, blamed the government for further aggravating the issue of statelessness, created by the ill-suited law through an organised recruitment of Bedouins to serve in the police force, the army and the National Guard. He described the recruitment in the following terms:

TABLE 3.3 KUWAIT ARMED FORCES, AS PER THE IISS *MILITARY BALANCE*

Year	Army	Air force	Navy (coast-guard)	Total Armed force	Reserves or para-military	Military service
1974–5	8,000	2,000	200	10,200	Not included	Conscription
1975–6	8,000	2,000	200	10,200	Not included	Conscription
1976–7	8,500	1,000*	200	9,700	Not included	18 months
1977–8	8,500	1,000*	500	10,000	Not included	18 months
1978–9	10,500	1,000*	500	12,000	Not included	18 months
1979–80	9,000	1,900*	200	11,100	Not included	18 months
1980–1	10,000	1,900*	500	12,400	15,000 police	18 months
1981–2	10,000	1,900*	500	12,400	15,000 police	18 months
1982–3	10,000	1,900*	500	12,400	18,000 police	18 months
1983–4	10,000	1,900*	500	12,400	Not listed	18 months
1984–5	10,000	2,000*	500	12,500	National Guard,[124] Palace, Border Guard	18 months
1985–6	10,000	2,000*	1,100 administered by the Ministry of Interior	12,000 'regular'	National Guard, Palace, Border Guard	Terms of service: 2 years university students: 1 year**
1986–7	10,000	2,000*	1,100 administered by the Ministry of Interior	12,000 'regular'	National Guard, Palace, Border Guard	Terms of service: 2 years university students: 1 year

* excluding 'expatriate personnel'.

** national service lasts for one year for university graduates and two years for the other conscripts and all men are supposed to receive a 30-day training annually, although few actually do.

Interestingly, the number of police forces is listed under 'Reserves or para-military'.

In the 1950s and 1960s, especially after independence, and in the light of Iraqi claims which threatened Kuwait's independence and integrity, Kuwait started to recruit a large number of bedouins to serve in the armed forces. Committees were set up by the Ministry of Defence to choose suitable and eligible bedouins. Selection depended mainly on a given person's tribe; a specific day was chosen for each tribe to bring several of its members to be introduced to the committees to enable them to make their selection ... The process of recruiting bedouins together with the lack of effective control of entry by land to Kuwait led to the entry into Kuwait of many thousands of tribesmen from Saudi Arabia, Iraq, Syria and Jordan, and additionally thousands of semi-bedouins, members of non- nomadic tribes, mainly from Iraq and Syria.[125]

In the nearby Sufayri in Saudi Arabia around 26 km northwest of Hafr al Batin (see Map 2.1), Professor Bruce Ingham, an anthropologist, witnessed the same phenomenon happening for the granting of Saudi nationality until the 1970s and 1980s: the Saudis accredited tribal sheikhs to register people as Saudis. The sheikhs signed a letter attesting to the applicant's entitlement through their tribal affiliation. Author of many studies on the Zafir tribe, Ingham also noted that the tribal subsections of the Humaid and Rufai', considered Iraqi tribes (*badiyat al Iraq*),[126] though having their summer quarters across the Euphrates, used to graze in winter in the north of Saudi Arabia, together with the Zafir. Knowing the region quite well, they claimed they were from the Zafir and had no problem registering as such.[127] In the absence of a clear notion of legality and identification, these practices illustrated the variable-geometry idea of common ancestry and tribal bonds,[128] possibly including ancillary tribes, as seen in the case of al-Rufai' and al-Humaid, which actually defies any state's endeavour to institutionalise family patterns.

In the midst of the confusion of tribal flocking to Kuwait, a certain logic nonetheless presided over the choice of recruitment. Since the beginning of the 1950s, conditions of life have been better in Kuwait than in neighbouring Saudi Arabia and Iraq. Bedouins first came to make a living, especially in the oil industry in Ahmadi, as pipeline guards, installation watchmen, etc.[129] It was easy to come and work, and in doing so, it was easier to get citizenship; 'tribes ha[d] relatives, cousins, Kuwait granted them the citizenship', Dr. Ahmad al-Khatib recalled.[130] To secure the loyalty of their recruits, the officers of the nascent Kuwaiti armed forces targeted certain tribes they trusted; and these trusted tribes were those whose sheikhs were in Saudi Arabia, the Mutair, the 'Ajman and also the 'Anaza. King Abd al-Aziz had close ties with the Rwala subsection of the 'Anaza, based in the northwestern region of Saudi Arabia, with whom he intermarried. It is in this context that the following quote, an extract from a thesis looking at the sedentarisation of a nomadic subsection of the Rwala in Northern Arabia, ought to be read:

> In 1963 a large proportion of the younger generation tribesmen left the Wadi [Sirhan] and joined the Kuwaiti Army, whilst others went to Sakaka, Kuraiat, Arar, Dammam, and Riyadh looking for jobs. Elders who remained viewed the migration of their sons as a loss of group unity.[131]

Whether through a decision or just the use by cousin tribes of their network resources, the sections of the tribes coming from Iraq – that is the 'Amara section of the 'Anaza but also the Shammar and the Zafir – were also hired under the same conditions.

A *bidun* source from the Iraqi Shammar concluded 'we came too late', adding 'the tribes and their sheikhs did not have much power. The government policies played a role, as the [government was the] main employer.'[132] Here a selection of families and employment histories will give a broad-brush idea of this period where no detailed picture is possible, with only fragmented oral sources and the classified nature of written sources.[133]

> My grandfather was a *badu* from the 'Anaza. Then, with the change in circumstances, the family mixed with other tribes. My father did not come back from Iraq where he was POW. He was in the military since 1968.[134]
>
> I am the third generation. My grand-dad came first and my father was born in Kuwait when there was no settlement. The family used to settle as shepherds during seasonal migrations. My dad was in the military, he was among the guards of the *suq*, which does not exist anymore. He went to Saad Abdullah College for police forces and stayed in the army and police until 1980.[135]

As a result, between 1962 when the Ministry of the Interior was established,[136] and the 1980s the *biduns* formed a clear majority in the armed forces, with figures as high as 70 per cent quoted.

Inflated support and demographics

Different reasons combined to explain the mass naturalisation of tribes. First, the overthrowing of King Faisal in Iraq and the coming to power of Abd al-Karim Qasim may have caused the government in Kuwait to turn to Saudi tribes and naturalise them in their numbers, among which were the Mutair, the 'Ajman and the Dawasir. As a result some tribespeople have had two nationalities. Secondly, the nationalists focus more on domestic politics to account for this decision. The 1962 constitution to which they had contributed a great deal was quite advanced in democratic terms. Although it held 11 out of the 14 ministries officially instituted in 1962, the Al-Sabah lost the advantage to the *hadar* Arab nationalists in the 1963 parliament. The royal family wanted to control the next parliament (s), to be elected in 1967 (and 1971). As a result, the government opened the door to naturalisation until the beginning of the 1970s.

In 1967, the then Minister of Guidance and acting Minister of the Interior, the powerful Sheikh Jabir al-Ali Al-Sabah, born to an 'Ajman mother,[137] mass naturalised the members of the 'Ajman tribe residing in Kuwait. As a result, all sources converge to note the large increase in the population of native Kuwaitis: from 220,000 in 1965 to 680,000 in 1980.[138] Ghabra[139] calculates that the number of people naturalised between 1965 and 1981 reached 220,000; Dr. Ahmad al-Khatib gives a similar estimation of around 160,000. Almost 80 per cent of those naturalised were from tribal origin, mostly from Saudi Arabia, swelling the numbers in support of the regime. If the precise number of the beneficiaries of these naturalisation measures is not known, there is one certainty in Kuwait: no *bidun* comes from the 'Ajman.

This policy of extra-legal naturalisations infuriated the *hadar* opposition, as illustrated by the position of Dr. Abdullah Fahd al-Nafisi,[140] who denounced it vehemently, and thereby, in 1979, lost his job at Kuwait University, and also his passport. This governmental strategy against its opposition reinforced the rigidity of the *hadar* conception of the citizenry. With the population increase being higher among the *badu* than among the *hadar*, the balance between the two tipped in favour of the former. Before the 1981 elections, the government readjusted the electoral constituencies drawn with the town as a primary focus in 1963, to reflect the new weight of the periphery. This reapportionment resulted in a significant increase in the number of Bedouin representatives and a dramatic decrease in the number of Shi'ites. The former constituted 56 per cent of the representatives elected in 1981, up from 50 per cent in the 1975 parliament.[141]

Figures are of utmost importance. With regard to the category of the *biduns* Longva notes:

> Before the war [the 1990 invasion], many expatriate residents in Kuwait were unaware of their existence as a separate social category, especially as the official census regularly counted them as Kuwaitis, a fact to bear in mind when we read the population and labor statistics.[142]

This last remark regarding the population and labour statistics points at another essential role of the *biduns* in the process of state formation in Kuwait. *Bidun* population inflated the national population, adding another 200,000 people around 1985 (see Chapter 1). Oddly, the presence of the *biduns* gave a certain legitimacy to the emirate of Kuwait as a national state.

So far, this chapter has contextualised the formation of the Kuwaiti social pact institutionalised by Law 15 of December 1959. The mode of self-identification according to the fluid logic of kin and patronage prevailed in both the *hadar* and *badu* populations, contrary to the nationalist myths of civic *hadar* and ethnic *badu*. Yet the definition of kin-based networks and subsequent alliances depends on socio-economic and political conditions as well as ideological considerations: in the balance of power between the sheikhs and the Arab nationalist Sunni elites, non-educated tribal populations, albeit pure Arabs, were perceived as being on the conservative side of the monarchical forces. They were indeed on the conservative side as a result of both cultural (rather than purely ideological) and economic considerations.

The exclusive character of the social pact, because of a mix of political – the fear of republican Arab nationalism – and economic – rent redistribution – led *de facto* to the obstruction of the naturalisation process. Yet the small number of the national population represented a real obstacle to both the regime stability and the state building process. This pushed the Kuwaiti authorities to recruit first in the near periphery from among the unlucky applicants for Kuwaiti nationality, but also to use their traditional networks and tap into their like-minded relatives in the neighbouring countries – starting with Saudi Arabia. The central concept of *wasta* – that is, gaining access through an intermediary, still largely in practice today[143] – ought to be explained here. Contrary to *backshish* (overt corruption practiced for financial gains) *wasta* implies trustworthiness. The individual being introduced to the ruler, leader or employer by an acknowledged loyal person would be considered trustworthy and deserving of the grace, favour or job he/she requested. While some observers, or new generations of Kuwaitis accustomed to nationalist myths of 'citizens in arms', see a paradox in the fact that the State of Kuwait relied on 'foreigners' to form the very heart of its defence, this book argues that they belonged to a strong sociological network whose trust-based links were used by the state, when faced with too many, or too politicised, migrants and a *de facto* obstructed naturalisation process.

As a result of both the exclusive character of the social pact and the state recruitment policies, the category of *biduns* combines very different cases. It is difficult to establish a typology of *biduns*: some of them are to be attributed to loopholes in the Nationality Law, especially its gender bias; some others can be attributed directly to government policies and the enormous incentives they created. One characteristic of the Nationality Law, in article 2, is that only the father can transmit nationality. This created a category of children without rights, the so-called 'children of Kuwaiti mothers', *abna' al kuwaitiyyat*, whether divorced or widowers.

These are the most invisible of the invisible. Their files have been 'under study,' sometimes for decades. Living in an all-Kuwaiti environment, they do not feel or appear socially as though they are part of the *biduns*. These cases arise when female Kuwaitis marry foreigners who begin a process of naturalisation. As this process can take a long time, the father may die or the parents divorce, as the latter raises the chances for the offspring to be granted nationality. However, if the children reach the legal age of the majority before the naturalisation process is complete, they end up not being Kuwaitis. If they were not registered with any embassy (as it is the case for children of Palestinians), they became stateless.

They are the tip of the iceberg of all the children born to Kuwaiti mothers who were obliged, though living their whole life in Kuwait, to take on their father's nationality, mainly Jordanian or Saudi. This generated frustration. In those cases, it is the private wealth of the family that would offset the absence of state allowances, and getting these children married becomes a real concern. A final legal refinement adds to this conundrum: the kind of citizenship held by the mother and relatives of the *biduns* whether first or second degree nationality.[144] When one is Kuwaiti *bi tajannus*, the article on the basis of which one was naturalised matters. In Kuwait, one is 'article 7 Kuwaiti' if the child or wife of a Kuwaiti *bi tajannus*, 'article 8 Kuwaiti', if the wife of a Kuwaiti *bi ta'sis* or 'article 3 Kuwaiti' if an orphan.

Second, the category of *biduns* comprises the individuals and their descendants who refused the second degree of nationality because they felt entitled to the first degree, as well as those whose file was rejected altogether.

Thirdly, there are *de jure* stateless people who never registered with the committees of nationality, whenever they arrived in Kuwait. They usually started their employment history in the oil facilities of Ahmadi as early as the 1940s. They later merged with a fourth type, recruited from the near region of northern Arabia who may have a previous nationality in Saudi Arabia, Jordan or Iraq. The category of the military, that is, the police and army, was treated separately with little transparency throughout the 1980s. Since the liberation of Kuwait, the relatives of *bidun* martyrs who fell during their service on the battlefields of the 1967 or 1973 Arab–Israeli wars, or at the hands of Saddam Hussein's troops during the invasion and liberation of Kuwait, form a category on its own, as they nurtured the hope of being better placed for a resolution of their undetermined status.

Finally there are all those who, as insiders of the system and looking and speaking enough like Kuwaitis, could take advantage of the category and who arrived in Kuwait in the 1980s.[145] This is the claim that the Kuwaiti authorities put forward to justify their pressure policy as of 1986. In the early 2000s when I first visited Kuwait, the entire category of *biduns* was associated with Iraqis who had come 'illegally', notwithstanding the issue of state employment in the armed forces or the subjective work of nationality committees.

The number of these Iraqis may have doubled the number of *biduns* on the eve of the Iraqi invasion. One example of such a family came into the international spotlight in a different context: Jihadi John, the executioner of the Islamic State, hailed from an Iraqi family that fled to Kuwait in 1987 and was born in Kuwait a year later. Living in Jahra, the Emwazi family eventually left for the United Kingdom in 1994, yet when the news broke in 2015, the father still lived and worked in Kuwait, at the Iraqi border, for Al-Abdali Agricultural Cooperative Society in Kuwait.

In conclusion, the category of *biduns* thus has no coherence apart from the administrative label assigned to them. In spite of some broad attested characteristics like their overwhelming presence in the military, the situations of the *biduns* in terms of socio-economic conditions, networks and rights enjoyed are very varied. The *bidun* category is far from the completely segregated group into which they have been fashioned by years of discriminatory policies.

This variety of cases and the interests linked to them (children of female Kuwaitis versus tribal soldiers) explains the variety of solutions put forward that insist on gender bias or war sacrifice. By bracketing this variety of cases together under the label of 'illegal migrants', the authorities hid their complexity as much as they blurred their actual policies, naturalising the 'children of Kuwaiti women' under their programme of statelessness reduction. The oppressive policies introduced in 1986 embodied an attempt by those in command of the modern Kuwaiti state to engineer and order a complex social reality of differentiated integration in order to fit it into rigid rationalised and legible administrative international categories.[146] This is what we called 'the manufacturing of illegality'.

CHAPTER 4

The Manufacturing of Illegality

[The government] handles labour problems with non-nationals as foreign policy problems (holding governments responsible for the docility of imported labor and vice versa-penalising non-nationals for the policy positions of their leaders).[1]

The previous chapter showed how, for domestic and international reasons, human resources that could be trusted were incorporated into the enterprise of state building. They could be trusted because they shared the same political culture, and also because their solidarity networks overlapped with parts of the communities that make up the Kuwaiti mosaic. These flows, difficult to regulate, eventually became uncontrollable.

The policy turn in the mid-1980s, officially formulated in 1986, illustrates the state's need to regain control. Refugees and expellees generated by political upheavals and the Iran–Iraq conflict mixed with *biduns* or added a layer of complexity to the *bidun* issue. Yet the government, in apparent ignorance of the variety of situations, put them all together under the category of 'illegal migrants'. As 'illegal migrants', who are presumed to have kept some connection with their home country, they then belong to state registered, international law sanctioned categories. Resorting to an internationally sanctioned vocabulary and discourses regarding border crossing movements disguised the origin of the *bidun* issue, pertaining to the creation of the modern state of Kuwait. The legal framework in which the *biduns* were institutionalised gave the state considerable leverage to closely scrutinise and regulate their lives and movements. This tremendous state power is discussed in this chapter as 'administrative violence', defined as the use of all possible administrative means to delegitimise claims to citizenship by anybody feeling some sense of entitlement.

However international humanitarian law, which seeks to reduce the category of statelessness, defies the logic of administrative violence. The core of the conflict between the state institutions set up in the second half of the 1990s to deal specially with the *biduns*, on the one hand, and the *biduns* and their advocates on the other, has – since the end of the second Gulf War in 1991 and even more during the 2000s – revolved around the recognition or not by the *biduns* of an attributed foreign origin. The *biduns'* capacity to survive lies in the fact that they have become part and parcel of Kuwaiti society, as well as in the inability of the Kuwaiti state to deport them. The *biduns* devised these survival strategies, elaborated with the help of that part of Kuwaiti society linked to them or sympathetic to their cause.

REGIONAL SECURITY AND ECONOMIC DOWNTURN

The 180 degree change in the government's policy towards the *biduns* took place in a dramatically changed international environment. The politicisation of Shiite transnational flows grafted onto traditional religious networks pushed the state towards more alignment in terms of border strengthening and population control.[2] The gradual politicisation of religious transnational networks in the 1970s was not the only transnational factor playing a role in influencing state structures and institutional organisations: the economic crisis of the 1980s, exacerbated by the collapse of the Suq al Manakh in Kuwait in 1982,[3] led to the adoption of the same reflex and discourse as in all the developed states facing economic crisis, that is, the revision of their policies of importing labour– a measure regarded as comparatively more flexible than other unpopular measures affecting citizens. However, in Kuwait, the role of migrants is double-edged since migrant workers are, more than anywhere else, excluded from society, while on the other hand, Kuwaitis are dependent on them, in contrast with non-rentier economies, where nationals are in competition with them.[4] This labour policy took a particularly schizophrenic outlook: rocked by waves of terrorist attacks on its own soil, the government of Kuwait – at least until 1985 – blamed the migrants, yet the number of targeted deportations orchestrated information campaigns to deflect public criticism had some intrinsic limits, so as not to unsettle the economic system. *Biduns* were thus relabelled as illegal migrants to satisfy both those afraid of the alien presence and those aware of the benefits of its presence.

The Regional Turmoil

The religious resurgence, or rather the adaptation of religion-inspired activism to the modern state system, represents one of the major structural changes to have affected Gulf politics since the 1970s. Shiite political Islam, which rose to prominence with the Iranian Revolution, in fact had a long history of diffusion, drawing on previously established patterns of religious interaction. The interlacing of political ideas adapted to the bounded nation states within the Shiite religious discourse dates back to the 1958 creation of the *Hizb al Da'wa al-islamiyya* (Party of the Islamic Call) in Najaf. The transnationalisation of these ideas is due first and foremost to the domestic conditions in Iraq, where the failure of the Da'wa project to overthrow the Ba'athist regime, and the dramatic reduction of its space for political action, led its leadership to seek bases abroad to guarantee the physical integrity of the movement. However, it also corresponds to a traditional pattern in the Kuwaiti Shiite community that used to bring Shiite clerics from prestigious *hawza*, particularly Najaf, in the absence of a tradition of high-level Shiite scholarship in the emirate.[5] The creeping Shiite activism went unnoticed by the Kuwaiti authorities. This is what Laurence Louër calls the 'dual positioning': the representative of Najaf in Kuwait was both an envoy of the *hawza* and of the political movement:

> being a delegate of the *marja'iyya* allowed him to stay on good terms with the Kuwaiti authorities for whom he was no more than a religious scholar doing his job in a population known for its loyalty to the ruling family.[6]

At the turn of the 1980s, the politicisation of transnational Shiite networks was a reality in Kuwait; it became a visible reality with the activist movement that formed around the Sunday lectures of Ahmad al-Muhri in the Sha'ban Mosque (*Masjid*) in August 1979 – during the period of dissolution of Parliament (1976–81).

Animated by a feeling of discrimination, in the aftermath of the Islamic revolution in Iran the Shiites in Kuwait organised a weekly gathering in *Masjid* Sha'ban to discuss the issue, as well as the return of parliamentary life in order to enforce the constitution and ensure equality – a grievance supported by Sunni Kuwaitis as well. Eventually, the government deemed the Sunday lectures potentially revolutionary. Indirectly, this movement had a double impact on the question of the *biduns'* issue.

First, it raised the core issue of the difference in nationality. As one Kuwaiti Shiite militant put it: 'It was not routine lectures: for the first time, the lectures talked about politics between Sunnis and Shiites and called for the application of the Constitution and the restoration of the Parliament',[7] two topics that were banned from discussion in the press at the time – the first one having been discredited as 'sectarian practices'. The core focus of the lectures was 'the concept of equality', a topic of concern to a wider Kuwaiti audience than just the Shiites to whom the lecture was delivered. Ahmad al-Muhri questioned 'the real meaning of equality', defining it in terms of equality of opportunity, equality of rights, equality between nationals and equality between genders. The *biduns* were part of this larger picture. Ahmad al-Muhri denounced the different levels of nationality and the different rights enjoyed by the sons of 'article 1 Kuwaitis' and the sons of naturalised Kuwaitis, that is 'article 7 Kuwaitis', deprived of political rights. He noted that, 20 years before, there was only one nationality and 'no *madat*' (different articles by virtue of which one is a Kuwaiti national), and that, at the time he spoke, only the governing elites were enjoying the first degree of nationality. In the context of widespread dissatisfaction concerning the two degrees of nationality (see Table 4.1), this discourse threatened the basis of the nationality system.

The success of the lecture series grew: 'From an audience of a few hundred at the beginning, the lectures managed to gather 1,000– 2,000 persons: added to the readership of the newspaper that covered the event, it may have reached 15,000 persons', according to the recollection of a Kuwaiti who attended the lectures.[8] The lecture

TABLE 4.1 ESTIMATION OF THE RATIO BETWEEN FIRST- AND SECOND-DEGREE CATEGORIES OF KUWAITIS IN 1975 AND 1985

	Number of registered voters (male Kuwaitis, above 21, first degree of nationality)[1]	Total number of male Kuwaitis above 20[2]	Percentage of first-degree Kuwaitis
1975	52,994	95,016	55,42%
1985	56,745	132,993	42,67%

NB: This is only an *imperfect* estimate, due to the inclusion of the 20-year age group in the total number.
1. Database of the Inter-Parliamentary Union (IPU). Available at http://www. ipu.org/parline/reports/2171_arc.htm (accessed 6 June 2017). Checked with the figures given by the Kuwait Politics Database (KPD), Georgia State University. The IPU quote a number of actual voters of 30,863, while the total of votes received by candidates in the KPD is 133,044. If all the voters had cast the maximum of five ballots (which is probably not the case), the number of voters would be 26,608.
2. Central Statistical Bureau, Population by Sex and Age groups, Census 1975 and 1985, *Annual Statistical Abstract* in 25 years 1990, p. 11.

series, because of the topic of popular concern as well as the diverse public that it attracted[9] had the potential to turn into a social movement.[10] The government, used to politics being performed in the semi-private space of the *diwaniyya*, the Kuwaiti form of *majlis*, rapidly showed signs of nervousness and forbade the event as contravening the 1979 decree-law No. 1965, regarding public meetings and assemblies that required prior authorisation. After his fourth lecture, Ahmad al-Muhri was arrested and jailed. His father Abbas had his nationality withdrawn[11] by decree 51/79, dated 16 September 1979, and as a consequence, so did all his family who had acquired the nationality by affiliation.[12] The authorities alleged that the grounds on which the nationality was attributed to the family were invalid and deported the 19 members of the family to Iran.

The *Masjid* al Sha'ban crisis had a second implication for the *bidun* question: the deportation of the al-Muhri family to Iran illustrated the growing tendency of the Kuwaiti government to 'define the opposition as foreign'.[13] Moreover, to put it in the regional context, the practice of massive deportations had largely been resorted to by Saddam Hussein's regime. From 1969 to 1989, the Iraqi regime expelled an estimated 130,000 Iraqi Shiites to Iran on the grounds that they were of Iranian origin or Faili Kurds, and stripped them of their nationality. Building on this precedent, the Ba'athist government also relocated tens of thousands of Kurdish families to the Arab south, following the razing of their villages.[14] The situation in Iraq, as well as the creeping radicalisation of the repression of the Shiites, had repercussions in Kuwait, where some of them sought refuge, starting with the members of al Da'wa. As Longva explains, '[the *biduns*'] ambiguous status as an unacknowledged population provided a human pool into which Iraqi refugees, draft dodgers, and infiltrators as well as absconding workers and illegal aliens could easily blend after getting rid of their identity papers'.[15] In London, for instance, members of the community of Iraqi Kurd migrants/refugees mentioned cases of *'bidun* Kurds', by which they meant Kurds displaced to southern Iraq who fled the country via Kuwait.[16] The Iran–Iraq War, following the proclamation of the Islamic Republic in Iran, had further destabilising effects on Kuwait. By siding with Saddam Hussein, the Kuwaiti government broke with its previous policy of neutrality vis-à-vis its powerful neighbours and allowed Iraqis to gain a foothold in Kuwait, tying the government's fate even more than before to that of the Iraqi internal turmoil. It also became increasingly exposed to the risk of infiltration by Shiite activists who, connected to Iranian transnational organisations, but mainly from Lebanon and Iraq, claimed responsibility for the car bombings in 1983[17] and the murder attempt on the Emir.[18] The progressive involvement of Kuwaiti Shiites in 1986–8 in violent actions, and the crackdown on the Shiites in the Kuwait armed forces, showed the government that 'it could use a degree of force, so long as it did not use it against every group at once'.[19] In this context, the fact that the *biduns* stemmed from tribes, stretching into Iraq, that included both Sunnis and Shiites – some of the latter possibly sympathetic to Iran – made the government particularly worried about their presence. Moreover, their role in the army had become more and more symbolic and less and less strategic, with the reflux of the Arab nationalist movement, the creation of the Gulf Cooperation Council in 1981 and the closer cooperation with the US, whose help was sought for the reflagging of Kuwaiti tankers.[20] As a result, and in a context of economic downturn, the *biduns* started to be seen as a financial burden.

The economic downturn

The onset of the economic recession in the 1980s made the State of Kuwait re-think the policy options it had adopted so far in domains other than security. The decrease in oil prices, which went below US$ 10 per barrel in 1986, created pressure for economic diversification and more productive activities (See Table 4.2 and Figure 4.1).

The Kuwaiti labour market was (and to a large extent still is) characterised by the concentration of Kuwaiti workers in unproductive employment in the public sector and the almost total dependence of the national economy on migrant labour. As in every modern state going through an economic crisis, the policy of importing labour was debated at that time. After the period of high oil prices, when both government expenditure and labour immigration witnessed a correlated rapid growth, the downturn, reflecting the collapse of world oil prices, did not result in the large scale re-export of foreign labour that was envisaged. 'The increase in renewals, which is in part a reflection of labor hoarding by some employers, has largely compensated for the falling level of new labor inflows and the growth in work permit cancellations and departures.'[21] By the middle of the 1980s, Kuwait had begun to import less and less labour from outside, in particular from Asia, and had come to rely more and more on the more settled stock of migrant labour already existing in Kuwait. In 1984, a conflict arose between the Ministry of Social Affairs and Labour and the Ministry of the Interior (headed by Sheikh Nawaf al-Ahmad) over the type of labour that should be allowed in Kuwait, especially the income threshold above which a migrant could bring his family into Kuwait. The Ministry of the Interior was willing to significantly increase this threshold out of consideration for state security.

TABLE 4.2   KUWAIT'S OIL REVENUES, 1968–2001

Year	Revenues in KD (millions)
1968	263.10
1969	243.00
1970	280.40
1971	297.70
1972	254.10
1973	505.90
1974	543.90
1975	2,056.50
1976	3,458.00
1977	2,598.30
1978	2,575.40
1979	3,036.00
1980	5,940.50
1981	4,434.20
1982	2,764.10
1983	2,334.60
1984	2,923.50
1985	2,493.80
1986	2,094.70
1987	1,483.90
1988	1,991.40
1989	2,035.10
1990	2,935.70
1991	246.10
1992	495.90
1993	2,085.30
1994	2,324.30
1995	2,784.80
1996	3,113.50
1997	3,935.90
1998	3,208.40
1999	2,254.40
2000	4,794.50
2001	4,528.00

Source: Central Bank of Kuwait (Abdullah Alhajeri, 'Citizenship and political participation in the state of Kuwait: the case of National Assembly (1963–1996)', PhD thesis, Durham University (2004), p. 84).

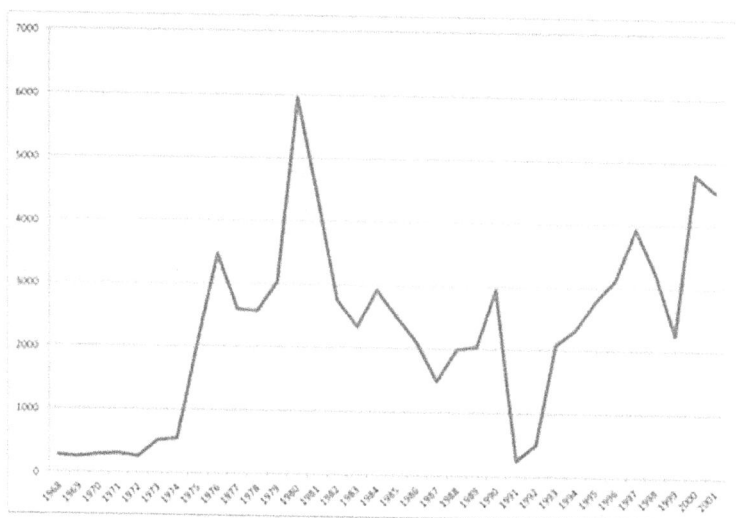

FIGURE 4.1   Kuwait's oil revenues, 1968–2001

The *biduns* employed in the armed forces belonged to the economically unproductive category. Kuwait's 1986–7 budget forecast oil revenues some 41 per cent down on their 1985–6 level.[22] Against the background of drastic economic downturn, forcing them into the category of non-Kuwaiti expatriates may have served a double purpose. First, it reduced the government payroll, especially in the aftermath of the crash of the Suq al Manakh and the government's decision, in December 1986, to launch a programme of land purchase to stimulate the economy.[23] Secondly, since socio-economic evils and insecurity always tend to be attributed to the influx of migrations to Kuwait, it may have defused public pressure to ask for a clampdown on migrant workers, whose presence was indispensable to the national economy and the financial interests of the merchant elite.

Moreover, the growing concern for migration control also went hand-in-hand with the advancement of identification and surveillance technology imported to Kuwait: the first civil data system, under the responsibility of the Minister of the Interior, Nawaf al-Ahmad al-Jabir, was made law on 25 April 1982.[24] It became compulsory for every resident, whether national or not, to carry an identification card (*bitaqa madaniyya*). It was instated between September 1982 and May 1983, roughly at the same time that around 50,000 to 100,000 illegal residents left Kuwait.[25] These efforts to limit the overall number of foreigners, especially those in illegal situations, paved the way for the categorising of the *biduns* with illegal migrants and other activist refugees.

On 29 December 1986, in the midst of an entrenched Iran–Iraq War and of an economic crisis, a select ministerial committee passed a secret decree that marked the official beginning of an oppressive policy towards the *biduns*. The decision, classified at the time, was reproduced by *Al-Tali'a* newspaper on 30 August 2003. In the absence of interviews with the main actors involved in the decision, who remain at the highest levels of power in Kuwait, I have relied on this document, whose authenticity has not been denied. The confidential decree gave new guidelines, divided into 12 main points. First, acknowledging that the immediate replacement of the *bidun* majority in the armed forces was simply impossible, their gradual replacement was set as a priority target. Most importantly, and what was tantamount to reclassifying the *biduns* as illegal, the decree prescribed that Law 17 of 1959 on the Residence of Aliens would be strictly applicable to the *biduns*. Until then, article 25 (h) of the Law had exempted them, as tribesmen (*afrad al 'asha'ir*), from complying with its requirement of sponsorship and residence permits. This paragraph (h) of article 25 was abolished in 1987. As a result, *biduns* were given six months to regularise their situation, that is to say, to provide the Kuwaiti authorities with the same required documents as those expected from foreigners who had entered the country in full compliance with the provisions of the Law on the Residence of Aliens for the previous 27 years.[26]

Due to the interdiction on illegal residents' eligibility to work in public institutions (including specifically benevolent societies or cooperatives),[27] *bidun* government employees had to produce a valid passport or risk losing their job. Moreover, the labour law in the private sector was also revised to raise the fines imposed on contravening companies. According to HRW, 'since Bedoons were not issued passports, thousands were dismissed from their jobs between 1987 and 1990 for failure to produce passports, Kuwaiti or otherwise'.[28] Directions were given to speed up the process of residence issuance for complying *biduns*, but also to refuse to officially register any marriage, should one of the two partners fail to provide the adequate official documentation, and to issue or renew driving licences and *bitaqa tamwiniyya*, which are cards giving access to state-subsidised food entitlement. Finally the transfer of 50,000 *bidun* children from public schools, costing the state a yearly KD 850 per child against KD 250 for private schooling, was viewed as a way to save KD 30 million for the public treasury. The private education institutions were not really provided to help to absorb the massive influx of new pupils year-to-year. Two points specifically pertained to the civil data system, namely the reinforcement of sanctions for false statements or withholding of information, and the cancellation of any name-changing process for *biduns*.

In addition to the immediate consequences of this secret decree, new measures were brought in in the following years to further augment the pressure on the *biduns*, such as the end of the tolerance for granting higher education scholarships abroad and the 1987 barring of *biduns* from Kuwait University's registration and state-subsidised health services. It began with the end being put to the widespread practice of treatment abroad, through introducing fees at hospitals to eventually refusing to issue birth and death certificates to the patients altogether. This series of measures was tantamount to a *de facto* denaturalisation.

ADMINISTRATIVE VIOLENCE

Formally, the 1986 decision was far reaching, as it deprived the *biduns* overnight of all the rights they had enjoyed while the state condoned their presence in the emirate, especially on its ministries' payrolls. In practice, though, it took years and the random events of the Iraqi invasion for it to be implemented. The question of state employment in the armed forces and attached state housing became quite complicated: mass layoff could not and did not occur in the Ministry of the Interior and Defence until after the 1990 invasion provided a suitable opportunity for such a drastic move.[29] The *biduns* were vilified as traitors in the blurred post-liberation period, doubly stigmatised as members of a defeated army and as sharing origins with the enemy. Longva recalls her pre-invasion fieldwork:

> It was generally agreed that they [the *biduns*] were concentrated in the outskirts of Kuwait in the lower-middle class areas where settled nomads lived. The children, who always gathered around me when I was on a visit in such areas, used to explain spontaneously without my asking: 'I am a real Kuwaiti, not an Iraqi,' or 'This is my best friend; he is not an Iraqi'. Upon inquiry, it was explained to me that the children meant to say that they were not bidoon. Clearly, there was a widespread opinion by the late 1980s that many Iraqis tried to pass as 'Kuwaiti stateless'.[30]

The association between *biduns* and Iraqis, seen as interchangeable, survived the Iraqi occupation of Kuwait, explaining the predicament of the *biduns* after the 1991 liberation as they were automatically suspected of sympathising with the occupiers if not of collaborating with them, especially in Saddam's Popular Army. In 2008, Abdullah Bishara, a former top-ranking Kuwaiti diplomat and Secretary-General of the Gulf Cooperation Council (GCC) from 1981 to 1993, summed up the issue of the *biduns*: 'the crises of 1961 and 1990, this is the whole problem'.[31] This long-lived association between *biduns* and Iraqis may have held true before the invasion, yet it fails to recognise several developments triggered by the liberation and the subsequent repression, starting with the dramatic drop in numbers, from 219,996 before the invasion to 122,576 in 2010[32] and 105,702 individual registered cases in 2015.[33] The invasion must have considerably reduced the number of Iraqi latecomers usurping the name of *bidun*. One *bidun* who fled to the UK noted that the number of Mutairi *biduns* was significant before the invasion but 'the war in 1990 also reduced the number of the *biduns* from this tribe [Mutair], because most of them entered Saudi Arabia and were granted the nationality [there]'. Electronic correspondence, 14 August 2008. For Sheikha Fawzia al-Salman Al-Sabah, this and other allegations that they supported Iran during the Iran–Iraq War were not verified. What is verifiable is the aim of the authorities to compress the number of *biduns* by all possible means, 'otherwise', she asked, 'what would be the purpose of not granting a death certificate?'[34] The fight is still on to clear their memories of this collective stigma.[35]

The concept of 'administrative violence' is intended to capture this enterprise to de- legitimise any historical claimants other than the dominant minority who monopolise the prerogatives to define citizenry. This *administrative* violence uses identification papers, official forms and certificates to exert financial and psychological pressure on the undesired people in order to force them out. The following section distinguishes between four different but linked mechanisms of the de-legitimisation of the *bidun* claims: the imposition of an identity rejected by the concerned persons, a *de facto* pauperisation of this category of the population, aimed at setting them apart from the Kuwaiti lower middle classes with which they were mixed. These are accompanied by a symbolic process of stigmatisation and a nerve-wracking absence of transparency.

1) Imposing a rejected identity
Since 1993 a special government unit under the Ministry of the Interior has been in charge of dealing specifically with the files of the *biduns*. From 1993 to 1996, the Central Committee (*Lajnat markaziyya*) was tasked with registering, regularising and overseeing *bidun* affairs. Established in 1996 by the Ministry of the Interior and based in 'Ardiyya, the Executive Committee for the Affairs of Illegal Residents (*Lajnat tanfiziyya li shu'un al muqimin bi-sura ghayr qanuniyya*) – shortened as Executive Committee, took over from the Central Committee. Its vocation is broadly to collect proof and presumptions of origin so as to attribute to the *biduns* a foreign nationality, supporting the claim that they are illegal migrants.

The evidence of foreign origin, however subjective, is stronger than the length of residence in Kuwait when it comes to qualifying or disqualifying an application for nationality. One *bidun* who claimed he could prove that his father was working in around 1951 in the oil company in Ahmadi before enrolling in 1957 in the Fahahil police had lost any hope of being naturalised because in 1975 the family's neighbour reported the Syrian affiliation of the whole family and denounced his father for registering, under his name, his paternal uncle in Kuwait.[36] On the basis of this gathering of information, *biduns* are assigned a foreign identity – most frequently Iraqi – which, in the light of their life experience in Kuwait, they refuse to endorse. 'There is here a fundamental misunderstanding between nationality, the official state recognition and origin, inferred from stated documentations', recognises Dr. Rashid Hamad Al-Anezi, a Kuwaiti academic and lawyer specialising in nationality issues.[37] Following the same genealogical logic, in September 1998 the Kuwaiti government decided that genetic tests would be required from all stateless residents to prove their Kuwaiti lineage. Taking biology as a criterion to determine the fate of the *biduns* did not seem to lead to more conclusive results than had the duration of their residence or their feeling of cultural affinity with Kuwait. It was later abandoned.

The Executive Committee is attributing a forced identity; it registers it in the files of the *biduns* who may learn about it later. For instance, *biduns* mention that when they go to the Ministry of Health to get their children's birth certificates or to court to get married, the ministry/court, in liaison with the Executive Committee, holds files under their name with the note '*min usul 'iraqiyya*', 'of Iraqi origin'. Ministries are instructed not to deal directly with the files of *bidun* families without referring the matter to the Executive Committee. The bone of contention is a formal acknowledgement of this attributed origin that would mean their citizenship claim would be dropped. In January 2007, as the government opened access to temporary driving licences, *biduns* refused to register for the document on the basis that the 'nationality' field was already filled with 'illegal resident' (*muqim bi-sura ghayr qanuniyya*), which made them *de facto* acknowledge a status they rejected.[38]

The Central System to Resolve Illegal Residents' Status (*al jihaz al markazi li-mu'alajat awda' al muqimin bi-sura ghayr qanuniyya*), which has come to be referred to as the 'Central System', was set up in November 2010, with the clear mandate to solve the vexed issue within a period of five years. It was created at a time when the Kuwaiti Parliamentary Committee for *Bidun* Affairs was pushing for Parliament to vote on a Law on Civil and Human Rights for the *biduns* (*qanun lil-huquq al insaniyya wa al madaniyya lil-bidun*), which the government prevented, according to Hasan al-Jawhar,[39] former head of the Parliamentary Committee for *Bidun* Affairs.[40] While still tasked with ascertaining *biduns*' national origins on the basis of cross-referencing data collected from all ministries and government agencies, the Central System boasts that it has gradually and selectively reversed the policy of rights deprivation, based on the Council of Ministers Decision No. 409/2011, promulgated on 6 March 2011, which granted them a set of civil and human privileges and facilities and claimed it included the content of the draft law.

The Central System has larger powers that the previous committees, affiliated with the Ministry of the Interior. The head of the Central System, Salih al-Fadala,[41] who has the reputation of being a staunch adversary of the *biduns*, has ministerial rank. Based in downtown Kuwait, unlike the preceding committees, the agency liaises with all the concerned ministries.

> Under Article 2 of the decree establishing the Central System, this agency may take all executive measures to resolve the status of this class. In turn, the agency is in constant, active contact with all government bodies, agencies, public institutions, and competent security bodies, which provide the Central System with the data and information it needs, derived from these bodies' records and official files. These files indicate the true nationality of the person claiming to belong to this class.[42]

The Central System claimed to have inherited 105,702 individual cases registered with the Central Committee, with the task of sorting them out. According to the government itself, 'approximately 12,000 illegal residents have not opened files with the Central System to Resolve Illegal Residents' Status and thus they have not been issued a review card',[43] or any form of identification card, meaning that they have no access to rights. Moreover, some files of *biduns*, with close ties to Kuwaiti nationals and as such with higher hopes of being naturalised are said to be lodged with the Supreme Committee and the Cabinet; there is also a bureau for *biduns* martyrs, the Martyr's Desk (*maktab al shuhada'*) for those who were killed while carrying out their duty in the armed forces.

The Central System takes particular care in facilitating the regularisation of *biduns* status by granting them a legal residents' permit of five years. To do so, it opened a special branch in the Mubarak al Kabir area on 6 May 2012 and since then, up until

February 2013, it claims it has registered the regularisation of 2,969 persons, most of them from Saudi Arabia (2,130 cases).[44] The Central System divided the *biduns* into three categories: 34,000 were deemed eligible for nationality and would hold a green card, valid for five years. Others would receive a red card, showing that they were disqualified from naturalisation because of a criminal record (around 900 cases) or they hold documents dating only to 1980 (8,000). Finally, the rest would receive a three-year yellow card and would be requested to come forward and regularise their status on the basis of their foreign nationality. It does not seem that the *biduns* registered with the previous 'committees' were automatically registered with the Central System, since the Central System stated that, although having 105,702 files, it delivered 79,198 cards, including renewal, replacement of lost cards and the issuance of new cards, up until 19 January 2013.[45] The Central System has at the time of writing issued two types of cards with different validity length, yet in June 2014 human rights' activists in Kuwait claimed that cards with validity as short as three months had been issued recently, hindering access to health services that require identification papers valid for at least three months.[46]

Foreign nationalities have also been on offer: 'outside the Executive Committee, you find persons selling forged passports for KD 2,000', asserted a *bidun* in 2008.[47] The traffic of forged passports is no secret[48] and the 'nationalities' concerned are that of the Dominican Republic, Somalia, Eritrea or Liberia. It is no secret to the Ministry of the Interior either, which is even said to encourage the traffic.

The principal consultant of the 2006–8 Parliamentary Commission for *Bidun* Affairs, describes the case of a *bidun* member in the armed forces who participated in the 1991 war of liberation:

> When he was sacked from the army, he was encouraged to change his civil status, through special offices designed to grant nationality of Eritrea, Liberia, the Dominican Republic and a few other African countries. He refused a sum of KD 4,000–5,000 offered to him to purchase the passport [in 2007].[49]

According to this source, 4,000 *biduns* employed in the Ministry of Defence did change their status by obtaining nationalities of foreign

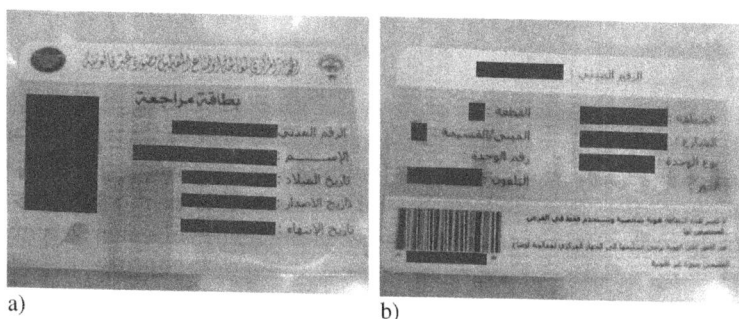

a)   b)

PHOTO 4.1   a–b Card issued by the Central System.
Note: On the back of the card it reads: 'This card is not considered a [proof] of personal identity. Should be used only in the cases prescribed for it'. This sentence was present in the previous identification cards for *biduns*.

countries, by virtue of secret bilateral agreements signed between Kuwait and these states. According to a *bidun* activist,[50] this practice peaked between October 1996 and July 2003 when the Ministry of the Interior was headed by Sheikh Muhammad Khalid al-Hamad Al-Sabah.

After denying its intention to strike a deal with the Comoros Islands to grant the *bidun* Comorian nationality for a long time,[51] the Ministry of the Interior Assistant Undersecretary for Nationality, Passports and Residency Affairs, Major-General Mazen al-Jarrah Al-Sabah,[52] made an announcement on 9 November 2014 stating that *biduns* would be granted 'special application forms for Comoros' economic citizenship', which would help them regularise their status as Comorian citizens – i.e., they would become foreign residents in the emirate and be given free residency permits and an incentive package, including the recovery of rights to employment, free education and health care.[53] The statement came as a materialisation of a previous public announcement on 15 May 2014 when the major-general said in a TV interview on *Al-Watan* that his country was negotiating with an unnamed 'Arab country' to grant them its nationality in exchange for economic benefits.[54] In this interview, Sheikh Mazen mentioned that the Central System, having studied the UAE–Comoros deal to naturalise Emirati *bidun*, was in the process of finalising the agreement in a proper legal manner, with the signatures of the heads of the 'Arab country' concerned.

The idea of buying a foreign citizenship to allow the *biduns* to stay as permanent residents and drop their claim on nationality has been around since at least 2008. In July 2008, the news of negotiations between the State of Kuwait and the Comoros Islands provoked a scandal in the archipelago, when the parliament of the Comoros refused to pass the first law granting economic citizenship to the Gulf *biduns*, rejecting it by 19 votes out of 33 MPs.[55] The bill stated that any person residing in a foreign country bound by a signed agreement with the Union of the Comoros was eligible for Comorian nationality. The amended law was nevertheless approved on 27 November 2008 by the Parliament of the Union of the Comoros (by 18 votes out of 33) and promulgated on 16 December 2008. It stipulated that:

> Article 1 The acquisition of economic citizenship through the decision of the public authority results from a decision made on the basis of an application filed by a major person holding the status of economic partner of the Comoros government [...]

> Article 2 Any person interested in obtaining economic citizenship in the framework of the economic investment programme in the Union of the Comoros should present a written request to the Independent National Commission.[56]

Kuwait-based businesses were among the initial actors who set up a policy of 'nationality offshoring', an expression coined by Noora Lori, who studied the UAE's case of statelessness, to describe 'a market solution to the 'problem' of migrant incorporation'.[57] The adoption of the law in December 2008 is to be credited to active visits by Kuwaiti businessmen.[58] The deal owes much to the fruitful bilateral relationship between the President of the Union of the Comoros, Ahmed Abdallah Mohamed Sambi (May 2006–May 2011), and Bashar Kiwan, a French-Syrian businessman, born, raised and residing in Kuwait, CEO of a Kuwait-based investment holding called the Comoro Gulf Holding (CGH) and affiliated to Kuwait Holdings.[59]

With 44.8 per cent of the 734,500 inhabitants below the poverty line, and 14 per cent of them being unemployed,[60] the Union of the Comoros seemed to offer prospects for development and infrastructure projects. The CGH positioned itself as the main country developer with a long-term vision of the Comoros as a tourist destination and a place where household consumption could be developed. Starting with the rehabilitation and expansion of the Itsandra Hotel, one of two international-standard establishments in Grande Comore, the CGH had obtained licences for investments to carry out projects in infrastructure, tourism, finance, commerce, media and communication, in particular to open a bank,[61] extend the Port of Moroni, establish a mobile phone company and develop air routes.[62] The economic influence of CGH, which described itself as the main private investor in the country, translated into political lobbying, whereby, according to a US cable, the 'CGH actively and openly lobbied for a controversial "economic citizenship law" that appeared to be rejected, then was passed at the National Assembly'.[63]

In the complicated arrangement struck between the Comorian presidency and certain Gulf States, the Kuwaiti holding was to be in charge of managing the investment disbursed in return for granting 'economic citizenship'. A Lebanese research consultancy firm carried out a survey to evaluate the preferences of *bidun* buyers potentially interested in economic citizenship, whose results formed the basis on which to attract investors into the construction of real estate projects.[64]

Whether it is because of the publicity attracted by the July 2008 scandal in Parliament or not, no deal was agreed between the Comoros and Kuwait at first. The idea seemed to be unacceptable in Kuwait because of the vocal opposition of some Members of Parliament, who did not hesitate to denounce it publicly.[65] The deal was nevertheless signed with the Emirati authorities:[66] it involved the down payment of USD$ 200 million, which represents slightly less than half of the pre-2008 gross domestic product (GDP) of the country;[67] USD$ 25 million of this was to be allocated to the government budget and USD$ 175 million to the realisation of big infrastructure projects. According to international donors to the Comoros trying to evaluate the amount and duration of this windfall and quoting the new vice-president, Mohamed Ali Soihili,[68] there had been a new bilateral agreement signed between Moroni and Abu Dhabi in October 2011, designed to be temporary (for a period of 18 months) but possibly renewable. Its stated objective was to grant certain members of tribes qualified as 'close to the authorities' a temporary passport with limited rights, for a sum of around USD$ 6,250, that would enable the holders to apply eventually (without any timeframe provided) for Emirati nationality. In the case of Kuwait, no such possibility has ever been put forward: the 2014 proposal entails no eventual granting of Kuwaiti nationality. On the contrary, it states that the children of holders of 'economic citizenship' will get original (*asli*) Comorian passports.[69]

In between, the relationship between Sambi and Kiwan fell apart. According to the Comorian press,[70] President Sambi issued a decree, 11-058/PR, on 23 April 2011, attributing the management of the Comoros trade centres, in charge of delivering economic citizenship, to the Emirati transport company of Esam al-Fahim, HSS Holding, for a period of five years. This breached the exclusive rights ceded to the CGH.

It is not clear why Kuwait changed its line towards the granting of Comorian citizenship, effective 'when the Comoros embassy opens in Kuwait'.[71] The new geo-strategic situation resulting from the Arab uprisings and the February 2011 *bidun* mobilisations clearly created new conditions for Kuwait to align with its more authoritarian, more daring and less ashamed Gulf neighbours.

The Kuwaiti decision took place in the context of a closing of GCC ranks: years of Kuwaiti and *bidun* mobilisation to fight for *biduns'* rights had contributed to preventing a certain conception of nationality being imposed top-down on the *bidun*, as has been the case in the UAE.[72] Yet, after the *bidun* uprising, Kuwait seems to have aligned its approach with the UAE's and coordinated its policy towards statelessness with that of other GCC countries: in April 2012, Salih Fadala, the head of the Central System, toured the GCC countries, in particular the UAE and Saudi Arabia, and 'exchanged views over illegal residents'.[73] The anti-tribal discourse and the revoking of nationality affecting opponents and naturalised people illustrated that, more than ever, if there is such a thing in Kuwait as *citizenship* understood as membership in a political community, it applies preferentially to those in the circles of power, that is, powerful *hadar* businessmen and non-dissenting *badu*. The rest hold only a *nationality*, which is an administrative document that can be disposed of.

2) Pauperisation: the denial of welfare benefits

In Kuwait services that are dependent upon the presentation of a valid civil ID (*bitaqa madaniyya*) have, since 1982, expanded far beyond the common issuing of official documents, whether passports or other, opening bank accounts or making financial transactions. Everyday life activities such as buying a mobile phone SIM card or consulting a general practitioner require identification too. Instead of a civil ID, *biduns* hold what is known as a security ID[74] – a form of registration with the Executive Committee, renewed annually, and stating clearly that it ought not to be taken as a proof of identity. Without ID cards, *biduns* have no access to state-provided health services, whether they are free for nationals or carry subsidised charges for foreigners.

Since 1986, the *biduns* have had to bear the cost of their children's education in private schools 'not those for foreigners, [understood here as schools for the sons of wealthy expatriates also frequented by the Kuwaiti elites] but those for Arabs with a lesser level'.[75] Under pressure from both sides, the *biduns* have to bear the expense of all the services that were once free for them, while their sources of income dropped when they became unlawful.

It is a little delicate to evaluate revenues earned by undocumented workers, all the more so in informal sector activities. Without any attempt at generalisation, a few instances can still suggest the scale of inequality or discrimination as regards income. It should be noted here that, however disturbing, this inequality is common currency when it comes to the Kuwaiti/foreigner divide. At the time the fieldwork was carried out, in 2006–7, the minimum monthly salary for a Kuwaiti civil servant was KD 900; in 2013, MPs suggested its level should be set at KD 1,500.[76] Meanwhile, the minimum wage in the private sector was set at KD 60 in April 2010,[77] and that for domestic workers at KD 45 in June 2015.[78] The monthly wage for *biduns* ranges from KD 100–50 to KD 600.

Biduns usually combine several different jobs; they also work long (er) hours. For instance, the employment in Sultan Centre supermarkets as a member of the security staff requires eight hours a day, with one day off a week. Like anywhere else, working illegally goes hand-in-hand with precarious employment conditions and the overhanging threats of being laid off overnight, or paid late, if at all. These conditions of course widen the divide between Kuwaitis and *biduns* to such an extent that the differential eventually comes to confirm, in a self-fulfilling effect, the line of argument of the Ministry of the Interior – through the voice of a former high-ranking member of the Central Committee, according to which, judging by their appalling living conditions, *biduns* are too poor to be anything but tribal migrants with no attachment to the land nor respect for the law and desperate to pick up the crumbs of Kuwait's wealth.[79] This reasoning shows how the static conception of Kuwaiti citizenry has turned very classist. Moreover, it is a self-fulfilling argument since part of the policy towards the *biduns* is precisely to dissociate them from the broader Kuwaiti population into which they were naturally integrated, and to stigmatise them in the eyes of the others.

3) Symbolic stigmatisation

The violence perpetrated against the *biduns* is usually not of a physical kind.[80] Kuwait is not a police state and its regime, if sometimes arbitrary, is not a brutal one. In absolute terms, Kuwait, 'country of plenty and safety' (*dirat khayr wa aman*), provides water, food and shelter, in the words of the head of the Executive Committee,[81] yet poverty is relative. The administrative violence depicted here is a

TABLE 4.3 ESTIMATES OF *BIDUNS'* MONTHLY EARNINGS

	Monthly earnings	
Type of occupation	Biduns	Kuwaitis (if applicable)
Messenger/envoy (*murasil*)[78]	KD 30	N/A
Taxi/bus driver	KD 90–100	N/A
Security staff at the door of supermarket	KD 120–150	N/A
Public sector (Ministry of Municipality)[79]	KD 100–200	KD 1000–1,500
Private sector (office employment)	KD 250–600	KD 1,200 and above

Source: interviews in Kuwait 2007–8.

structural and symbolic violence: structural as it is indeed the arbitrariness of the social hierarchy in Kuwait that is itself violent. The social hierarchy in Kuwait is determined by the arbitrariness of nationality or circumstances of birth, which themselves stem from the global injustice that is being concentrated in the tiny emirate. In the case of foreigners, the internalising of the norm of a world divided into sovereign units disciplines and stifles any feeling of envy or entitlement. The *biduns*, on the contrary, have contemplated – and sometimes still contemplate – the possibility of being naturalised. As a result they feel the entire extent of this inequality. They cannot understand why they cannot get basic support like others of their kind, such as disability allowance, pension benefits, and widow allowances – let alone the privileges reserved for Kuwaitis.

Secondly, administrative violence is symbolic certainly not in the sense that it is unreal, but in the sense that it belongs to the register of the state staging its full power: all the *bidun* informants without exception noted that the worst part of their daily life is the humiliating encounter with the state embodied in its police forces, the Executive Committee and the various ministries. Some *biduns* complain about the fact that they can spend up to four hours at a police station whenever they need to report something: 'When you say you are a *bidun*, it is as if you were not a human being.'[828384] Likewise, in a special report on *bidun* youth, one of them wondered why the police always patrol the ring roads that lead to areas known to be populated only by *biduns*.[85] In 2007, members of the National Assembly called on the Ministry of the Interior to change the members of the Executive Committee, who had been in the same employment since 1996 and were accused of mistreating and harassing the *biduns*.[86] While the responsibilities of the Executive Committee were renewed in October 2008,[87] its new secretary acknowledged the poor working conditions and poor services offered by committee employees, asking for better treatment and material, in an interview with *Al-Nahar*.[88]

The denial of state endorsement of the most important milestones of life – certificates of birth, marriage and death – is the extreme form of the almighty state. In the case of marriage certificates, the refusal on the part of the state to issue official certificates unless the *biduns* sign a document declaring themselves illegal led to circumventing practices whereby the couple marries but then registers a case in court against the bride or groom so that the whole family comes to testify in court that the marriage occurred. The judgment issued by the court, albeit falling short of a marriage certificate, serves as an official document declaring there was indeed a marriage.[89]

Biduns are excluded, and need to be seen as excluded, from the official and public sphere in all its guises: on a TV programme, *Behind the Doors*, on the channel *Al-Ra'i*, dated 11 June 2007, the Salafi Member of Parliament, Ahmad Baqir,[90] former Minister of Justice, walked out of the studio when he found out that he was unwittingly put in the presence of a *bidun* Islamic preacher, whom he was not willing to face. It must be added that Ahmad Baqir was, as a Minister of Justice, accused by MPs of preventing the employees of his ministry from attesting to marriage contracts for *biduns*, in violation of the constitution and human rights principles.[91] The plight of the *biduns* cannot but serve as a deterrent example, for any new frauds planning to try and claim they are a part of the category. There might still be candidates arriving from northern Saudi Arabia to Jahra. As a result, *biduns* live in a nerve-wracking situation as impostors waiting to be unmasked.

Finally, it is a stigmatising process, cutting off this part of the population by uprooting their links with the rest of the Kuwaitis. The process of discrimination and stigmatisation induced by the administrative procedures is a perverse and self-reinforcing one: as seen above, the approach of the Ministry of the Interior is to simply identify them as greedy and parasitic. Yet the pauperisation that results from their exclusion from state services contributes to the unintended strengthening of another stigma. By drawing attention to the destitution of this particular population in need, and all the obstacles they encounter in their daily lives, the Kuwaiti human rights organisations that are intending to gather support for them further estrange them not only from the less sympathetic parts of the Kuwaiti population but also from the Kuwaiti women who used to intermarry with them.

4) Absence of transparency

More often than not the various encounters with the state take the form of a legal trap, sometimes with aspects of a Kafka novel, compounded by a complete lack of transparency and visibility regarding the data respectively held or required by the administration to be eligible for naturalisation.

In 2000, the National Assembly voted in two laws on 'gradual naturalisation': one pledged to naturalise 2,000 persons a year (Law 22) and the other (Law 21) amended article 5 of the 1959 Nationality Law by adding a new paragraph 3, in addition to the other two relating to the *khidmat jalila* (paragraph 1) and *abna' al kuwaitiyyat* (paragraph 2). According to paragraph 3 of article 5, the new requirements for people to be considered for naturalisation include proof of residence in Kuwait in or before 1965, a permanent stay in Kuwait until the issuing of the Law 21, as well as the same financial, religious and security conditions prescribed by article 4, notably the absence of a criminal record (*qayd amni*).

Yet the yearly quota of naturalisations has not been transparently handled: it proved to include more than the *biduns'* files, as many thought it would, but still concerned the naturalisation of artists and special personalities by virtue of exceptional services rendered to the state. Moreover, the law has not been applied consistently over the past decade: the Executive Committee cited a figure of 3,517 individuals naturalised for the years 2000 and 2001,[92] a figure that included minors, while until then only persons of full legal age were counted.[93] It even ceased to be applied after that date with only hundreds of naturalisations being carried out, as in 2007.

The most likely people to be naturalised and included in the rarely-applied yearly quotas are the sons of female Kuwaitis, but they are just scratching the surface of what is referred to as 'the *bidun* question'. Secondly, a lot of cases are barred from consideration for naturalisation because of criminal convictions. The definition of criminal offence includes, in particular, registering as a *bidun*, when presumptions exist that one might not be, which may be punishable as 'false information' or the crime of forgery.

In this cunning game of disputed identity, the state and its administrative maze largely crush the individual, as illustrated in the below case:[94]

> Mr A registered as a *bidun* with the Kuwaiti administration is presumed to be of Egyptian origin: Mr A requested the Egyptian authorities to provide him with any official proof (birth or electoral records) mentioning his name in order to qualify for Egyptian nationality. In the absence of formal record, his naturalisation application is rejected, his appeal against the Egyptian Ministry of the Interior lost. Provided with the proceedings of the lost trial, the Kuwaiti court pronounced the following sentence:
>
> – Mr A is not a stateless *bidun* as his presumed origin is known, albeit non- ascertained;
> – Mr A is not an Egyptian national; although he may be held to be so this will nevertheless not constitute his being one if he is not such according to the law of the Republic of Egypt;
> – Finally, Mr A is found guilty of giving 'false information' for his registration as a *bidun* and given a suspended sentenced for the crime of forgery, being punishable to up to nine years in jail according to the Kuwaiti penal law.

His file joined the pile of others whose cases are barred from consideration for naturalisation because of their criminal – sometimes political – convictions (*quyud amniyya*). *Biduns* testified in 2007:

> The Central Committee attached to Ministry of the Interior started to shift the battle onto the legal ground and brought cases to the court. Between 1998 and 1999, four cases of *biduns* were condemned for forgery. This was a new solution being tried. Yet the Higher Court issued a judgment against the decision of the Committee.[95]

Moreover, according to official sources, 16,500 to 18,000[96] collaborated with the Iraqi Popular Army during the invasion, while 5,000 others were involved in drug- and assassination-related crimes.[97] The diplomatic enmity and international political considerations undoubtedly complicated the issue but to an unknown extent, especially in the case of Iraq. However, fieldwork in Iraq was simply unimaginable in 2006, and we can only presume that the inter-state dimension exacerbated domestic administrative violence in the region. In 2014, however, according to the Central System's spokesperson during an interview,[98] only 900 individuals had been rejected for naturalisation under its mandate on account of their cooperation with the Iraqi Popular Army. Yet the basis for giving security blocks has been extended: Human Rights Watch mentioned the case of 'unspecified security restrictions'.[99] The new restrictions might have affected activists, among others, including those who participated in the banned demonstrations. Some human rights groups believe there may be as many as 30,000 *biduns* with security blocks against them.[100] This inflation is noted by a *bidun* in 2014: 'the holding power of the first [*bidun*] generation has eroded: now everybody is security flagged'.[101]

BIDUNS' SURVIVAL STRATEGIES

Living conditions

The majority of the *biduns* live in popular housing or *buyut sha'abiyya* located in Jahra (Tayma) and Sulaibiyya at the periphery. Constructed in the 1970s, the *buyut sha'abiyya* constituted the housing benefits attached to employment in the armed forces: they represented a solution to housing issues at a time when *biduns* recalled living in hut-like *'ashish*. Made initially of 200 m² ground floor concrete houses lined up in parallel streets, they are now overwhelmed with the unauthorised addition of more rooms. Obviously, housing has not kept pace with demographic growth: when a new generation take over a lease, they share the house between brothers. For instance, two brothers, sons of a soldier who had joined the Kuwaiti army in 1974, shared the same popular housing in Sulaibiyya. The two families counted 14 members; as a result of this overpopulation, a third brother left the house to rent outside the area.

While the monthly rent in the popular housing districts amounted in 2008 to KD 50, particularly low by Kuwait standards, it reached KD 250–300 a month (excluding bills) for a middle class housing outside *bidun* areas.

What strikes the visitor in the popular housing areas is threefold: first, a feeling of over-crowding and lack of space as the habitat has not kept up with the general evolution of living standards. *Biduns* have added rooms to accommodate new family members or their

South Asian drivers, constructed ad hoc parking shades for the ever-increasing number of cars, infringing on the streets, turning them into *de facto* one-way roads. Secondly, the overall feeling of destitution is linked to the deficient provision of public goods, visible in the poor maintenance of roads pitted with scattered potholes and the accumulation of large volumes of refuse typical of Third World slums, as well as crumbling mosques with their loose loudspeaker wires and cracks in the paint and the minaret's walls. This leads to a third remark: the sheer contrast with the neat and tidy wealthy Kuwaitis' residential areas, or even the expatriate areas with many-storey buildings.

'This housing is a humiliation' or 'the future of the houses is to be demolished' are the feelings of the interviewed *bidun* inhabitants of these areas.[102] The simplistic but quite common identification of the residents with their squalid environment and, more particular to Kuwait, of the individuals with their economic status, is part of an invisible violence that is the lot of the majority of the *biduns*. As a result, the new generations have left the popular housing to rent in lower-class expatriate areas like Farwaniyya, Jlib al Shuyukh, Sabah al Salim and further south on the road towards Ahmadi. They joined the other *biduns*, who never benefited from the state housing of the armed forces, around Umm al Hayman and in any other affordable accommodation (Khaitan, Hawalli).

The diversity of the *biduns'* situation is wider than it may seem at first sight, in respect to employment. Work for *biduns* depends on their resourcefulness and their connections but also their luck, as no rules and no contracts, apart from the trust in the good faith of their employers, regulate their professional activities.

Although the door of the public sector is closed to them, *biduns* still work in many areas of the public sector.[103] While their number and percentage in the armed forces is not known with any certainty they have not been replaced, as was planned in the 1986 decree, and the question of their recruitment was again on the agenda.[104] Likewise, discussions were engaged to hire them in employment affected by staff shortage, as nurses,[105] teachers[106] or clerics.[107]

At the bottom of the Kuwaiti social hierarchy, but still a buffer between Kuwaitis and expatriates, albeit at the mercy of both, the

PHOTO 4.2   a–c *Biduns'* popular housing.
Source: Author's own pictures.

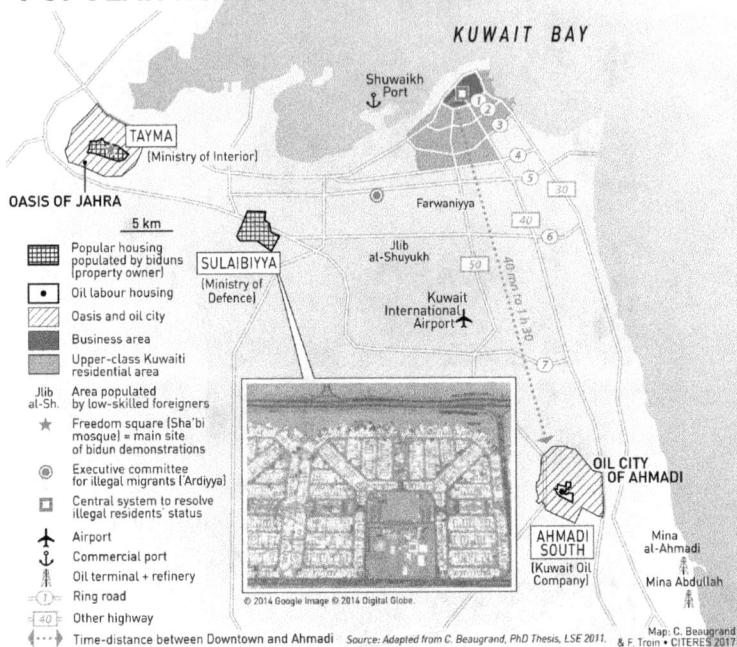

POPULAR HOUSING IN KUWAIT

KUWAIT BAY

Shuwaikh Port

TAYMA
[Ministry of Interior]

OASIS OF JAHRA

Farwaniyya

5 km

Popular housing populated by biduns (property owner)

Oil labour housing

Oasis and oil city

Business area

Upper-class Kuwaiti residential area

Jlib al-Sh. Area populated by low-skilled foreigners

★ Freedom square (Sha'bi mosque) = main site of bidun demonstrations

◉ Executive committee for illegal migrants (Ardiyya)

▢ Central system to resolve illegal residents' status

⊥ Airport

⚓ Commercial port

Oil terminal + refinery

Ring road

40 Other highway

Time-distance between Downtown and Ahmadi

SULAIBIYYA
[Ministry of Defence]

Jlib al-Shuyukh

Kuwait International Airport

OIL CITY OF AHMADI

AHMADI SOUTH
[Kuwait Oil Company]

Mina al-Ahmadi

Mina Abdullah

© 2014 Google Image © 2014 Digital Globe.

Source: Adapted from C. Beaugrand, PhD Thesis, LSE 2011.

Map: C. Beaugrand & F. Troin • CITERES 2017

MAP 4.1   Popular housing in Kuwait

biduns work mainly in a semi-formal sector, especially beyond the fourth ring road. 'Semi-formal sector' is defined here as a sector made of traders and merchants whose businesses belong firmly in the formal sector in terms of goods and services, but these businesses are run with a necessary ignorance of the officially sanctioned and mandated rules and procedures.[108] This is to be distinguished from completely informal sector activities such as mobile vendors – children selling fragrance sprays at the traffic lights – and stationary stalls of mixed nuts and cold water on the pavements. Some *biduns* specialise in the retail of second-hand consumer goods, such as electronics, household appliances and particularly cars. *Biduns* form a perfect channel between Kuwaitis, from whom they buy or collect the unwanted goods, which represent quite a significant volume considering the frenetic consumption culture,[109] and expatriates to whom they re-sell them.

They trade not so much on the black market *per se* as on a parallel market such as the Friday market, south of the fourth ring road (before Andalus), far away from the high-street brands in the lower tier of what is seen as a dual system of consumption in Kuwait. Car-related business is a particularly flourishing one: a few *biduns* work in garages, on car repairs and second-hand car sales in Jahra (though those with technical skills are more often than not Iranian, Pakistani or Syrian); they sell repaired cars at the car auction in Amghara, east of Jahra, and take a commission. An open secret, which does not seem to affect the reputation of its well-known Salafi owner from the Sultan merchant family, is the fact that the whole security personnel of Kuwait's Sultan Centre shopping centre is staffed by *biduns*.

As far as office jobs are concerned, the variety of *bidun* employment is almost impossible to track. *Biduns* occupy petty jobs at the reception areas of tailors' shops and work as couriers (*mandub*) for law practices. They also hold more qualified or computer-literate occupations such as freelance IT support specialists, employees in the real-estate sector, in customer services for electronics brands and as secretaries and journalists in newspapers. Some *biduns* are prominent columnists or artists, whether photographers, poets or novelists, fully integrated into the intellectual landscape of the country and the Gulf. This is explained by the fact that the generation in the employment market today has benefited from the pre-1990s free education – from the younger having completed secondary education to the older who may hold higher educational qualifications and even doctorates. Educated *biduns* have such a deep knowledge of the country and its society, and bring such important skills, that they were hired in the campaign headquarters of some Kuwaiti candidates.[110]

Intertwining with the middle classes

Kuwait is not a surveillance state; this provides *biduns* with some interstices for private networks of survival and solidarity. Shafeeq Ghabra uses the expression 'politics of survival', which, in the case of Palestinians, highlights the pivotal role of the family in order for the group to survive and to maintain its cohesiveness under circumstances of dispersion.[111] We prefer to use the term 'survival strategies' but our core question here is comparable to that of Ghabra: how do family-based groups mobilise their resources in the absence of state protection – and further, here, under the duress of administrative pressures? *Biduns* have kept groups afloat through the mobilisation of family resources, particularly those of their Kuwaiti members, as well as patronage links, on the one hand, but also the politicisation of the issue in Kuwait over the last decade, on the other. The mobilisation of solidarity networks helped to provide for material needs. The gradual emergence of the *biduns* as a non-ethnic disenfranchised minority enabled them to take a common position in reaction to state policies.

As seen above, in their type of employment *biduns* survive because the oil wealth reaches them or trickles down to them through three main channels: their Kuwaiti relatives; charities; and the concessions made by the government under pressure from Kuwaiti nationals.

Though the topic is quite embarrassing, the *biduns* who are kin-related to Kuwaiti nationals are supported in one way or another by these Kuwaiti relatives. *Bidun* children are reported to be brought up with Kuwaiti families, even using illegal means to obtain state allowances and secure places in Kuwaiti schools by registering them under that family's name. *Biduns* also mentioned the generosity, as well as the opulence, of Kuwaitis who would sometimes give them KD 400 on the day they met.

When asked about what kind of aid they received, most of the *biduns* cited the government-run *bayt al Zakat*, as well as the state-subsidised mosque and charities. The *bayt al Zakat* distributes free staple food once every three months. As for the Kuwaiti religious charities, they are famous for their financial strength. The most active is the Salafi Society for the Revival of the Islamic Heritage (*jama'iyyat Ihia' al turath*) followed by the Muslim Brothers' social branch. Shiite *biduns* note the better organisation of the Sunni charities that, subsidised by the government, provide significant support of a solely material kind. They regret the pressure for conversion or need for *taqiyya* – the Shiite theologically-endorsed possibility of lying about one's true faith in the case of danger – that goes together with this help, and go as far as seeing in it the tacit approval of the government to keep the sectarian balance unchanged, or in favour of the Sunni creed.

Finally, a typical phenomenon in Kuwait, especially over the last decade, is to see the pervasive state give back via different channels what it had denied or taken by different means. This is the logic behind the granting of Passport-article 17, which speaks more of a *laissez-passer*.[112] At first, these temporary passports were granted as a convenience, especially for pilgrimage, but they did not mention the holder's nationality. When they were re-instated after their issuance temporarily ceased,[113] directives were issued to and by foreign embassies not to accept these passports when issuing visas. It also goes without saying that they are not valid in the GCC zone of free movement. Only Syria and Iran accept them. As for the rest of the countries, including the European Union the rules are not clear.

The most important achievement for the *biduns* was the establishing by the government of two charity funds (*al sunduq al khayri*), financed by the Ministry of Religious Endowment, with a budget of KD 4 million a year each and the objective of easing the lives of the *biduns* in the domains of health and education. Though versions diverge, the creation of these funds is often credited to the efforts of the independent Shiite MP Dr. Hasan al-Jawhar, together with two prominent members of the royal family, the lawyer Sheikha Fawzia al- Salman Al-Sabah and the daughter of the late Emir Jabir al-Ahmad, Sheikha Awrad, who adopted the cause of the *biduns*.

Both funds are aimed at alleviating the costs of private clinics and private schooling[114] for the young stateless barred from public schools and hospitals. As one interviewee put it,[115] education, though costly, has become the only way to salvation or to make up for the congenital discrimination. He proudly told me that with his Business Administration diploma obtained in 2002 through distance learning at the University of Jordan, he could train employees of various government bodies on meeting preparation and minute writing, which represented a much enjoyed recognition of skills and know-how. In the domain of higher education, *biduns* have seized opportunities in the opening of the Kuwait branch of the Arab Open University (AOU), with its policy of an open door to stateless people, and cheaper fees (KD 600/year) than other private universities, like the first private university in Kuwait, the Gulf University for Science and Technology, known as GUST, and opened in 1997. A quarter of the AOU's first batch of the five-year course's graduates in 2007 was made up of *bidun* students.

The appropriation of the cause of the *biduns* by prominent Kuwaiti figures and organisations enabled the part of the Kuwaiti society affected by the issue to organise its mobilisation and the first-ever campaigns and protests. In addition to liberal personalities on the Kuwaiti political scene, the Kuwait Society for Human Rights (KSHR), the Human Rights Committees of the powerful Kuwait Bar Association (KBA) and the Graduates Association played a powerful role in the citizens' mobilisation.

The support that the *bidun* cause has gathered throughout the 1990s from Kuwaiti nationals, which blossomed in the 2000s, is of utmost importance. The way the *biduns'* grievances have always been presented to me by Kuwaiti nationals on their behalf, as if the *biduns* were minor persons unable to speak for themselves, had been quite puzzling at first. It does make sense, though, in light of the 1968 Military Law as well as the 1986 secret decree that required cooperation from the Ministry of Information, in order to forbid the entire press to publish any article or complaint related to the *bidun* category.[116]

The interdiction on speaking about the issue seemed to have been literally blown apart, in three steps. First, Kuwaiti nationals have been able to afford to criticise the policy of the government, within certain boundaries. In Kuwait, the nationality-based hierarchy is so entrenched that the existence of a law does not necessarily help in cases of major complaint lodged by non-nationals; the backing of a Kuwaiti national to support the claim of a foreigner in the face of another Kuwaiti or of the state is indispensable. Without under-standing this considerable power of Kuwaiti citizens, despite their inability to interfere in terms of the sovereign matter of nationality, one cannot fully appreciate the significance of the involvement of prominent Kuwaiti figures. Secondly, this support and frame for action given by Kuwaitis provided the opportunity to the previously muzzled *biduns* to *speak* for themselves. That is the significance of the event '*Al bidun yatahaddathun*' [The *Biduns* Talk], held on 4 November 2006 in the amphitheatre of the Kuwait Bar Association and organised by the KSHR, in the presence of the prominent human rights activist, Dr. Ghanim Al-Najjar, Sheikha Awrad and all the MPs who support the cause. The issue of the *biduns* has since been widely debated in the press and on TV, whether on the religious programme of sheikh Nabil al-'Awadi, *sa'at saraha*, the 'Hour of Truth',[117] on the *Al-Ra'i* channel in December 2006 or on Dr. Shafeeq Ghabra's weekly *Diwaniyya* programme on 6 February 2007. Both TV programmes allowed *biduns* to intervene, give their testimonies and express their difficulties. Moreover, the *biduns'* situations are widely discussed on internet forums specially designed for the purpose (See Table 4.4).

In addition, the issue is debated on websites dedicated to tribal confederations that have flourished since 2007. Though the reliability of the data placed on these websites is doubtful, it is important to reflect on the significance of the recent multiplication of websites focusing on the history of tribes (as well as *hadar* great families). In the case of tribal confederations, internet pages revive the past glory as a sort of golden age, and recreate virtual and cross-border solidarity. The proclaimed support to *bidun* 'brothers' in Kuwait plays a unifying role in this process of solidarity building. It seems, though, that the resurrection of the tribal, and particularly transnational, identity reflects the pressure for more opportunities and social equality emanating from the *badu* part of the population that was last integrated in the polity.[118]

TABLE 4.4   SAMPLE OF WEBSITES DEDICATED TO THE *BIDUNS*

http://www.bedoon.org.kw	KSHR website
http://www.kuwbedmov.org	Website of Muhammad Wali al-'Anazi, *bidun* living in London, UK.
http://www.bedoon.net	*muntada lajnat al kuwaitiyyun al bidun* (shut in 2012)
http://www.bedoon.cc	
Muntada al Fursan	*kuwaitiyyun bila huwwiyya* (shut in 2012)
http://www.bedoonrights.org	Network founded by Kuwaiti-stateless advocate Mona Kareem

Note: in 2008, almost all the websites' headers reproduce the official pictures of the Emir Sheikh Sabah al-Ahmad Al-Sabah (r.2006) and the Crown Prince Sheikh Nawaf al-Ahmad Al-Sabah, as a sign of allegiance.

Thirdly, despite the fact that the *biduns'* community, as a purely administrative category, lacks cohesiveness, Kuwaiti nationals managed to form an advocacy group, the *Bidun* Popular Committee or *Lajnat sha'abiyya* (*li qadayia al bidun*). Founded in 2006, the *Bidun* Popular Committee provides a platform for *biduns* to react to official measures and policies in a coordinated way and in liaison with their Kuwaiti supporters. It enables them to try to present a united front to the government and the Executive Committee, as was the case in January 2007 with regard to the issuance of temporary driving licences.

Campaigns, protests and efforts to raise awareness of the issue of the *biduns*, like the day of action organised in front of the National Assembly on 28 October 2008,[119] have increased in recent years. Many *biduns* feel that their cases are being used in Kuwaiti internecine arguments between politicians. Nevertheless, the implications of the *bidun* question are larger than interpersonal political rivalries and electoral gains. While the original alchemy between the diverse components of the Kuwaiti citizenry is subtle, the inclusion of the *biduns* into the polity would raise the question of a possible evolution of this status quo – what we call the 'renegotiation of the social pact'.

In conclusion, under the guise of a battle against illegal migration, the Kuwaiti government targeted not only newcomers and infiltrators but also an entire category of people that it had earlier tapped into for recruitment and turned into a liability for the state, in the dangerous context and daunting challenges of the first Gulf War and a sharp economic downturn. While severing the migration networks of near-foreigners, it maintained the regulated influx of other foreigners essential to its economy and the leisure of its citizens.

While the inward flow of near-foreigners might have been slowed, this policy has both limits and long-lasting consequences. For sure, the number of people who want to be naturalised has been reduced, sometimes by artificial means (such as the granting of African or South American nationalities). The consequences of the utilisation of the human resources drawn from the northern Arabian region cannot be reversed or erased. This is particularly true because of the transnational foundations of Kuwait's society. Part of

the Kuwaiti population originating from the same tribal background is intertwined with the *biduns* or feels sympathetic towards
them in a context where the conflict between state and society has
evolved.

The crackdown on the *biduns* in the 1990s also coincided with the
end of the political alliance between the ruling family and its *badu*
loyal support. Emir Jabir al-Ahmad had bolstered tribal forces in the
1980s to counter vocal opposition forces (Arab nationalist and Shiite
Islamists).[120] Yet as of the 1990s this political space was already filled
with dissenting voices stemming from two main sources, the tribes
and Sunni Islamists. A new generation of tribespeople, born in the
1960s–70s, highly educated, has fallen out with the old hierarchies,
customs and 'blind obedience' of their fathers and rose to
prominence. From the Mutran tribe, Musallam al-Barrak is the most
prominent tribal icons of Parliament, continuously re-elected from
1999 to 2012: a born orator, he made his reputation as an MP by
opposing draft laws that he saw as encouraging corrupt practices (he
supported the reduction of constituencies from 25 to five in 2006 to
discourage vote buying) and by confronting fellow lawmakers or
ministers and officials in the cut and thrust of parliamentary
debates.[121] Secondly, albeit in an invisible manner, class-based
concerns, formulated either in liberal or Islamist terms, have started
to divide the historical identity of the *hadar*, opening avenues for
common platforms with the *badu*.

Pressures for more equality have emerged in the domestic debate
around the *biduns* issue in the 2000s which certainly represent a move
to limit inherited privileges. Another type of pressures exerted by the
human rights organisations to put an end to the phenomenon of
statelessness also plays a complex role in this domestic game.

CHAPTER 5

The Emerging 'Cause' of the *Biduns*: Supporters and Opponents

Il n'est pas de problème si difficile qu'une absence de solution ne finisse par résoudre.[1]
[No problem is so difficult that an absence of solution cannot eventually resolve.]

More than 50 years after the issuance of Law 15 on Nationality and Law 17 on the Residence of Aliens, the disputes that resulted from loopholes in the legal system are still unresolved. For the last 30 years, the promises to find a 'radical' or definitive solution have fared no better. The 2010 newspaper headline 'Kuwait: Council sets plan to solve Bedoun issue'[2] rings hollow,[3] as did the triumphalist headline '1981 will be the year of nationality! *Al-Siyasa* publishes arrangements to obtain nationality'.[4]

Yet things have undeniably evolved. The state's calculated decision to force the *biduns* out of the country bore fruit. Not only did it more than halve their number in 20 years, from over 250,000 at the beginning of the 1990s to under 100,000 at the end of the 2000s, it also downgraded their claim from an entitlement to nationality to a guarantee of basic rights. By a rather clumsy manipulation of juridical categories, Kuwait aligned itself with the discourse on immigration prevalent in the majority of sovereign states. This alignment, which resulted from the interaction between international organisations and domestic, state and non-state, actors, is what is meant here by the 'internalisation' of the accepted illiberal practices towards migration based on the norms of the sovereign state system.

This chapter first discusses the internal debate as it unfolds on the Kuwaiti political scene. It begins by explaining how the opponents to the naturalisation of the *biduns* understand citizenship. The term 'economic understanding of citizenship' is used to suggest that the right to participation in political decision making pertains mostly to the issue of economic redistribution. It also analyses the equivocal arguments deployed by the proponents of the cause of the *biduns*, which oscillate between outright naturalisation and recovery of civil rights. It then looks at the impact of international human rights organisations and advocacy groups on the domestic debate. Finally, against the background of these three perspectives, it discusses the current position of the government in light of the obstacles to a rapid resolution of the problem.

POLITICISATION OF THE *BIDUN* ISSUE: THE INTERNAL DEBATE

The Gulf States have tended to be treated as exceptional cases because of their reliance on oil, their authoritarian regimes and their demographic makeup. However, when it comes to the impact of immigration on nationalism, they are very much like any other society where citizenship is largely defined in terms of access to welfare state benefits.

The citizens of welfare states tend to fear that the inclusion of newcomers into the citizenry would result in a real, or *perceived*, reduction of their socio-economic benefits. State expenditure is considered a pie to be shared: the greater the number of shares, the smaller their size. This rather simplistic logic, neglecting the complexities of public budgets and the variety of possible allocations, is not peculiar to the Gulf. It is very much behind the illusionary objective of 'zero immigration' put forward by certain conservative parties and all the far right parties in Europe – as well as the US Trump administration. The electoral dividends that can be reaped from such arguments are well known. Moreover, the extension of citizenship or other rights to migrants – and stateless/paperless/undocumented people or *sans-papiers* – creates a conflict of interests between established residents and newcomers. It challenges the existing power structure and creates competition on the labour market. This is particularly true of illegal employment niches such as the building trade, the clothing industry in France, light industry and agriculture in the southern United States, to mention only a few examples. Any change in the distributive balance is thus perceived as a zero-sum game. Rather than confronting popular discontent, it is politically easier to opt for the status quo – to the great satisfaction of employers of undocumented workers.[5] Kuwait is no different. However, its peculiar economic structure exacerbates this perception: the pay of civil servants is 'better thought as a monthly disbursement from the national trust fund' rather than being tied to services rendered; the 'size of the stipends paid to citizens' depends more on 'politics and the price of oil in world markets, rather than local labour markets', while 'the number of citizens hired by the government is driven not by government need for employees but instead by the supply of citizens, with most new entrants to the job market receiving a position'.[6] Apart from positions based on ethical motives, the nationals, who see no political allies in a category that anyway cannot vote or can vote only through the Kuwaiti women married to *biduns*, tend generally to oppose the cause of the *biduns*. On the contrary, those who try to unsettle the status quo might see an advantage in denouncing one of its most visible dysfunctions and putting pressure by stoking up frustrations.

Protecting the welfare privileges

Overall, Kuwaiti public opinion does not favour the cause of the *biduns*. The question of national identity and nationality is sensitive in any country. But in Kuwait the trauma of the invasion, during which *bidun* foot soldiers were collectively stigmatised as traitors or cowards, is reminiscent of post-World War II Europe, with the associated issues of collaboration, military defeat and the displacement of the population in the face of the enemy. The *bidun* issue, linked to the humiliating occupation, got stalled in the decade following the 1990 Iraqi invasion, while Kuwaitis were hoping for a prompt solution in the aftermath of the liberation. As a result, the majority of Kuwaitis have become indifferent to an issue perceived as insoluble. According to one *bidun*, who frequently contributes to the press and internet forums, in 2008, out of a limited press readership of 10 per cent of Kuwaitis, perhaps 2 per cent might have an interest in the issue.[7] Moreover, the Arab Spring[8] episode pushed Kuwaiti nationals to turn in on themselves, concentrating on their own political issues in times of upheavals and confrontation with the government, rather than focusing on the disenfranchised.

Although not fully representative, albeit significant, I was invited to observe an all-female class given at the Faculty of Political Sciences of Kuwait University on the topic of the *biduns*, which the lecturer had discussed in his 1996 textbook. What struck me was certainly not the students' animosity towards the *biduns*, but rather their benevolent detachment. While only one girl said she would have agreed to marry a *bidun*, what these girls found problematic, or 'the biggest mistake' of Kuwait, was the naturalisation of the foreign wives of Kuwaiti men after five years of marriage, while that of South Asian spouses seemed to them a heresy. All in all, the *biduns* appeared to be little different from other (Arab) foreign workers, certainly deserving rights but not equality.

The greatest opposition to the cause of the *biduns* comes from the economic elites or the wealthiest *hadar* families. That resistance was corroborated by the quantitative analysis of Youssef Ali[9] and it is omnipresent in my qualitative interviews. The *biduns* and their supporters have a particular term to designate that category: they are the 'blue-blooded' (*al dima' al zarqa*), that is to say, those who think of themselves as being of a superior pedigree. The category cuts across religious orientations, whether Islamist or 'liberal' – the latter referring in the Kuwaiti context to an approach that is secular – but uses the same nationalist language.

Not all merchant families are staunch adversaries to a resolution favourable to the *biduns*. A few names were frequently mentioned in my interviews as being particularly averse to any relaxation of the pressure exerted on the *biduns* because they took public positions.[10] Among them, Abd al-Aziz Al-'Adsani's[11] position towards the *biduns*, as well as the support he received in the press, provide a good illustration of the line of argument of certain merchants. As early as 1994, Abd al-Aziz al-'Adsani demand[ed] a review of all nationality files [suspecting that] only 4 per cent of the *biduns* qualify for citizenship'.[12] Replying to the MP Khudayr al-'Anazi's promise to release official papers to facilitate access to health and education services, as well as birth certificates and driving authorisations, al-'Adsani requested a full investigation into the *biduns'* files so as to deny these papers to those having a criminal record. As al-'Adsani put it, 'the security dimension is more important than the humanitarian one'.[13] Social conflict or conflicts of interest are presented in conservative nationalist terms as security 'threats to the nation'. This is a very common process among states, which is far from peculiar to Kuwait: increasingly, for instance, it is the case in the stigmatisation of the Muslim migrant communities in Europe.[14] It is all the more acute in Kuwait because of the Iraqi invasion and the bureaucratic traps described above. More original are the reasons put forward in defence of the credibility of Abd al-Aziz al-'Adsani's stance:[15] in addition to the public functions he assumed, his wisdom comes from his stemming from 'a respectable family of long involvement in social and political activities' (*usra 'ariqa*).[16]

Apart from security,[17] the other line of argument resorts to economic reasons, such as those given, for instance, by Yusuf Muhammad al-'Adsani, MP and speaker of the 1980–4 parliament, in an article dated 29 March 1983 in *Al-Qabas*, 'The naturalisation of 1,000 persons a year will give the state an extra burden to carry'.

However, according to Sheikha Fawzia al-Salman Al-Sabah it is less a matter of security or economics than one of fear on the part of the *hadar* who are being outnumbered by the *badu* in the proportion of 40–60 per cent, and feel that any enlargement of the polity would jeopardise their economic privileges.[18] The sociological and identity cleavage here clearly overlaps with class interests.[19]

Feeling themselves under siege, the *hadar* cling to their civic and political legacy as state builders, but their domestic and international socio-economic position has evolved since the days of independence. As a consequence, so has their conception of citizenship. In light of these changes, the two Kuwaiti conceptions of state membership described by Longva, quoted earlier and re-stated by Tétreault as cited below, need to be revisited here:

Urban Kuwaitis, on the other hand, understand citizenship as *jinsiyya*, from the root verb *jns*, meaning 'to make alike, to assimilate, to naturalise' ... There is an idea of similarity and horizontal solidarity ... [*Jinsiyya*] does not posit *a priori* an idea of hierarchy and supreme authority. In this sense, it is much closer to the Western concept of citizenship ... the urban Kuwaitis relate this notion [*jinsiyya*] with a territorialised community ... previously the town, toady the nation-state, rather than with a particular leadership.

The tribes in Kuwait understand nationality and citizenship in the sense of *tabi'iyya*, which can be translated as the 'following' of or 'allegiance' to a leader, in this case Kuwait's ruling family. The root verb of *tabi'iyya* means, among other things, to walk behind someone, to be subordinate to, to be under someone's command. The concept is clearly built on an idea of hierarchy and vertical allegiance.[20]

For sure, the idea of *jinsiyya* is close to the Western concept of citizenship or *muwatana*. The bond between them and the State of Kuwait is indeed indissoluble: they are nationals *and* citizens in the sense that their entitlements are rights that the sudden whim of a ruler could not possibly question. First and foremost, their first-degree nationality is immune to denaturalisation, except in extreme cases of high treason or *lèse-majesté*. This is the case in most democratic countries and is applied on the basis of a legal text as a sentence on security grounds.[21] Ben Herzog shows that the definition of loyalty and the grounds justifying revoking citizenship in the United States have evolved over time and are now part and parcel of the discourse on the war against terror.[22] Kuwait has taken a similar path, with the denaturalisation of Kuwaiti members of al-Qaeda involved in jihadist movements in Iraq and Afghanistan. Sulayman Abu Ghaith's first-degree citizenship was revoked by a council of ministers' decree after he appeared in October 2001 on Al Jazeera News as the official spokesman of al-Qaeda. Since Abu Ghaith is an original Kuwaiti citizen, his family was not concerned by the termination.

For cases that threaten state interest or security, Nationality Law (15) of 1959 differentiates between withdrawal applying to naturalised citizens and termination applying to original Kuwaiti citizens.[23] Based on this distinction, in the event of withdrawal, citizenship may be withdrawn from family members who acquired it by affiliation (article 13, paragraphs 4 and 5), which is not the case for the termination.[24]

The case of the denaturalisation of al-Muhri and the 18 members of his family appeared shocking to Kuwaitis because it involved all the members of the al-Muhri family.[25] The most current grounds on which nationality is withdrawn are the mistakes that allegedly occurred in the naturalisation process or the interdiction of the dual nationality, *izdiwaj al jinsiyya*.[26]

The suspicion surrounding the loyalty of dual nationality holders predates the 1959 Nationality Law. The internal crisis caused by the Malik affair in 1957 is worth mentioning. Fahd al-Malik, from a family remotely related to the Al-Sabah, was a close advisor to King Abd al-Aziz Al-Saud until 1948, when he moved to Kuwait and became the senior companion of Sheikh Jabir al-Ali. In Kuwait, Fahd Al-Malik began to act as though he were not subject to the rulers' authority: he began claiming desert land, erecting buildings without permission and in one case, in November–December 1956, seized land in the Fahahil area by tearing up a Kuwaiti's land title deeds.[27]

In order to subjugate al-Malik's excesses, the Kuwaiti government forced him to declare whether he was Saudi or Kuwaiti. Upon his answer that he was a Saudi, he and his family were ordered to leave Kuwait by 15 May 1957. Yet instead of doing so they 'barricaded themselves within the family compound'. The Abdullah Mubarak's security forces punished their transgression of the ruler's authority. On 15 May, the family compound was bombarded with heavy artillery – eight al-Malik were killed, five injured and 35 captured.[28]

The issue of the Kuwaiti nationality held by Saudis or vice versa is an acute one in Kuwait today. Yet it seems that the way it has been handled by the Kuwaiti government since the 1950s has depended very much on the regional balance of power in northern Arabia. In the face of the growing Iraqi threat, Kuwait had been more lenient towards Saudi frauds and more cautious towards Iraqi ones. Another important event in Kuwait bore witness to this trend: in 1980, Khalid Khalaf, a Kuwaiti lawyer who took on Iraqi nationality, was also stripped of his nationality because of the interdiction on dual nationality. The 'decrees of nationality withdrawal' (*sahb al jinsiyya*), published in the press, were frequent during the troubled first half of the 1980s. For instance, on 18 May 1980 *Al-Qabas* reproduced decrees nullifying nationalities granted in 1962 and 1963; on 23 August 1983, decision nullifying decrees of 1966 and on 3 March 1985, another one nullifying a decree of 1962, all ending with the mention 'all the dependents who were naturalised along with them/him are deprived of their nationality'. These decrees still exist at the time of writing. In the context of the US-led occupation of Iraq, Kuwait seems to be more assertive towards its Saudi neighbour.

In fact, the question of the dual nationality has risen as a prominent one to counter tribal opposition. On 21 July 2014, in the midst of the deadlock between the government and the opposition movement made up of an alliance of tribes and Islamist forces, five people were stripped of their Kuwaiti nationality, soon followed by ten others on 10 August 2014. These included Ahmad al-Shammari, owner of *Al-Yawm* TV station and newspaper, mouthpiece of the opposition, and was decided on the basis of the fact that his activities undermined the country's security and stability (*tahdid amn al qawmi*). So also were the former MP Abdullah al-Bargash,[29] from the 'Ajman who is close to the scientific Salafi movement, and, officially related to his involvement in Syria, Nabil al-'Awadi, a Salafi preacher. Other than in the case of the Shiite anti-Sunni preacher Yassir al-Habib in 2010, who left to go to the United Kingdom, no Kuwaiti national seemed to have been deprived of his nationality for political motives since 1979 and the denaturalisation and deportation to Iran of the Muhri family. The rest of the denaturalised are Bedouins from the Mutran and Shammar suspected of forgery in the naturalisation process (*tazwir al tajnis*): this political gesture, by Cabinet decree, signified a clear warning to tribes that were integrated later in the Kuwaiti citizenry.

Second, the *hadar* aristocracy, like the rest of the male and female Kuwaitis – except those newly naturalised and members of the armed forces – has secured political rights. Since the re-establishment of the National Assembly after liberation in 1992, the ruling family have found it difficult to create an authoritarian coalition capable of supporting a non-constitutional suspension of Parliament. However, political participation occurs within the limits of a hybrid democratic system where Parliament has the power to block government action, through the threat of interpellations and votes of no confidence, without the responsibility of rule that would come from the formation of the government by parliamentary parties, led by a commoner prime minister.[30] This kind of political participation is diametrically opposed to the self-governing ideal substantially linked to democratic understandings of citizenship: instead of the self-regulation of social conflict regarding the allocation of budget resources, the ruling family, and the patriarchal figure of the emir, is put in the position of an arbitrator of welfare redistribution between the *hadar* bourgeoisie and *badu* employees. The result of this political structure, coupled with the welfare provisions, is not, as Marshall predicted, an equalising of opportunities, but rather the exacerbation of social conflict over the rent redistribution to which the *hadar* private sector was the first to get access. Contrary to the Marshallian logic,[31] social rights have proved unable to ameliorate inequalities inherent to capitalism. It is not entirely accurate to state that the conception of citizenship as Marshallian state-given rights led to a passive and privatistic practice of citizenship in Kuwait.

Of course, it cannot be denied that in the Gulf States, unlike in Western democracies, welfare provisions have not served the primary purposes of labour market regulation 'as part of the continual perfection of democratic ideas'.[32] They have, rather, aimed at legitimising the regime by transforming traditional powers into authoritarian powers.

> Rulers in the wealthiest [Gulf] states offer an upscale variant of developmentalism. Celebrating materialism and the regime's ability to realize its subjects' wildest shopping fantasy, these rulers work to move people from the marketplace of ideas to the marketplace. This government-sponsored orgy of consumption has indeed been largely embraced by the national population of the oil-producing states.[33]

This consumerist dimension, oddly in tune with the neo-liberal turn of the 1980s and 1990s 'that marks the end of the liberal concept of citizenship with the return of citizenship to the market',[34] is still very much present at all levels of the Kuwaiti society. It is particularly salient and conspicuous for the wealthiest, whom the *biduns* denounce as the 'consumer class'.

Yet the Kuwaiti merchant families are not only consumers, they have become global investors: the class of merchants was a pillar of the Kuwaiti social pact. Starting with only relative wealth and the habit of dealing internationally through business networks, they amassed fortunes domestically. This occurred thanks to state policies that forced foreign enterprises to enter into business alliances with a local partner and granted them most of the government contracts. This wealth, massively invested abroad in real estate and securities, generated huge revenues at the time of 'asset appreciation in industrial countries, to the point that their wealth and earning abroad surpassed their wealth and earnings at home. Consequently, their dependence on the goodwill of ... [the] government was reduced'.[35] Contrary to the bourgeoisie in other Gulf States, the Kuwaitis have been quite slow to invest back into Kuwait when the economic liberalisation opened up new investment opportunities at home.[36] They preferred to invest their capital in the UAE or Bahrain when they chose to repatriate it to the region. This is because of the looming threat posed by the rule of Saddam Hussein until 2003, as well as the hindrances imposed by Parliament, whose majority, representing civil servants, prefers the government to distribute revenues directly rather than investing in infrastructure projects, and exerts strong pressure to curb the monopolies on the attribution of public contracts to the great family business like al-Khurafi contractors.

What does this all mean for the conception of *jinsiyya* and *tabi'iyya*? These cultural categories have evolved and now mask other interests, whether one calls them nationalist, as Longva does,[37] revisiting her own work, or economic, as I am inclined to do, for three main reasons.

First, the Kuwaiti globalised bourgeois class has bonds outside of its country of origin. This has two main consequences: the relative weakening of 'the horizontal solidarity' because of the competition in the market place[38] and the relative loosening of ties with the 'territorialised community'. Its position belies both Miller's defence of a nationality-based citizenship, as the divorce from the salaried citizens is profound, and Linklater's optimistic hope for a supra-national cosmopolitan citizenship.[39] They are part of 'a network of connections and functional interdependencies which has developed within certain important sectors of the 'global market', above all finance, technology, automation, the manufacturing industry and the service sector' that Danilo Zolo equates with what 'Western cosmopolitans call "global civil society"',[40] and to which Kuwaitis do not pretend to belong, adhering to family lines.[41] In no way does this mean a detachment from the State of Kuwait as core business provider rather than 'nation state'. According to Luciani, the desire of Gulf businessmen to invest at home originates from the realisation that if they become alienated from their countries of origin, they will carry no weight as major international business characters. Their international status depends on their association with their countries of origin, which offer by far the best opportunities for investment and growth, much better than those offered by the industrial countries.

> The comparative advantage of the Gulf bourgeoisie lies exactly in being the protagonist in the development of the Gulf and of the Arab world more broadly rather than in the real estate market in Mayfair, Knightsbridge, and Belgravia ... Hence the Gulf bourgeoisie is, on the one hand, substantially autonomous from the state, but on the other hand, very much committed to the development of their countries of origin – and to demands from the state that it should vigorously promote it.[42]

These multi-level economic interests coupled with multiple places of sojourn or abode, shed new light on the official narrative according to which *hadar* are state builders with an interest in the public good, as exemplified by the 1960s and 1970s golden age, as opposed to the influx of *badu* who do not care about a land with which they have no link but are only interested in getting money from the state.

The second reason to revisit the *badu*/*hadar* conception of citizenship is the fact that the alleged *badu* allegiance towards a leader rather than the territorial sovereign state does not hold true. The now long-settled Bedouin populations have obviously accepted the logic and legitimacy of the state system and the rules of the Kuwaiti democratic game. Their absence of identification with and commitment to the national community is attributed to their 'backward' traditions,[43] coming from Saudi Arabia, as well as, in the eyes of the more secular *hadar*, to their Islamist orientations, particularly Sunni. However, *badu* and Islamist MPs from the fourth and fifth constituencies, that is to say the constituencies beyond the fourth ring road,[44] raise demands that are closely associated with the concepts integral to the nation state model, such as popular sovereignty, social equality and democratic accountability. Although they sometimes indulge a certain populism tinged with Islam or tribal values, their demands reflect less a 'vertical allegiance' and the acceptation of the 'hierarchy' than pressures for changes in the redistribution pattern. Moreover, the fact that the *biduns* are as reluctant as the rest of the Kuwaitis to opt for an exit strategy in spite of the pressure exerted against them bears witness at least to a similar kind of attachment to the place.

Thirdly, Longva's cultural approach proves questionable when justified by resorting to the analysis of Ibn Khaldun (1332–1406) and its notion of group feeling or *'asabiyya*, that transcends each individual and explains political loyalty and recognition of the superiority of the leader.[45] Though the term is never used to refer to the *hadar*, the group feeling is widely shared among long-settled urban families too. The familial solidarity and hierarchy is staged in the ritual of the *diwaniyya*, the Kuwaiti traditional *majlis* for men, it is also very tangible in the handling of businesses that stay exclusively in the hands of the family. The difference with the *badu* is a matter of scale as the *badu* identity and source of social pride lies in the cultivation of longer genealogies and wider networks. In the end, the only ones who adhere to the *tabi'iyya* notion of citizenship seem to be the rulers: though their hereditary rule is inscribed in article 4 of the constitution and was reasserted during Kuwait's occupation, part of their legitimacy is drawn from the patriarchal myth that portrays the emir as the father of his people and the polity as a family story. The emir appears as the paternal figure who cares for the unity and cohesion of his family, and as such intervenes to calm down and arbitrate the recurrent conflicts between the executive and the legislative powers. The Kuwaitis are happy to comply with this harmless myth and their head of state, but they also know where their interests lie.

To sum up, the different social classes' conceptions of citizenship in Kuwait have evolved together with their respective positions and their integration within the wider global context. They even seem to be inverted: the general tendency is not towards greater inclusion but a fairer distribution among the nationals. Yet those who push for greater social equality among nationals seem more favourably inclined towards the *biduns*; they are eager to see nationality and consolidated citizenship rights going hand-in-hand, although commitment and responsibility to the community are not prominent in their rhetoric. On the contrary, the state-protected bourgeoisie, integrated into some informal global networks and whose civic virtues are still celebrated, lean towards a differentiated notion of citizenship, decoupled from nationality in a multicultural context – the *badu* culture being almost a separate one marked by profiteering.

These general tendencies should not obscure the variety of other reasons mentioned to me to support a stance opposing the *biduns*. Among them is the fear of competition over jobs and privileges that occur mostly at lower levels of government employment but also at higher levels. Luciani notes that 'with time, the successful business-people would tend to attribute their success to their own business acumen and appetite for risk rather than to their access to the state generosity'.[46] The emergence of a new generation reinforces this sentiment as it whittles away at the qualitative difference between good and bad business instinct.

Some *biduns* employed in the private sector and eager to acquire management qualifications underlined the how some members of the new generation of merchant families lack the business acumen and dedication of their forefathers, as well as modern qualifications, and think that their privileges are threatened by the skills of the *biduns*. The *biduns'* qualifications are a controversial topic, and are largely generation dependent; yet, the fact that some of them are doing well in the private sector is attested to by another accusation made about them, according to which they are as rich as Kuwaitis because they work in three different employments.

According to the author of a special report for the Parliamentary Commission for *Bidun* Affairs submitted in December 2006, the social elites who hold commercial, economic and historic power constitute a powerful lobby against the naturalisation of the *biduns*. They exert an important pressure on the government, brandishing arguments for the preservation of Kuwaiti national identity, the economic cost of naturalisation and the social and security impact on society.

The question of the economic cost (*taklifa/kulfa maliyya* or *iqtisadiyya*), for those wielding it, is not only a matter of figures but also of identity. At the time of writing, the author knows of no proper economic evaluation of the various scenarios for solving the *bidun* issue. Without any doubt, the fall of oil prices in the summer 2014, which weighed heavily on the Kuwaiti budget, has further lessened the chances of a solution favouring sizeable, let alone wholesale, naturalisation. The economic argument consists of making a gross calculation of the overnight naturalisation of around 120,000 *biduns*, listing the following items:

- housing benefit per family: KD 50,000–70,000;
- health cost per person per year: KD 5,000–7,000;[47]
- education cost per child per year over 12 years: KD 1,200–2,400;
- employment guaranteed by article 41 of the 1962 constitution;
- social services, subsidised utilities (water and electricity) and food staples.[48]

The total figure put forward is KD 600 million for the naturalisation of 100,000 *biduns*. However, no official study or parliamentary document ever confirmed or disconfirmed this estimate. In most of the cases, though, the bottom line of the addition is not drawn: it is sufficient for Kuwaitis to make the first line multiplication of 20,000–24,000 families (according to whether one counts a five- or six-member family) by the amount of the housing benefit (KD 50,000–70,000) – that is KD 1–1.68 million – to feel the anticipated pressure on their public services.

This adverse economic shock, for those who fear it, would require adjustments and probably mean the end of the subsidised provision of water, electricity and food and a return to market prices, as well as an uncertain future for free domestic phone calls, education and municipality services (street cleaning or waste collection). Naturalisation, for those who evaluate the massive cost, would constitute a liability on future generations that they cannot morally create. It is beyond the scope of this research to try to reach a more accurate estimate, but it can nevertheless note that, although a core concern, the government way of dealing with the *bidun* issue usually dodges the issue, as it is very unpopular.

The scenario of overnight mass naturalisation to be credited to the generosity or wisdom of the ruler and on which he could capitalise politically – as was done in Bahrain in 2001 – is very unlikely. The issue is too divisive in Kuwait; it brings back the haunting trauma of the invasion. The controversy paralyses decision makers more than it pushes them to take any decisive initiative. Finally, numbers only make sense in comparison. Whatever the result of the above addition, it ought to be presented together with the figures of the government budget in excess of KD 12.68 billion in 2007-8,[49] examples of expenditure items from the 2007-8 state budget – such as KD 2.4 billion transfer payments to the Public Institution for Social Security, KD 203 million in Emiri grant to the public or the total payment of salaries and wages of KD 1.95 billion[50] – as well as other long-term liabilities, for instance its defence budget of KD 1.32 billion in 2005.[51] No absolute cost calculation would ever hide the fact that *in fine* the decision is a political one regarding the future orientation of the society.

The opposition to naturalisation by part of Kuwaiti society takes place in the wider context of a double insecurity. The first pertains to the decline of Kuwait, which has become backward vis-à-vis other Gulf States while it used to be the most developed one among them. This vision of decline is supported by the fact that Kuwaitis may have to wait ten years for accommodation. This feeling, particularly widespread among businessmen in the private sector since the invasion, is blamed on either the paralysing role of a *badu* dominated and undisciplined Parliament or lack of vision by the rulers.[52]

The second fear is felt across the whole Kuwaiti class spectrum (and elsewhere in the Gulf), namely, that of losing control over their own country to the 65 per cent alien majority. The history of Kuwait's population is one of very limited naturalisation, which worked as a strong signal to dissuade any would-be claimant. Naturalisation is not part of the Kuwaiti citizenship ethos. Nothing could be more opposed to Kuwaitis' self-perception than the idea of multiculturalism or the idea of participatory citizenship in the space of their city (-state).

On the contrary, hierarchy is essential to their social being: nationals should benefit from the oil revenues first, which then trickle down to foreign labour. In the words of Michael Herb, alien workers are an 'item of luxury consumption' present in the country to 'generate convenience' at a minimal cost.[53] Longva provides a very accurate analysis of this phenomenon of contra-distinction:

> Even more than the privileges it imparted, what really gave citizenship its significance was the presence of the disproportionately large non-citizen population. Not only would the privileges have been concretely fewer without this presence, but also their enjoyment and appreciation would not have been the same for lack of contradistinction.[54]

Many Gulf specialists have also noticed how the nationality-based privileges have indeed begun to be perceived as dues, irreversible and impermeable to any change, and even expected to be always increased.

> The Kuwaiti population has gotten so used to its privileges that it is ready to support ever more extreme measures to deny them to anyone else, even to the extent of contemplating rules that would make it difficult for Kuwaiti citizens to marry non- Kuwaitis without giving up their children's right of citizenship.[55]

Though entirely true, this misses a dimension that appeared during my interviews and probably emerged as a consequence of the slow and secure growing of the Kuwaitis' capital, namely a certain deterritorialised perception of this privileged identity. If the oil revenues were to be equally shared among the 2.8 million population, 'what would be the benefits?' and 'would anybody then stay in Kuwait?', asked an interviewee from the Kuwait Economic Society, trying to deduce what a Kuwait naturalising foreigners or *biduns* would look like.[56]

Of course such statements should not be taken at face value; it is a way of reviving a longstanding tradition of Kuwaiti merchants to leave when they run out of opportunities in the port-city, as their attachment is, above all, to their network of contacts and business opportunities and those prevail over their obedience to the rulers. It reminds us of the defection of three Kuwaiti pearl traders who, in

1910, left Kuwait with their fleet and crew for Bahrain to avoid the ban on diving declared by Sheikh Mubarak Al-Sabah in order to levy military forces. Though the merchants have lost their financial power vis-à-vis the ruling family to oil revenues, it is a way of putting additional pressure on the Al-Sabah.

Finally what it also means is, firstly, the deep-rooted classism of many Kuwaitis who do not mind getting acquainted with the world's jet set but loathe rubbing shoulders with the masses, whether in Jahra or Bangkok, and, secondly, a clan tendency to stick together among relatives wherever they go, be it London, Geneva or Beirut. This behaviour may be interpreted as a reaction to globalisation, which brings the most extreme forms of inequality to Kuwait through the channel of labour migration, embodied at its top end by the advisory services of former UK Prime Minister Tony Blair and at its bottom level by the Bangladeshi gardeners watering the flowerbeds of the ring roads. The very forms of inequality found in Kuwait derive from the position of the emirate in the wider world. *Bidun* integration highlights the mechanisms through which international differentiation via economic privileges has turned, in multi-national societies, into a valued identity to which only the fewest people can make claim. It also shows how international dynamics in the countries at the interface between the First and Third Worlds are leading to a defensive rather than a participatory idea of citizenship. The security and criminality questions surrounding the *bidun* class are part and parcel of this obsidional nationalism.

The deprivation of *biduns*' rights poses two important questions: first, the correlation between socio-economic exclusion, on the one hand, and criminal offences and the propensity to join terrorist groups, on the other, and, secondly, the link between unsettled identities and the resort to violence. The national security argument more often than not is used to mask other conflicts over redistribution or social equality. Security is also used to define the opposition as foreign or, in the context of migration, inassimilable. In the case of Kuwait, the *biduns* conflate the image of 'enemies of the nation', since the 1990 Iraqi invasion of Kuwait, with that of a demographic group with a high crime rate. According to the daily *Al-Watan*,[57] 21,500 *biduns* cannot be considered at all for naturalisation because of their criminal records: 16,500 allegedly collaborated with the Iraqi Popular Army during the occupation and 5,000 are involved in drug- or homicide-related crimes. These figures were revised in 2014, with the Central System rejecting 900 individual files for naturalisation on account of their cooperation with the Iraqi Popular Army. Yet the basis for imposing security blocks has been extended to include different forms of law violations, including, since 2011, participation in illegal gatherings.

Opponents to the *biduns* highlight the offences that they have committed against Kuwaiti law, starting with the fact that they breached the Law on the Residence of Aliens. As a consequence, the *biduns* are also guilty of false statement and forgery with regard to their identity and true entitlements. This line follows exactly the official one, according to which the *biduns* are still hiding their original passports. 'The state [interests] are above humanitarian [concerns]; its law and sovereignty must be respected: any individual whose situation is illegal shall bear the consequences', states Khalifa al-Khurafi.[58] This line of argument clearly sees the deprivation of rights as a punishment on individuals in irregular situations.

Nevertheless, another perspective is emerging concerned with the social cost of this pressure policy and also, albeit silently, with its backfiring effect in terms of terrorism, and ironically, state security. The first signs of the long-term human cost of the crackdown policy start to be visible even inside the fourth ring road. Those probably played a role in the redressing of the most threatening and long-lasting effects of the governmental hard line, and particularly in the removing of the obstacles put in the way of access to education for *bidun* children.

The following is now part of the Kuwaiti landscape: when the traffic light turns red on the second or fourth ring road, a six to eight-year old child passes between the cars to sell bottles of air freshener for KD 1. Other teenagers sell mixed nuts and cold water under a sunshade along the Arabian Gulf Street. Until the 2000s, most of the *biduns*, whatever their age, had access to at least a basic education.[59] Now, cases appear of teenagers, born for instance in 1993, who are illiterate, which means that many of the white-collar jobs occupied hitherto by other *biduns* will be inaccessible to the new *bidun* generation. A study commissioned by the Ministry of Interior and focusing on criminality among the various national groups in Kuwait showed that the crime rate of the *biduns* is second only to that of the Egyptians.[60] The *bidun* existence outside the rule of law is an open door to impunity for those abusing the *biduns'* situation. It is also the open door to illicit activities.

Most of the newspapers in Kuwait devote one of their local pages to in-brief reports of crimes. I took a closer look at the 'local news' in the *Kuwait Times* during the first half of 2007. Table 5.1 gives an overview of the results.

Without overestimating the conclusions to be drawn from these observations, a few remarks can nevertheless be made. Apart from the atypical knife fight and graffiti that might be a strategy to get a basis on which to claim political asylum, drink driving, drug and sexual abuse are, comparatively, also common offences found in briefs related to cases involving Kuwaiti citizens or expatriates. Reports of thefts are also widespread among Kuwaitis, particularly against their domestic personnel, as well as among expatriates, usually among themselves. Sexual abuse almost exclusively involves foreign women, particularly Southeast Asians. Drug smuggling consists of picking up sacks on the coast containing, usually, 50 kilograms of hashish, and thrown from speedboats coming from Iran.[61] This task is most commonly carried out by Iranians, Pakistanis or *biduns*, although the consumers are largely nationals.

What seems peculiar to the *biduns* is the theft of cars, buses and spare parts, in a society where the car is king.[62] Some of them may be used for youth entertainment, some recycled in the garages,[63] but some are also smuggled to Iraq and Saudi Arabia. On 20 March 2007, the Kuwaiti police broke up a 'gang of automobile smugglers … specialising in stealing and smuggling luxury vehicles out of the country', in this case to Iraq. The people arrested were three drivers from Iraq and Iran, three *biduns*, a Kuwaiti employee of the Ministry of Defence, driving vehicles with forged licence plates, and an Egyptian customs representative 'found in possession of a huge quantity of licence plates, forged official documents and firearms'.[64] Instead of accepting the forced institutionalisation of their status as illegal migrants, some *biduns* stayed in informal circles, or rather

TABLE 5.1 CRIMES COMMITTED BY *BIDUNS*

Offenders				Victims			
No.	%	Type of crime	Location	No.	%	Type of crime	Location
6	30	Theft among which:	Jahra, Fahahil, Jlib al Shuyukh,	2	10	Theft of money	Jahra
4	20	*vehicles*	Farwaniyya, border posts	2	10	Sexual abuse	Riqqa,
1	5	*burglary*	(Salmi, 'Abdali)				'Ardiyya
1	5	*mobile phones*					
4	20	Gun firing (3) and knife fight (1):	Sulaibiyya, Jahra				
2	10	Consumption of drugs or alcohol	Ahmadi, Jahra				
2	10	Drug smuggling	Fintas				
1	5	Sexual abuse	Riqqa				
1	5	Graffiti of public buildings	Kuwait City				

Source: 'Local news', *Kuwait Times*, February–July 2007; 20-incident sample.

were pushed towards another kind of informal non-state action, the underground trade that has particularly flourished since the destruction suffered in neighbouring Iraq. This links the *bidun* issue to those of radicalisation, political violence and sectarianisation.

The second question of utmost importance is that of their involvement in jihadist cells in the context of the 2003 US-led attack on Iraq, first, and then, less than a decade later, in the context of the Syrian crisis and the rise of the Islamic State across Iraq and Syria. During the 2000s, this involvement in violent actions was less discussed in the Kuwaiti public debate than their alleged collaboration with the Iraqis in 1990–1. The latter question unified Kuwait while the former is extremely divisive among Kuwaitis, since the rise of jihadist movements has involved Kuwaiti nationals first and foremost.[65] There is no doubt about its sensitivity: a clear correlation between the outcast *bidun* category and the networks fighting US troops in Iraq and later Baghdad and Damascus' armies would show the limits of the policy of pressurising the *biduns* into confessing their 'real nationality'.

Bidun involvement in political violence has come about only in the framework of extremist transnational Islamist movements present in the country and comprising Kuwaitis as well as foreigners. Never have the *bidun* organised violent actions to claim rights or end their plight; on the contrary, the sole protest movement in the wake of the Arab uprisings opted for peaceful means of mobilisation.

Yet since the first *bidun* actions in the framework of the Lions of the Peninsula Brigades (*Kata'ib usud al Jazira*), a violent organisation linked with Iraqi and Saudi branches of al-Qaeda[66] that fought the US presence in Kuwait in the first half of the 2000s,[67] *bidun* involvement seems to have taken greater visibility, in line with the rise of jihadi calls. In 2005, following a shootout with the Kuwaiti police forces,[68] out of 37 suspects, 25 Kuwaitis and seven *biduns*[69] were tried for 'joining an illegal organisation, carrying out terrorist acts, participating in the killing of several policemen and plotting to attack US forces and citizens in the emirate'.[70] Six militants were sentenced to death,[71] four upheld in the appeal's verdict, among whom were three *biduns* and three Kuwaitis.[72]

Ten years later, the criminal investigation into the 26 June 2015 attack on the Shiite Imam Sadiq Mosque in Kuwait, which killed 26 people and left more than 200 others injured, led the public prosecution to charge 29 in the attack, out of which five were Kuwaitis, seven Saudis, three Pakistanis, and 13 *biduns*.[73] While the suicide bomber was identified as a Saudi national, the inquiry led to the arrest of three Kuwaiti *biduns*: the driver of the car who took the bomber to the mosque, collected the explosive belt from Saudi accomplices at the southern border and allegedly confessed to being part of the Islamic State, the owner of the car, and the car owner's brother.

The complicity of *biduns* in political violence, however, reflects a broader trend of Islamic empowerment and radicalisation affecting Kuwaiti politics. This empowerment follows the convergence of interests between tribes and Islamist movements, including the Muslim Brotherhood and Salafi movements, that originated from non-tribal (*hadar*) Kuwaitis. While socialisation in these movements functioned as a vehicle for upward mobility for a new generation of tribal youth, tribal allegiances, conversely, have helped Islamists gain electoral victories, especially since 2006. The *biduns* have been exposed to the political doctrines of Sunni Islamists via two channels.

First, as a people derived mainly from transnational tribal backgrounds (mostly 'Anaza, Shammar and Zafir, composed of both Sunnis and Shiites), the *biduns* inhabit the Kuwaiti 'tribal' periphery, where Salafi currents are well implanted, in particular the activist party *Hizb al Umma*. The case of 'Amir al-'Anazi, the head of the Lions of the Peninsula Brigades, who died in 2005, illustrated these transnational and tribal connections: a preacher at the Malik bin 'Awf Mosque in Jahra in the adjacent area to the Popular Housing, he was fired by the Ministry of Awqaf and Islamic Affairs on 2 January 2005, shortly before the incidents, for his extremist ideas and frequent visits to Iraq. The mosque where he preached was the meeting point for Kuwaitis of tribal backgrounds, employees of the Ministries of Awqaf or Defence, Saudis as well as *biduns*.[74]

Secondly, the influence of the Salafis and Muslim Brothers grew among *biduns* due to their financial influence, distributed through powerful charities, including the Salafi Society for the Revival of the Islamic Heritage (*jama'iyyat Ihia' al turath*) and the Muslim

Brotherhood's Association for Islamic Reform (*jama'iyyat al Islah*). The Shiite foundations, such as the Social Society for Culture (*jama'iyyat al thaqafa al ijtima'iyya*), score rather poorly by comparison. *Biduns* of Shiite persuasion blame the absence of government funding of Shiite organisations, which is an old Shiite grievance in Kuwait.[75] In order to benefit from the financial or material help provided by the Salafis, the *biduns* need to subscribe to their rigorous interpretation of the Sunni creed, so that nowadays there are strong religious pressures for the Shiite *biduns* to convert to Sunni Islam. 'Moneywise, it is better to be Salafi', assures a Shiite pro-*bidun* activist, quoting the example of Muhammad Wali al-'Anazi, founder of the Kuwaiti Bedoons Movement, 'originally a Shiite from Iraq, who turned into a Salafi'.[76]

The Sunni radicalisation of the *biduns* has been growing since 11 September 2001 (9/11) when the *bidun* neighbourhoods were visited by al-Qaeda promoters offering to aid a man's whole family financially if he went to jihad. This radicalisation also has to do with the fact that many young *bidun* men grow beards in the hope to find a job in charities, according to a *bidun* activist.[77] Because the *biduns* stem from mixed sectarian tribes, the sectarianisation of the community is a new phenomenon.

The Arab Spring and the wars in Libya and Syria have also played a role in this process of radicalisation. As the Syrian war galvanised some of Sunni religious movements, in particular the Salafis', the politicised *biduns* were also part of the momentum. According to the same *bidun* activist, *bidun* Salafis repeatedly brought the Syrian and Libyan examples to the *biduns*: 'They are impressed by the radical fights over there and think the *bidun* community has no reason not to fight on such a level.' Some answered the call to fight the holy war: Abu Azzam al-Kuwaiti, deputy commander of Jabhat al-Nusra in Qalamoun, made the news in March 2014 when he was seen releasing the Maloula nuns after an agreement reached between Jabhat al-Nusra and the Syrian government. A few days later he fell on the battlefield during combat in Yabroud. As a sign of cooperation between *bidun* and nationals among the jihadist movements, he was hailed as a 'martyr' not only by his *bidun* relatives in Jahra but also by Islamist former members of parliament, Ja'aman al-Harbash (Muslim Brotherhood from the 'Anaza tribe) and Walid al-Tabtabai (*haraki* Salafi from an urban background).

The temptation to fight in Syria and Iraq is also shared by certain young affluent Kuwaitis, whose number on the battlefield was estimated at 70 at the beginning of 2015.[78] In conclusion, *biduns'* involvement in political violence cannot be separated from the bigger picture of Islamist empowerment and its increasing connection to tribes, and transnational networks that have taken a radical turn in the face of regional events (notably in Syria). While the Kuwaiti state has brandished the security threat as an efficient means to widen the distance between the Kuwaitis and the *biduns* and delegitimise the latter's claims in the late 1980s and throughout the 1990s, the current situation of a real intermeshing of *biduns* and nationals in violent religious movements has not triggered the same anti-*bidun* rhetoric nor the same securitisation of the issue as before.

On the contrary, the pressure exercised by pro-*bidun* Kuwaitis has borne some fruit, with the Council of Ministers Decision No. 409/2011, promulgated on 6 March 2011, granting *biduns* a set of civil and human privileges and facilities that they were hitherto denied. The security-humanitarian conundrum had pushed many Kuwaitis to call for the end of the policy of human rights violation. The next section explores the mobilisation among Kuwaiti nationals who expressed dissatisfaction with the way the government had let the issue snowball, making the solution increasingly difficult and costly in both human and financial terms.

'Give the biduns their human rights'

The opponents of the naturalisation of the *biduns* form a relatively homogenous group, with mainly economic and security concerns and motivated by the fear of losing privileges and social peace, cloaked in nationalist terms. Conversely, the supporters of the *biduns'* cause come from various contexts, with different motives and different proposals for solutions.

The proponents of a policy change towards the *biduns* form a very heteroclite group. The cause is mainly defended by Shiite activists and politicians, *Badu* MPs overlapping with certain Sunni Islamists, some liberals and two prominent female members of the royal family. As opposed to the Sunni *hadar*, Shiite *hadar* are seen as generally more favourably disposed towards the *biduns*. MP Hasan al-Jawhar[79] has been a prominent figure in the defence of the *biduns'* rights; head of the *Bidun* Popular Committee, he was also the first president of the influential Parliamentary Committee for *Bidun* Affairs established in July 2006.[80] He belongs to a generation of Kuwaiti politicians who arrived in the political arena at the end of the 1990s and whose credibility had not been affected by previous, sometimes deemed 'opportunistic', positions, like Ahmad Sa'dun,[81] or sectarian statements (Adnan Abd al-Samad)[82] in the 1980s. Ahmad Sa'dun was among the first of the deputies to attack the government head on for its muddled nationality policy in the 1980s. As of 1981, he asked for the official number of people who had acquired nationality (first- and second-degree) since independence.[83] During the electoral campaign for the 1985 parliament, of which he was elected speaker, he became famous for his speech warning the government that it was sitting on a time bomb because of the way it handled the granting of nationality.[84] This famous 'time bomb' expression referred to the '65,000 persons consider[ing] themselves Kuwaitis and 46,000 [who] appl[ied] for the nationality',[85] and the fact that nationality was granted to a lot of ineligible people, while it was denied to some others who were qualified to become Kuwaiti citizens. At the time, the claims from 25,000 Kuwaitis to be Kuwaitis 'by origin' were ignored. This discourse is seen as ambiguous and double-edged. For some it denounced the situation of *biduns*, yet for others it pointed to them, in the troubled context of the 1980s, as a threat. Head of the Popular Bloc (*takattul al 'amal al sha'abi*), founded in 1999 as an alternative to the liberals or Islamists and closer to evolving social needs, Sa'dun kept his oppositional line to the government, his advocacy of parliamentary life and civil rights guarantees but presented himself, when interviewed, as a staunch Kuwaiti democrat rather than human rights activist or a partisan of balance with the *badu*. The name of Abd al-Samad was strongly associated with the claims for equality between levels of nationality in the 1979 Shiite movement in the Sha'ban Mosque.[86]

On the contrary, Dr. al-Jawhar's involvement has proved consistent and enduring, which has given him consideration as more genuine than other MPs. His name is now somehow associated through the *Bidun* Popular Committee with the action of the two

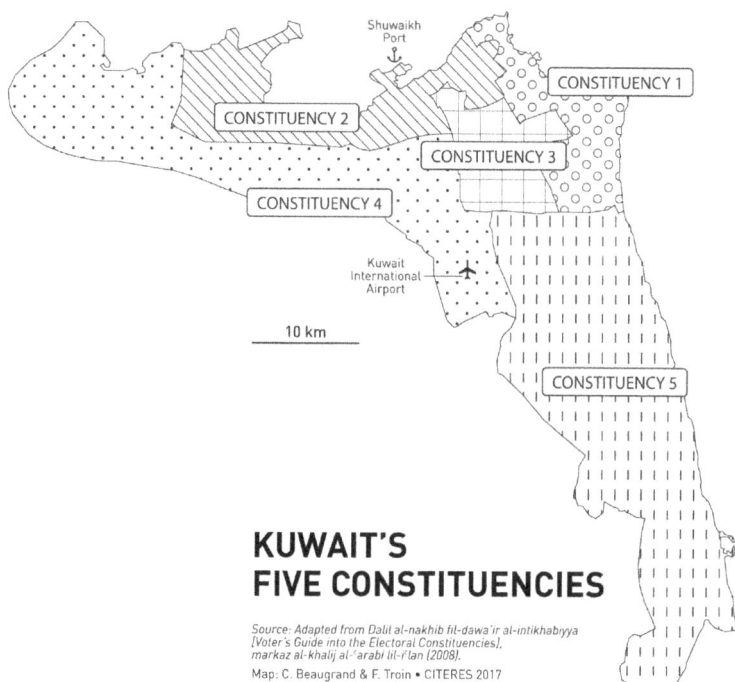

MAP 5.1   Kuwait's five constituencies

female members of the royal family, Sheikha Awrad and Sheikha Fawzia. These two sheikhas entered the *bidun* debate with reputations of neutrality: as members of the royal family they are considered to be above political squabbling and interests. Sheikha Awrad is a daughter of the late Emir Jabir al-Ahmad al-Jabir Al-Sabah, whose life was saved by the sacrifice of two *bidun* bodyguards on 25 May 1985,[87] while Sheikha Fawzia is a lawyer. The two sheikhas stress their thirst for justice based on the rule of law.

Dr. Jawhar's position is at the crossroads between two sometimes overlapping groups of proponents of the *biduns'* cause: the Shiite *hadar* and the Popular Bloc. The first group includes MPs Adnan Abd al-Samad, Abd al-Muhsin Jamal, Ahmad Lari, supportive of *khatt al imam*, the Imam Khomeini line (Imamis) and Yusuf Zalzala.[88] Shiites will sometimes explain this position as emanating from a feeling of commiseration that Shiites, themselves oppressed, share with any kind of oppressed people. This subjective interpretation has a political implication though: changing the status quo through an enlargement of the citizen basis could be to the advantage of the Shiite minority. The reasons behind this argument somewhat echo those of the 2006 debate surrounding the reduction of constituencies from 25 to five, which included the battle against clientelism and government intervention in the elections.

Two arguments run parallel to each other: the first assumes that the majority of the *biduns* are Shiite and that the *biduns'* naturalisation would *in fine* increase the number of co-religionist voters. Yet the sources that I interviewed and that were among the most familiar with the *biduns'* issue, Dr. Jawhar and Dr. al-Waqian, who both had access to government resources via Parliament's Commission for *Bidun* Affairs, affirm that the majority of the *biduns* are Sunnis, which could be explained by some phenomenon of conversion within the group. According to the second line of argument, the clear winners of this new political support would certainly be the tribes, because of their relations with the *biduns*; the losers would indisputably be the Sunni *hadar*, who would be in direct competition with reinvigorated tribal religious conservatives. Eventually the underpopulated second constituency would have to be adjusted and the representation of the Sunni *hadar* would be affected.[89] Finally, while Sunni *hadar* families like the Ghanim have kept a foot in both economics and politics, putting pressure on the government via the powerful Chamber of Commerce, there is a bigger chasm between great Shiite merchants (Bahbahani, Ma'arafi) and politicians. To sum up, 'for most Sunnis [the economic elite], retaining undiminished economic and political clout is more tangible than abstract concepts of building shared citizenship among Shia and Sunnis'.[90] The limitation of the considerable *hadar* Sunni power would also benefit the *hadar* Shiites.

The second group that sympathises with the fate of the *biduns* is the oppositional Popular Bloc. In addition to Ahmad al-Sa'dun and the Imami Shiites, it includes tribal MPs like Musallam al-Barrak,[91] from the Mutair, and Muhammad al-Khalifa (Shammari).[92] As opposed to the MPs mentioned above, these MPs run in *badu* constituencies. Beyond the fourth ring road, in what are now the fourth and fifth constituencies, there are no 'liberals' or Shiite MPs, who have become somehow *hadar* categories. The 'Wild West' or fourth constituency is the fiefdom of northern tribes – 'Anaza, Shammar, Zafir – but also the powerful southern tribe of the Mutran as well as the Rashayida. The 'Wild South' belongs to the 'Ajman and 'Awazim. The political landscape is dominated by tribal politics (primaries or *fara'iyya*) until 2008, when the Ministry of the Interior forbade them, and the rise of Sunni Islamist movements, said to be the result of Saudi influences. The MPs from tribal backgrounds who systematically support the *biduns'* cause are based in areas actually affected by the presence of *biduns*: Muhammad al-Khalifa and Khudayr al-'Anazi,[93] both of whom were elected in Jahra al Jadida, the constituency including Sulaibiyya, and the suburbs surrounding the 'old' or historic Jahra around the Red Castle. Sa'dun Hamad (al-'Utaybi) represents the district of Ahmadi,[94] the area of the oil installations where many *biduns'* family histories started, while Ghanim al-May', from the 'Awazim,[95] is the MP for the neighbouring popular Sabahiyya. Together with Jawhar, these four MPs formed the Parliamentary Commission for *Bidun* Affairs that did not outlive the aborted parliamentary session of 2006–8, in spite of certain tangible achievements like the charitable funds.

Supporting the cause of the *biduns* often means issuing statements in favour of their rights and raising awareness of their plight. The MP Khudayr al-'Anazi was a prominent example of this battle of words on all fronts during his 2006–8 mandate: he was present at the conference of November 2006, 'The *Biduns* Talk'.[96] In December of the same year he denounced the decision of the Ministry of Awqaf and Islamic Affairs to reduce the number of *bidun* pilgrims from 1,250 in 2005 to 500, whose officials he expected to be 'religious people who fear God and help Muslims to perform their rituals and not an intelligence or security agency'.[97] In January 2007, in the midst of the release of temporary driving licences for *biduns*, he hosted a gathering together with MPs Hasan Jawhar and Muhammad Khalifa at his house in Jahra to warn the *biduns* not to fall into the trap of signing an official document acknowledging their illegal status.[98] On 17 April 2007 I attended his lecture at Kuwait University on 'The *Biduns* and Kuwaiti Society': he raised the issue of 'faraway suburbs' with '29 individuals in popular housing' and the government inconsistencies at the heart of the *hadar* elite reproduction system. In December he called for the unification of nationality;[99] he was still battling with the Minister of Defence, Sheikh Jabir al-Mubarak Al-Sabah over the naturalisation of the *bidun* employees of his ministry[100] when the National Assembly was dissolved. He was not re-elected in May 2008. Like others before him, he came up against the brick wall of the government's investigation committees and the unshakable status quo, and did not deliver much on his promises.

This absence of effective results never fails to raise the question of the credibility of pro-*bidun* politicians, accused not only by the Minister of the Interior and adversaries alike but also by disillusioned *biduns*, of using the issue for electoral purposes or as a tool for bargaining with the government. As a matter of fact, MPs mostly from the fourth (Mutran, 'Anaza) but also from the fifth ('Ajman) constituency have multiplied their declarations of support for *biduns'* humanitarian demands and their willingness to 'solve their problems'.

Working separately but with the same electorate, part of the Salafis also expressed their position in favour of the *biduns*. The Salafi Movement, renamed so in 1997, urged the government and the National Assembly to cease the injustice and the discrimination against the *biduns* by demanding the abolition of Decree Law 98 of 1996, which forbids passing any official papers concerning the *biduns* without the prior clearance of the Executive Committee. It also urged the government to commit to the 1954 Convention relating to the Status of Stateless People, which would grant the *biduns* the full human rights enjoyed by nationals, such as the right to work, to education and to get married, as well as freedom of movement in accordance with the principle of the Islamic Shari'a.[101]

The *Hizb al Umma* (the Party of the Islamic Nation), created in January 2005 by three members of the Salafi Movement (*harakat al salafiyya*), among them Hakim al-Mutairi and Husain al-Sa'idi, offered a very articulate argument against the current nationality policy of the royal family. In addition to the standard Salafi calls for an Islamic society and Islamic-based legislation, as well as for Islam to be the state's religion, the *Hizb al Umma*'s programme proclaims its faith in a multi-party system and the peaceful alternation of power. Its call for the adoption of political parties – exemplified by the name itself, *hizb* or 'party', which caused it to be sued and considered illegal – is based on the sovereignty of the nation and a developed notion of citizenship (*muwatana*). In his online article '*tabi'un la muwatinun*' (Subjects not citizens), with the subtitle 'Gulf people and the issue of citizenship',[102] Hakim al-Mutairi, General Secretary of the party, rejected the official version, which depicts the relation between ruled and ruler as one between father and children. Beginning from the fraternal equality among believers, he argues for a relationship of equals between all members of the society, whether female[103] or male, large or small, rich or poor, ruled or ruler. This implies a sharp criticism of the legitimacy of the six ruling families of the Gulf Cooperation Council (GCC) countries, whose privilege to rule[104] he sees as inherited from British colonialism, and he describes as a feudal and tribal (*iqta'i* and *'asha'iri*) system based on allegiance and subjection to the sheikhs (*tabi'iyya wa ra'awiyya*),[105] lacking both religious legitimacy and the international legitimacy drawn from the people's representation. Apart from the religious inspiration, the argument resembles an anti-monarchical discourse against arbitrary privileges and the concentration of power, land and wealth in the hands of the few royal families who represent nobody but themselves. He denounces the fact that 'six royal families preside over the destiny of 30 million Gulf people'. As a result, the ruling families conceive nationality as a royal prerogative: they alone grant and withdraw it at their whim, disregarding the right of people who have lived on the land for centuries.

The right of abode (*haqq al ujud bil-ard*) is core to the position of the members of *Hizb al Umma*:[106] following the position of Muhammad 'Abduh, they consider that there is no such a thing as a Muslim without nationality. People should be nationals of the country in which they are settled, in which they live with their families and in which they make a living. And the *biduns* who belong to the artificially divided Arabian Peninsula are no exception.

In addition to this Islamist rhetoric, the *Hizb al Umma* underlines its attachment to constitutional provisions and refers to the international discourse of human rights and the 1948 Universal Declaration of Human Rights (UDHR) to point out the deprivation of individual rights but also the absence of possible judiciary or legislative[107] resort for *biduns* to claim their rights. Like the *badu* MPs, members of the *Hizb al Umma* have first-hand knowledge of the issue and its complex links with the emergence of an educated and ambitious class of *badu*. The Head of the Political Bureau until June 2006, Husain al-Sa'idi, for instance, is from a large Jahra family, affiliated with the Zafir. He studied theology in Mecca; his elder brother was promoted to general in the Kuwaiti army; his younger brother was a student at the American University of Kuwait; and yet another brother, of first-degree citizenship, married a *bidun* Zafiri. The brother of this *bidun* spouse was born in 1990 and educated in a school for *biduns*. A student at the Gulf University for Science and Technology (GUST), he struggled to pursue his higher education and planned to complete his surgery studies in the Ukraine. The combination of a high level of education and the frustration of not being able to achieve and bring about change explains to a certain extent the positions of Husain al-Sa'idi and his like in the *Hizb al Umma*.[108] Husain al-Sa'idi later disagreed with the other leaders of the party over the participation in the 2008 elections. He left the party to run in the fourth constituency but was not elected.[109]

Finally, and diametrically opposed to the Salafi's thinking, whose position remains both anti-Shiite[110] and ambiguous towards labour migrants, there is the voice of the so-called 'liberals', which is to say the non-religious voice. They are mostly composed of intellectuals, academics and journalists, who use their columns in prominent daily newspapers to defend principles of human rights and humanitarian needs, the dignity of the person and tolerance of others. They come from all areas and write in the prominent journals: Ali al-Baghli,[111] former MP and Minister of Oil, head of the Kuwait Society for Human Rights (KSHR), writes in *Al-Qabas*, while two renowned scholars – Dr. Sami Khalifa and Dr. Salah al-Fadli – contribute to *Al-Ra'i*.[112] The editorial team, around Saud al-'Anazi, keeps the famous organ of the Arab nationalist press, *Al-Tali'a*, alive. The newer *Al-Jarida* receives the pro-*bidun* articles of at least six authors,[113] among whom is Dr. Ghanim Al-Najjar, academic in Political Sciences in Kuwait University, human rights expert and consultant for the UN Office of the High Commissioner for Human Rights. Finally, the academic

Dr. Faris al-Waqian and the *bidun* artist Karim Haza', founding member of a literary cenacle 'the Tuesday's cultural gathering' (*multaqa al thulatha' al thaqafi*) were contributors to the now closed *Awan*. According to Karim Haza', intolerance in Kuwait can be explained by poorly understood religion, tribal traditions and lack of education or 'enlightenment'.[114] For the new generation of *badu*, the *bidun* issue illustrates the lack of integration of the periphery and the absence of social equality in Kuwait. Kuwaitis don't hesitate to speak about 'racism' in Kuwait. The definition of the term, borrowed from the Western lexicon to frown upon discrimination, is usually vague and its historical loading, linked to invalidated scientific beliefs, does not apply to the region. What undeniably exists is first a very strong social hierarchy based on the international 'ranking' of nationalities – or the countries' wealth or development. Lastly, there is a deep-seated divergence in the camp of supporters of the *biduns'* cause. This is largely reflected in the very different views they hold about a possible solution, on a wide spectrum, from proponents of the granting of civil rights to advocates of naturalisation.

Apart from the recurrent leitmotiv according to which 'the *biduns* who deserve nationality should be granted it', advocates of a solution to the issue share a very narrow common platform. The decade-long policy of rights deprivation led to the shifting of the terms of the debate, the scaling down of claims – in short, the clear decoupling of nationality as the formal aspect of state membership, understood as papers and basic needs, and citizenship as the enjoyment of full civil and political rights and participation in the body politic. This is obvious in the prioritisation of the issues between the increasing ranks of those who stress the urgency of tackling human rights needs and the fewer and more radical who favour a straightforward granting of full rights, including nationality but also political rights. In its extreme form, the first stance is illustrated by the following statement:

> 'We will no longer push for granting citizenship to qualified Bedouns as we are more concerned about giving them their most basic civil and human rights' says MP Hussein Quwaian Al-Mutairi.[115] Speaking to the *Arab Times* Sunday, Al-Mutairi admitted many Bedouns deserve the Kuwaiti citizenship but their fundamental human and civil rights are more important than their nationality.[116]

Many proposals to grant *biduns* their 'basic', 'humanitarian' or 'civil' rights leave the question of their naturalisation in particularly vague terms – if it is envisaged at all. The various draft bills suggest in strikingly similar wordings giving the *biduns* freedom of movement (through issuing IDs, passports, driving licences), the right to obtain official documents (marriage, birth and death certificates) and the right of access to education and health care. Some include the right to benefit from priority housing or employment in the public sector. These proposals are presented as 'temporary solution[s] to the bedoon problem until reaching a final settlement',[117] yet, 'asked about the nature of the sought final settlement, Tabtabae said it should naturalise people who deserve citizenship and take legal measures against those who don't'.[118] This is tantamount to putting the question of naturalisation off *ad Kalendas Graecas*; the idea of 'naturalising deserving *biduns*' is, in legal terms, quite ill-defined. It is all the more so given the malleable nature of the security clearance required from the *biduns* to obtain nationality. It is not uncommon in Kuwait to read about erroneous naturalisations that result in the stripping of the granted citizenship after 'reports about security restrictions' on concerned individuals who have 'criminal and financial cases registered against them' and even cases allegedly 'related to the security of the State'.[119] It should be noted here that the list of people deserving naturalisation and presented to the Council of Ministers might include a cocktail of extremely varied cases – including Saudi nationals or recently married foreign wives. One staunch supporter of the *biduns*, MP Ahmad al-Mulaifi, independent but with Sunni Islamist inclination, was reported to admit that

> on allegations that some MPs used the naturalization issue to gain the voters' trust ... he had some reservations on the names included in the list of Bedouns qualified for naturalization. He said even the government raised doubts on some of the names included in the list.[120]

The absence of MPs' responsibility for final decisions not only in this but also in other matters explains the existence of (and the blame for) the extravagant promises made to win votes. What is striking here is that the discourse surrounding the *bidun* issue has converged with the discourse on the treatment of migrants in other countries, especially Western democracies. The comparison between *biduns* and

Mexicans in the US, favourable to Kuwait, is sometimes ventured.[121] Moreover, a deputy of the National Assembly proposed the introduction of the US model of the 'Green Card' for some expatriates with long residence in the country, including *biduns*.[122] Although this proposition is aimed at re-establishing some sense of clear legal requirements, it makes its own the governmental premise that *biduns* ought to be treated like migrants.

The international context in which the Kuwaiti debate is framed has been geared in previous decades towards a neo-liberal view of citizenship that conceives the citizen as a consumer. This implies that the social citizenship and its equalising function in Marshall's work is being replaced by the private matter of material consumption, requiring only regulating bodies to secure its effectiveness. Migrants are thus welcome to circulate, work and enjoy the services and environment but the republican commitment to the community is no longer a necessity, while political participation is undertaken mostly in order to check the excesses of power (voting out corruption) or promote sectional interests.

The liberalisation in Kuwait manifested by the enfranchisement of women in 2005 did not lead to any new or inclusive concept of citizenship. On the contrary, there has been a rapprochement with the practice in other developed countries.[123]

The few advocates of the cause of the *biduns* who have a clear vision of a naturalisation scheme emphasise the link between naturalisation and investment in human resources. Hasan Jawhar, after positing the same distinction between civil rights for all and citizenship, criticises the 2000 Law on Gradual Naturalisation as a waste of time. Should it ever be applied it would take over 20 years to naturalise the *bidun* population. Moreover, he criticises the law for its undifferentiated approach towards *biduns'* skills. He sees the creeping phenomenon of underemployment (*bitala muqanna'a*) in the country and the waste of skills that graduate *biduns* who do not have access to work at their level of qualification represent. In line with his efforts on the funding of education for young *biduns*, he advocates a naturalisation plan that would be based on clear criteria and the principles of justice and national economic needs.[124] Abdullah Bishara, former Secretary General of the GCC, argues along the same lines, noting the paradoxical presence of *c.*600,000 Indians and 80,000 *biduns* ready to integrate in Kuwait and concluding that it is not normal to have *biduns* and at the same time to bring in Egyptians or foreigners. For him, *biduns* present a minimal security risk in the long term by comparison with migrant labourers. They are 'loyal, trustworthy' and hard workers as they usually have two jobs despite the insecurity of their employment. Thus they should be integrated as much as possible in the labour market and their naturalisation would be better.[125]

In addition to economic value, proposals for solutions put forward various categories of statelessness that should be dealt with as a priority. MP Ahmad al-Mulaifi blatantly contradicted the government line of argument when he openly asked to prioritise the files of those who earlier refused Kuwaiti citizenship according to the second article of the law, or second-degree nationality.[126] All, starting with Sheikha Award and Sheikha Fawzia, agree that the relatives of the *biduns* who died while serving in the armed forces or those who served loyally in the armed forces should be treated with the honours that the fatherland reserves for its defenders.[127] Lastly, few supporters advocate a radical solution that refuses to dissociate civil or basic rights from other political rights and privileges. This position of principle, tainted with religious argument, was held by members of *Hizb al Umma*; it is also the stance of Faris al-Waqian, developed in the comparative study he prepared for the Parliamentary Commission for *Bidun* Affairs entitled 'Enquiry into the solutions to the *bidun* question in the context of the [evolving] understanding of civil rights and the experience of neighbouring countries'.[128] In this study, al-Waqian criticises the piecemeal solution, or what he ironically calls the solution 'in instalments' (*al taqsit al murih*), by which he refers to the time-consuming process of fighting for the issuing of a driving licence one day and a birth certificate the next, and so on, which only contributes to the 'electoral show'. He favours a comprehensive solution that would include civil and political rights together.

Contextualising the issue, he sees two contradictions: first between the democratic system in Kuwait and the exclusion from the citizenry of part of its population despite the growing acceptance worldwide of the *jus soli* principle, and second the proclamation of gender equality, with the enfranchisement of women in 2005 and, still, the impossibility of women passing their Kuwaiti nationality on to their children or husbands.[129] Stressing his belief in social justice and equality, he considers the full 'rights of *biduns* as legal and universal and not as a gift'.[130] His position is rather isolated: the promotion of the systematic application of the rule of law is somehow alien to the political culture of the patronage-based emirate of Kuwait. The Kuwaiti system, where politics are played as much through the social game as through political associations, makes the findings of citizenship studies and literature on statelessness sometimes difficult to apply in a one-dimensional way. On the contrary, there is a two-way appropriation and compliance with the international human rights discourse and organisations.

INTERNATIONALISATION OF THE *BIDUN* ISSUE

External pressures for a solution

The previous section has shown the complex social and political dynamics in Kuwait that must be dealt with both by international human rights organisations and the government, to which they address most of their recommendations. International non-governmental organiations (INGOs) and international (governmental) organisations (IOs) have played a determining role in denouncing the Kuwaiti government's discriminatory policy as it was fully applied in the aftermath of the Iraqi invasion. The internationalisation of the issue has led to a double-edged interaction between local and international actors: the intervention of external actors has led many Kuwaitis, particularly the victims of the Iraqi occupation, to work together with the international bodies, and more generally to adopt their pervasive discourse and vocally request solutions. Twelve years after the 1995 Human Rights Watch (HRW) reports, Khudayr al-'Anazi was saying: 'This issue should not be delayed so that no solutions from outside are imposed on us.'[131] At the same time, the resort to INGOs and IOs has been increasingly presented as a threat, their reports resented as a stain on Kuwait's international image and used to put pressure on the government. All Kuwaitis, whether for or against a change in the current policy of pressurising the *biduns*, understandably fear an externally imposed solution, although a decade of non-compliance, even in the face of the past US promotion of democracy in their northern neighbour, has shown the unlikelihood of such a scenario – which has become even more unlikely with the turmoil engulfing the Middle East since 2011, the war in Syria and the rise of the self-proclaimed Islamic State.

Ironically, the Iraqi invasion of Kuwait, albeit easy to explain because of the unleashing of violence it rendered possible, played a major role in creating the conditions for both hardening the crackdown on the *biduns* and placing the country at the heart of a powerful civil society movement, on the one hand, and under the scrutiny of INGOs, on the other.[132] After the liberation of Kuwait, the *bidun* issue was part of a broader human rights crisis that included the crimes of the occupiers but also, those of the occupied. The questions of Kuwaiti prisoners and missing persons in Iraq, war crimes and human rights violations committed under the occupation, as well as reparations brought the International Committee of the Red Cross (ICRC), Amnesty International (AI)[133] and the various United Nations (UN) agencies dealing with compensation[134] and tackling refugees and other humanitarian needs into the country. Following the occupation, which represented a period of survival in the absence of a state, Kuwaiti citizens, victims of the Iraqi aggression, set up the Kuwaiti Association to Defend War Victims (KADWV). Dr. Ghanim Al-Najjar, who had been held prisoner in Iraq, was a prominent activist in the KADWV which, together with the Arab Human Rights Organisation, was the first to be allowed to operate in post-1991 Kuwait. The question of the prisoners of war (POWs) never ceased to engage Kuwaiti civil society until after the 2003 attack on Iraq, when their hopes of finding the POWs somewhere in the liberated jails of the Ba'athist regime were finally dashed. In 1992 the National Assembly created a Parliamentary Commission for the Defence of Human Rights. The local human rights NGOs and Parliamentary Committee were there to stay.

Yet the international human rights organisations that came to scrutinise the Kuwaiti emirate in the aftermath of liberation did not restrict themselves to the violations perpetrated by the Iraqis: the martial law trials, accusations of collaboration that led, among other things, to the deportation of a large part of the Palestinian community, and associated unprecedented legal issues[135] were soon the objects of investigation.[136] It is in this context that the repression of the *biduns* continued. As things gradually calmed down and went back to normal the question arose with renewed prominence; the first HRW report solely dedicated to the issue, *The Bedoons of Kuwait: Citizens without Citizenship*, issued in August 1995,[137] marked a huge rupture in the visibility of the statelessness phenomenon. The Kuwaiti authorities had tolerated, at least outside the two unconstitutional suspensions of the Parliament (1976–81 and 1986–92), criticisms of the management of issues surrounding nationality provided the discussion remained a strictly Kuwaiti matter.[138]

For the first time in around 30 years, the issue went public internationally. The trauma of the invasion, as said above, rendered feasible the resort to an international audience and condemnation in the case of the *bidun* issue. This was a great step: as one *bidun* in the UK put it in 2009, there are limits to what a Kuwaiti on the payroll of the government can say. Yet at the same time this external pressure has been felt as humiliation. The inextricable presence of the *biduns* is internalised by most Kuwaitis, whatever their stance, as a stain on their international reputation – a stain that other Arab countries, with no better human rights records, are only too happy to utilise.

Statelessness in the first place, and even more the pressure policy exerted against *biduns*, represent for the INGOs a gross violation of the principle of non-discrimination. By labelling the *biduns* illegal migrants, Kuwaiti decision makers used the institutionalised category of international law to evade the actions of the transnational INGOs. An article published in *Al-Watan* on 5 September 1994 reported MP al-'Adsani saying that 'when the government established the [Executive] committee, it called it the Committee for Illegal Residents which protects Kuwait from international condemnation'.[139]

Yet this political manoeuvre did not completely protect the country from international condemnation: party to the Covenant on Civil and Political Rights (CCPR) that came into force in 1996, Kuwait became engaged in the process of reporting on its human rights situation. By virtue of article 40 of the covenant, which made it compulsory for states party to the covenant to report on their situations, Kuwait submitted its initial report on 8 December 1999.

This ushered in an interactive process of points to clarify, questions and answers between the government of Kuwait and the Human Rights Committee (of the United Nations's Office of the High Commissioner for Human Rights (OHCHR) in charge of monitoring the implementation of the CCPR), making the former accountable for its promises and also policy turns. The United Nations High Commissioner for Refugees (UNHCR), represented at the time by Maureen Laing, is also following up and watching any stepping back.[140] Moreover, while Kuwait thought it would be immune from international condemnation by grouping together *biduns* and migrants, the latter also became increasingly the focus of the IOs' attention, and both issues are often treated together.[141]

The substantial collaboration with a growing number of IOs (for instance the International Organisation for Migration) and INGOs, one of the most active on the *bidun* file currently being Refugees International, led to a wide appropriation of the discourse of these organisations by an increasing proportion of local actors. Nonetheless, this unified discourse has had a double-edged effect. For sure, it halted the tendency towards greater financial than psychological pressure on the *biduns*, yet it also contributed to the process of stigmatisation of the category. The NGOs graphically highlight the plight of the *biduns*, presenting them in *dishdasha* and *ghutra* without a face (Refugees International),[142] or with a *shmagh* wrapped around their head,[143] hiding their face (KSHR) or with ankles and wrists bound by chains, with their head down.

Though this triggers feelings of sympathy, it also adds to the stigmatisation of this part of the population, in a society where poverty is clearly seen as the attribute of foreigners. Overall, it reinforces the government line of trying to estrange the *biduns* from Kuwaiti society when they are historically part and parcel of the social pact. While some *biduns* accept being victimised, as many others refuse this representation of *biduns* as weak people, at least based on the information gathered during our fieldwork. The Kuwaiti *Biduns'* Congregation movement, for example, shows a brandished combative fist.

Biduns are proud of their education, skills and steadfastness under duress and in the face of discrimination. Obliged to toil for their living, they mock the idleness and the ignorance of those too used to being served and thus no longer able to acquire any skills. Some of those who could invest in education at the Arab Open University (AOU), abroad or through distance learning, are confident that their qualifications will logically and economically become indispensable and that they will be redeemed by their resourcefulness and strength of will. Even the most disillusioned, such as the man who has given up hope altogether of getting married or being naturalised because of the mistakes of his father, who brought members of his Syrian family to Kuwait in the 1970s, speaks of his fight for employment with some pride, and recalls with amazing precision every single sheikh who headed the Ministry of the Interior and Defence since Sheikh Saad Abdullah became Crown Prince in 1978.

Although the recommendations of the INGOs would find it simply impossible to look at every situation where naturalisation is barred by a criminal record or prior counter-security accusations, some of them need special mention and discussion. In addition to recommending systematic registration at birth,[144] the access to 'civil registry, social services, education and access to due process in court', Refugees International also urges the 'revis[ion of] the nationality law to bring it into conformity with more progressive legislation in the region, particularly regarding the equal right of women to pass on nationality to children'.[145] Building on the precedent of granting women voting rights on 16 May 2005, this recommendation could bear some fruit. The goal of the government and its allies is obviously not to enlarge the citizenry, or to do so keeping tight control of the process. Yet it has no long-term interest either in disappointing a significant part of its female population, particularly the mothers of the *abna' al kuwaitiyyat* (children of Kuwaiti women), who can enjoy nationality but still feel discriminated against, especially now that women possess the right to vote. Tackling the two issues together would help stop the stigmatisation of the destitute *bidun* while reintegrating them progressively into society, through mixed marriage, hitherto not an option for *bidun* men or Kuwaiti women, and integrating them into the citizenry.

Buying time ... until when?

In conclusion, having seen the positions of the various stakeholders involved in the issue of the *biduns* in Kuwait, from the opposition of historic *hadar* economic elite to the Al-Sabah, to the new increasingly independent *badu* political forces as well as the international actors whose work influences the decisions of strategic support from powerful state actors, the following question remains: what are the options left to the Kuwaiti government?

In spite of the widespread belief that a comprehensive and radical solution can be found,[146] as already suggested above with the case of Kuwaiti women, the issue of the *biduns* may well be the tip of the iceberg of decades of inconsistencies in the handling of nationality in Kuwait. The *biduns* who are still claiming their entitlement to rights and nationality in Kuwait are the most visible aspect of the phenomenon; yet the circles of Gulf exiles suggest a wider extent if the deadlock is to be broken. A study made among Bahraini exiles showed that, although they were granted Canadian, Swedish and British nationalities, all of the Bahraini exiles, with the exception of the Free Bahrainis in London, decided to return to their country in spite of all they had to give up in terms of material enjoyment and professional careers.[147] Like the Bahrainis, the feeling among *biduns* in exile is that of an unrepaired injustice: 'I belong to the 'Anaza and I feel I have the right to belong to any Gulf country, because this area is my place of origin and also the 'Anaza have been living in this region for ages.'[148]

Moreover, there is the problem faced by British solicitors of finding a legal ground for asylum requests by *biduns*. *Biduns* also note that being granted asylum cannot be founded on political grounds or oppression and that it has become increasingly difficult since 9/11, especially in Canada and Australia, the primary destinations for *biduns* in the 1980s and 1990s. As a result across the world there are cases, whose number is of course impossible to evaluate, of *biduns* who became stateless again in Western countries following the rejection of their asylum applications.[149] Finally, the fate of the *biduns* officially from Iraq, who came back to their country of origin during the 1990 invasion and 1991 Gulf War and stayed there at a time when the Kuwaiti border with Iraq was closed, has remained undocumented. However, claims of an unknown magnitude exist on this front as well, as shown by the unpublished document 'Statement regarding the group of unfairly-treated *biduns* in Iraq. Open information campaign in solidarity with them'.[150]

Secondly, the issue of the *biduns* has shown the limits of the mode of government adopted by the Al-Sabah decision makers, who either take a consensual approach as fathers of the nation or else pit different parts of the population against one another to maintain the political advantage. The question of the inclusion or exclusion of the *biduns* divides the Kuwaiti polity deeply along lines of divergent and irreconcilable interests. In that sense, it reveals the real sense of democratic politics based on a consensus of the rules of the debate but strong confrontation of arguments. There can be no solution that would please both *hadar* and *badu*. The Kuwaiti rulers are caught between two parts of their citizenry, running the risk if it moves in either direction of losing the support of either the economic elite or the numerous middle class. The most radical *hadar* economic elite is inflexible in its unwillingness to compromise. Its historic and financial might renders the loss of its support extremely perilous. At the same time, the pressure from Parliament becomes more intense and the executive power seems to be weakening in face of its head-on approach. Losing credibility in the face of a democratically elected parliament would jeopardise the support of the international community so firmly secured by the Al-Sabah since the 1990–1 crisis as well as the united front of the ruling family and its pre-1990 parliamentary opposition.[151] This domestic deadlock explains the desperate attempts by the Kuwaiti authorities to find solutions outside the Kuwaiti citizenry by dealing with third party countries that are willing to negotiate their nationality entitlements. They also hope that the two opposing factions of the Kuwaiti population will eventually come up with a mutually acceptable solution that would preserve the unity of Kuwait. Knowing the incommensurable nature of arguments put forward, this consensual solution may take a long time.

Finally, the issue of the *biduns* touches upon the very tense relations between Kuwait and its two powerful neighbours. The riddle of Kuwaiti relations with Iraq is well known, poisoned by decades of mistrust. However, relations with Saudi Arabia, with its profound discomfort at the memory of the battle of Jahra as a national symbol, are not easy either. The problem of dual nationality among Saudi tribes is a recurrent one; Saudis who were hired in Kuwait did not necessarily renounce their Saudi nationality or, say, destroy their passports. Since the early days of oil exploitation, the material situation has been far more advantageous in Kuwait than in Saudi Arabia, especially in its northern region, far from Riyadh. The trend of Saudi immigration *stricto sensu* to Kuwait and the deep-running ties of intermarriage remain. Our observations in Jahra, though impossible to generalise in any way, show that young Saudi males still come and stay with their uncles, work in decent and skilled jobs and obtain nationality. This is corroborated in a statement from the MP Jawhar, pointing in the direction of Saudi Arabia to find the origins of the majority of the *biduns*, as well as the figures released by the Central System where *biduns* who have recovered Saudi nationality figure prominently (See Table 1.2). In any case, not only the absence of granting nationality but also the granting of nationality itself with a complete absence of transparency is problematic in Kuwait, as illustrated by the MP Ahmad al-Mulaifi's contesting the validity of half of the 570 naturalisations granted in January 2008, while '5,000 people, who fully qualify for citizenship, have been waiting for years because they have no influence': 'We have discovered serious violations in the list of people who were granted citizenship and we will not remain silent. This is a sensitive issue that relates to the country and its sovereignty.'[152]

The secrecy surrounding the whole process of nationality granting by Emiri decree will certainly render the solution to the *bidun* issue, but also to the wider issue of nationality definition, a long one. By contrast with the 1960s, any change to the Nationality Law or, rather, nationality and naturalisation *practices*, will have to involve all the Kuwaitis. Nationality-linked challenges lie ahead with the new waves of Syrian migrants, whose status is tantamount to refugees or stateless, since the return to their home country seems extremely far away.

CHAPTER 6

Sans-papiers Mobilisation in an Oil Monarchy

It is not about naturalisation, it is about existing.[1]

On 18 February 2011, a week after the fall of Hosni Mubarak in Egypt and just a few days after the Bahraini and Libyan uprisings, more than a 1,000 *biduns* took to the streets in Tayma, the faraway periphery of Kuwait, where most of them live. At the end of the Friday prayer in the Sha'bi Mosque,[2] bordering the exclusively popular housing area, a handful of politically aware *biduns* gathered, soon joined by hundreds more, asking for a solution to their legal status and demanding citizenship, free education, free health care and access to jobs. Security forces dispersed them with water canons, tear gas and smoke bombs, wounding 30 and leading to the arrest of more than 50 protestors.[3] Eighty demonstrators were also reported concomitantly in Sulaibiyya.

The year 2011 marks an important rupture in the established order and hitherto practices of the *bidun* struggle. It was the first instance of a *bidun*-organised street demonstration. The *biduns* recalled only one precedent, when they opposed the decision by the Kuwait Oil Company (KOC) housing authorities who were asking them to return their low-income housing in Ahmadi.[4] The incident ended with the authorities rescinding the order. According to a *bidun* living in Ahmadi, 'this was a circumscribed event. Since it involved the first generation of *biduns* who built the country, the government felt some compassion'.[5] In 2011, nobody had foreseen the *bidun* uprising and it was considered spontaneous, even though the government later started searching for ringleaders in Kuwait and among the most vocal political exiles in London. According to interviewees, the mobilisation had been called for by social media: 'There was a call on Facebook by Muntada al Fursan and *kuwaitiyyun bila huwwiya* calling for a protest in front of the Mosque al Sha'bi.'[6] None of the existing *bidun* movements acknowledged organising the protest, although their members wholeheartedly recognised that they had participated in it.

The majority of the people who gathered at the exit of the Sha'bi Mosque in 2011 were male, young and middle-aged *biduns* from the second and third generations. They chanted various slogans such as: '*Bidun* until when?', 'Kuwaitis! Kuwaitis!', 'Death rather than humiliation', 'Freedom', 'Dignity' and 'When the people want to live' (*Idha al sha'ab yawman arada al haya*), the last verse of the Tunisian national anthem. These particular *bidun* generations had few educational skills, since most of them would have reached the age of secondary schooling in the 1990s–2000s, when access to public schools was gradually denied to them. The use of social media played a huge role in mobilising them.

The protest movement went through various phases, corresponding to different strategies, before gradually petering out. In the weeks following the 18 February 2011 protest, the *biduns* first offered gestures of goodwill to Kuwaiti public opinion in order to promote solidarity: they organised a massive campaign of blood donation to the Kuwaiti blood bank, the 'Friday of Blood Donation', and handed out fresh flowers during a 'Flowers Day'. Then, the initial strategy of reaching out to Kuwaiti nationals lost momentum with the latter themselves being involved in massive protests demanding the fall of the government of Sheikh Nasir al-Muhammad. The *bidun* protest was reignited in December 2011 with international landmark dates like the 'Day of Non-violence' (2 October), 'Human Rights Day' (10 December), and the 'Monday of Dignity' (*yawm al karama*) on 19 December.

In the run up to the anniversary of the first demonstration, 'protests were held every week', a *bidun* activist recalled,[7] 'the number of protesters reached thousands, which is a high proportion compared to the total number [of *biduns*]'. In early 2012, in an attempt to thwart the movement, the Ministry of the Interior issued a statement saying that it would not authorise the continuation of public demonstrations. On 13 February 2012 *biduns* defied the ban and went ahead with their scheduled protest, which was eventually repressed by Special Security Forces and led to the arrest of all the *biduns* hitherto known for their involvement in the cause. This arrest brought a new generation of *bidun* leaders to the fore: new to activism, the new leaders adopted a more direct strategy, mixing marches, campaigns demanding the entry of *bidun* students at Kuwait university, the schooling of *bidun* children[8] and sit-ins in front of the Ministry of Education, with methods of action that had hitherto not been used by *biduns*, such as hunger strikes and the cycle of imprisonment/call for release.

This chapter thus raises the questions of why and how did the *bidun* community mobilise, despite their being particularly destitute and marginalised, and who mobilised along with them? In her book on the undocumented migrants or *sans-papiers'* collective action, Johanna Siméant underlines the fact that *sans-papiers* mobilisations are never only the pure deed of *sans-papiers*: they are also shared by 'support persons', who have various motivations and goals.[9] In the case of the *biduns*, the relationship with support from Kuwaiti citizens is a complex and contradictory one. The rise of the *bidun* movement owes a great deal to the 'solidarity activism' of Kuwaiti citizens throughout the 2000s. Moreover, the firing of *biduns* from the Ministry of Defence and the Interior, relieving them of the duty of confidentiality required from those serving in the security forces, has led them and, even more, the new *bidun* generation, to intermingle with the rest of the society, as they seek employment in new economic sectors and speak out a little more freely. At the same time, there is a tendency for some emerging *bidun* figures to claim greater autonomy from the support of Kuwaiti nationals, seeking a more confrontational stance with the state and trying to break with what they consider a patronising attitude towards them. Finally, this chapter will raise the question of the results of this new form of struggle and assess the gradual shifting of the terms of the debate.

FROM PUBLIC MEETING TO TAKING TO THE STREETS

The first *bidun* movements, as a form of entry into activism, were geared towards raising awareness. The activities of the *Bidun* Popular Committee, composed mainly of Kuwaiti citizens, constituted the first phase for the involvement of *biduns* in their own cause. Until then, the lack of *bidun* action resulted from a mix of fear on the part of the *biduns* and a 'divide and rule' strategy on the part of the government.[10]

Enrolled in security forces on the basis of their loyalty, having experienced miserable housing conditions and owing everything to the State of Kuwait, the first generation of *biduns* did not dare raise their voices to ask for rights, nor did it dare criticise the Kuwaiti royals or hierarchical superiors for their treatment. Expecting to be eventually naturalised, the *biduns* waited and feared that any wrongdoing would jeopardise the chance of theirs being among the few selected files. As a result of their vulnerable situation, they also feared loosing their jobs or their houses, and even being deported – although this never happened. Since 1993 and the actual demolition of the informal housing in Umm al Hayman and, in 1997, the KOC's attempt to reclaim the South Ahmadi houses, the *biduns* living in popular housing have feared that they would be expelled in turn.[11]

The support of the Popular Committee, led by Kuwaiti nationals, played a tremendous role in breaking down fear among the *biduns* and bridging the gap with Kuwaiti society. The gap was, first and foremost, a physical and geographic one, as *biduns* lived in distant suburbs where most of the citizens would never go, unless they had relatives there. Hasan al-Jawhar, one of the founding members of the Popular Committee, recalled:

> I said at the meeting of the Popular Committee in a big tent in Jahra where we invited Khudayr al 'Anazi: "we need to move the *bidun* issue from the peripheral areas to the centre" ('*min al manatiq al kharijiyya ila al manatiq al dakhiliyya*').[12]

After the meeting where the previous words were uttered, the next conference was held in the capital city, with Dr. Ghanim Al-Najjar. It was considered a 'breakthrough'. The conference in question was

the event *Al bidun yatahaddathun* [The *Biduns* Talk], held on 4
November 2006. A *bidun* noted:

> It broke the fear among the *biduns*. A lot of them feared to attend
> the conference. Dr. Ghanim [Al-Najjar] had to reassure them by
> saying that no measure would be taken against them if they spoke and
> that there would be no security forces outside. [The presence of]
> Sheikha Awrad, the daughter of the [late] Emir [Jabir] was a real
> guarantee.[13]

Moreover, the Popular Committee helped in uniting the *bidun*
category, whose members' claims were dispersed because of the
shame attached to their stigmatised status and the ensuing egoistic
expectation that the solution to their plight could only come on an
individual basis through a nominal decree of naturalisation. The
various categories of *biduns* included those with relatives holding
citizenship – whose files are sometimes sitting on the *majlis al 'Alia* in
the cabinet – those married to Kuwaiti women and their children,
those employed in the security forces, the families of the *'bidun*
martyrs'[14] and those present in the 1965 census.

After 2008, *bidun* members of the Popular Committee started to
organise by themselves and formed *bidun*-run (unregistered) societies.
In February 2008, 12 *biduns* founded the Kuwaiti *Biduns'* Congregation (*Tajammu'*)[15] with the aim of alleviating the *biduns'* suffering,
demanding the recovery of human rights for all *biduns* while leaving
the issue of their naturalisation for later. 'We gave up on
naturalisation; yet since there was a consensus on the recovery of
rights, we thought it would be easier to obtain them.'[16] Three months
later, in May 2008, 15 *biduns* created another organisation, the
Kuwaiti *Biduns'* Committee (*Lajna*), with the aim of securing civil
rights or naturalisation for those *biduns* who were best placed to
obtain them. Both organisations emphasised their Kuwaiti character
in the names that they chose, and both were composed of *biduns* with
some sort of advocacy experience as event organisers, lobbyists of
Kuwaiti MPs, or managers of webpages, most of them in the
framework of the Popular Committee activities.

Yet while acknowledging the tremendous role played by the
Popular Committee, members of these two groups highlighted
the limits from which sprang the need for *bidun*-run organisations.

The face of the Popular Committee was only Kuwaitis. *Biduns* were in
the background. Yet they wanted to participate in the decisions; they
wanted more than roundtables and conferences, more activities and
actions like the demonstration to demand that the Parliamentary
Committee for *Bidun* Affairs be maintained in the 2008 legislature,

stated one of its *bidun* member.[17] Another complained: 'I suggested
applying the [charity] funds [for education] to "educational
institutes" and not only schools, but they did not follow my
suggestions.'[18] As an instance of their work, the *Tajammu'* worked
closely on the bill on the 'human and civil rights' proposed by the
Parliamentary Committee for *Bidun* Affairs at the end of 2009. The
voting session at the Majlis al Umma was scheduled for 10 December
2009, yet the government prevented the MPs from reaching the
building to vote, so that the session was postponed twice until the
government formed a special committee to study the issue, involving
the Popular Committee, the Kuwait Society for Human Rights and
the Kuwait Economic Society. The special committee issued a
roadmap document that formed the basis of the five-year mandate of
the Central System to Resolve Illegal Residents' Status created in
November 2010. The Council of Ministers Decision No. 409/2011
largely took over the dispositions of the draft bill of 2009.

Finally, a third (single person) group, the Kuwait Bedoons
Movement, was founded in exile in London by Muhammad Wali al-
'Anazi, who has become a prominent advocate of the *bidun* cause.
Muhammad Wali's trajectory is somewhat different as he is the only
one acting politically from outside Kuwait. Muhammad Wali left
Kuwait in 1991 to go to the United Kingdom. He created the Kuwait
Bedoons Movement's website in 2006. He presents himself as a
Salafi and notes that his website is all he has as he leads no
organisation. 'Yet the website is useful for activism to go against the
voice of the government.'[19] Muhammad Wali is seen as the first one
to speak openly of the *bidun* issue: from the United Kingdom, he
gave interviews to prominent media, noting 'before, we could not
go to the TV'.[20] Although he claims no followers, the *bidun*
community widely respects him for not mincing his words and the
government of Kuwait largely sees him as benefiting from the
biduns' trust.

In the years between 2008 and 2011, the Kuwait-based *bidun* organisations worked on concrete practical actions, in the domain of human rights; as for the Kuwaiti *Biduns'* Committee (*Lajna*), it focused on getting birth and marriage certificates and was involved in the work of the charity fund, for education, *al sunduq al khayri*. The *Tajammu'* tried to organise sit-ins, in particular on the day of the vote on the bill on human and civil rights at the parliament, but security forces mainly prevented them from visible actions. It is against this backdrop of growing *bidun* activism that the 18 February 2011 *bidun* mobilisations ought to be analysed.

Street protest: new generations, new repertoire of actions
The 2011 protest movement marked a clear rupture with hitherto contentious practices of *biduns*. It goes without saying that the Arab Spring had a clear impact as a trigger for the *bidun* protest movement: 'We took our inspiration from Egypt. I was in contact with groups there: we thought that Egypt was the beating heart of the Arab world. [The protest there] was on *Al Jazeera* 24/24.'[21] As in other Arab countries, social media played a significant liaising role. The sociology, the place and the nature of the protest constituted innovations.

The participants in the demonstration were for the first time almost exclusively *biduns*. A member of the first generation of *bidun* activists noted:

> As of 2009, there was pressure from the youth. [When Fadala, famous for its anti-*bidun* stance was nominated at the head of the Central Sytem, *biduns* were wondering]: 'how come this person who is against the *biduns*, is mandated to solve the issue?' This clearly broke our hopes. The protestors were simple people who were against Fadala.[22]

Contrary to previous events, which involved mostly educated *biduns* interacting with Kuwaiti supporters in settings typical of the urban culture in Kuwait (such as clubs or societies), the street protestors were drawn from the lower layers of the *bidun* community. 'The new generation has nothing to loose, it is poorly educated: between 1995 and 1997, it went to education institutes in Jahra, Riqqa, Jlib al Shuyukh. It is a lost, a broken generation.'[23] Unlike their fathers, some of whom still held long-term jobs with ministries or public institutions, this new generation has not known stable state employment and works mainly in the private sector, making them less wary of losing their jobs should they demonstrate.

Secondly, the *biduns* brought their fight onto their own territory, in the distant suburb of Jahra, among the popular housing: the destitute areas provided spaces for politicisation and the performance of transgressive acts.[24] Moreover, by renaming in the wasteland adjacent to the Sha'bi Mosque, the 'Freedom Square', the *biduns* created a site dedicated to contestation, where the act of protest could be replicated and thus the protest as an event commemorated.

Thirdly, the adoption of spontaneous demonstrations as a contentious action was an act of defiance in itself. As 'illegal residents', according to the 1979 Law on Public Gathering, the *biduns*, just like other foreigners, are not allowed to demonstrate or even organise – hence the unregistered nature of the above-described movements. However, in the double context of the Arab Spring coupled with the entrenched political crisis in Kuwait that brought many citizens on to the streets, the *biduns* enacted and performed this right in a mimetic way. More than an awareness-raising campaign, seeking support among citizens, the sustained demonstration campaign at a time when citizens' street protests led to the fall of the prime minister (28 November 2011) constituted a clear political contestation gesture. Moreover, while the first demonstrations were geared towards winning the hearts and minds of Kuwaiti nationals, through goodwill gestures (donating blood, flowers and the release of white balloons on 19 July 2011) so as to avoid their actions being felt as threatening, the new leadership of the movement has taken a more confrontational position towards the state.

Over time, the *bidun* leaders of the new generation started to criticise the fact that, at the outset of the protest, demonstrators exhibited portraits of the emir and symbols of the emirate as a way to prove their loyalty and neutralise the suspicion of being foreigners or disloyal. Unlike their parents, who did not dare to criticise the emir or the royal family, the young *biduns* explicitly identify the emir and his government as the source of their problems. Part of this resentment comes from the fact that an Emiri decree appointed Salih Fadala as the head of the institutions meant to solve their issue. 'Fadala has very strong ties with the Emir. When he was an MP, he made very racist comments about the issue of the *biduns*, and against their naturalisation. Yet, the Emir gave him full authority', according to a *bidun* member of Group 29 a group created in the wake of the *bidun* protests with the aim of proposing solutions to the *bidun* issue (G29: see below).[25] Among the *bidun* interviewees, the same aphorism came back several times: 'the Central System is a fourth power, after the legislative, the executive and the judiciary power. It functions parallel to the rest of the state institutions'.[26] Conversely, the spokesperson of the Central System stated: 'Salih Fadala was chosen exactly for that: because he is known for being tough on naturalisations.'[27] The *biduns* have lost faith that their ordeal will ever been solved under Sabah al-Ahmad.

Furthermore, the new generation of *biduns* also started to adopt a narrative whereby they have been victims of injustice. The vocabulary has changed: *biduns* talk about 'historical injustice' towards them and even, emphatically, a 'process of cleansing' (*'amaliyyat tasfiyya*) to eradicate rather than solve the phenomenon. Moreover, some *biduns* do not back away from using the vocabulary of threat, intimidation and fearlessness. 'In 2012 and 2013, we blocked streets, we wanted to scare people so as to send a message.'[28] A leading figure of a newly created movement also explains: 'since 2012, I have chosen a theme for the campaign each year. 2012 *khuruj al mubagha* (exit oppression), 2013 *al bidun qadimun* (here are the *biduns* coming), 2014 *bil hajar ya sadiqi'* (With a stone, my friend!)'[29], referring to the Palestinians. How did this change of attitude come about?

The protest crackdown acted as a catalyst for the emergence of new movements. During the 2011 protest campaigns, the various movements supporting the *bidun* cause went through different fortunes. First, although remaining in existence, the Popular Committee was on the decline. According to a founding member, 'Kuwaitis have changed their priorities; the *badu* are under pressure from the government'.[30] Secondly, the *bidun* self-run movements that had been working in the orbit of the Popular Committee, and as a result had their leaders clearly identified in the public sphere, were severely repressed during the February 2012 showdown.

In 2012, as the *bidun* movement defied the government ban on demonstration, the entire leadership of the two *bidun* activist groups, the Congregation and the Committee (*Tajammu'* and *Lajna*), known and visible in the public sphere, was arrested. The groups' leaders were held in custody for 40 days, accused of calling for demonstrations and possessing links with foreigners. They were later released on bail. As a result of the pressure exerted against the Kuwaiti *Biduns'* Congregation, four of the 12 founding members sought asylum abroad. The website Muntada al Fursan, close to the unregistered Kuwaiti *Biduns'* Committee, was shut down.

Although badly hit, these groups have nevertheless maintained their activities. The Kuwaiti *Biduns'* Congregation is documenting the demos, the arrest, providing help with the lawyers, paying the bails, and helping the international organisations. As for the Kuwaiti *Biduns'* Committee, it seems to focus more on securing and allocating the various aid and funds, including from Sunni charities. This mention of sectarian affiliation counts among the rare occurrences when sectarian affiliation was referred to in the context of the *bidun* struggle.

During this process of recomposition of the *bidun* activist scene, two new groups emerged: one among Kuwaiti nationals, Group 29, the second among the *bidun* base, *al Muwatinun al Kuwaitiyyun al Bidun* (Kuwaiti *Bidun* Citizens). Despite their clear disagreements on tactics and strategies, they share a lot in common, belonging to the same generation, being internet-literate and proficient in social media, and not hesitating to resort to attracting the international community's attention to break the stalemate. These groups emerged as a consequence of the crackdown on pre-2011 *bidun* movements.

On 19 February 2012, three Kuwaiti nationals who were present at the prohibited *bidun* demonstrations were arrested. This included the future founder of the all-female Kuwaiti organisation, created formally in April 2012 and named Group 29. Moreover, with the arrest of the entire *bidun* leadership, a new generation of *bidun* activists came to the fore to fill the void: they displayed greater charisma and did not hesitate to continue taking to the streets, being arrested, contesting judicial decisions and hunger striking. From this group of youths, an informal group emerged from the protest movement, calling itself *al Muwatinun al Kuwaitiyyun al Bidun* (the Kuwaiti *Bidun* Citizens).

Group 29 was founded by seven women, all highly educated and all but two married. They already possessed experience of some kind in collective actions,[31] but none specifically in pro-*bidun* groups. They present themselves as liberal. The name Group 29 refers to article 29 of the 1962 Constitution, which states: 'All people are equal in human dignity, and in public rights and duties before the law, without distinction as to race, origin, language or religion.' The group possessed a dedicated website (http://www.group29q8.org) and a Facebook page. Its stated objectives are to 'fight against any form of discrimination and strengthen the principles of humanity and social justice'.[32] Coming themselves from a minority group, as Kuwaiti women, the leaders focus on the *bidun* issue. Many have *biduns* in their families or have themselves experienced statelessness, as 'children of Kuwaiti mothers' or as the only *bidun* nuclear family in a wider all-Kuwaiti family.[33] The group has no formal membership but includes both Kuwaiti and *biduns*.

During interviews with members of the group, a general distrust towards politicians appeared: as opposed to playing the rules of politics, the group wants practical results.

G29 is the first group that does not involve politicians. We want to deliver. What would otherwise happen in ten years? The politicians will use us and that's it. G29 had tangible results when we protested for university entry for *biduns*.

stated a *bidun* member of G29.[34] 'MPs agitate a lot but behind closed doors they change their minds', added another Kuwaiti member.[35] According to one funding member: 'G29 wants practical solutions, like the entry in government schools or the employment of *bidun* doctors.' Based on the observation that 'naturalisation is not going to happen overnight', the group's objective it to 'integrate *bidun* into the society'.[36]

As a result, Group 29 was involved in a successful campaign in favour of the right to education: it helped outstanding *bidun* pupils to enter Kuwait University. It also contributed to the reporting of international organisations, including the Universal Periodic Review report on Kuwait; it ran a TV programme called '*halqa*' (circle) and issued official statements criticising the government policies. In April 2013, it organised an international conference with the objective of putting pressure on the state to recognise *biduns* as a stateless people. In this way, it hoped to force the state to issue official identification papers for the *biduns*, which, according to Group 29, has still not been done for those who are not registered with the Central System.

Although it is not clear exactly how the informal group *Muwatinun* came into being, it is usually acknowledged that the April 2013 conference created a rift among activists for the *bidun* cause, specifically about the recognition of *biduns* as a stateless people. An organising member of G29 mentioned that 'after the conference we came under attack: *biduns* don't think they are stateless, they think they are Kuwaitis'.[37] Likewise, *Muwatinun* members stated: 'At the G29 conference, they wanted to change from *biduns* to stateless. This would allow the government to deport us: we are Kuwaiti *biduns*. Stateless means "we are not sure that you are Kuwaiti".'[38]

Al Muwatinun al Kuwaitiyyun al Bidun gathered young who can be described as 'mobilisation entrepreneurs' and sought to build charismatic figures, whose fame has been eclipsed by jail sentences. *Muwatinun* has 'no legal existence, no formal structure, no hierarchy. It wants to solve the issue of the *biduns*'.[39] Typical of other Arab Spring movements, it appears above all to be a loose electronic platform to coordinate marches and protest, with a highly visible presence on social media. Contrary to the two pre-2011 *bidun* movements, *Muwatinun's* members have had no prior experience of activism. According to one leader of the group, *Muwatinun* gained its own independent line after the Kuwaiti *biduns' Lajna* and *Tajammu'* repression in February 2012, when they split over the opportunity to issue a joint statement condemning the crackdown.

The group's main characteristic is that its members, leaders and followers, are *biduns*. The main leaders have reached higher education levels, but most of the grassroots members have not. For instance, the visible faces of the movement, the two Abd al-Hakim al-Fadli (having the same name) are both fluent in English. Born in 1976, they are from the 'lost generation' who went to high school in the 1990s, but they also count among the few who managed to get an education despite government restrictions and are proud of it.

The first, one, from Jahra and referred to as 'the doctor', is a dentist, who studied for five years in the Ukraine on his own funds, and as a consequence, is also fluent in Russian. The second was born in Umm al Hayman and now lives in Ali Sabah al Salim. He first studied automative engineering at a local institute for industry, which did not amount to a baccalaureate. In 2007, his car manufacturer employer enrolled him in a training programme, where he was trained in reverse engineering, completing with an online bacca-laureate. Since 2012 he has been pursuing business English 'to communicate to the world'. As shown by Johanna Siméant, in the case of *sans-papiers* mobilisation, 'the model of relative frustration' explains the fact that 'the persons most deprived of resources, and as such poised to having accumulated grievances, are not necessarily those who get involved in mobilisations. On the contrary, frustration can result from a rise of expectations that are not fulfilled'.[40] This explanation fits the case among the *biduns* of the new generation: the leaders are those who have accumulated some form of educational and economic capital, in a relatively better situation than others, but who are exposed to discrimination in their job career.[41] 'The doctor', for instance, notes that after 11 years of practice, he is in charge of the professional evaluation of Kuwaitis with a year of practice; yet in his encounter with the police, he faces people who do not 'even know what stomatology means'. Education is cherished as the only way to build a self different from the one assigned by the Kuwaiti state. During a conversation with leaders of the *Muwatinun* movement, different statements were expressed on the value of education as a benchmark of merit, denied on the sole basis of their birth.

> Education is the element that reverts the given order or hierarchy: your real identity is your competences. I don't need a document from the state to ascertain my identity.
>
> Our difference with the *Lajna*? They give in stereotypes, and especially on the issue of poverty. They accept the funds for education, which endorses the principle of education as a charity [gesture]. This idea is the biggest crime ever: it is a soft way to kill the *biduns* little by little.[42]

This education capital and the new ideas it articulates confer to a few *bidun* leaders of *Muwatinun* a certain charisma. As noted by Brokstad Lund-Johansen, the demonstration gave a feeling of action and fulfilment, and *biduns* 'expressed a sense of pride that they were part of a bigger movement.[43] 'The choice of action is therefore strongly related to [*Muwatinun'*]s formation of a collective identity'. The *Muwatinun* leaders are clearly the instigators of action on the ground. Abd al-Hakim al-Fadli does not hesitate to tour *bidun* areas, to convince *biduns* and give them advice. He said: 'It is a civil movement: we went from house to house and ask to go out for demonstration.'[44] Likewise, another *bidun* activist recalled: 'as the intelligence confiscated all his personal belongings, he [Abd al-Hakim al-Fadli] went riding from *diwaniyya* to *diwaniyya* with leaflets advertising the non-violence day [2 October]'.[45]

From their work, the mobilisation entrepreneurs have emerged as charismatic figures. They are charismatic because they embody the figure of the combatant (*manadil*). Abd al-Hakim al-Fadli is admired because he is fearless: 'he takes it on to the street and goes to jail'.[46]

Abd al-Hakim was sentenced to two years in jail in 2012: 'it was the first heavy sentence for expressing opinion'. He thus stayed 103 days in jail between 12 December 2012 and 25 March 2013 before being sentenced again in 2014. Another *bidun*, Abdullah 'Atallah, also broke the taboos surrounding the Emir and braved the government:

> 'Atallah is not popular because he is a Salafi yet his [February 2014] arrest is a whole different story. He came to the protest with the intention to address and challenge the Emir himself, saying that the sweet talk was gone and that *biduns* had entered a new phase. He thought: if Kuwaitis can challenge the Emir and get years in jail, why not us? [47]

This refers to the sentencing to five years in jail of Musallam al-Barrak, emblematic figure of the opposition, for rhetorically addressing the person of the Emir in a speech he pronounced in October 2012 in which he warned him 'we will not allow you' to go down the path of autocracy.

The two *bidun* leaders were arrested in February 2014: Abd al-Hakim was charged with offences including 'damaging police patrol cars' and 'inciting rebellion' and released on 8 April, while Abdullah 'Atallah, charged with 'insulting the Emir', 'illegal gathering' and 'damaging police property (car)', was released on 15 June 2014 on bail.[48] In an act of defiance against the inability to make claims, they started a hunger strike on 18 March 2014.[49] Unlike other *collective* hunger strike movements of *sans-papiers*, the protest here functioned as a way to manufacture heroes, emerging from among the *biduns'* ranks, figures who stood firm in the face of state violence and did not hesitate to put their own bodies at risk. Contrary to the representation of the *biduns* as shameful, hidden and faceless victims of the state oppression, the hunger strike appears as a personified and defiant gesture exposing state violence.

The *bidun* movement has evolved greatly since the end of the 2000s: from a rather homogeneous movement instigated by Kuwaiti nationals mostly moved by humanitarian concerns and united by the unanimous request for human rights, it has taken on a form of autonomy, but also diversified and fractured. It now appears as divided regarding the attitude to adopt towards citizens and the notion of citizenship itself.

Results of the protest actions

What did the post-2011 movement eventually achieve?

According to Dr. Faris al-Waqian: 'The government changed its tactics, not its strategy'.[50] Undeniably, the *biduns* have not reached their rhetorical goal of 'solving the problem', whether this refers to the recovery of their basic rights or an outright naturalisation. On 6 March 2011, the Council of Ministers promulgated Decision No. 409/2011, which granted them 11 facilities – a set of civil and human rights, including access to health and educational services (under certain conditions of registration), and the issuing of birth, marriage, divorce, and death certificates, as well as driving licences. Yet although the decision implemented by the Central System gradually and *selectively* reversed the non-recognition, it still considers *biduns* 'illegal residents', and their access to services remains dependent on the possession of cards issued by the Central System.

Furthermore, the Central System divided the *biduns* into three categories: 34,000 were deemed eligible to receive nationality. Another 8,000 are disqualified from naturalisation because they have criminal records or hold documents dating only up to 1980. Finally, the remaining *biduns* were requested to come forward and regularise their status on the basis of their foreign nationality. To add to the complexity, the Ministry of the Interior made an announcement on 9 November 2014 stating that *biduns* would be granted 'special application forms for Comoros' economic citizenship', which would help them regularise their status as Comorian citizens – i.e., that they would become foreign residents in the emirate and be given free residency permits.[51]

The government's line towards the *biduns* has remained unchanged but its tactics have been revamped and its communication refined. One of the most tested practices of the Kuwaiti rulers is the 'divide and rule' strategy: it has used it against its own citizens to thwart opposition, promoting Bedouins against *hadar* opposition in the 1980s or Shiites against Sunni Islamists. It also made use of it to prevent any common movement to emerge among the *biduns*. The official line is to naturalise a fraction of the *biduns* and discard the claims of as many others. Yet, since 2010, the Central System has changed the policy of keeping some secrecy around the *biduns'* issue and files. First, its building, contrary to the previous committee in charge of the *biduns* near the industrial zone of 'Ardiyya, is located in Kuwait City, giving it new administrative visibility. The head of the institution, Salih al-Fadala, regularly meets with representatives of human rights organisations and foreign diplomats, and is willing to be seen doing so.[52] The Central System has a department of Public Relations and Media that issues booklets tracking 'facts and figures' and posting in what appears as full transparency.

Yet while the government's line has not changed, the protest movement initiated in 2011 resulted in the broadening of the debate on rights that was initiated by Kuwaiti human rights activists in the mid-2000s and endeavours to question national identity timidly. Several scholars of citizenship studies have argued that citizenship, as an evolutionary rather than a fixed concept, can be interpreted in a way that accommodates actors who, although unrecognised as such, constitute themselves, through the concrete acts of claiming their rights, as political and legal subjects. This is the meaning of the concept of 'acts of citizenship'. Engin Isin and Greg Nielsen suggest that

> to investigate citizenship in a way that is irreducible to either status or practice, while still valuing this distinction, requires a focus on those acts when, regardless of status and substance, subjects constitute themselves as citizens or, better still, as those to whom the right to have rights is due. But the focus shifts from subjects as such to acts (or deeds) that produce such subjects.[53]

This approach has often been applied to the struggles of undocumented people, when they manage to impose themselves as fully-fledged interlocutors of a government willing to consider naturalisation. How to assess the impact of the *biduns'* actions, which, although falling short of bringing them out of illegality, turned them nevertheless into political subjects?

In their struggle, *biduns* performed some acts through which they articulated political subjectivities to claim rights that they were not entitled to exercise. The first of these was the right to demonstrate, prohibited for foreigners in Kuwait and *a fortiori* for the 'illegal' foreigners that the *biduns* represent in the eyes of the State of Kuwait. As a result of the *bidun* protest, Kuwaiti lawyers seized the Constitutional Court in order to clarify whether *biduns* were allowed to demonstrate;[54] they obtained a mitigated judgment that did not positively assert the right to demonstrate but emphasised the absence of sentences stipulated in the 1979 Law regulating demonstrations.[55]

The French scholar Johanna Siméant, looking at the hunger strikes of *sans-papiers*, suggests focusing on the forms of action dictated by certain circumstances and engendering new ones rather than on the profound causes of a mobilisation. She sees in this methodology a way to question the way people – in particular those most deprived of resources – decide to adopt new forms of action that at first may seem heterodox. She notes that protest techniques such as striking, considered banal nowadays, marked a rupture the first time they were performed or enacted, as they were not socially considered as possible.[56]

Since 2011 the *biduns* have been using new juridical means that, albeit at the disposal of any Kuwaiti or foreigner, were unavailable to them before. Many *biduns* were sent to jail and had to face courts.[57] This resort to the judicial system eventually disrupted the way in which the Central System, exclusively in charge of them, tries to prevent the *biduns* from contacting the rest of the public administration. The Central System, whose head has ministerial rank, is responsible with liaising between *biduns* and all the concerned ministries.[58] By being put on trial and jailed, the *biduns* force the state to recognise them and acquire the status of legal subjects, moving from a position where they are neither subjects nor objects of the Kuwaiti laws. Some *biduns* now claim that they are 'not afraid to go to ministries or to court' or 'to enter the local police station'. Moreover, by declaring a hunger strike to protest their detention conditions, *bidun* protesters also adopted contentious actions hitherto used by the Kuwaiti citizens when considering themselves political detainees: this was the case of journalists and political activists, whose number tended to grow since the 2010 political unrest.[59]

Finally, the *biduns* and pro-*bidun* activities have broadened the terms of the debate on citizenship and identity. Through their various actions, pro-*bidun* rights activists have sought to break the monopoly of the state as attributing identities and status. Actions have tried to make the *biduns* subject to national law (in the case of the Constitutional Court seizure) or international law (in the case of the status of statelessness).

Finally, from a tiny fringe of *Muwatinun* activists there emerges a radical questioning of the national identity as it has been built, and its arbitrariness. The leaders of the *Muwatinun* resent the role of interface with international organisations played by the Kuwaitis, who talk just enough human rights 'language' to satisfy their international interlocutors while not jeopardising the interests of the government. 'We operate underground, as intellectuals', states Dr. Abd al-Hakim al-Fadli.[60] The claims of *Muwatinun* are non-negotiable: they demand fully-fledged naturalisation for all *biduns* – apart from those who broke the united struggle and went on to solve their own cases by purchasing faked passports in the 2000s. *Muwatinun* members seek support from foreign activists rather than that of the Kuwaiti political and economic elite, and articulate a new discourse that they know signifies a complete rupture with the prevailing conception of citizenship in Kuwait. This new conception of citizenship breaks with passive citizenship practices like voting or participating in the processes of wealth allocation. It asserts itself outside the multiple networks of authority and patronage prevailing in Kuwait.

Bidun activists debate how to conceive of citizenship. They criticise, for instance, the *biduns* who at the outset of the protests exhibited portraits of the emir and symbols of the emirate in order to prove their loyalty and neutralise the suspicion of being 'foreigners'. A prominent *bidun* noted:

[at first] they were trying to position themselves in tune with the 'people' but our features are darker. The fact that they are overdoing this loyalty is a message to the Kuwaiti society that we are like you. Still they feel they need to prove something! We don't realise that we don't need to be like them. Like for the Iranian Kuwaitis, the diversity can be recognised. We are not urban, *hadar*, that's it. How don't we realise our position of difference?[61]

In other words, the entrenched loyalty expressed by the *biduns* illustrates the lack of multi-cultural understanding of citizenship interiorised by the *biduns* themselves, who feel that despite their most radical claims to outright naturalisation they have to emulate *hadar* Kuwaitis – look like them, behave like them and talk like them. Mona Kareem, a *bidun* who sought asylum in the US, where she studied literature, and a great source of inspiration for the *biduns* who remained trapped in Kuwait, notes: 'When I realized my *bidun* identity, I saw the role of Kuwaitis in producing this.'[62] There is an interesting comparison here to shifting minority immigrant discourses in the United States in the 1960s among groups like Latinos and Asian-Americans: like the *biduns*, who feel close to Kuwaitis but excluded from them, the latter felt simultaneously included, in comparison with African-Americans, and excluded, compared to other 'white ethnic' immigrants, from a sense of belonging to the dominant white, middle-class American culture in the post-World War II period. As a result, and drawing inspiration from the Black Power movement, many minority immigrant groups began to focus less on assimilation and more on embracing their cultural differences as Americans. Although the phenomena are comparable, the recognition of cultural difference is very different in Kuwait, whose core citizenry acknowledges different sects and socio-cultural backgrounds but for which diversity framed in terms of national origins is inconceivable.

As a matter of fact, the internalisation of a stigmatised origin from northern Arabia or southern Iraq is still so powerful that it does not leave any room for a diversity of origin in the national identity.

> *Biduns* were tribal, from the Northern tribes: we needed to hide our origins as much as possible particularly that our grand parents were from Southern Iraq. For instance, my Mum had a tribal accent, but my uncle always taught me not to talk like her.[63]

THE PROSPECTS, FROM NATURALISATION TO COMMODIFICATION OF NATIONALITY

The persistence of the *biduns'* claims is an important challenge to the rentier system in Kuwait. The government's handling of the issue is often described as 'poor' and inefficient by Kuwaiti citizens, whatever their stance, and the absence of solution for 30 years dissatisfies most of them, fearing that the country's human rights record have put it in disrepute – barely answered by the nomination of the Emir Sheikh Sabah al-Ahmad as 'humanitarian leader of the world' in September 2014. The government has promised to solve the issue almost since its inception in the early 1980s but has never managed to do it in a credible way. Rather, the government has appeared to take ad hoc and inconsistent measures, usually under pressure, in order to deflate domestic and international criticism, buying time and managing the issue rather than solving it. The Council of Ministers Decision No. 409/2011, promulgated on 6 March 2011, that granted *biduns* a set of 11 civil and human rights, and facilities came first, in the midst of the *bidun* uprising, and second as the response of the executive power to the big push made by Parliament that consisted in having the same measure voted and enacted as a law with full force.

Moreover, the regime's usual way of co-opting open opposition to its rule is being challenged on several fronts with the new *bidun* mobilisation. In the absence of foreigners' organised mobilisation, it is almost the first time that the state has had to face political opposition from a group whose acquiescence it cannot buy with traditional rent distribution mechanisms. In the face of the 2011 demonstrations, the government reacted with a mix of repressive measures (water canon, tear gas and arrests) and concessions (decree 409/2011 facilitating the obtaining of certificates of birth, death, marriage and divorce). Repression has emboldened some *bidun* leaders and earned them admiration from other young *bidun* men that I interviewed, who talked about their 'charisma'. This fighting for a cause also inspired young Kuwaiti activists. Yet the state is caught in a double bind: as far as concessions are concerned, its room for manoeuvre is limited, as any measure aiming at alleviating social and economic conditions of the *biduns*, let alone prospects of naturalisation, is mostly perceived by the citizens as a threat to their own privileged position. Certainly, in 2011 as *biduns* mobilised while citizens were themselves in political ferment, denouncing the corruption of the former prime minister,[64] the government tried to contain dissent of the latter by distributing rent gifts of KD 1,000 per citizen. This technique proved insufficient to curb the citizen protest movement but also increased the frustration of the deprived *biduns*. Yet it managed to keep the two protest movements separate. The *biduns* interviewed on the relations between the *bidun* and opposition movement[65] since 2011 did not hide their disappointment with the lack of support from the citizens' protest movements. They noted that only when the anti-corruption movement began to be treated harshly, with detentions and interdictions to demonstrate, did it feel more sympathetic to the *bidun* movement and attended *bidun* demonstrations, supporting the right to peaceful protest. Yet the growing pressure placed on the Kuwaiti opponents with the jailing of Musallam al-Barrak and decrees of denaturalisations over summer 2014 made them focus on their own priorities: the idea is now that if the opposition manages to obtain a reform of the government to break the royal family's monopoly on sovereign portfolios, then the situation of the *biduns* could have a little chance to evolve.[66]

So far, these prospects seem to be further away than ever as the government severely cracked down on the opposition. As part of a counter-revolution move and as a powerful deterrent, Kuwait resorted to denaturalisation of selected political opponents and citizenship stripping of tribe's members. In 2014 and 2015, 33 people were stripped of their Kuwaiti nationality –which affected a larger number of people since the withdrawal of an individual's nationality implies the revocation of that of his offspring. Ironically, the withdrawal of the citizenship from Kuwaiti nationals placed the reform of the 1959 Nationality Law on the agenda of the opposition with calls to set limits on the executive practice of nationality withdrawal or statelessness production. Yet, the issue of citizenship withdrawal from nationals and that of the *biduns* remained distinct.[67]

Under such circumstances what are the *biduns'* prospects for a solution?

At the moment, prospects for naturalisation of the *biduns* are very meagre. In April 2017, the government refused a proposal by Parliament to grant Kuwaiti nationality to at least 2,000 *biduns* in 2017.[68] The 2011 protest movement led to piecemeal improvements, yet they must be taken with a pinch of salt. *Biduns* have been re-admitted to Kuwait University under the pressure of the campaign by pro-*bidun* movement G29 and *Muwatinun*, and with a quota of 100 in 2013 and 150 in 2014. Secondly, the government boasts that the Decision 40 restored the *biduns'* civil and human rights, including the delivery of official papers, as well as access to health and education. Yet a closer examination of the measure makes it clear that not all *biduns* would equally benefit from the measures, as they usually require identification papers or cards issued by the government's authorities.[69] *Biduns* with no registration, or invalid, expired and blocked cards are likely to be refused the '11 facilities' granted by the government. Further to the dividing of the *biduns'* registered files, in 2010, into green (eligible for the application for nationality), yellow (requested to regularise their situation) and red cards (disqualified for naturalisation as a result of a criminal record),[70] it is to be expected that those who benefit from the easing measure are only the green-card holders, while the number of red-card holders is increasing due to criminal convictions linked to participation in demonstrations. In fact, the main outcome of this categorisation is to entrench the idea that only a limited number of *biduns* (34,000) is potentially eligible for naturalisation, while the remaining 80–100,000 would have to drop their claims.[71] This seriously reduces the scope of the *bidun* issue but the solution for all the cases remain far away: thousands of cases are said to have amended their status but the number of regularised cases is far from reaching 80,000.[72]

The 'children of Kuwaiti mothers' are better placed for naturalisation. They have usually been the beneficiaries of previous naturalisation measures, solving unsatisfactory family situations within Kuwaiti families. Denied the financial advantages attributed to the children of nationals, many women, unable to cope with the costs attached to their 'citizen' status, divorced 'on paper' so that their children became eligible for citizenship. Unlocking the *bidun* deadlock could come from an empowerment of women, who would be able to pass nationality on to their children and husbands, measures that were passed in other Arab Muslim countries, Morocco, Egypt and Syria and has been contemplated in Bahrain since January 2014.[73] This could open up a gradual solution.

The idea nevertheless seems to prevail that the extremely complex *bidun* puzzle can be comprehensively solved at once, in a top-down matter, without engaging with reflection on access to nationality as a longer-term process. Avoiding this debate only enables the Gulf rulers, unwilling to enlarge the polity, to buy time and opt for as narrow a polity as possible to retain the regime's legitimacy.

Until now, the line of the Central System has not changed as its mandate consists in the delivery of a comprehensive solution to the *biduns'* issue. Its communication line is to release a series of figures supporting the gradual diminishing of the *biduns'* numbers, used as concrete evidence of the efficacy of its work (even if this numerical decrease is artificial, as some cases are deliberately not registered).[74]

Moreover, without much consistency or information about how the solution put forward by the Central System will be articulated with this new proposition, the Ministry of the Interior announced on 9 November 2014 an alternative way to solve the *bidun* issue, following in the footsteps of the UAE. Kuwait seemed to have aligned its approach on nationality with the UAE's and coordinated its policy towards statelessness with that of other Gulf Cooperation Council (GCC) countries: the existence of a vocal parliament and years of Kuwaiti and *bidun* mobilisation, though leading to no solutions, contributed to preventing a certain conception of nationality being imposed top-down on the *bidun*, as has been the case in the UAE,[75] yet the counter-revolution triggered by the Arab Spring may have provided the conditions for such a policy turn.[76] Kuwait seems to have considered striking a deal with the Comoros Islands by which the *biduns* would be able to apply for the Comorian 'economic citizenship' and, as a result, regularise their status in Kuwait and obtain work and residency permits. The implementation of the deal was made conditional on the opening of a Comorian embassy in Kuwait, so that it is too early at the time of writing to say if *biduns* – especially the red-card holders and most vulnerable, will actually apply for the nationality of an archipelago whose name they have barely heard before. Nevertheless, the first reactions of *bidun* activists were extremely negative, feeling that they were being 'sold' without their consent. Two years after the announcement was made, however, the government is denying any agreement with the Comoros islands,[77] which points at some internal disagreement as to which strategy to adopt, and which also might be explained by the changes in political and economic circumstance in the Comoros Islands.[78]

The design of an 'economic citizenship' by which a state gets rid of residents on its territory it deems 'undesirable' raises important theoretical questions. This idea does not come out of the blue: by outsourcing their nationality issue, Kuwait and the UAE do nothing but bend the existing practice of providing nationality – rather than citizenship[79] – for money. In other words, they make use of an identified worldwide trend by which granting the advantages of naturalisation is used as an incentive to attract foreign money to a given country by providing tax exemptions and/or mobility and access.

Some precedents do exist, especially in the fiscal havens of the Caribbean, where invested money is exempt from taxes, as in St Kitts and Nevis and the Dominican Republic.[80] The latest cases at the time of writing belong to the European Union (EU) – Cyprus, Malta, Austria[81] and Bulgaria. For example, cash-strapped Cyprus set up a 'scheme for naturalisation of investors in Cyprus by exception' on 24 May 2013. It mainly targets non-EU residents (read: Russian investors) on the island, who, through the acquisition of EU citizenship, would get access to the Schengen Area and visa facilitation around the world in addition to free access to 160 countries.[82] Nationality has become a real business: private companies such as Henley & Partners or 101 Immigration Inc. specialise in advising wealthy individuals on how to obtain several passports to ease their life and their mobility, as well as governments on how to attract high-net-worth individuals. The idea that nationality can be bought and sold is gaining greater currency for the select few who can afford it.

Yet the main difference of economic citizenship in the Comoros Islands lies in the fact that, although the scheme is designed to develop the country, those concerned in the scheme are not applying for it willingly. In the case of Comorian nationality, the practice is tantamount to ascribing a national bond that *desubstantiates* and *deterritorialises* the citizenship bond to make it purely formal and material (that is, a passport). As a well-informed source on a Comorian blog sums it up:[83]

> What is certain, is that the beneficiaries of this citizenship are not economic partners of the government of the Comoros, as stipulated in the law, but rather individuals who appear sometimes in the 'news in brief' section of the Gulf press.

Even worse, documents prepared by foreign consultancies to evaluate the profitability of the economic citizenship schemes showed that the *biduns* were posited to be 'consumers' and 'real estate purchasers' in a wider plan that would make Kuwaiti enterprises responsible for the development of low- to middle-class residential areas.[84] This is how the 'commodification of citizenship' differs from the 'purchasing of passports' for jetsetters: it empties out any political bond to reduce only to the level of a commodity or worse of a potential for consumption and thus profits. Or, to put it differently, it strips nationality of its meaning.

Kuwait's hesitation regarding this commercial option take place in the context of a growing instability around nationality in all the GCC countries but also in liberal democracies in the face of the security challenges posed by the aftermath of the Arab uprising[85] (be it Daesh, for most, or Hezbollah, in Bahrain and Saudi Arabia, or the Muslim Brothers in the UAE). All the GCC countries have started stripping their opponents of their citizenship, on the grounds of being a 'state security threat'. Kuwait has followed suit: the anti-tribal discourse on dual nationality and the revoking of nationality affecting opponents and naturalised people illustrates that, more than ever, if there is such a thing in Kuwait as citizenship understood as membership in a political community, it applies preferably to those in the circles of power, that is, powerful businessmen and non-dissenting Badu. The rest hold only an administrative document that can be disposed of.

The desubstantiation and deterritorialisation of the citizen bond first, but then also of the national bond, is pushed to its extreme in the case of economic nationality: it is the logical result of two decades of dissociation between the right to nationality, on the one hand, and a generation-long place of abode and anchorage in the national community, on the other. It is also the next step in two decades of rights deprivation, when nationality has come to mean nothing but papers, almost in their material dimension. Moreover, the commercialisation of nationality to buy time officially to eradicate claims to naturalisation ought to be set in the Gulf context, where migrant workers can be conceived of not only as labour – that is, through the perception of their work utility/power – but as a sheer source of revenue by the virtue of their presence.

This economic conception, finally, is the one that has largely prevailed in the global migration system. Kuwait, by turning a domestic issue of a dysfunctional naturalisation process into illegal migration, has clearly placed itself and the *bidun* human rights issue in the broader international context of migration practices and discourses in developed countries, where one sees a growing contrast between an educated class, for whom nationality is not a problem as the internationalisation of careers means less pressure for integration via naturalisation,[86] and the increasing number of illegal workers, paid abusively low wages, on which entire sectors have come to depend,[87] whose reality of no rights enjoyment is becoming increasingly problematic in liberal democracies.

Conclusion

The issue of the *biduns*, from its origin in the early oil days, its increasing complexity in a troubled regional environment up to the different solutions put forward by the State of Kuwait to try to solve it, is certainly one of the most intractable questions in the modern Gulf States. It helps highlight a wider range of phenomena that relate to the formation of modern states, the process of national identity building and the evolution of the understandings of nationality – its materiality and its relationship with territory.

This book's originality lies in the fact that it has sought to take seriously the views of the excluded bottom-tier of Gulf societies, in addition to the other voices that are usually heard. Focusing on this liminal, invisible and heterogeneous group known as *biduns*, previously overlooked by academics, the book will contribute to the rapidly emerging literature on Kuwait and the Gulf on marginalised groups that addresses various issues related to migrant labourers, second-generation non-nationals and disenfranchised citizens such as women or young people.

Complementing the perspective of the state or its enfranchised citizens, this book uses the narratives, accounts and memories of *biduns* as they chose to impart them, and offers a complex vision of the recent past of the Kuwaiti Emirate. To do so, it presents a multitude of visions and perceptions of the past and present, all of which share the common feature of contesting – in some cases completing, in others openly confronting – the official state narrative of the *biduns'* illegal presence on Kuwaiti territory. As such, it challenges the idea that the *whole* of the issue resides in the dishonesty of fraudulent people attracted by economic opportunities, adding layers of complexity to the simplistic story and depicting how, for want of an adequate solution, the problem has continued to snowball since its inception.

Seeking to offer alternative visions or counter-narratives on the sensitive issue of the state-endorsed discriminatory treatment of the *biduns* is a difficult endeavour. The information I gathered on the *biduns* as a group is necessarily patchy and fragmented, so that I could not build a comprehensive view of the category currently perhaps only available to the Central System to Resolve Illegal Residents' Status, which holds the majority of the *biduns'* files – although we know for certain that some cases are not registered with the Central System. This book is thus only a first attempt in knowledge production about Kuwait's *bidun* margins.

In order to look into the *bidun* phenomenon, the book breaks with the official narrative but also enlarges the vision of human rights literature. It draws on different academic disciplines: political science, international relations and anthropology. This multi-disciplinary approach was required to show the connection between the local and the transnational labour dynamics and regional conflicts, and the relations between the state and its society in both creating and exacerbating the *bidun* question in Kuwait. The book posits that the plight of the *biduns* cannot be analysed without referring to economic factors, prevailing discourses on citizenship and national myths, issues of domestic security and foreign policy (the peculiar situation of Kuwait in the face of its three powerful neighbours), transnation-alism and the ebb and flow of oppositional politics.

Analysing the emergence of the *bidun* issue helps us to show how the distinction between citizens and foreigners is problematic and results from a long process embedded in historical circumstances. It forces us to think hard about the origin of the distinction built in the context of migration and consider how it has become an accepted and unquestioned part of the Gulf societies.

What emerges in the book is the evolution of the association between nationality and territory: in the pre-modern state era, the understanding of belonging is not necessarily territorial. The *bidun* issue originates in a phase of territorialisation of nationality when residence means belonging. Yet, in the context of globalisation, when millions of people have multiple citizenship and millions more lack the nationality of the country where they reside or work, the book also identifies a growing tendency to deterritorialise nationality or dissociate nationals from their place of abode or, rather, separate the place of abode from the granting of nationality.

Statelessness, far from being an accident in modern Gulf state building, is part and parcel of it. The extremely complicated issue of the *biduns* illustrates the passage from a sheikhly emirate to a modern nation state, involving the definition of fixed borders, the shift from premodern to national paper-based identities, the integration of nomadic tribes into new oil economic structures. In fact, the *bidun* riddle represents the long-lasting consequences of the revolution of 'the national' or the introduction of thinking along national lines, bringing new conceptions of security and legitimacy. With the adoption of the modern nation state, tribespeople no longer played any part in securing territorial sovereignty guaranteed by the recognition of the international community, nor in ensuring the regime's legitimacy henceforth based on the norms of popular and state representation of its national people. When the Bedouin pastoral economy collapsed due to the internationalisation of the oil-based economy, the question of their integration into different national polities was a difficult one, with long-lasting consequences.

While the State of Kuwait has concentrated its effort on writing a national history centred first and foremost on the maritime and *hadar* identity of the city-port, this research has presented recollections of less glorious histories written at the poor margins of the capital city. It resurrected the times when shanties sprawled at the far periphery, near the oil production site, the oasis or Jahra, or just at the doors of the rapidly expanding city. It evoked the Bedouins, and others, flocking to Kuwait,[1] the government housing policies desperately trying to eradicate informal housing areas that claimed victory over the shanties, which stubbornly reappeared. This book, in short, described the flipside of the modern development, and considered it as a necessary background to understand the emergence of the *bidun* issue. It resurrected names given to slums areas that have been demolished and erased today, the housing scheme reserved for certain ministries' employees and, above all, it recalled the tenacious hopes for housing and an improved life, and hopes of seeing one's name on naturalisation decrees.[2]

Throughout the book we gradually see that state policies, with sometimes unintended results, play a great part in shaping sociological realities. First, the research shows that, away from the port-city where the modern state is being put in place and in the context of migration from regions further away (British (former) colonial empire or the Levant), the delineation between citizens and aliens took place at a different scale, in the desert periphery, on the Bedouin margins, upon which the embryonic state has had little grip. Downtown, the immigration policies and the *importing* of foreign labour necessary to the development of the country created the archetype figures of the 'alien other': the Western oil engineers, the Indian and Pakistani white-collar workers, etc. On the Bedouin margins, a process of 'othering' occurred among newcomers from the desert. The fracture line between Kuwaiti Bedouins and non-Kuwaiti Bedouins started to develop as the abstract notion of 'nationality' turned into a concrete reality endowed with a material dimension and differentiating between those who would get a state-funded housing and services and those who would not. There is a gap between nationality as defined in law and the way it is concretely understood and enacted on the periphery. Initially expressing a technical or procedural issue (naturalisation files being processed), the terms of the *bidun* question have thus shifted towards economic ground, with the first drop in oil prices. This is when the state as a paternalist employer turns into a business manager.

Secondly, the research looked into the emergence of the sociological category of *biduns*, which is somehow inconsistent and groups very different kinds of people together. The only shared feature among all the *biduns* is their administrative status and the state's specific policies towards them. In the 1980s, the disappearance of *biduns'* utility among the state employees went hand-in-hand with their being seen as a security threat, so that they were clearly vilified as Iraqis, but also associated with cheating, as 'illegal', and all the prejudices linked to being categorised as destitute, prone to theft, crime and dishonesty. Nowadays, this rhetoric still prevails, increasingly taking the shape of transnational networks of jihadists enrolling among *biduns* –stigmatising the whole group – as a result of two decades of the proselytising activities of Islamic charities offering financial support to the young unemployed *biduns*.[3]

Interestingly and as in other cases of discriminated migrant minorities, the actors themselves have appropriated the identity of *biduns*. This appropriation of the *bidun* identity owed much, first, to the mobilisation of Kuwaiti nationals in raising *biduns'* self-awareness and supporting their cause. The mobilisation of the citizens to support the rights of the *biduns* emerged against the opposition of a majority of Kuwaitis: opponents to the cause clearly embody the anti-immigration discourse common to most of the welfare states, a phenomenon described by Longva as the 'ethnicization and the rise of ethnopolitics' as a result of a competition over social advantages.[4] The Kuwaiti-led actions resulted in decompartmentalising the different *bidun* categories and rendered possible the formulation of collective claims rather than, or alongside, individualist strategies for naturalisation that *biduns* were nurturing.

Biduns gradually re-appropriated their own discourse and agency, feeling constrained in their position as victims. *'Bidun'* was originally a label assigned to them by various public institutions filling in the blank 'nationality' line; they now claim it as their own but add 'Kuwaiti *bidun'*, pointing to their national feeling of belonging and their collective experience as a discriminated-against sociological group. The 2011 mobilisation movement, although largely extinguished five years later because of strong state repression, has brought to the fore a new *bidun* generation that is not afraid of contesting the state in public spaces, sometimes with a quest for individual identity and fame. This generation was born in Kuwait and believes it has nothing to lose in articulating a counter-narrative about the unjust treatment of which they feel they are the victims and about alternative ways to understand citizenship. Whatever the end result, the *biduns* are part and parcel of Kuwait's social history that has yet to be written.

APPENDIX

Family Tree of the Al-Sabah

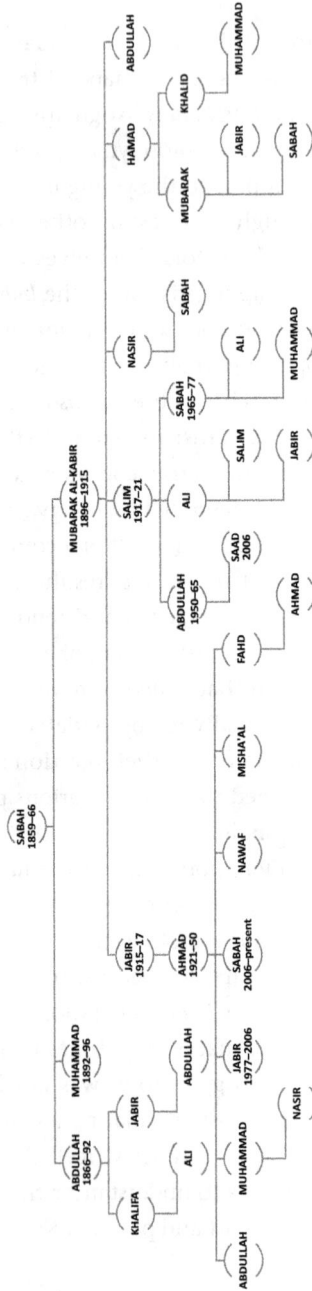

SABAH
1859–66

MUHAMMAD
1892–96

MUBARAK AL-KABIR
1896–1915

ABDULLAH
1866–92

KHALIFA

JABIR

ALI

ABDULLAH

MUHAMMAD

ABDULLAH

NASIR

JABIR
1915–17

AHMAD
1921–50

SABAH
2006–present

JABIR
1977–2006

NAWAF

MISHA'AL

FAHD

AHMAD

SALIM
1917–21

NASIR

HAMAD

ABDULLAH

ABDULLAH
1950–65

ALI

SABAH
1965–77

SABAH

MUBARAK

KHALID

SAAD
2006

SALIM

JABIR

ALI

MUHAMMAD

JABIR

SABAH

MUHAMMAD

Notes

CHAPTER 1   FROM INVISIBILITY TO STIGMA: WHO ARE THE
BIDUNS?

1. Fuad I. Khuri, *An Invitation to Laughter: A Lebanese Anthropologist in the Arab World* (Chicago, IL: University of Chicago Press), p. 120.
2. A blend of coastal *khaliji* (Gulfian), different tribal Central and North Najdi dialects infused with Persian, Indian and English influences.
3. Bruce Ingham, 'Notes on the dialect of the Dhafir of north-eastern Arabia', *Bulletin of the School of Oriental and African Studies* 45/2 (1982), pp. 245–59, p. 245.
4. *Dishdasha* is the gown worn by Gulf men, '*iqal*, the black rope fixing the traditional headwear, which is called *ghutra* when it is white.
5. I am fully aware of the polysemy of the words 'nationality' and 'citizenship'. In this book, I hold that 'nationality' refers to the international and formal aspect of *state membership* while 'citizenship' defined as the *possession* within a particular state of full *civil and political rights*, stresses more its national and actual aspect -the contents of these rights varying across states.
6. Technically, this is the Emiri decree 15 with regard to Nationality Law. It is later referred to as a 'law'.
7. Bedouins ought to be differentiated from *biduns*, although the two sometimes overlap. See later in the chapter.
8. This was, for instance, the case of the family of the executioner of the Islamic state, Mohamed Emwazi, nicknamed Jihadi John, who fled Iraq to Kuwait in 1987 before seeking asylum in the United Kingdom in 1994.
9. Atossa A. Abrahamian, *The Cosmopolites: The Coming of the Global Citizen* (New York: Columbia Global Reports, 2015).

10. Noora Lori, 'Unsettling state: non-citizens, state power and citizenship in the United Arab Emirates', PhD thesis, Johns Hopkins University (2013), p. 174.
11. Alice Bloch and Sonia McKay, *Living on the Margins: Undocumented Migrants in a Global City* (Bristol: Policy Press, 2016).
12. Abrahamian, *The Cosmopolites*.
13. Francesco Ragazzi, 'Post-territorial citizenship', in Sonika Gupta and Sudarsan Padmanabhan (eds), *Politics and Cosmopolitanism in a Global Age* (New Delhi: Routledge India, 2015), pp. 489–97.
14. 'Convention on Certain Questions Relating to the Conflict of Nationality Laws', The Hague, 12 April 1930 (The Hague Convention). Available at http://eudo-citizenship.eu/InternationalDB/docs/Convention%20on% 20certain%20questions%20relating%20to%20the%20conflict%20of% 20nationality%20laws%20FULL%20TEXT.pdf (accessed 6 June 2017).
15. Maarten P. Vink, Arjan H. Schakel, David Reichel, Gerard-René de Groot and Ngo Chun Luk, 'The international diffusion of expatriate dual citizenship', paper presented at the 22nd International Conference of Europeanists, Paris, France, 8–10 July 2015.
16. 'Migrant citizenship' is an emergent form of Philippine membership that requires insurance from the Philippine state that employment overseas be accompanied by rights and obligations that come with it. Robin M. Rodriguez, *Migrants for Export: How the Philippine State Brokers Labor to the World* (Minneapolis, MN: University of Minnesota Press, 2010). India created the new legal categories of non-resident Indians (NRI) and Persons of Indian Origin (PIO) to rekindle links with ethnically defined Indians living abroad, the PIO being granted visa and investment advantages without political rights.
17. Frederick Anscombe, 'An anational society: Eastern Arabia in the Ottoman period', in Madawi Al-Rasheed (ed.), *Transnational Connections and the Arab Gulf* (New York: Routledge, 2004), pp. 21–38; Claire Beaugrand, 'Émergence de la "nationalité" et institutionnalisation des clivages sociaux au Koweït et au Bahreïn', *Chroniques yéménites* 14 (2007), pp. 89–107 and 'Deconstructing minorities/majorities in parliamentary Gulf States (Kuwait and Bahrain)', *British Journal of Middle Eastern Studies* 43/2 (2016), pp. 234–49.
18. Robert Kiefe, *La nationalité des personnes dans l'Empire Britannique* (Paris: Rousseau & Cie, 1926), pp. 169–79.
19. Joseph H. Carens, 'The rights of irregular migrants', *Ethics and International Affairs* 22 (2008), pp. 163–86; Mae M. Ngai, *Impossible Subjects. Illegal Aliens and the making of Modern America* (Princeton, NJ: Princeton University Press, 2004).
20. We need not look far back in time to find such occurrences, with the refusal of certain Baltic states to grant nationality rights to their Russian minorities or, even in the Gulf, with the sudden attempt by the Qatari regime in 2005 to strip the Ghafran section of the Murra tribe of their

citizenship allegedly for holding the Saudi citizenship. (P.K. Abdul Ghafour, 'Qataris stripped of citizenship cry foul', *Arab News*, 2 April 2005). The measure was met with vocal campaigns denouncing it as a violation of international charters.

21. I recognise, following Esra Bulut, that the term itself is inadequate and that it would be more accurate to use the word 'trans-state' as by-passing the state; yet this confusion between state and nation is such a deep-rooted one in International Relations (IR), that I shall stay with the common IR use. Esra Bulut, '"Friends, Balkans, statesmen lend us your ears": the trans-state and state in links between Turkey and the Balkans', *Ethnopolitics* 5/3 (2006), pp. 309–26, p. 310.

22. Sami N. Khalifa al-Khaldi, 'Al "bidun" fil Kuwait ... bayn al huquq al madaniyya wa al tajnis' [The *biduns* in Kuwait ... between civil rights and naturalisation], unpublished manuscript (2007), p. 11.

23. Stephen Castles 'Guestworkers in Europe; a resurrection?', *International Migration Review* 40/4 (Winter 2006), pp. 741–66.

24. Paul Dresch, 'Foreign matter: the place of strangers in Gulf society', in John W. Fox, Nada Mourtada-Sabbah and Mohammed al-Mutawa (eds), *Globalization and the Gulf* (London: Routledge, 2006), pp. 200–22, p. 200.

25. Jacques Derrida, *Les marges de la philosophie* (Paris: Éditions de Minuit, 1972), pp. xix and xxiv.

26. 'Le texte écrit de la philosophie (dans ses livres cette fois) déborde et fait craquer son sens' (ibid., p. xix). (Translation mine).

27. 'La marge, la marche, la démarcation passent ici entre dénier et déconstruire' (ibid., p. xvii). (Translation mine).

28. In October 2011 two young Saudi bloggers were even sent to jail for 15 days after uploading a ten-minute documentary on poverty in Riyadh – although the video was not the first provocative video of their web show 'Mal'oub 'alayna' ('We are being Fooled').

29. Short for *ma qasarti* or *ma qasarta*.

30. Madawi Al-Rasheed and Robert Vitalis, *Counter-narratives: History, Contemporary Society, and Politics in Saudi Arabia and Yemen* (London: Palgrave Macmillan, 2004), p. 1.

31. Mary Ann Tétreault, *Stories of Democracy: Politics and Society in Contemporary Kuwait* (New York: Columbia University Press, 2000).

32. For Marx, a class is defined by the ownership of the means of production or the absences thereof that obliges people to sell their labour power: see Karl Marx, *Capital*, 3 vols, numerous editions, first published in English 1952.

33. For an overview of the literature on the struggle of undocumented migrants in Europe, see Ruud Koopmans, Paul Statham, Marco Guigni and Florence Passy, *Contested Citizenship Immigration and Cultural Diversity in Europe* (Minneapolis, MN: University of Minnesota Press, 2005); Anne McNevin, 'Political belonging in a neoliberal era: the struggle of the sans-papiers', *Citizenship Studies* 10/2 (2006), pp. 135–51;

Iker Barbero, 'Expanding acts of citizenship: the struggles of Sinpapeles migrants', *Social and Legal Studies* 21/4 (2012), pp. 529–47. For the French case of *sans-papiers*, see Étienne Balibar, Monique Chemillier-Gendreau, Jacqueline Costa-Lascoux and Emmanuel Terray, *Sans-papiers: l'Archaïsme Fatal* (Paris: La Découverte, 1999); Johanna Siméant, *La Cause des sans-papiers* (Paris: Presses de Sciences-Po, 1998); Pierre Barron, Anne Bory, Lucie Tourette, Sébastier Chauvin and Nicolas Jounin, *On bosse ici, on reste ici! La grève des sans-papiers: une aventure inédite* (Paris: La Découverte, 2011). For North America, see Anne McNevin, 'Undocumented citizens? Shifting grounds of citizenship in Los Angeles', in Peter Nyers and Kim Rygiel (eds), *Citizenship, Migrant Activism and the Politics of Movement* (New York: Routledge, 2011), pp. 165–83; Peter Nyers, 'The regularization of non-status immigrants in Canada: limits and prospects', *Canadian Review of Social Policy* 55 (2005), pp. 109–14.

34. Engin F. Isin and Kim Rygiel, 'Abject spaces: frontiers, zones and camps', in Elizabeth Dauphinee and Cristina Masters (eds), *The Logics of Biopower and the War on Terror: Living, Dying, Surviving* (Basingstoke: Palgrave Macmillan, 2007), pp. 181–203, p. 184.

35. Siméant, *La Cause des sans-papiers*, p. 25: 'les mobilisations "de" sans-papiers, précisément, ne sont jamais *uniquement* des mobilisations de sans-papiers. Elles sont autant le fait de populations que nous qualifierons de "soutiens" ....' (translation is mine).

36. Engin F. Isin and Greg M. Nielsen (eds), *Acts of Citizenship* (London: Zed Books, 2008); Engin F. Isin, *Citizens Without Frontiers* (London: Bloomsbury, 2012).

37. Gérard Noiriel, *État, nation et immigration: vers une histoire du pouvoir*, (Paris: Editions Belin, 2001), p. 61. '"Le sens que nous donnons aux mots, loin d'être neutre, véhicule souvent la vision des vainqueurs, le regard de ceux qui ont réussi à imposer leur vision des choses"' (translation mine).

38. Ahmad M. Abu Hakima, *The Modern History of Kuwait, 1750–1965* (London: Luzac, 1983). The Bani 'Utub are also considered to be the ancestors of the Al-Khalifa and Al-Thani royal families in Bahrain and Qatar, as they left Kuwait to settle first in Zubara on the Qatari Peninsula before the Khalifa clan split off again and cross to the island of Bahrain in 1783 where it has ruled until now.

39. Mostafa A. Sagher, 'The impact of economic activities on the social and political structures of Kuwait (1896–1946)', PhD thesis, University of Durham (2004). Available at http://etheses.dur.ac.uk/1266/ (accessed 6 June 2017).

40. Ibid.

41. Jill Crystal, *Oil and Politics in the Gulf: Rulers and Merchants in Kuwait and Qatar* (Cambridge: Cambridge University Press, 1990).

42. Anthony B. Toth, 'Tribes and tribulations: Bedouin losses in the Saudi and Iraqi Struggles over Kuwait's frontiers, 1921–1943', *British Journal of Middle Eastern Studies* 32/2 (2005), pp. 145–67.

43. Eran Segal, 'Rulers and merchants in pre-oil Kuwait: the significance of palm dates', *British Journal of Middle Eastern Studies* 41/2 (2014), pp. 167–82.

44. Sagher, 'The impact of economic activities', p. 216.

45. Dawn Chatty, *From Camel to Truck: The Bedouin in the Modern World* (New York: Vantage Press, 1986).

46. Jill Crystal, *Oil and Politics in the Gulf* and *Kuwait: The Transformation of an Oil State* (Boulder, CO: Westview Press, 1992).

47. Chatty, *From Camel to Truck*, p. 1.

48. Some present-day politicians even include the *hadar* settled tribes in villages like Jahra.

49. Khaldoun H. Al-Naqeeb, *Society and State in the Gulf and Arab Peninsula: A Different Perspective*, trans. L.M. Kenny, amended Ibrahim Hayan (London: Routledge, 1990); Abdulkarim Al-Dekhayel, *Kuwait: Oil, State and Political Legitimation* (London: Ithaca Press, 1999); Jacqueline S. Ismael, *Kuwait, Social Change in Historical Perspective* (Syracuse, NY: Syracuse University Press, 1982); Muhammad G. Rumaihi, *Beyond Oil: Unity and Development in the Gulf* (London: Saqi Books, 1986).

50. Rivka Azoulay and Claire Beaugrand, 'Limits of political clientelism: elites' struggles in Kuwait fragmenting politics', *Arabian Humanities* 4 (2015). Available at http://cy.revues.org/2827 (accessed 6 June 2017).

51. Parliament was dissolved unconstitutionally twice: between 1976 and 1981 and again between 1986 and 1992.

52. Tétreault, *Stories of Democracy*.

53. Women received the right to vote and contest in elections in 2005.

54. Anh N. Longva, 'Nationalism in pre-modern guise: the discourse on *hadar* and *badu* in Kuwait', *International Journal of Middle East Studies* 38/2 (2006), pp. 171–87.

55. Ibid., p. 172.

56. Farah Al-Nakib, 'Revisiting *hadar* and *badu* in Kuwait: citizenship, housing and the construction of a dichotomy', *International Journal of Middle East Studies* 46/1 (2014), pp. 5–30, p. 5.

57. Ibid., p. 5.

58. Anh N. Longva, *Walls Built on Sand: Migration, Exclusion, and Society in Kuwait* (Boulder, CO: Westview Press, 1997).

59. International Crisis Group (ICG), 'The Shiite question in Saudi Arabia', *Middle East/North Africa Report* No. 45, 19 September 2005; Mamoun Fandy, *Saudi Arabia and the Politics of Dissent* (London: Palgrave Macmillan, 1999); Toby Matthiesen, *The Other Saudis: Shiism, Dissent and Sectarianism* (Cambridge: Cambridge University Press, 2014).

60. Mary A. Tétreault and Haya Al Mughni, 'Modernization and its discontents: state and gender in Kuwait', *Middle East Journal* 49/3 (1995), pp. 403–17.

61. Pascal Ménoret, *Joyriding in Riyadh: Oil, Urbanism, and Road Revolt* (Cambridge: Cambridge University Press, 2014); Amélie Le Renard, *Femmes et espaces publics en Arabie Saoudite* (Paris: Dalloz, 2011).

62. Ménoret, *Joyriding in Riyadh*.
63. Mitya Underwood, 'Going nowhere fast: analysing the joyriders of Saudi Arabia', *The National*, 17 July 2014. Available at http://www.thenational. ae/arts-lifestyle/going-nowhere–fast-analysing-the-joyriders-of-saudi-arabia (accessed 6 June 2017).
64. Shafeeq Ghabra, 'Palestinians in Kuwait: the family and the politics of survival', *Journal of Palestine Studies*, 17/2 (Winter 1988), pp. 62–83, p. 65.
65. According to Mai Al-Nakib the population of Palestinians in Kuwait was made up of a first wave following the 1948 Nakba, consisting of urgently required teachers, engineers, doctors, civil servants, scientists, technicians and labourers. Between 1957 and 1965, the Palestinian population grew from 15,173 to 77,712. The second wave, which also included the families of Palestinians already in Kuwait, followed the 1967 war as well as Black September in Jordan: in 1970, the number of Palestinians in Kuwait had reached 147,696. In terms of percentage of the entire population, Palestinians went from 7.3 per cent in 1957 to 20 per cent in 1970. The first wave arrived with only travel documents while the second wave had usually obtained a Jordanian passport (different from the Jordanian nationality). Mai Al-Nakib, '"The people are missing": Palestinians in Kuwait', *Deleuze Studies* 8/1 (2014), pp. 23–44, p. 24.
66. Longva, 'Nationalism in pre-modern guise', p. 184.
67. Rashid H. Al-Anezi, 'A study of the role of nationality in international law with special reference to the law and practice of Kuwait', PhD thesis, University of Cambridge, Cambridge (1989), pp. 4–8; Ghanim Al-Najjar '*Qadiyya In'idam al jinsiyya fil Kuwait*' [The issue of lacking nationality in Kuwait], unpublished manuscript (2005), pp. 6–7; al-Khaldi, 'Al "bidun" fil Kuwait …', pp. 6–8.
68. James C. Scott, *Seeing Like a State: How Certain Schemes to Improve the Human Condition Have Failed* (New Haven, CT: Yale University Press, 1998), p. 2.
69. Technically the 1959 Emiri decree 17 on the Residence of Aliens, referred to later as a law.
70. Mohammed Al-Fahed, 'An historical analysis of police in Kuwait: prospects for the future', PhD thesis, University of Exeter, Exeter (1989), p. 2.
71. Ibid., p. 251.
72. Gérard Noiriel, 'Du "patronage" au "paternalisme": la restructuration des formes de domination de la main-d'oeuvre ouvrière dans l'industrie métallurgique française', *Le Mouvement Social* 144 (1988), pp. 17–35, p. 19.
73. A labour office opened in 1954 in Kuwait and the Ministry of Labour and Social Affairs, which issued work permits, in 1955. At this point 60 per cent of the workers had entered Kuwait 'illegally', that is without the appropriate authorisation document. Shamlan Y. Alessa, *The*

Manpower Problem in Kuwait (London: Kegan Paul International, 1981), p. 32.

74. These include also Syria (the *maktumun*, literally 'the muted' Syrian Kurds) in the Middle East, the Baltic states (the so called 'permanent residents' of Russian or Russified origin) apart from Latvia, Nepal (the Lhotshampa, expellees from Bhutan), Bangladesh (the Muslim Biharis), Burma (the Rohingyas of the western Arakan state) and seven countries in southeast Asia (people of Zomia highlands) as well as the Democratic Republic of Congo (Banyarwanda) in Africa, to quote just the most well-known cases. For the Nepalese case: Michael Hutt, *Unbecoming Citizens: Culture, Nationhood, and the Flight of Refugees from Bhutan* (Oxford: Oxford University Press, 2006). For the people of Zomia: James C. Scott, *The Art of Not Being Governed: An Anarchist History of Upland Southeast Asia* (New Haven, CT: Yale University Press, 2009).

75. United Nations High Commissioner for Refugees (UNHCR), 'Nationality and reduction of statelessness: international, regional and national perspectives', special issue of *Refugee Survey Quarterly* 25/3 (2006), pp. 203–5.

76. New Human Rights instruments have appeared: the 1979 Convention on the Elimination of All Forms of Discrimination against Women (CEDAW) invested the right to nationality with the more tangible principles of non-discrimination and equality before the law, while the 1966 International Covenant on Civil and Political Rights (CCPR) and the 1989 Convention on the Rights of the Child (CRC) made it more subtle and less rhetorical by substituting it with the right to 'acquire' a nationality. Kuwait is state party to 13 international instruments, among which are the CCPR, the CEDAW and the CRC.

77. Lori, 'Unsettling state'.

78. 'Government to provide Article 17 documents to "eligible" Bedoun; panel criticizes "Bedoun" as inhuman', *Arab Times*, 19 December 2006.

79. Al-Naqeeb, *Society and State in the Gulf and Arab Peninsula*; Crystal, *Oil and Politics in the Gulf*; Crystal, *Kuwait*; Rania Maktabi, 'The politics of citizenship in Kuwait – membership and participation in a rentier state', paper presented at the 13th Annual National Political Science Conference, Hurdalsjoen, Oslo, 5–7 January 2005.

80. Hazem Beblawi and Giacomo Luciani, *The Rentier State* (London: Croom Helm, 1987).

81. Crystal, *Oil and Politics in the Gulf*, p. 79.

82. Longva, 'Nationalism in pre-modern guise', p. 184.

83. Michael Herb, 'A nation of bureaucrats: political participation and economic diversification in Kuwait and the United Arab Emirates.' *International Journal of Middle East Studies* 41/3 (August 2009), pp. 375–95.

84. Article 4, regulating succession matters, stipulates the emir's choice for a crown prince needs to be approved by an absolute majority of

Parliament. If a new crown prince fails to win Parliament's approval, the emir submits the names of three eligible members of the family to Parliament, which then selects one of them.

85. With the notable exception, in the pre-national era, of the attempts by Abd al-Aziz Al-Saud to use tribal allegiances to extend the territory of his kingdom as far as possible northwards.

86. Fred Halliday, *Arabia without Sultans* (London: Saqi Books, 1974), pp. 421–3. Saddam Hussein did not: he sought to enrol as many *biduns* as possible in his Popular Army of Occupation and later used the issue as a bargaining and pressurising tool on Kuwait in the years after 1991, reportedly sending alleged *biduns* to demonstrate at the border and to demand their return to Kuwait. Yet his main argument was based on historical documents.

87. Herb, 'A nation of bureaucrats'. Michael Herb, *The Wages of Oil: Parliaments and Economic Development in Kuwait and the UAE* (Ithaca, NY: Cornell University Press, 2014).

88. Except in Oman, where the nationality law was designed to integrate populations repatriated from Zanzibar. In Bahrain, the issue was solved in 2001 by the then sheikh, Hamad Bin Isa Al-Khalifa, who, as a sign of royal generosity (*makruma*), granted Bahraini nationality to between 10,000 and 20,000 *biduns* of mostly Iranian ('*ajam*) origin in an attempt to diffuse social and sectarian tensions. In the United Arab Emirates, the issue came into the limelight in October 2006 when the president, Sheikh Khalifa Bin Zayd Al-Nahyan, pledged to solve the issue once and for all, which led two years later to the process of registration of nationality applications. Since 2011 it has been handled through the granting of Comorian passports. In Saudi Arabia and Qatar, statelessness has not yet come to be a prominent issue, though it is certain that it affects the Kingdom significantly. Whether or not it affects Qatar to the same extent is doubtful, but it certainly exists there.

89. Lori P. Boghardt, *Kuwait amid War, Peace and Revolution: 1979–1991 and New Challenges* (Basingstoke: Palgrave Macmillan, 2006), pp. 67, 71, 86; Laurence Louër, *Transnational Shia Politics: Religious and Political Networks in the Gulf* (London: Hurst & Co., 2008), pp. 172–6.

90. Although the number is not known, this is attested by a Bahraini Shiite activist who was exiled in 1981 and later granted asylum in Canada until 2001. He recalled at the time the *bidun* refugees from Kuwait. Interview, Bahrain, February 2007.

91. For instance, a quick look at three years of the immigration debate in the UK will suffice to convince us: in May 2006 'Dave Roberts, a senior official in the Immigration and Nationality Directorate (IND), [prompted by questions regarding the number of illegal migrants ordered to leave the country who actually did so] admitted he did not have the "faintest idea" how many illegal immigrants were in Britain' (Nigel Morris, '"Soft targets" picked on for deportation, say refugee

campaigners', The *Independent*, 18 May 2006. Available at http://www. independent.co.uk/news/uk/this-britain/soft-targets-picked-on-for-deportation-say-refugee-campaigners-478629.html (accessed 2 June 2006); see also 'Illegal immigrants not "hunted"', BBC News, 17 May 2006. Available at http://news.bbc.co.uk/1/hi/uk_politics/4985744.stm (accessed 2 June 2006); Alan Travis, 'MPs shocked by fresh immigration revelations', The *Guardian*, 17 May 2006. Available at https://www. theguardian.com/uk/2006/may/17/immigration.immigrationandpublic services (accessed 2 June 2006)). This follows and strangely echoes the 2005 declaration by Charles Clarke, the then Home Secretary, that 'he did not know how many illegal immigrants there were in Britain' in the midst of a row over the concealment of official estimates on illegal immigration (David Leppard and Robert Winnett, '500,000 illegal migrants, says Home Office', *The Sunday Times*, 17 April 2005. Available at https://www.thetimes. co.uk/article/500000-illegal-migrants-says-home-office-3t9spqqpvf3 (accessed 2 June 2006)). These few examples could be multiplied.

92. Nadeya S.A. Mohammed, *Population and Development of the Arab Gulf States: the Case of Bahrain, Oman and Kuwait* (Aldershot: Ashgate, 2003): xiii-xiv.

93. Human Rights Watch (HRW), *The Bedoons of Kuwait: 'Citizens without Citizenship'* (New York: Human Rights Watch, 1995). Available at https:// www.hrw.org/reports/1995/Kuwait.htm (accessed 26 August 2017).

94. Department of Public Relations and Media, *Illegal Residents: Facts and Data (2013)*, pp. 22–3.

95. Available at https://www.csb.gov.kw/Socan_Statistic_EN.aspx?ID=18 (accessed 6 June 2017). These statistics include the number of *biduns* in the total Kuwaiti population.

96. Available at https://www.csb.gov.kw/Socan_Statistic_EN.aspx?ID=18 (accessed 6 June 2017). These statistics exclude the number of *biduns* in the total Kuwaiti population, including retrospectively for dates until 1985.

97. HRW, *The Bedoons of Kuwait*.

98. Department of Public Relations and Media, *Illegal Residents: Facts and Data (2013)*, pp. 22–3.

99. It is also referred to as the Central Statistical Office (CSO).

100. Parliament was dissolved twice in an unconstitutional way, that is without the calling of new elections within the two months following the dissolution: once between 1976 and 1981 and again between 1986 and 1992.

101. Query on 9 November 1984, Rashid H. Al-Anezi, *Al bidun fil Kuwait [The Biduns in Kuwait]* (Kuwait: Dar al Qurtas, 1994), p. 1. See also 'Interior Minister: 200,000 "bidun" claim nationality', *Al-Anba'*, 18 November 1985.

102. The figure is mentioned in *Al-Siyasa*, 28 September 1983, 17 October 1983, 8 May 1984 (articles by Nabil Suwidan), and then in reply to the MP, Khaled al-Wasmi, on 17 May 1984 in *Al-Watan* and *Al-Ra'i al 'Amm*.

103. HRW, *The Bedoons of Kuwait*.
104. Ibid.
105. In particular a report handed over to me from the Parliamentary Committee for *Bidun* Affairs and based on official estimates of the Ministry of Planning, gave the following figures: 119,000 *biduns* in 2000 and 104,000 in 2006.
106. Department of Public Relations and Media, *Illegal Residents: Facts and Data (2013)*, pp. 23–4.
107. US Embassy in Kuwait, *Human Rights Report*, 2013, p. 14. Available at http://kuwait.usembassy.gov/human_rights.html (accessed 24 August 2015, no longer available).
108. Human Rights Watch, *World Report 2014: Kuwait*. Available at http://www.hrw.org/world-report/2014/country-chapters/kuwait?page=2 (accessed 6 June 2017).
109. Access to Arabic archives required huge linguistic efforts; some details may have been lost in translation, due also to the time constraints.
110. The complete title being: 'shu'un al dakhiliyya wa taqsimat al idariyya-wizarat al dakhiliyya/ shu'un al jinsiyya, al jinsiyya wa al tajnis, qanun al jinsiyya/ sahb al jinsiyya, fa' bidun jinsiyya'.
111. In 1977 the new emir eventually chose his rival, Sheikh Saad Abdullah, putting an end to his efforts.
112. 'Damaging our reputation' is a recurring attack proffered by the MPs against the government's handling of the problem while 'embarrassing the country in the eyes of the world' is a potent threat from proponents of the *bidun* cause against their opponents.
113. In total, I met with 20 *biduns* at the time of my research. To gain their trust, I privileged repeated and in-depth interviews over a greater number: I met with half of them several times, sometimes over years, meeting them again in 2014. I met the families of four interviewees on several occasions and was invited to the homes of three of them. Otherwise, most interviews were carried out in coffee shops or on work premises. One of the difficulties was the preference by some *biduns* to hold collective interviews: on the one hand, it can be explained by their feeling more at ease, but on the other hand, it made the interview far less focused and the information drawn less original or creative, as many would sometimes just agree with what was said.

　　The sample included *biduns* naturalised as children 'of Kuwaiti mothers', as well as *biduns* from various backgrounds, met through different channels so as to avoid tapping into the same network. All the interviewees were from the second or third generation of *biduns*. I met no *bidun* over 60 years old. All of my interviewees, apart from one female (when not talking about the family), were male, of working age and in a form of professional activity, from salaried jobs to precarious independent jobs; two were laid off from the armed forces. Finally, while around two-thirds of those interviewed were Shiite, sectarian affiliation was a topic of conversation only to the extent that it affected the help provided by Kuwaiti charity organisations at the end of the 2000s decade. This was different when I returned in 2014 as some *biduns* mentioned it as a dividing line among various *bidun* groups.

CHAPTER 2   THE TRANSNATIONAL FOUNDATIONS OF THE KUWAITI EMIRATE

1. C. Victor Müller, *En Syrie avec les Bédouins. Les tribus du désert* (Paris: Ernest Leroux, 1931), p. 331 (Translation mine).
2. Ahmad Al-Khatib, *Al Kuwait: min al imara ilal dawla [Kuwait: from an Emirate to a State]* (Casablanca: Al markaz al thaqafi al 'arabi, 2007), pp. 7–8, p. 331.
3. George Joffé, 'Concepts of sovereignty in the Gulf Region', in Richard Schofield (ed.), *Territorial Foundations of the Gulf States* (London: UCL Press, 1994), pp. 78–93, pp. 85–6.
4. For instance, after their victory over the forces of Abd al-Aziz Al-Saud in the summer of 1915, the 'Ajman sought refuge in Kuwait for fear of retaliation, where Mubarak welcomed them. The Kuwaiti contingent, led by his son Salim, had indeed failed to provide support to its Saudi allies.
5. It is debatable whether these taxes can be assimilated into the *zakat* (act of financial worship) since the Gulf sheikhs did not make any claim to give a religious legitimation to their authority.
6. Salwa Alghanim, *The Reign of Mubarak Al-Sabah: Shaikh of Kuwait 1896–1915* (London: I.B.Tauris, 1998), pp. 136–7.
7. Rosemarie S. Zahlan, *The Origins of the Arab United Emirates: A Political and Social History of the Trucial States* (London: Macmillan, 1978), p. 6.
8. Anh N. Longva, 'Nationalism in pre-modern guise: the discourse on *hadar* and *badu* in Kuwait', *International Journal of Middle East Studies* 38/2 (2006), pp. 171–87, p. 184.
9. The abstract of Mohammed Al-Fahed's thesis, completed in 1989 and dealing with the police in Kuwait, reads: 'Rapid culturalisation (sic) occurred and a large influx of *immigrants* and *non-Kuwaitis* entered the country, leaving Kuwait with more than one half of its population being non-Kuwaiti. Although a large portion of these non-Kuwaitis have a tribal, Bedouin heritage and are predominantly Arab and Muslim, their loyalty to the ruling family and ability to elevate their social status has become threatening to Kuwait's social and political structures' (emphasis added). Mohammed Al-Fahed, 'An historical analysis of police in Kuwait: prospects for the future', PhD thesis, University of Exeter, Exeter (1989).
10. The Hamad Desert stretches north-westwards between Syria and Saudi Arabia.
11. Interview, Kuwait, 7 January 2007.

12. Interview, Kuwait, 30 August 2007.
13. For the reasons why and how the Al-Sabah turned from tribal sheikhdom to a ruling dynasty established in the port of Kuwait see Ahmad M. Abu Hakima, *The Modern History of Kuwait, 1750–1965* (London: Luzac, 1983) and Alan de Lacy Rush, *Al-Sabah: History and Genealogy of Kuwait's Ruling Family, 1752–1987* (London: Ithaca, 1987).
14. The position was taken over by his son (1941–54) and grandson until Kuwait's independence.
15. The book uses both the name Abd al-Aziz (bin Abd al-Rahman Al-Saud) which is the correct name used in Arabic to refer to the founder of the Saudi state, and Ibn Saud, mainly used in European languages albeit erroneously since Saud is the name of the lineage and not of his father as implied by 'Ibn'/son.
16. Reidar Visser, *Basra, the Failed Gulf State. Separatism and Nationalism in Southern Iraq* (Münster: LIT Verlag/Transaction Publishers, 2005), p. 152.
17. Hanbali for the Najdi and Zubayri, Akhbari for the Shiites from Bahrain and al-Hasa, Usuli for the *'ajam.*
18. Philip S. Khoury and Joseph Kostiner (eds), *Tribes and State Formation in the Middle East* (Berkeley, CA: University of California Press, 1990), p. 8.
19. Hamad M. Al-Sa'ydan, *Al mawusu'a al kuwaitiyya al mukhtasara* [*Small Encyclopaedia of Kuwait*], vol. 2 (Kuwait: KFAS, 1992-3), p. 1079.
20. The dialect of the city of Kuwait borrows a lot of words from Farsi and Hindi.
21. Mohammad S. Al-Haddad, 'The effect of detribalisation and sedentarisation on the socio-economic structure of the tribes of the Arabian Peninsula: Ajman tribes as a case study', PhD thesis, University of Kansas (1981), p. 44.
22. Ibid., pp. 44, 56–7.
23. Jacqueline S. Ismael, *Kuwait, Social Change in Historical Perspective* (Syracuse, NY: Syracuse University Press, 1982), p. 25.
24. Abd al-Aziz. M. Al-Mansur, *Dirasat fi tarikh al Kuwait, al Kuwait wa 'ilaqat-ha bi 'Arabistan wa al Basra bayn 'am 1896–1915* [*Studies in Kuwait's History: Kuwait's Relationships with Arabistan and Basra between 1896 and 1915*] (unknown: Matba'a Labib, 1970), p. 14.
25. Touvia Ashkenazi, 'The 'Anazah tribes', *Southwestern Journal of Anthropology* 4/2 (Summer 1948), pp. 222–39, p. 231.
26. John F. Williamson, 'The political history of the Shammar Jarba tribe of al Jazirat 1800–1958', PhD thesis, Indiana University (1975).
27. Yitzhak Nakash, 'The conversion of Iraq's tribes to Shiism', *International Journal of Middle East Studies* 26/3 (1994), pp. 443–63, p. 445.
28. Interview with a member of the family al-Mulla, Kuwait, 20 May 2008.
29. Alghanim, *The Reign of Mubarak Al-Sabah*, p. 22, pp. 27–8.
30. Alan J. Villiers, *Sons of Sinbad* (New York: Charles Scribner's Sons, 1940).
31. Anonymous, 'The monthly record', *The Geographical Journal* 40/3 (1912), pp. 330–9, p. 331.

32. Madawi Al-Rasheed, *Politics in an Arabian Oasis: The Rashidis of Saudi Arabia* (London: I.B.Tauris, 1991), p. 144.

33. In August 2010, the Sunni *hadar* MP Ahmad al-Sa'dun blamed the government for being '100 per cent responsible' for the creation of the *bidun* issue, in 'Al hakumat al kuwaitiyya tutalib bil tadqiq fi qanun 'al bidun' wa al nuwab yatahhimun-ha bikhtilaq al azma' ['The Kuwaiti government demands some more verifications for the law on the *biduns*; MPs accuse it of aggravating the crisis'] *Al-Khalij*, UAE, 15 August 2010.

34. Harold R.P. Dickson, *The Arab of the Desert: A Glimpse into Badawin Life in Kuwait and Saudi Arabia* (London: George Allen & Unwin Ltd, 1949), p. 267.

35. Su'ad M. Al-Sabah, *Saqr al khalij: Abdullah Mubarak Al-Sabah [The Falcon of the Gulf: Abdullah Mubarak Al-Sabah]*, 4th edn (Kuwait: Dar Su'ad Al-Sabah lil nashr wa al tawzi', 2000), p. 34.

36. Sheikh Ahmad al-Jabir al-Mubarak and Sheikh Ali al-Salim al-Mubarak, two of his grandsons, both had offspring from 'one 'Ajman tribal lady', Wadiha, from a subsection of the Ibn Huthlayn (Violet Dickson, *Forty Years in Kuwait* (London: Allen and Unwin, 1971), p. 19). The sons of Sheikh Ali al-Salim and Wadiha were Salim and Jabir al-Ali al-Salim. Jabir al-Ali, future Minister of Information (1975–8), became a prominent figure within the ruling family: orphaned at an early age, he was educated with the sons of the Abdullah al-Salim and would be a future candidate for the title of crown prince.

37. Alghanim, *The Reign of Mubarak Al-Sabah*, p. 87. Intermarriage with the Mutair occurs again in the Al-Sabah family as Sheikh Jabir al-Ahmad al-Jabir Al-Sabah is said to have married Mutairi women.

38. The alliance with the 'Ajman was a enduring one: following their victory against the forces of Abd al-Aziz Al-Saud in the summer 1915, thanks to the defection of the Kuwaiti contingent led by Salim al-Mubarak allied to the Saudis, the 'Ajman, fearing the Saudi retaliation sought refuge in Kuwait, where they were accepted by Mubarak (Sultan bin Kalid bin Huthlayn, *Tarikh qabilat al 'Ajman: dirasat watha'iqiyya [History of the Ajman Tribe: Documentary Study]* (Kuwait: Manshurat zat al salasil, 1998), pp. 102–15).

39. Article 4 states: 'Kuwait is a hereditary emirate, the succession to which shall be in the descendants of the late Mubarak Al-Sabah.' Mubarak had seven sons, out of which the descendants of four (Jabir, Salim, Hamad and Abdullah) have claims to the throne nowadays, although traditionally the Jabir and Salim branches alternated at the head of the state.

40. Zahlan, *The Origins of the Arab United Emirates*, p. 6.

41. Ahmad M. Abu Hakima, *Histoire moderne du Koweït, 1750–1965* (Unknown, 1992), p. 139; Alghanim, *The Reign of Mubarak Al-Sabah*, p. 97.

42. Ibn Huthlayn, *Tarikh qabilat al 'Ajman*, p. 98.

43. John H. Mueller, *Koweit, Cadillac et Coca-Cola* (Paris: Robert Laffont, 1963), p. 247. (Translation mine).

44. All were from branches of the Al-Sabah and had some experience in desert battles: Sheikh Ali al-Khalifa al-Abdullah Al-Sabah, the son of Mubarak's nephew, who died in the battle of Sarif, Sheikh Abdullah al-Ahmad Al-Sabah, son of the Emir, and Sheikh Sabah al-Nasir al-Mubarak. The last-named, mentioned many times during field interviews with *biduns* and dwellers of Jahra, remained attached to the desert: known, like his grandfather Mubarak, as Amir al badiya, Sabah al-Nasir had a castle in 'Ardiyya, that is in the desert periphery at the time. A school was named after him in Jahra.

45. It involved Ali al-Salim al-Mubarak Al-Sabah, heading the Kuwaiti forces made up of Bedouin horsemen and motorised vehicles, Ali Khalifa al-Abdullah, his cousin Abdullah Jabir al-Abdullah, Abdullah Ahmad Al-Sabah and Sabah al-Nasir al-Mubarak. Upon the death of Ali al-Salim during the battle, the Emir appointed Abdullah al Jabir al Abdullah commander of the defence cavalry and infantry outside the wall.

46. Musa G. Al-Hatim, *Tarikh al shurta fil Kuwait* [*History of the Police in Kuwait*] (Kuwait: Dar al Qurtas, 1999), pp. 16–19.

47. Kamal Osman Salih, 'The 1938 Kuwait Legislative Council', *Middle Eastern Studies* 28/1 (January 1992), pp. 66–100, p. 68.

48. Prevent and counter theft in open markets, preservation of public order, safety of people and property and control of public morals, including control of the coffee shops.

49. He was liable for any theft in the *suqs* during the night or the lunch break.

50. Al-Hatim, *Tarikh al shurta fil Kuwait*, pp. 22–4.

51. Abdulmohsen Y. Jamal, 'Political opposition in Kuwait', PhD thesis, University of Sunderland (2003), p. 131.

52. Simon C. Smith, *Kuwait, 1950–1965: Britain, the Al-Sabah and Oil* (Oxford: Oxford University Press, 2000), p. 12.

53. Al-Khatib, *Al Kuwait*, pp. 38–9.

54. '*rijal ashkali-him ghariba 'arat al sudur, kathifi sha'ar al ra's ka al nisa'.*' (translation mine).

55. Jill Crystal, 'Public order and authority: policing Kuwait', in Paul Dresch and James Piscatori (eds), *Monarchies and Nations: Globalisation and Identity in the Arab States of the Gulf* (London: I.B.Tauris, 2005), pp. 158–81, p. 166.

56. Talal Almutairi, 'Police-community relationship in Kuwait: public relations perspective', PhD thesis, University of Stirling (2013), pp. 21, 137–8.

57. Sheikh Sabah al-Salim Al-Sabah headed the police forces from 1953 to 1959.

58. As assistant, Abdullah Mubarak was in charge of public order outside the wall, a vast programme that included territory control (*ishraf al badiya*). The whole Rashayida tribe were said to be entirely loyal and devoted to him.
59. He was seconded by Sheikh Abdullah al-Ahmad al-Jabir Al-Sabah. See the Kuwait Politics Database. http://www2.gsu.edu/~polmfh/database/DataPage1910.htm.
60. Ghanim Al-Najjar, 'Challenges of security sector governance in Kuwait', Working Paper 142, Geneva Center for Democratic Control of Armed Forces (2004), p. 3. He evaluates the number of men in charge of dealing with security issues in general to be around 500 at the end of the 1940s.
61. Mueller, *Koweit, Cadillac et Coca-Cola*, p. 68.
62. Major Abdullatif Faisal al-Thuwayni was director of the Public Security, later the Police and Public Security (1959–62). He became Undersecretary of the Ministry of the Interior (1962–81), before eventually being appointed advisor to the Amir's Diwan (1981).
63. Al-Najjar, 'Challenges of security sector governance in Kuwait', p. 4.
64. In the publication of a monthly magazine for the armed forces entitled '*humat al watan*' ['Guardians of the nation'], Abdullah Mubarak mentioned that 'the force towards the creation of which he was working was nothing but part and parcel of the forces of the original Arab entity' (Al-Sabah, *Saqr al khalij*, p. 94). 'Wa laysat hadhihi al quwa alati na'mal li-insha'-ha illa juz'an mutammiman li-quwa al kian al 'arabi al asil.' (translation mine).
65. Ibn Saud first refused it then finally endorsed it when they were supplemented with the two 'Uqair protocols (2 December 1922).
66. Quoted in Moudi M. Abdul-Aziz, *King Abdul-Aziz and the Kuwait Conference, 1923–24* (London: Echoes, 1993), p. 57.
67. Farah Al-Nakib, 'The lost "two-thirds": Kuwait's territorial decline between 1913 and 1922', *Journal of Arabian Studies* 2/1 (2012), pp. 19–37, pp. 34–6.
68. Article 3, Bahra Agreeement, quoted in Abdul-Aziz, *King Abdul-Aziz and the Kuwait Conference*, p. 110.
69. Abdullah al-Ali al-Zamil, quoted ibid., p. 26.
70. Marcek Kurpershoek, *Arabia of the Bedouins*, trans Paul Vincent (London: Saqi Books, 2001), p. 13.
71. Bruce Ingham, *Bedouin of Northern Arabia: Traditions of the Al-Dhafir* (London: Kegan Paul International, 1986), pp. 19–20, p. 43; Visser, *Basra, the Failed Gulf State*, p. 127.
72. Carl R. Raswan, 'Tribal areas and migration lines of the North Arabian Bedouins', *Geographical Review* 20/3 (1930), pp. 494–502, p. 497; Ashkenazi, 'The 'Anazah tribes'', p. 236.
73. Visser, *Basra, the Failed Gulf State*, p. 127.
74. Ibid., pp. 126–8.

75. Ibid., pp. 128–30, 157–8.
76. Ibid., p. 126.
77. Zahlan, *The Origins of the Arab United Emirates*, p. 64.
78. Anthony B. Toth, 'Tribes and tribulations: Bedouin losses in the Saudi and Iraqi Struggles over Kuwait's frontiers, 1921–1943', *British Journal of Middle Eastern Studies* 32/2 (2005), pp. 145–67, p. 149, 157.
79. Ibid., p. 166.
80. Martin Pratt and Janet A. Brown (eds), *Borderlands under Stress* (London: Kluwer Law International, 2000).
81. Zahlan, *The Origins of the Arab United Emirates*, pp. 69–70.
82. Müller, *En Syrie avec les Bédouins*, p. ix (translation mine).
83. The former head of the Central Committee, the organisation of the Ministry of the Interior responsible for the *biduns*, differentiated between two phases: the first being when the *hadar* built the country and the state and the second represented by the influx of *badu* as of 1985 who do not care about the territory and have no link whatsoever to it. Interview, Kuwait, 3 June 2008.
84. Visser, *Basra, the Failed Gulf State*, p. 18.
85. John C. Wilkinson, 'Nomadic territory as a factor in defining Arabia's boundaries', in Martha Mundy and Basim Musallam (eds), *The Transformation of Nomadic Society in the Arab East* (New York: Cambridge University Press, 2000), pp. 44–62.
86. Khaled O. Al-Radihan, 'Nomadic sedentarisation with special reference to the Shararat of Northern Saudi Arabia', PhD thesis, University of Wales, Swansea (2001), p. 101.
87. Ibid., p. 139.
88. Donald P. Cole and Soraya Altorki, 'Production and trade in North Central Arabia: change and development in 'Unayzah', in Martha Mundy and Basim Musallam (eds), *The Transformation of Nomadic Society in the Arab East* (New York: Cambridge University Press, 2000), pp. 145–59, p. 150, 154.
89. Al-Radihan, 'Nomadic sedentarisation', p. 78.
90. James C. Scott, *Seeing Like a State: How Certain Schemes to Improve the Human Condition Have Failed* (New Haven, CT: Yale University Press, 1998), p. 4. See the Homs military college both as the institution of middle-class integration and a nationalist symbol. Patrick Seale, *The Struggle for Syria: a Study of Post-War Arab Politics 1945–1958* (London: I.B. Tauris, 1986), p. 37. See also the rationale for the conscription in Iraq and the issue it encountered as the Yazidis did not want to mix with other segments of the population. Nelida Fuccaro, 'Ethnicity, state formation, and conscription in postcolonial Iraq: the case of the Yazidi Kurds of Jabal Sinjar', *International Journal of Middle East Studies* 29/4 (1997), pp. 559–80.

91. Fuad I. Khuri, *Tribe and State in Bahrain: the Transformation of Social and Political Authority in an Arab State* (Chicago, IL: University of Chicago Press, 1980).

92. With the dramatic consequences that this could have made the state become dictatorial.

93. John. B. Glubb, *Arabian Adventures: Ten Years of Joyful Service* (London: Cassell, 1978), pp. 97–8.

94. Robert A. Fernea, 'State and tribe in southern Iraq: the struggle for hegemony before the 1958 revolution', in Robert A. Fernea and William R. Louis (eds), *The Iraqi Revolution of 1958: the Old Social Classes Revisited* (London: I.B.Tauris, 1991), pp. 142–53, p. 145. '*Ashira* is a tribe's section.

95. For instance, in 1967 part of the reason the elections were confiscated is that the sheikhs felt they were unable to compete with the rhetorical skills of the nationalist opposition. Robert L. Jarman, *Sabah al-Salim Al-Sabah, Amir of Kuwait 1965–77: A Political Biography* (London: London Centre of Arab Studies, 2002), p. 216.

96. In a report dated 5 May 1967, the World Health Organisation commented on the health situation in Kuwait: 'Up to 21 April, 12 cases with six deaths of clinically confirmed variola major have been reported. These cases are in Shaddadia, Maqwa'a and 'Awazim, all districts on the western borders of Kuwait. Inhabitants of these districts are nomads. The original or index case has been traced. This person had contact with other nomads from an adjacent country' (World Health Organisation (WHO), *Weekly Epidemiological Record* (Geneva: World Health Organisation, 1967), p. 219).

97. Alawadi, Abdulhadi M., 'Low- and middle-income housing in Kuwait', *Habitat International* 4/3 (1979), pp. 339–44, p. 342.

CHAPTER 3   FROM SHANTY BEDOUINS TO ILLEGAL RESIDENTS

1. *Al-Watan*, Kuwait, 9 May 1985.

2. Anh N. Longva, 'Neither autocracy nor democracy but ethnocracy: citizens, expatriates and the socio-political system in Kuwait', in Paul Dresch and James Piscatori (eds), *Monarchies and Nations: Globalisation and Identity in the Arab States of the Gulf* (London: I.B.Tauris, 2005), pp. 114–35, p. 114.

3. Michael Herb, *The Wages of Oil: Parliaments and Economic Development in Kuwait and the UAE* (Ithaca, NY: Cornell University Press, 2014).

4. 'Citizenship in the Gulf States: conceptualization and practice', in Nils A. Butenschøn, Uri Davis and Manuel S. Hassassian (eds), Citizenship and the State in the Middle East: Approaches and Applications (Syracuse, NY: Syracuse University Press, 2000), pp. 179 – 97.

5. This was changed immediately in 1960 to ten years.

6. Rashid H. Al-Anezi, *Al jinsiyya al kuwaitiyya [The Kuwaiti nationality]*, 4th edn (Kuwait City: Kuwait University, 2005), pp. 285–315. The minimum periods of compulsory residence to be eligible for naturalisation were raised again in 1980 to 15 and 20 years for Arabs and non-Arabs respectively.

7. For ten years initially, then 20 years as of the Law 70/1966 prescribing it. It was amended in 1986 (Decree-Law130/1986) to add another ten years, which makes 30 years in total, as of the date of naturalisation, and brought down to 20 years in 1995 as of the date of naturalisation.

8. Mary A. Tétreault, *Stories of Democracy: Politics and Society in Contemporary Kuwait* (New York: Columbia University Press, 2000), pp. 44–6.

9. Anh N. Longva, *Walls Built on Sand: Migration, Exclusion, and Society in Kuwait* (Boulder, CO: Westview Press, 1997), p. 24.

10. Tétreault, *Stories of Democracy*, p. 43, 46.

11. Ibid., p. 46.

12. Sula Al-Naqeeb, 'The question of citizenship and integration in Kuwait: looking at the Bidoun as a case study', MA thesis, School of Oriental and African Studies, London, 2006, p. 27.

13. The most famous case was the cancellation of a planned joint-venture (K-Dow) signed between Dow Chemicals and Petrochemicals Industries Co of Kuwait (PIC) in December 2008, under the pressure of the parliament threatening to interrogate the then Prime Minister, Sheikh Nasir Muhammad Al-Sabah. This cost PIC, a subsidiary of the state-owned Kuwait Petroleum Corporation, US$ 2.16 billion in damages, following the decision of an arbitration court of the International Chamber of Commerce. Ed Crooks and Camilla Hall 'Dow Chemicals wins $2.2 bn in Kuwait damages', *The Financial Times*, 24 May 2012.

14. The writing off of consumer debts occurred twice in the history of the country, in 1982 after the crash of the Suq al Manakh, a parallel stock exchange where investors speculated on borrowed money, and after the 1991 liberation. Yet the issue resurfaced sharply in 2010, dividing the country between the economic elite and the government, on one hand, and the 'populist parliament' on the other. In January 2010, Parliament passed a plan worth US$ 23.3 billion, according to which the government would assume the responsibility of some loans while the banks were required to waive the accumulated interest. The government derailed its implementation (as the measure did not gather two-thirds of Parliament's vote). In April 2013, Parliament passed a new law covering some personal loans taken from 2002 until 2008 and their interest for a value of US$ 2.61 billion, the MPs arguing that consumers had paid overcharged interest.

15. On 26 October 2008, Kuwait's Central Bank ordered the suspension of the Gulf Bank's shares and a restructuring plan to cover (KD375 million) US$ 1.4 billion in currency derivative losses; 'Kuwait's Gulf Bank sees first

quarter profit after bailout', Reuters, 11 April 2009; 'State of the GCC banking system', *International Financing Review/Middle East Report*, 2010.

16. Jill Crystal, *Oil and Politics in the Gulf: Rulers and Merchants in Kuwait and Qatar* (Cambridge: Cambridge University Press, 1990), pp. 212–54.

17. The role of Ja'far in the facilitation of the naturalisation of foreigners is not ascertained: according to a later interview, Ja'far stated that 'the Law had been enacted on the personal initiative and instruction of the late Ruler Sheikh Ahmad al-Jabir. There appears to have been no request from the British authorities or even knowledge on their part of the fact that a law had been enacted' (Rashid H. Al-Anezi, 'A study of the role of nationality in international law with special reference to the law and practice of Kuwait', PhD thesis, University of Cambridge, Cambridge (1989), pp. 161–2). Yet the British held 'Izzat Ja'far as an 'undesirable person': they insisted on the suspension of the 1948 Nationality Law straight away as, fearing Arab nationalism, they thought that the law had 'been drawn by ... Izzat [Jaffer], on an Egyptian pattern, in language which is probably designed to ensure livelihoods for the fraternity of the Egyptian Bar'; British archives document dated 5 December 1950 and quoted ibid., p. 164.

18. Ahmad al-Khatib, *Al Kuwait: min al imara ilal dawla [Kuwait: from an Emirate to a State]* (Casablanca: Al markaz al thaqafi al 'arabi, 2007), pp. 77–87.

19. Fred Halliday, *Nation and Religion in the Middle East* (London: Saqi Books, 2000), p. 38.

20. Crystal, *Oil and Politics in the Gulf*, pp. 78–80.

21. Interview, Kuwait, 26 May 2008.

22. In article 7 of the 1959 Nationality Law, Law 44 of 1994 added a clause stating that the offspring of second-class citizens born in Kuwait are also counted as first-class citizens. Ironically this enabled them to vote in the 1996 election, whereas their fathers were not able to do so and had to wait until the 2000 elections, because, naturalised at the earliest in 1965 (at the end of the work of the nationality committees), they had to wait 30 years and register a year prior to the election.

23. Farah Al-Nakib, 'The lost "two-thirds": Kuwait's territorial decline between 1913 and 1922', *Journal of Arabian Studies* 2/1 (2012), pp. 19–37.

24. Jerzy Zdanowski, *Slavery in the Gulf in the First Half of the 20th Century: A Study Based on Records from the British Archives* (Warsaw: Askon, 2008), p. 183.

25. The four main neighbourhoods in Old Kuwait City were: Qibla, Sharq, Murqab and al-Wasat. They enclosed smaller quarters like *firij* al-Hasawi, al-Mutran, al-Balush, al-Shuyukh, al-Jana'at, al-Nusf, al-Fadala, representing a couple of streets populated by related families.

26. Khalid Al-Mubaylish, *Al 'awa'il al kuwaitiyya fil ahia' wa al qura al qadima [The Kuwaiti Families in the Old Neighbourhoods and Villages]* (Kuwait: Sharikat al siyasi lil nashr wa al tawzi', 2007).

27. Emiri decree No 5 of 1960 published in the official journal *Kuwait al-Yawm*, issue 267. I thank Abdulrahman Alebrahim for pointing this to my attention.
28. Interview with Sheikha Fawzia al-Salman Al-Sabah, a Kuwaiti lawyer defending the cases of *biduns*, Kuwait, 30 August 2007.
29. Claire Beaugrand, 'Émergence de la "nationalité" et institutionnalisation des clivages sociaux au Koweït et au Bahreïn', *Chroniques yéménites* 14 (2007), pp. 89–107.
30. Al-Anezi, 'A study of the role of nationality in international law', pp. 256–7.
31. Electronic correspondence, 21 August 2008.
32. Al-Anezi, 'A study of the role of nationality in international law', p. 257.
33. Ibid., p. 257.
34. Electronic correspondence, 17 August 2008.
35. Hamad M. Al-Sa'ydan, *Al mawusu'a al kuwaitiyya al mukhtasara* [*Small Encyclopaedia of Kuwait*], vol. 2 (Kuwait: KFAS, 1992-3), p. 1124. *'Ajam* are Gulf residents of Persian origin.
36. Steven Heydemann, 'Social pacts and the persistence of authoritarianism in the Middle East', in Oliver Schlumberger (ed.), *Debating Arab Authoritarianism: Dynamics and Durability in Nondemocratic Regimes* (Stanford, CA: Stanford University Press, 2007), pp. 21–38, p. 25.
37. Soraya Altorki, 'The concept and practice of citizenship in Saudi Arabia', in Suad Joseph (ed.), *Gender and citizenship in the Middle East* (Syracuse, NY: Syracuse University Press, 2000), pp. 215–36, p. 215.
38. Andrzej Kapiszewski, 'Non-indigenous citizens and "stateless" residents in the Gulf monarchies', *Krakowskie Studia Miedzynarodowe* 2/6 (2005), pp. 61–78, p. 65.
39. Rania Maktabi, 'The Gulf Crisis (1990–1991) and the Kuwaiti regime: legitimacy and stability in a rentier state', PhD thesis, Department of Political Science, University of Oslo (1992), p. 27.
40. Together with the other naturalised people (articles 4, 5, 7 and 8), the children of naturalised fathers were deprived of their political rights until after the period stated in article 6. However, in 1994 (Law 44) the Law was amended and stated that children of naturalised fathers born in Kuwait were considered as Kuwaiti *asli*.
41. The singer Nawal, *bidun* born to a Kuwaiti mother *bi-tajannus* or by naturalisation, is an exception. Up to the time of writing she had not obtained nationality. Also, the Bolivian passport might be interpreted as a sign of being originally *bidun*.
42. *Al-Nahar*, Kuwait, 2 January 2008 reproduced the emiri decree granting the nationality to 573 persons for the year 2007, out of which 17 were for special services, among whom were the al-Hadhal.
43. Human Rights Watch (HRW), *The Bedoons of Kuwait: 'Citizens without Citizenship'* (New York: Human Rights Watch, 1995), pp. 32–3.
44. The paragraph no longer exists in the current law.
45. Al-Anezi, 'A study of the role of nationality in international law', p. 257.

46. Interview, Kuwait, 30 August 2007.

47. Mohammed Al-Fahed, 'An historical analysis of police in Kuwait: prospects for the future', PhD thesis, University of Exeter, Exeter (1989), p. 25.

48. Ibid., p. 3.

49. Ibid., p. 2.

50. Ibid., p. 6.

51. Farah Al-Nakib, 'Revisiting *hadar* and *badu* in Kuwait: citizenship, housing and the construction of a dichotomy', *International Journal of Middle East Studies* 46/1 (2014), pp. 5–30.

52. Miriam Ababsa, Baudouin Dupret and Eric Denis (eds), *Popular Housing and Urban Land Tenure in the Middle East* (Cairo: American University in Cairo Press, 2012).

53. Allan Hill, 'The population of Kuwait', *Geography* 54/1 (January 1969), pp. 84–8.

54. Jahra (mainly Mutair), Dimnah, now Salmiyya (mostly 'Awazim), Fintas, Abu Halifa and Shuaiba.

55. Study published in *Al-Ra'i al 'Amm* on 17 March 1978, 'Dirasa 'ayn mushkilat al 'ashish fil Kuwait' [Study in the question of the *ashish* in Kuwait]. According to the study, there were shanties as early as 1936. Al-Moosa ('Bedouin shanty settlements in Kuwait: a study in social geography', unpublished PhD thesis, SOAS, University of London, 1976', p. 58) also notes the existence of shanties in Maqwa'a near the first oil field discovered in Burgan on 22 February 1938. The first oil shipment was exported on 30 June 1946.

56. Ibid.

57. Reem I. R. Alissa, 'Building for oil: corporate colonialism, nationalism and urban modernity in Ahmadi, 1946–1992', PhD thesis, University of California, Berkeley (2012), p. 39.

58. 'The plan for the house designed for the labour force had only two rooms, an inner courtyard and a miniscule store and cooking area furnished only with a stove and a sink.' Alissa, 'Building for oil', p. 49.

59. 152 senior, 144 junior staff and 240 artisans.

60. Artisans were mostly Pakistanis.

61. Alissa, 'Building for oil', p. 57.

62. Ibid., pp. 82, 128.

63. Including inside the town's wall at least in 1951, as shown in an aerial picture of Kuwait. Al-Moosa, 'Bedouin shanty settlements in Kuwait', p. 58.

64. *Al-Qabas*, 15 August 1972: '1,500 'a'ilat muhaddida bil-tasharrud' [1,500 families facing imminent risk of homelessness]. This affected the areas of Doha, Jahra, Farwaniyya, Jlib al Shuyukh, Sayhad al 'Awazim, Shadadiyya, al Maqwa'a and Sulaibiyya.

65. Al-Moosa, 'Bedouin shanty settlements in Kuwait', p. 64.

66. Colin Buchanan and Partners, *Studies for National Physical Plan for the State of Kuwait and Master Plan for the Urban Area, Second Report: The Short Term Plan* (Kuwait: Kuwait Municipality, 1971), p. 45.
67. Singular: Dussari. The Dawasir is a tribe considered from the South of Kuwait, whose traditional territory stretched as far as Bahrain and Qatar.
68. Inteviews, Tayma and Ahmadi, 23 April 2014. Electronic correspondence, 19 August 2008.
69. *Al-Ra'i al 'Amm*, 'Dirasa 'ayn mushkilat al 'ashish fil Kuwait'.
70. *Al-Fajr*, 1958 (precise date unknown), Al 'ashish lil-kuwaiti ... wal zahab al aswad lil-musta'mir!! [The *'ashish* for the Kuwaiti ... and the black gold for the coloniser!!].
71. Al-Moosa, 'Bedouin shanty settlements in Kuwait', p. 96.
72. Gradually, people in mixed areas (Bedouin and urbanite) tended to swap lots so as to live in a more homogenous social environment.
73. At an average cost of KD 5,190 (reimbursed on a monthly basis of KD 3.750 to KD 15).
74. It includes both Kuwaitis and what would be later considered as *biduns* in the 1985 census.
75. Al-Moosa, 'Bedouin shanty settlements in Kuwait', pp. 118–292.
76. Ibid., pp. 297 and 299.
77. At an estimated cost of KD 800 and provided to its occupant at a monthly rent of KD 7.
78. The number of housing included in the first Scheme of Popular Housing was 14,992, distributed between three areas. Only half of the planned units were built.
    - Mina Abdullah: 4,992 units planned.
    - Jahra (al Na'im): 2,594 out of the 5,000 planned.
    - Al 'Ardiyya (later cancelled): 5,000 planned.

    As a result of the failure of the scheme, building on the third site in 'Ardiyya was cancelled and used for low-income houses instead. Kuwait News Agency (KUNA), 'Al Kuwait insha'at al buyut al sha'abiyya badilan li-zahirat al 'ashish' [Kuwait established popular housing to replace the shanties], KUNA, 22 February 2004.
79. In a later Channel One TV programme, the popular housing is described as 'temporary' for Kuwaitis waiting to move to other types of better accommodation.
80. Kuwait News Agency (KUNA), 'Al Kuwait insha'at al buyut al sha'abiyya badilan li-zahirat al 'ashish' [Kuwait established popular housing to replace the shanties], KUNA, 22 February 2004.
81. *Al-Ra'i al 'Amm*, 'Dirasa 'ayn mushkilat al 'ashish fil Kuwait'.
82. *Al-Anba'*, 'Lajnat al 'ashish tajtama' al sabt li-wad'a khuttat izalat al 'ashish' [The Committee for the *'ashish* meets on Saturday to draw a plan for the eradication of *'ashish*], 7 September 1978.

The number of units built in the framework of the second Scheme of Popular Housing by December 1979 was distributed between:
- 4,150 housing units in Jahra (zone A and B) for 35,000 persons;
- 5,546 in Sulaibiyya for 43,257 persons.

Al-Qabas, '7,375 baytan hakumiyyan bil-sulaibiyya li-sukan al 'ashish' [7,375 government houses in Sulaibiyya for the people from the *'ashish*], 16 March 1978.

83. Ibid.
84. *Al-Siyasa*, '700 bayt sayatamm tawuzi'-ha fil Jahra' [700 houses will be distributed in Jahra], 10 September 1978.
85. *Al-Siyasa*, '800 'asha mutabaqiyya fi anha' al Kuwait' [800 'ashish remain in different places of Kuwait], 14 June 1980.
86. *Al-Qabas*, 'Qabl an nahtafil bil zikra al thaniyya li-izalat akhar 'ashish' [Before celebrating the second anniversary of the eradication of the last *'ashish*], 2 February 1984.
87. *Al-Qabas*, "'Awdat al 'ashish laysat zahira mukhifa' [The return of *'ashish* is not a frightening phenomenon], 10 February 1984; *Al-Qabas*, 'Tarakhis li-zara'ib al mashiyya tatahawwal ila masakin lil-bashara' [Licenses for animal pens turned into habitations for human beings], 5 August 1985.
88. There are still areas in Kuwait that are referred to as *jawakhir* – Kabd and al Hajn, in the desert east of Ahmadi, south of Sulaibiyya.
89. *Al-Qabas*, 'Tarakhis li-zara'ib al mashiyya …'.
90. Ibid.
91. It is beyond the scope of this book but it would be interesting to link the episodes of the Iran–Iraq War with the influx of undocumented migrants, who sometimes sought asylum in third countries.
92. Interview, Kuwait, 29 April 2014.
93. Interviews, 'Ardiyya, 27 May 2008.
94. Alissa, 'Building for oil: corporate colonialism', p. 111.
95. HRW, *The Bedoons of Kuwait*, p. 34.
96. Confidential telegram, 3 June 2009. Wikileaks. Available at https://www.wikileaks.org/plusd/cables/09KUWAIT558_a.html (accessed 6 June 2017).
97. In KUNA, 22 February 2004, 'Kuwait insha'at al buyut al sha'abiyya badilan li-zahirat al 'ashish', the director of Rental Housing at the Public Authority for Housing Welfare mentioned that popular houses in Jahra (Na'im) and Umm al Hayman were destroyed. The most likely interpretation is that he was referring to the informal settlement inhabited by the *biduns*.
98. In the article of *Al-Qabas*, 'la niyya li-hadm al buyut al sha'abiyya fil Sulaibiyya wa Tayma. Lil musajjilin hata 31/8/1987, "al sakaniyya" tastaqbil al yam talabat mashru 'Umm al Hayman', 3 September 1997, the PAHW asserted, as in the article's title, that it had 'no intention to demolish the popular housing in Sulaibiyya and Tayma. For those registered until 31/8/1987, the PAHW accepts applications today for the Umm al Hayman project'.

99. *Al-Siyasa*, 'Al-Qallaf: sharikat naft al Kuwait qarrarat tarad 'al bidun' min masakin-ha fi ghyiab majlis al Umma' [Al Qallaf: the Kuwait OIl Company decided to expel the *biduns* from its houses in the absence of Parliament], 24 August 1997.
100. Interview, Ali Sabah al Salim, 22 April 2014.
101. Interview, Ahmadi, 29 April 2014.
102. Colin Buchanan and Partners, *Studies for National Physical Plan*, Second Report, p. 12.
103. *Al-Ra'i al 'Amm*, 'Dirasa 'ayn mushkilat al 'ashish fil Kuwait'. The article indicates that the source is the 1970 census.
104. Al-Moosa, 'Bedouin shanty settlements in Kuwait', p. 82.
105. This nevertheless leaves open the possibility of extra-legal naturalisations, since Buchanan does not state the source of the figures.
106. As a result, Kuwait has had a different policy towards the Soviet bloc, being the sole Gulf state having relations with the USSR and the Eastern European countries. Ghanim Al-Najjar, 'Challenges of security sector governance in Kuwait', Working Paper 142, Geneva Center for Democratic Control of Armed Forces (2004), p. 5.
107. Interestingly, the interview of a former Soviet general, who visited the Egyptian front during the War of Attrition for a *Russian Today* TV programme celebrating the fortieth anniversary of the 1973 war and belittled the seriousness of the Kuwaiti troops, sparked a debate in the Kuwaiti press, with former combatants giving a great deal of detail on the role and operations of Kuwaiti contingents (The Q8ping, 23 October 2013. Available at https://www.youtube.com/watch?v = 0OySWlVEV0s (accessed 6 June 2017)). See in particular the reply made by the retired brigadier, Sa'adi Falah al-Shammari, in *Al-Anba'*, 'Al-Shammari: al quwwat al kuwaitiyya mumaththila bi-luwa' al Yarmuk 'amalat fil-khuttut al amamiyya min jabhat al qital al misriyya did al 'adu al isra'ili akthar min 7 sanawat' [Shammari: the Kuwaiti forces, represented by the Yarmouk Brigades worked at the fore of the Egyptian battlefront against the Israeli enemy for more than 7 years], 10 November 2013. Available at http://www.alanba.com.kw/ar/kuwait-news/421681/10–11–2013 (accessed 6 June 2017).
108. *Al-Ra'i*, '"Al Difa'a" tarudd 'ala mughalatat jeneral rusi: butulat al jaysh al kuwaiti tadrab fi 'umq al tarikh' [The MoD replies to the false statements issued by a Russian general: the heroism of the Kuwaiti Army strikes at the heart of history], 30 October 2013. Available at http://www.alraimedia.com/Articles.aspx?id=462469 (accessed 6 June 2017). For a full recollection of the Kuwaiti troops' operations in the 1967 war, see *Al-Watan*, 'Dawr al jaysh al kuwaiti fi harb Huzayran 1967' [The Role of the Kuwaiti army in the June 1967 war], 5 June 2014. Available at http://alwatan.kuwait.tt/articledetails.aspx?id=363192 (accessed 6 June 2017).

109. Miriam Joyce, *Ruling Sheikhs and Her Majesty's Government, 1960–69* (London: Frank Cass, 2003), p. 90. The document referred to by Joyce is FCO 8/144 PRO. Neil Partrick mentioned in his thesis that, as for Iraq, it 'had dispatched troops to the battlefield via Jordan, as they had done in 1948'. Neil Partrick, 'Kuwait's foreign policy (1961–1977)', PhD thesis, London School of Economics (2006), p. 81.

110. *Al-Watan*, 'Dawr al jaysh al Kuwaiti fi harb Huzayran 1967'.

111. *Al-Anba'*, 'Al-Shammari: al quwwat al kuwitiyya'.

112. Partrick, 'Kuwait's foreign policy', p. 184. Partrick also quotes a editorial by *Al-Ra'i al 'Amm*, 1 December 1974 (FCO 8/2193) that bemoans the muted response of Arab capitals in the face of an Iraqi territorial penetration: 'it is surprising that Egypt and Syria, which are aware of the sacrifice made by Kuwait in the context of the Arab battle, have not lifted a finger to maintain Arab solidarity.'

113. By order of military operations No. 3967. See 'Madha qaddama al 'Arab li-Misr fi harb Oktober' [What did the Arabs contribute to Egypt during the October war], *Al-Masri al Yawm*, 2 October 2014. Available at http://www.almasryalyoum.com/news/details/536573 (accessed 6 June 2017).

114. A tank battalion, an infantry battalion, two companies of artillery, an anti-aircraft company and a commando company of the Kuwait 25th Commando Brigade.

115. Al-Najjar, 'Challenges of security sector governance in Kuwait', pp. 4–5.

116. Ibid., p. 5.

117. Interview, Kuwait, 26 May 2008.

118. Jasim al-Qitami, a member of the Arab Nationalist Movement, was elected in 1963's parliament before resigning in 1965, together with all the members of the opposition. See the Kuwait Politics of Georgia State University: Database. Available at http://www2.gsu.edu/~polmfh/database/positions7.htm (accessed 6 June 2017). He was elected again in 1975 and 1985 in Qibla.

119. Al-Najjar, 'Challenges of security sector governance in Kuwait', p. 7.

120. Military service was suspended between 2001 and April 2015 when the National Assembly passed a new law to reinstate it, as of 2017.

121. Al-Fahed, 'An historical analysis of police in Kuwait', p. 246. Al-Fahed notes: 'lower ranks of the Kuwaiti police force are filled by non-Kuwaitis who are not only perceived by the community as second-class citizens, but are in fact, socio-ethnically deprived because they are only birth certificate holders' (ibid., p. 3).

122. Ibid., p. 230.

123. Longva, *Walls Built on Sand*, pp. 50–1.

124. The National Guards were established in June 1967, when Kuwaiti troops were first sent to Egypt. Contrary to the army and the police, from which they are independent and where other nationalities are allowed to serve

either as soldiers or officers, the National Guards are made up of volunteers from among nationals.

125. Al-Anezi, 'A study of the role of nationality in international law', pp. 256–7.

126. Abd 'Awan al-Rawdan, *Mawusu'at 'asha'ir al 'Iraq: tarikh, ansab, rijalat, ma'thir [Encyclopaedia of Iraq's Tribes: History, Genealogy, Men and Deeds]*, 2nd edn (Amman: Al Ahlia lil-nashr wa al tawzi', 2008), p. 233, pp. 314–5; Bruce Ingham, *Bedouin of Northern Arabia: Traditions of the Al-Dhafir* (London: Kegan Paul International, 1986), pp. 29–30.

127. Information he gathered in Kuwait in 1977. Interview, London, 20 March 2009.

128. The linguistic or dialect factor represents nevertheless an identifiable limit to this extensive definition.

129. Mohammed H.S. Ebrahim, 'Problems of nomad settlement in the Middle East with special reference to Saudi Arabia and the Haradh project', PhD thesis, Cornell University (1981), p. 66.

130. Interview, Kuwait, 26 May 2008.

131. Khaled O. Al-Radihan, 'Nomadic sedentarisation with special reference to the Shararat of Northern Saudi Arabia', PhD thesis, University of Wales, Swansea (2001), p. 137.

132. Interview, Shuwaikh, 7 June 2008.

133. It is not even sure that these sources exist at all. They may have been destroyed or stolen by the Iraqis during the 1990–1 invasion, like the major part of the Kuwaiti official archives.

134. Interview, Sulaibiyya, 14 May 2008.

135. Interview, Kuwait City, 8 June 2008.

136. The Ministry of Defence was set up in 1964, and the two posts held together in 1965 by Saad al-Abdullah, which explains why in Kuwait police and army are often confused.

137. Saad Abdullah was then Minister of the Interior (1964–78). Jabir al-Ali al-Salim became Minister of Guidance and Information in 1964. In June 1965, when the journal *Al-Siyasa* was founded he was believed to be the real owner, 'who was seeking to position himself for the position of Crown Prince'. Kjetil Selvik, 'Elite rivalry in a semi-democracy: the Kuwaiti press scene', *Middle Eastern Studies* 47/3 (2011), pp. 477–96, p. 482. After the death of Abdullah al-Salim in November 1965 and the choice of Jabir al-Ahmad as Crown Prince, he was re-appointed Minister of Information, a position he kept until 1971. After being left out of cabinet for four years, he was appointed Minister of Information and Vice-Prime Minister in 1975 until 1981. Although the "most prominent candidate' to be Crown Prince in 1977 when Jabir al-Ahmad became Emir', he was sidelined. John E. Peterson, 'The nature of succession in the Gulf', *Middle East Journal* 55/4 (2001), pp. 580–601, p. 586. Peterson writes because 'he was too abrasive and uncontrolled'. Recent articles in the Kuwaiti press, based on British archives of 1978, recall that

he was chosen because he was not seen in a positive light by Kuwaiti families (*a'ila*) whereas he enjoyed a strong support among the tribal leaders (*zu'ama' al qaba'il*). Available at http://www.nationalkuwait. com/forum/index.php?threads/47717/; http://www.alqabas.com.kw/ Articles.aspx?ArticleID=465373&CatID = 557 (accessed 6 June 2017).

138. Abdul-Reda Assiri, *The Government and Politics of Kuwait: Principles and Practices* (Kuwait: Al-Watan Printing Press, 1996), p. 139.

139. Shafeeq Ghabra, 'Kuwait and the dynamics of socio-economic change', *Middle East Journal* 51/3 (Summer 1997), pp. 358–72, p. 364.

140. Abdullah F. al-Nafisi, *Kuwait: al ra'i al akhar* [*Kuwait: the Other Perspective*] (London: Ta-ha Advertising, 1987).

141. Lawson, Fred H., 'Class and state in Kuwait', *MERIP Reports*, No. 132, 'The future of the Gulf' (May 1985), pp. 16–21, p. 20.

142. Longva, *Walls Built on Sand*, p. 51.

143. Interview with a *bidun* naturalised Kuwaiti in the 2000s, Kuwait, 12 December 2005. This *bidun*, an employee of a ministry, noted that he had his job thanks to a *wasta*, his driving licence because his mother was Kuwaiti, and that he had obtained a temporary passport, renewable every year, to go abroad thanks to a *wasta*. As a result he went to study abroad in the hope that this would increase his chances of getting naturalised.

144. Articles 1 and 2, according to which one obtains the first degree of nationality, are simple: article 1 concerns the persons who can actually prove their continuous residence in Kuwait since 1920; article 2 concerns their children.

145. Physical appearance and linguistic abilities constitute limits to this seemingly extensive definition. It is quite unlikely that an Egyptian from Middle Egypt will ever be seriously taken for a *bidun*. Prof. Bruce Ingham, London, 20 March 2009.

146. James C. Scott, *Seeing Like a State: How Certain Schemes to Improve the Human Condition Have Failed* (New Haven, CT: Yale University Press, 1998), p. 3.

CHAPTER 4   THE MANUFACTURING OF ILLEGALITY

1. Jill Crystal, 'Civil society in the Arabian Gulf', in Augustus R. Norton (ed.), *Civil Society in the Middle East*, vol. 2 (Leiden: E.J. Brill, 1996), pp. 259–86, p. 264.

2. Laurence Louër, *Transnational Shia Politics: Religious and Political Networks in the Gulf* (London: Hurst & Co., 2008), pp. 103–49.

3. Parallel to the official Kuwait Stock Exchange, the Suq al Manakh was an unofficial, unregulated and highly speculative stock market, trading foreign companies' shares in Kuwait. Fed by the wealth that accrued to the country further to the 1973 and 1979 oil crises, the speculative

bubble burst in August 1982, the value of securities collapsed and the government shut the Suq al Manakh.

4. Marwan R. Asmar, 'The state and politics of migrant labour in Kuwait', PhD thesis, University of Leeds, Leeds (1990), p. 157; Michael Herb, *The Wages of Oil: Parliaments and Economic Development in Kuwait and the UAE* (Ithaca, NY: Cornell University Press, 2014).

5. Louër, *Transnational Shia Politics*, p. 113, 115. *Hawza* is a seminary where Shiite clerics are trained.

6. Ibid., p. 111.

7. Interview, Kuwait, 16 January 2007.

8. Kjetil Selvik notes that 'more than 100 magazines, monthlies and weeklies were created in the 1960s and 1970s, and the expansion also included several dailies'; 'Elite rivalry in a semi-democracy: the Kuwaiti press scene', *Middle Eastern Studies* 47/3 (2011), pp. 477–96, p. 481.

9. Including Sunnis and Shiites who did not follow the Imam Khomeini line, *khatt al imam*.

10. Louër, *Transnational Shia Politics*, p. 170.

11. Article 14 of the 1959 Nationality Law states three cases leading to nationality termination: enrolment in a foreign army; collaboration with a foreign country at war with Kuwait; or a crime committed abroad and considered as treason in their home country. Article 13 regulates the cases of nationality withdrawal for naturalised Kuwaitis (arts 3, 4, 5, 7, 8), which are far more numerous and include the 'threat to the highest interest of the state and its security'.

12. See the decree of reinstatement of nationality, 23 March 1997. Available at https://www.cmgs.gov.kw/Electronic-Services/Decrees/Decree-Result. aspx?qry=المهري&sMode=0&sOption=0&pSize=1000 (accessed 6 June 2017).

13. Jill Crystal, 'Public order and authority: policing Kuwait', in Paul Dresch and James Piscatori (eds), *Monarchies and Nations: Globalisation and Identity in the Arab States of the Gulf* (London: I.B.Tauris, 2005), pp. 158–81, p. 179.

14. Andrew Whitley, 'Minorities and the stateless in Persian Gulf politics', *Survival* 35/4 (1993), pp. 28–50, pp. 32, 37.

15. Anh N. Longva, *Walls Built on Sand: Migration, Exclusion, and Society in Kuwait* (Boulder, CO: Westview Press, 1997), p. 51.

16. Background information, London, November 2009. Their number is impossible to evaluate.

17. In late January 1984, the trial judging the authors of the December 1983 bombings involved 25 individuals: 17 Iraqis, three Lebanese, three Kuwaitis and two *biduns*. All of the Iraqis were Shiites, and most admitted belonging to al Da'wa. At least two of the Lebanese were Shiite.

18. Lori P. Boghardt, *Kuwait amid War, Peace and Revolution: 1979–1991 and New Challenges* (Basingstoke: Palgrave Macmillan, 2006), p. 76.

19. Crystal, 'Public order and authority', p. 176.
20. Chookiat Panaspornprasit, *US–Kuwaiti Relations, 1961–1992: An Uneasy Relationship* (London: Routledge, 2005), pp. 88–112.
21. John S. Birks, Ian J. Seccombe and Clive A. Sinclair, 'Migrant workers in the Arab Gulf: the impact of declining oil revenues', *International Migration Review* 20/4 (1986), pp. 799–814, p. 810.
22. Ibid., p. 805.
23. Jill Crystal, *Oil and Politics in the Gulf: Rulers and Merchants in Kuwait and Qatar* (Cambridge: Cambridge University Press, 1990), p. 100.
24. Law No 32 of 1982 on the System of Civil Information. It will later become the Public Authority for Civil Information.
25. Boghardt, *Kuwait amid War*, p. 68.
26. Exceptions were made though for those employed in the military or *biduns* married to Kuwaitis as well as an enigmatic non-defined category of 'those who deserve the nationality' (*sic*).
27. In Kuwait, local supermarkets are called 'cooperatives' because they are collectively owned, in shares, by the male citizens of the residential area.
28. Human Rights Watch (HRW), *The Bedoons of Kuwait: 'Citizens without Citizenship'* (New York: Human Rights Watch, 1995), p. 10.
29. Mohammed Al-Fahed, himself a member of the police force, who completed his thesis on ways to improve the efficacy of the Kuwaiti police in 1989 does not mention any such policy nor possibly envision it in his criticisms or recommendations; 'An historical analysis of police in Kuwait: prospects for the future', PhD thesis, University of Exeter, Exeter (1989).
30. Longva, *Walls Built on Sand*, p. 73n.10.
31. Interview, Kuwait, 8 June 2008.
32. Figures quoted in the National Assembly session by the MP Ahmad al-Sa'dun, 'Al hakumat al kuwaitiyya tutalib bil tadqiq fi qanun 'al bidun' wa al nuwwab yatahhamun-ha bi-ikhtilaq al azma' ['The Kuwaiti government demands some more verifications for the law on the *biduns*; MPs accuse it of aggravating the crisis'] *Al-Khalij*, UAE, 15 August 2010.
33. According to the official institution set up in November 2010 to close the file on this particular type of 'illegal resident', the Central System to Resolve Illegal Residents' Status. Yet, some *bidun* activists estimate that the real number of *biduns* in Kuwait is as high as 240,000, reflecting the government's failure to update its statistics – based on the fact that many children of *biduns*, lacking proper birth certificates, do not appear in the figures. Interview, Kuwait, 26 April 2014.
34. Interview, Kuwait, 30 August 2007.
35. In an article dated 23 December 2007, 'Al-Barrak wa Al-May' yantaqadan al ta'amul 'ghayr al insani' ma' milaf 'al bidun' [Al-Barrak and Al-May' criticise the inhuman way in which the *bidun* file is handled],

in *Al-Qabas*, the MP Mussallam al-Barak demonstrates the extent to which the allegation that half of the armed *biduns* were traitors is baseless.

36. Interview, Kuwait, 27 May 2008.
37. Interview, Kuwait, 13 December 2005.
38. 'Bedoun to get driving licenses from Jan 6, 2007', *Arab Times*, 2 January 2007 and 'Bedoons fear driving licenses may be used against them', *Kuwait Times*, 11 January 2007.
39. Also referred in this book as 'Hasan Jawhar'.
40. Interview, Kuwait, 29 April 2014.
41. Also referred in this book as 'Salih Fadala'.
42. Government of Kuwait, 'Report on the Human Rights Watch report and response to its questions and inquiries', further to the 13 June 2011 Human Rights Watch, 'Prisoners of the past, Kuwaiti Bidun and the burden of statelessness', p. 6. Available at http://www.hrw.org/sites/default/files/reports/Response%20of%20the%20Kuwaiti%20Government%20to%20HRW_0.pdf (accessed 6 June 2017).
43. Ibid., p.11.
44. Official booklet handed over by the Central System to Resolve Illegal Residents' Status, Department of Public Relations and Media, *Illegal Residents: Facts and Data* (2013), pp. 41–2.
45. Ibid., p. 43.
46. Email exchange and phone conversations, 4 June 2014.
47. Interview, Kuwait, 8 June 2008.
48. 'Open letter to Mr David Blunkett, Head of the Home Office of the United Kingdom; a false passport is the only way to become a citizen', by the Harrow Kuwaiti Community Association, reproduced in *Kuwait Community News* 4 (May–June 2004), p. 5. A forged British or Canadian passport is reported to be valued at £5,000 or KD 2,500.
49. Interview, Kuwait, 5 March 2007.
50. Skype interview, 9 November 2014.
51. The day following the Comorian parliament's refusal to pass the text on 'the economic citizenship', the Kuwaiti ambassador in Cairo and non-resident ambassador to the Comoros, Dr. Rashid al-Hamad, stated that no Kuwaiti official had discussed with Comorian counterparts the status of the Kuwaiti *bidun*. Kuwait News Agency (KUNA), 'Stateless issue not raised in Kuwait–Comoros talks – Al-Hamad', 27 July 2008. Available at www.kuna.net.kw/ArticleDetails.aspx?language=en&id=1927583 (accessed 20 November 2014). During his visit to the Gulf the same year, the Minister of Foreign Affairs of the Comoros, Ahmed Ben Said Jaffar, stated that there had been no 'official' demand on the part of the Kuwaiti government regarding the *bidun* file, yet he was unofficially in touch with the Ministry of the Interior via the UAE.
52. Sheikh Muhammad al-Khalid al-Hamad had been again appointed Minister of the Interior and Deputy Prime Minister on 4 August 2013.

53. Muhammad al-Sharhan, 'Al-Jarrah to *Al-Jarida*: *Bidun* to the Comoros Islands', 9 November 2014, *Al-Jarida*. Available at http://m.aljarida.com/pages/news_more/2012693535 (accessed 12 March 2015).

54. See the interview: www.alaan.cc/pagedetails.asp?nid=188135&cid=30 (accessed 12 March 2015).

55. 'Still no place to call home for Arab Bidoon', *Agence France Presse*, 26 July 2008, according to which the deal was to naturalise 4,000 Gulf *biduns* (from the UAE, Kuwait and Saudi Arabia) for a sum of US$ 100 million; 'Human rights body to study the plight of 'stateless' tribes', *Arab News*, Riyadh, 29 July 2008; *Al-Anba'*, 31 October 2008. In the article 'Passeports comoriens en vente libre pour les sans-papiers du Golfe', *Le Monde*, 15 March 2009, the figures are 4,000 *biduns* from Kuwait, while the UAE would have already pledged an immediate payment of US$ 200 million. The deal included in addition to pledge from Gulf countries to invest in Comoros, every applicant for nationality should pay US$ 2,800 to develop the Comoran local economy.

56. Translation mine. A first National Commission was created by a decree on 10 January 2009, but never convened. It was replaced by a second one under a new abrogating decree in October 2011.

57. Lecture at the Institute for the Transregional Study of the Contemporary Middle East, North Africa, and Central Asia Brown Bag Lunch, 23 April 2013. See also Noora Lori, 'Unsettling state: non-citizens, state power and citizenship in the United Arab Emirates', PhD thesis, Johns Hopkins University (2013).

58. See the report of the visit by the then foreign affairs minister, Sheikh Muhammad Sabah al-Salim, in a US diplomatic cable: WikiLeaks, 'Kuwait FM in Comoros to discuss investment', 19 February 2008. Available at www.wikileaks.org/plusd/cables/08ANTANANARIVO136_a.html (accessed 12 March 2015).

59. For the complete history of the genesis of the economic citizenship, see Atossa A. Abrahamian, *The Cosmopolites: The Coming of the Global Citizen* (New York: Columbia Global Reports, 2015).

60. World Bank, 'Comoros'. Available at http://data.worldbank.org/country/comoros (accessed 22 December 2013).

61. Federal Bank of Commerce, 'Lettre du Président'. Available at www.bfcbanque.com/president_letter.php (accessed 12 March 2015).

62. 'Since its establishment in the Comoros in 2006, the holding has set up the Federal Bank of Commerce, created the newspaper *Albalad* and bought the Itsandra Hotel, which it is refurbishing. CGH estimates its currents investments in the country at €35 million'; Nations Unies, *Guide de l'investissement aux Comores: Opportunités et Conditions* 2011, p. 13 (translation mine). Available at http://unctad.org/fr/docs/diaepcb2011d4_fr.pdf (accessed 20 December 2013). The presentation brochure of the company, headed by Sheikh Sabah al-Jabir al-Mubarak, presents a broader list of companies, including media activities

(*Al-Waseet*, a classified newspaper; Concord Media, outdoor advertising; *Layalina*, a magazine that proved very successful in Kuwait; and Quadri, a printing house); telecommunications (Tawama); and construction (the Combined Group, a Kuwait-based enterprise that set up a Comorian subsidiary, the Comoro-Combined Group, in June 2009). Comoro Gulf Holding (CGH), 'From vision to decision'. Available at http://comoros-islands.com/images/articles/File/cgh%20profile.pdf (accessed 20 December 2013; no longer available).

63. WikiLeaks, 'Gulf investment group influence in the Comoros', 5 January 2009. Available at www.wikileaks.org/plusd/cables/09ANTANANARIVO2_a.html (accessed 12 March 2015).

64. See the evaluation of the business plan of the Jannet al Kamar project by an advisory firm; KPMG, 'Jannet al Kamar', Cormoros, January 2010. Available at http://www.consolatocomore.it/modulistica/Jannet_Al_Kamar_combined_FINAL_KPMG_for_CGH.pdf (accessed 30 August 2015).

65. According to a US-based journalist, Bashar Kiwan tried to no avail to lobby opposition MPs such as Musallam al-Barrak to rally the idea of 'economic citizenship'; Skype interview, 24 May 2015.

66. The involvement of Saudi Arabia remains unknown, though it is mentioned sometimes in the Comoros press.

67. According to the World Bank, the GDP was US\$ 595 million in 2012 and had been US\$ 46.5 million in 2007. World Bank, 'GDP (current US\$)'. Available at www.data.worldbank.org/indicator/NY.GDP.MKTP.CD?page=1 (accessed 20 December 2014).

68. Concerns surrounding the massive payments arise from the fact that they are not traceable: in a reply to parliamentary questions in June 2013, the finance minister, Mohamed Ali Soilih, distinguished between two parts of the bilateral agreement, one being subject to parliament's scrutiny, the other being in the exclusive purview of the government, as the agreement included a confidentiality clause.

69. 'The head of the household will receive a passport and nationality, both called "economic documents" [*ithbatan iqtisadian*], whereas the children will be granted an original Comorian passport and nationality'; al-Sharhan, 'Al-Jarrah to *Al-Jarida*'. This provision, together with the one that states that *bidun* committing crimes could be deported, seems to be quite new in relation to the assurance usually given to the Comorians, namely that the *bidun* would never be residents of the islands (and thus in contradiction of the spirit of the law in Annex 1).

70. 'Bataille autour de la citoyenneté', *L'Archipel* 242, 16 March 2012.

71. Al-Sharhan, 'Al-Jarrah to *Al-Jarida*'.

72. The conditions of the arrest of the *bidun* blogger Ahmed Abdul Khaleq on 22 May 2012, as he was summoned to regularise his legal status and accept a Comorian passport in exchange for his current ID, illustrated the same administrative ascribing of identity as the Kuwaiti *bidun* suffered from when they were obliged to carry identity documents stating 'illegal

resident'. See Human Rights Watch, 'UAE: free blogger activist', 28 May 2012. Available at www.hrw.org/news/2012/05/28/uae-free-blogger-acti vist (accessed 12 March 2015).

73. Kuwait News Agency (KUNA), 'Kuwaiti official in charge of illegal residents arrives in Dubai', 3 April 2012. Available at http://www.kuna. net.kw/ArticlePrintPage.aspx?id=2231582&language=en (accessed 12 March 2015).

74. It is better translated as identification card: the Arabic refers to a 'reference card' (*bitaqa muraja'a*), like in a 'reference number'.

75. Interview with *biduns*, 'Ardiyya, 27 May 2008.

76. Habib Toumi, 'Kuwaiti MPs want monthly minimum wage raised', *Gulf News*, 24 February 2013. Available at http://gulfnews.com/news/ gulf/kuwait/kuwait-mps-want-monthly-minimum-wage-raised-1. 1150274 (accessed 6 June 2017). Yet the bill did not seem to have been passed.

77. Nasra M. Shah, 'Kuwait revised labor laws: implications for national and foreign workers', *Asian and Pacific Migration Journal* 20/3–4 (2011), pp. 339–63, p. 356.

78. B. Izzak, 'Kuwait's MPs pass laws to regulate domestic workers and to establish human rights body', *Kuwait Times*, 18 June 2015. Available at http://news.kuwaittimes.net/pdf/2015/jun/18/kt.pdf (accessed 6 June 2017).

79. Interview, Kuwait, 3 June 2008.

80. Type of multi-task job consisting in carrying out petty tasks involving a ride (delivering post, getting documents stamped etc.).

81. The figures for the Ministry of Municipality are mentioned in an article of *Al-Jarida*, 25 April 2008, according to which the Executive Committee reported that 101 *biduns* were working in the Ministry of Municipality for a salary of KD 100, while a Kuwaiti would earn KD 1,500 for the same task.

82. Though cycles of detention in deportation centres and liberation due to their illegal status are reported by human rights organisations.

83. 'Al Shabab "al bidun"… min yamluk al hal?' [*Bidun* youth: who has the solution?], *Al-Qabas*, four-page special report, 4 November 2007. *Dira* is the Kuwaiti word to refer to the country or homeland.

84. Interview, Sulaibiyya, 14 May 2008.

85. 'Al-Qabas Al Shabab "al bidun"… min yamluk al hal?' [*Bidun* youth: who has the solution?], *Al-Qabas*, four-page special report, 4 November 2007.

86. 'Bedoons unveil new plan of action: "We will embarrass them in front of the world"', *Kuwait Times*, 25 January 2007.

87. 'Appointment of five General Directors and the Secretary of the Executive Committee for the Affairs of Illegal Residents', *Al-Shahid*, 26 October 2008. Available at http://alshahed.net/index.php?option= com_content&view=article&id=4068&catid=31:03&Itemid=419 (accessed 6 June 2017).

88. 'Brigadier General Othman urges officers of the Committee to deal with their interlocutors in a civilized way', *Al-Nahar*. Available at http://www. annaharkw.com/annahar/Article.aspx?id=156306 (accessed 6 June 2017).

89. 'Lying to get married: the maze of Bedoon marriage', *Kuwait Times*, 19 February 2007.

90. Salafi MP in Mansuriyya from 1985 continuously until 2006.

91. 'Kuwaiti MP seeks to quiz minister', *Khaleej Times*, Dubai, 5 January 2005.

92. Sami N. Khalifa al-Khaldi, 'Al "bidun" fil Kuwait … bayn al huquq al madaniyya wa al tajnis' [The *biduns* in Kuwait … between civil rights and naturalisation], unpublished manuscript (2007), p. 12.

93. Ghanim Al-Najjar, 'Qadiyya In'idam al jinsiyya fil Kuwait' [The issue of lacking nationality in Kuwait], unpublished manuscript (2005), p. 12.

94. Interviews in a lawyer's office, Kuwait City, 13 December 2005.

95. Interview, Kuwait City, 17 January 2007.

96. The upper figure was given by Dr. George Braidi, Chief of Mission, International Organization for Migration, during an interview, Salmiyya, 22 July 2007.

97. 'Masdar masu'ul lil-Wasat: 21 500 min 'al bidun' 'alay-him quyud amniyya tahul dun tajnis-him' (From a trusted source to *Al Wasat*: 21,500 *biduns* have criminal records hindering their naturalisation), *Al-Wasat*, Kuwait, 16 January 2008.

98. Interview, Kuwait, 29 April 2014.

99. Human Rights Watch, 'Prisoners of the past: Kuwaiti bidun and the burden of statelessness', 13 June 2011, p. 41. Available at http://www. hrw.org/sites/default/files/reports/kuwait0611WebInside.pdf (accessed 9 July 2015).

100. Home Office Country Information and Guidance, 'Kuwaiti Bidoon', 3 February 2014, p. 17.

101. Interview in Ahmadi, 22 April 2014.

102. Interviews, Sulaibiyya, 14 May 2008; 'Ardiyya, 27 May 2008.

103. For instance, thirty-six were employed on a contractual basis in the Ministry of Municipality; 'Bedoon employees should prove nationality', *Kuwait Times*, 28 April 2008.

104. An article in *Kuwait Times* dated 9 February 2008 and entitled 'Bedoons in the police' stated: 'The Ministry of the Interior sent a request to the fatwa and legislative department about the legitimacy of recruiting bedoons in the police department … Other committees in Saad Al-Abdullah Academy are now reviewing the files of bedoon men who want to enroll in the academy'. According to G29, a Kuwaiti civil society organisation devoted to solving the *bidun* issue, quoting Abdullah al-Tamimi, the head of the Parliamentary Committee for *Bidun* Affairs, approximately 350 are still in the police and 500–600 in the army: interview, Kuwait, 16 April 2014.

105. 'Ministry of Health plans to hire Bedoon nurses', *Kuwait Times*, 8 February 2008. Interview with *bidun* whose sister studied nursery hoping she will be hired: 'Ardiyya, 27 May 2008. This recruitment though was plagued with a scandal of abuse of the *bidun* nurses. A human rights activist explained in an article 'Campaign addresses the plight of the biduns', *Kuwait Times*, 21 October 2008: 'the government tricked them into registering for a nursing course, where they were forced to pay a KD 3,000 fee. After graduating from the three-year course, they are still unemployed as the public sector demands that their fathers are currently employed as military officers'. One of G29 campaigns, in 2013, focused on obtaining *bidun* employment in the Ministry of Health.

106. 'Civil Service commission sets criteria for Bedoon teachers', *Kuwait Times*, 10 September 2008.

107. 'Bedoon men as clerics', *Kuwait Times*, 18 March 2008.

108. Mehran Kamrava, 'The semi-formal sector and the Turkish political economy', *British Journal of Middle Eastern Studies* 31/1 (2004), pp. 63–87.

109. Sulayman N. Khalaf, 'Gulf societies and the image of unlimited good', *Dialectical Anthropology* 17/1 (March 1992), pp. 53–84.

110. This was the case, for instance, of the campaign of an independent *hadar* candidate, in the third constituency (see Map 5.1). Interview, Kuwait, 8 June 2008.

111. Shafeeq Ghabra, 'Palestinians in Kuwait: the family and the politics of survival', *Journal of Palestine Studies*, 17/2 (Winter 1988), pp. 62–83.

112. According to article 17 of the Passports Law No. 11 of 1962, a passport can be delivered for the non-Kuwaiti civil servants working for the state of Kuwait if they are endowed with a temporary mission outside of the country.

113. 'Government to provide Article 17 documents to "eligible" Bedoun; panel criticizes "Bedoun" as inhuman', *Arab Times*, 19 December 2006.

114. According to Brigadier Faisal al-Sinnin, Head of the Executive Committee, in *Al-Qabas*, 4 November 2007, the Education Fund concerned 16,000 students per year, spread across 60 private schools.

115. Interview, 'Ardiyya, 8 June 2008.

116. *Al-Tali'a*, Kuwait, 30 August 2003.

117. DVD, 'hilqat al bidun' [The *biduns*' circle], from 'The Hour of Truth', by Sheikh Nabil al-'Awadi, *Al Ra'i* TV and *Bidun* Popular Committee. See on Sheikh al-'Awadi's website, 'The Hour of Truth', dedicated to the *biduns'* situation on 25 November 2006: http://www.emanway.com/content/7283/ (accessed 30 September 2017).

118. See Sebastian Maisel, 'The construction of virtual identities: online tribalism in Saudi Arabia and beyond', in Sherin Hafez and Susan Slyomovics (eds), *Anthropology of the Middle East and North Africa: Into the*

New Millennium (Bloomington, IN: Indiana University Press, 2013), pp. 285–300.

119. 'Buramya calls for public protest', *Kuwait Times*, 28 October 2008; 'Bedoun protest for "basic rights"', *Arab Times*, 28 October 2008.

120. In 1981, the government increased the number of electoral districts from ten to 25, in a gesture largely seen as favouring peripheral tribal constituencies by inflating their electoral weight.

121. On 21 April 2017, he was released from jail after serving a two-year sentence for addressing critically the Emir in a speech pronounced in October 2012.

CHAPTER 5   THE EMERGING 'CAUSE' OF THE *BIDUNS*: SUPPORTERS AND OPPONENTS

1. Henri Queuille, 1886–1970, head of the French Cabinet under the Fourth Republic. Translation mine.

2. *Arab Times*, Kuwait, 14 February 2010.

3. One of my *bidun* informants even suggested I enquire into the similar pattern of promises made to the *biduns* by comparing the archives of the Kuwaiti papers and the present press. Interview, Kuwait, 8 June 2008.

4. *Al-Siyasa*, 3 January 1981.

5. Emmanuel Terray, 'Le travail des étrangers en situation irrégulière ou la délocalisation sur place', in Étienne Balibar, Monique Chemillier-Gendreau, Jacqueline Costa-Lascoux and Emmanuel Terray (eds), *Sans-papiers: l'archaïsme fatal* (Paris: La Découverte, 1999), pp. 9–34, pp. 18–32.

6. Michael Herb, 'A nation of bureaucrats: political participation and economic diversification in Kuwait and the United Arab Emirates', *International Journal of Middle East Studies* 41/3 (August 2009), pp. 375–95, p. 382.

7. The significance of the figures lies less in their accuracy than in the perception, by the interviewee, of the very scant interest for the issue of the *biduns*. Interview, Kuwait, 26 April 2008.

8. I am aware of the limitations of this expression but use it out of convenience for the episode of popular uprisings that engulfed the Arab world as of December 2010.

9. Youssef Ali, 'Statelessness and citizenship rights in the Middle East: the case of Kuwait', *DOMES: Digest of Middle East Studies* 15/1 (Spring 2006), pp. 62–76.

10. Ironically, Salih al-Fadala, the future head of the Central System to Resolve Illegal Residents' Status, is perceived as one of them: he was deputy (1981, 1985, 1992, 1999, 2003 and 2006) of 'Adiliyya. 'Bedoon sue ex-MP' *Kuwait Times*, 13 March 2008. See for instance, as public statement: 'Khalifa al-Khurafi: al bidun dukhala'... hadhihi wajhat nazari wa la tafasil' [Khalifa al-Khurafi: *Biduns* are intruders ... this is my point of view, full stop], *Haraka* 57/4, 26 February 2007. Khalifa is member of the municipal council.

11. Deputy (1992, 1996 Kaifan) General-Secretary of the Organisation of Arab cities since the establishment of its headquarters in Kuwait in 1967 and president of the Audit Office since March 2009.
12. Title of an article in *Al-Watan*, 5 September 1994.
13. Title of an article ibid.
14. Gérard Noiriel, *A quoi sert 'l'identité nationale'?* (Marseille: Agone, 2007), p. 73.
15. Abdullah al A. Al Tuwayjri, 'Kalimat al haqq bi hadha al rajul' [This man speaks rightly], *Al-Qabas*, 8 February 2008.
16. One of the most prominent members of the family was Khalid Sulayman al-'Adsani, the secretary of the Legislative Council of 1938 (*majlis tashri'i*) and author of 'Nisf 'am lil-hukm al niabi fil Kuwait' ['Half a Year of Parliamentary Rule in Kuwait'], 1947, unpublished manuscript. The family is well-known for its judges and conciliators.
17. See Nadia Eldemerdash 'Being and belonging in Kuwait: expatriates, stateless peoples, and the politics of citizenship', *Anthropology of the Middle East* 10/2 (Winter 2015), pp. 83–100. Eldemerdash argues that the building of the Kuwaiti identity is based on portraying migrants or stateless people as external threats, among other things.
18. She employed a very significant vocabulary to make this point, referring to the urban historic distinction overlapping the socio-economic divide: 'yakhaf yusharikun min nahyiat iqtisadiyya dakhil al sur' [They [*hadar*] are afraid that they [*biduns*] come to share in the economy 'within the wall'.]. Interview, Kuwait, 30 August 2007.
19. Farah Al-Nakib, 'Revisiting *hadar* and *badu* in Kuwait: citizenship, housing and the construction of a dichotomy', *International Journal of Middle East Studies* 46/1 (2014), pp. 5–30.
20. Mary A. Tétreault, *Stories of Democracy: Politics and Society in Contemporary Kuwait* (New York: Columbia University Press, 2000), p. 47.
21. Sandra Mantu, *Contingent Citizenship: the Law and Practice of Citizenship Deprivation in International, European and National Perspectives* (Leiden: Brill, 2015).
22. Ben Herzog, *Revoking Citizenship: Expatriation in America from the Colonial Era to the War on Terror* (New York: New York University Press, 2015).
23. Fatemah Alzubairi, 'Kuwait and Bahrain's anti-terrorism laws in comparative and international perspective', Masters degree dissertation, University of Toronto (2011), pp. 30–4.
24. Article 14 regarding termination of citizenship states that the termination may be decreed in the following cases: '1. If the person joins the military service of a foreign state and has remained despite being ordered to leave by Kuwait's government; 2. If the person worked to the benefit of a foreign country that is at war with Kuwait, or whose political relations with Kuwait have ended. 3. If the person's regular residence was abroad and he joined an organisation whose purpose is to undermine the social or economic system of Kuwait, or if [the Kuwaiti courts] convicted him of

crimes that the state decides affect his loyalty towards his country. In these cases, the citizenship can be terminated solely from the individual at fault, and not from those who earned it due to him.'

25. In 1997 they were allowed back to Kuwait and only one son of Abbas al-Muhri, Ahmad, refused the emir's grace and preferred to stay in London. Interview with a Shiite activist, Kuwait, 8 July 2007.

26. 'Khalid Khalaf has withdrawn his Kuwaiti nationality', *Al-Qabas*, 8 December 1980. 'Khalid Khalaf renounces his Iraqi nationality. His attempts to get his Kuwaiti nationality back are rejected', *Al-Qabas*, 15 December 1980.

27. Robert L. Jarman, *Sabah al-Salim Al-Sabah, Amir of Kuwait 1965–77: A Political Biography* (London: London Centre of Arab Studies, 2002), p. 49.

28. Ibid., p. 50.

29. He was MP in 2008 and February 2012, in the fifth constituency (See Map 5.1).

30. Herb, 'A nation of bureaucrats', p. 380.

31. Thomas H. Marshall, *Citizenship and Social Class and Other Essays* (Cambridge: Cambridge University Press, 1950).

32. Douglas E. Ashford, 'L'Etat Providence à travers l'étude comparative des institutions', *Revue Française de science politique* 39/3 (June 1989), pp. 276–95, p. 295.

33. Jill Crystal, 'Authoritarianism and its adversaries in the Arab world', *World Politics* 46/2 (January 1994), pp. 262–89, pp. 280–1.

34. Gerard Delanty, *Citizenship in a Global Age: Society, Culture, Politics* (Buckingham: Open University Press, 2002), p. 20.

35. Giacomo Luciani, 'Linking economic and political reform in the Middle East: the role of the bourgeoisie', in Oliver Schlumberger (ed.), *Debating Arab Authoritarianism: Dynamics and Durability in Nondemocratic Regimes* (Stanford, CA: Stanford University Press, 2007), pp. 161–76, p. 170.

36. Mays Abdel Aziz, 'Rethinking FDIs and development: the case of Kuwaiti investments in Jordan', Masters dissertation, Paris School of International Affairs, Paris (2014), pp. 29–34.

37. Anh N. Longva, 'Nationalism in pre-modern guise: the discourse on *hadar* and *badu* in Kuwait', *International Journal of Middle East Studies* 38/2 (2006), pp. 171–87, p. 186.

38. For instance the bitter rivalries between Muhammad al-Saqr and Jasim al-Khurafi, Speaker of the Parliament, on the one hand, and, on the other, Muhammad al-Saqr and Sheikh Nasir al-Muhammad Al-Sabah, Prime Minister, related to the acquisition of shares in each other's companies.

39. Andrew Linklater, 'Cosmopolitan citizenship', in Kimberley Hutchings and Roland Dannreuther (eds), *Cosmopolitan Citizenship* (New York: St Martin's Press, 1998), pp. 35–59; David Miller, 'Bounded citizenship', Ibid., pp. 60–82.

40. Danilo Zolo, *Cosmopolis: Prospects for World Government* (Cambridge: Polity, 1997), p. 137.

41. In that sense, they are either nostalgic of a regionally framed 'cosmopolitan citizenship' as developed in its historical sense by Sami Zubaida, 'Cosmopolitan citizenship in the Middle East', *Open Democracy*, 20 July 2010. Available at https://www.opendemocracy.net/sami-zubaida/cosmopolitan-citizenship-in-middle-east (accessed 6 June 2017).

42. Luciani, 'Linking economic and political reform', p. 171.

43. Such as the *niqab* covering women's faces, the high fertility rate, gender discrimination, sometimes even the wearing of the *shmakh* (red checked headwear) at other times than winter.

44. The number of constituencies was reduced from 25 (two MPs per constituency) to five (ten MPs per constituency) in 2006 in an attempt to reduce electoral corruption and vote-buying.

45. Ghassan Salamé, '"Strong" and "weak" states: a qualified return to the *muqaddimah*', in Giacomo Luciani (ed.), *The Arab State* (London: Routledge, 1990), pp. 29–64, p. 32.

46. Luciani, 'Linking economic and political reform', p. 170.

47. According to 'taklifa al ta'min al shamil al sihhi li-shakhs fil Kuwait' [quote for a personal complete health insurance in Kuwait]. It should be noted that the health system in Kuwait includes all the costs of treatments abroad for the patient and a relative.

48. These figures are all based on interviews with informed sources, in particular at the Kuwait Economic Society, Kuwait, 11 July 2007 or at the parliament, *Majlis al Umma*, 2 July 2007.

49. 'KD12.68bn revenues estimated in Kuwait budget for 2007/08', *Kuwait Times*, 28 January 2008. Compare with the 2006–7 revenues of KD8.32 billion. The article is based on official figures.

50. 'Record oil prices lift Kuwait budget surplus to KD11.4bn', *Kuwait Times*, 6 May 2008. The source for the article's figure is the National Bank of Kuwait's 'Economic brief on the oil market and budget developments'.

51. International Institute for Strategic Studies (IISS), *The Military Balance* (London: Routledge, 2006), p. 195.

52. Michael Herb, *The Wages of Oil: Parliaments and Economic Development in Kuwait and the UAE* (Ithaca, NY: Cornell University Press, 2014).

53. Herb, 'A nation of bureaucrats', p. 387.

54. Anh N. Longva, *Walls Built on Sand: Migration, Exclusion, and Society in Kuwait* (Boulder, CO: Westview Press, 1997), p. 47.

55. K. Celine, 'Kuwait living on its nerves', *MERIP Reports* 130 (February 1985), pp. 10–12, p. 12.

56. Interview, Kuwait, 11 July 2007.

57. 'Masdar masu'ul lil Wasat: 21,500 min 'al bidun' 'alay-him quyud amnia tahul dun tajnis-him' [From a trusted source to *A-Wasat*: 21,500 *biduns* have security files hindering their naturalisation], *Al-Wasat*, 16 January 2008.

58. 'Khalifa al-Khurafi', *Haraka*, 57/4, 26 February 2007.
59. For instance, a *bidun* artist, born *c.*1975, completed high school but could not continue his studies at the university before the invasion because 'at the time there were no private universities outside Kuwait University'; as for a *bidun* born in 1980, he had no chance of completing high school.
60. Interview with Faris al-Waqian, Kuwait, 17 January 2007. I did not obtain a copy of this study so that methodology and criteria adopted remain unknown.
61. *Kuwait Times*, 23 June 2007.
62. Pascal Ménoret, *Joyriding in Riyadh: Oil, Urbanism, and Road Revolt* (Cambridge: Cambridge University Press, 2014).
63. 'Tyre specialist held', *Kuwait Times*, 28 February 2007: 'Jahra Police arrested a bedoon in Taima while stealing the tyres of a car. During interrogation he confessed that he specialised in stealing tyres from several cars especially from the Fahahil area. Police filed a case and referred the man to the authorities.'
64. 'Gang smuggling stolen cars busted in Jahra, *Kuwait Times*, 20 March 2007. The article states that: 'On interrogation [the thefts] confessed to stealing 20 vehicles totally valued at KD 80,000, but detectives speculated the number to exceed 30'.
65. Zoltan Pall, 'Kuwaiti Salafism and its growing influence in the Levant', *Carnegie Endowment for International Peace*, 7 May 2014. Available at http://carnegieendowment.org/2014/05/07/kuwaiti-salafism-and-its-growing-influence-in-levant-pub-55514 (accessed 6 June 2017).
66. Al-Zarqawi in Iraq and the Saudi terrorist cell of 'the Al Haramayn Brigades'.
67. Falah A. al-Mdaires, *Islamic Extremism in Kuwait: From the Muslim Brotherhood to al-Qaeda and Other Islamist Political Groups* (London: Routledge, 2010), pp. 187–90.
68. The gun battles in Hawalli, Umm al Hayman, Salmiyya and Mubarak al Kabir's governorate between the Kuwaiti security forces and members of the organisation 'the Lions of the Peninsula Brigades' left four policemen dead and ten wounded. It also cost the lives of two civilian passersby and eight militants, including two Saudis, in addition to the head of the organisation, 'Amir Khulaif al-'Anazi, who died in custody.
69. The 37 included a woman, the wife of 'Amir al-'Anazi, Nuha al-'Anazi. The four other nationalities were as follows: two Jordanians, one Saudi, one Australian, one Somali.
70. 'Kuwait tries suspected Al-Qa'idah-linked militants', *Agence France Presse*, 24 May 2005. 'Kuwait prosecution demands death for 34 militants', *The Peninsula*, Doha, 12 June 2005. At a later session on 25 September 2005 the public prosecutor asked for the death penalty for all the defendants.
71. In addition to the death sentences, one person received a life sentence, 22 were condemned to prison sentences ranging from four months to 15 years, while the remaining seven were acquitted – Nuha al-'Anazi had meanwhile succumbed to cancer.

72. 'Six Qaeda-linked militants sentenced to death in Kuwait', *Khaleej Times*, Dubai, 27 December 2005; 'Planned attacks on US troops; court jails three Bedouns', *Arab Times*, 18 January 2007. Al-Mdaires (*Islamic Extremism in Kuwait*, p. 189) writes: 'a short time after this conviction [27 December 2005] the court changed the death sentences to life sentences for the six LPP [Lions of the Peninsula Phalanges, here translated as Lions of the Peninsula Brigades] members' with no further reference'.

73. The rest charged with involvement in the attack included five Saudis, three Pakistanis and another unnamed person at large. See 'Kuwait court frees 11 suspects in Shia mosque attack', *The New Arab*, 6 August 2015. Available at http://www.alaraby.co.uk/english/news/2015/8/6/kuwait-court-frees-11-suspects-in-shia-mosque-attack#sthash.000LkoRB.dpuf (accessed 6 June 2017).

74. '30 held in Kuwait as hunt for suspects continues' *Gulf News*, Dubai, 13 January 2005.

75. Graham E. Fuller and Rend R. Francke, *The Arab Shi'a: The Forgotten Muslims* (New York: Palgrave, 1999), p. 169.

76. Interview with a member of the *Bidun* Popular Committee, Kuwait, 28 July 2007.

77. Correspondence with the author, 8 March 2014.

78. Peter R. Neumann, 'Foreign fighter total in Syria/Iraq now exceeds 20,000; surpasses Afghanistan conflict in the 1980s', International Centre for the Study of Radicalisation and Political Violence, Department of War Studies, 26 January 2015. Available at http://icsr.info/2015/01/foreign-fighter-total-syriairaq-now-exceeds-20000-surpasses-afghanistan-conflict-1980s/ (accessed 26 August 2015).

79. Deputy of Hawalli in 1996, 1999, 2003 and 2006, then of the first constituency in 2008 and 2009. Labelled Shiite independent, he belonged to the Popular Bloc (*takattul al sha'abi*) in 1999 and 2003 but also ran together with the Shiite Islamists of the Imam Khomeini's Line in 2008, to whom, though usually independent, he is known to be close.

80. See the history of the committee at http://www.kna.kw/clt/run.asp?id=950#sthash.7Ure7FFf.dpbs (19 July 2005; no longer available). The current president of the Committee for Solving the Status of those of Undetermined Nationality (*lajna mu'alajat awda' ghayr muhaddidi al jinsiyya*) is also a Shiite, independent, Abdullah al-Tamimi, from the fifth constituency.

81. Liberal deputy, elected continuously ten times since 1975, first in Khaldiyya, after 2006 in the third constituency until February 2012. He later joined the opposition, boycotting the December 2012 and 2013 elections. He was speaker of the 1985 parliament, which was dissolved unconstitutionally, as well as of the first two post-invasion parliaments of 1992 and 1996.

82. Shiite deputy of Sharq between 1981 and 1999, defeated in 2003, elected in Rumaythiyya in 2006 and in the first constituency since then until

2013. Member of the Social Society for Culture in 1985, Popular Bloc in 1999 and then the Shiite Islamic National Alliance (*tahaluf al islami al watani*) movement affiliated with Al Da'wa movement, created in the aftermath of the Iranian revolution.

83. *Al-Anba'*, 31 October 1981.

84. 'Al-Sa'dun warns the Kuwaiti government against a time bomb "because of nationality"', *Al-Dustur*, Jordan, 17 February 1985.

85. 'The issue of nationality is like a bomb that could explode at any time: 65,000 persons consider themselves as Kuwaitis and 46,000 apply for the nationality' *Al-Qabas*, 14 February 1985.

86. Interview with an Imami Shiite activist, Kuwait, 16 January 2007, according to whom Adnan Abd al-Samad gave the fifth lecture at the *Masjid al Sha'ban*, which made his fame and helped his entry into Parliament in 1981.

87. 'Al haqiqa fi 'uyun shuhudi-ha' [The truth through the eyes of its witnesses], DVD, Kuwait Movies Corporation, 2007; given to me by Sheikha Fawzia, Kuwait, 30 August 2007.

88. Ahmad Lari, from the Islamic National Alliance, was deputy of Sharq in 2006, in the first constituency in 2008 and twice in 2012; defeated in 2013, he won in a by-election in 2014 in the second constituency. A former member of the Social Society for Culture, Abd al-Mushin Jamal was deputy of Mansuriyya in 1981 and 1992, then of the Shiite district of Da'iyya in 1999 and 2003. Yusuf Zalzala, a doctor of economics and seen as a moderate Shiite, defeated the members of the Islamic National Alliance in Sharq in 2003 and was elected in the first constituency in 2009, December 2012 and 2013.

89. The second constituency counted around 40,000 voters against, above 90,000 for the tribal fourth and fifth, 55,000 and 65,000 for the third (mixed) and first (roughly Shiite). 'Dalil al Nakhib fi dawa'ir al intikhabiyya' [Voter's guide into the electoral constituencies], *markaz al khalij al 'arabi lil-i'lan* (2008), p. 221.

90. Fuller and Francke, *The Arab Shi'a*, p. 171.

91. Vocal opposition deputy elected in 1996, 1999, 2003 and 2006 in Jlib al Shuyukh, and in 2008, 2009 and February 2012 in the fourth constituency; member of the Popular Bloc before he took the lead of the opposition against the government and then against the amendment to the electoral law, by an Emiri emergency decree, reducing the number of candidates voters can elect from one to four.

92. Deputy of Jahra al Jadida from 1999 to 2006; member of the Popular Bloc.

93. Elected in 2006 only, under the banner of the Islamic Constitutional Movement (*harakat al dusturiyya al islamiyya*), Kuwait branch of the Muslim Brotherhood and with the blessing of his tribe in the primary.

94. Elected as an 'independent' but close to the government in 2006 – with the endorsement of his tribe – and in the fifth constituency in 2008 and 2009 and then again in December 2012 and 2013.

95. Candidate of his tribe, he was elected as an 'independent' but was close to the government in 2003, 2006 and in the fifth constituency in 2009.

96. *'Al bidun yatahaddathun* [The *Biduns* Talk], DVD, Kuwait Society for Human Rights, 4 November 2006.

97. 'MP blasts government over inhumane bedoon policies', *Kuwait Times*, 1 December 2006.

98. 'Bedoons unveil new plan of action: "we will embarrass them in front of the world"', *Kuwait Times*, 25 January 2007.

99. 'Government not dragging feet on law to naturalise 2,000 Bedouns' *Arab Times*, 15 December 2007.

100. 'Solve nationality issue soon: Al-Enezi', *Kuwait Times*, 4 February 2008.

101. Al-Mdaires, *Islamic Extremism in Kuwait*, pp. 59–60.

102. Hakim al-Mutairi, 'tabi'un la *muwatinun*' [Subjects not citizens]. Available at www.ommah.net (accessed 19 July 2005; no longer available).

103. This is a prominent difference between Hakim al-Mutairi and other members of the Salafi Movement.

104. Inscribed in article 4 of the 1962 Kuwaiti constitution.

105. *Ra'awiyya* or subjection is drawn metaphorically from the Arabic root 'to graze'.

106. Online article by Hakim al-Mutairi 'The *bidun* issue and its legal solution'. Available at www.ommah.net (accessed 24 May 2005; no longer available).

107. Since the executive is not always bound by the legislature; separation of powers is a core demand of the *Hizb al Umma*, which asked, for instance, for a separate inquiry, reporting to the Ministry of Justice rather than the Ministry of the Interior, into the death in custody of 'Amir al-'Anazi, head of the Lions of the Peninsula.

108. Interview, Kuwait, 29 May 2008.

109. Carine Lahoud-Tatar, *Islam et politique au Koweït* (Paris: Presses Universitaires de France, 2011).

110. In 2003 'Awad Bard al-'Anazi, MP of Jahra al Jadida was as famous for his anti-Shiite stance and proposal to withdraw nationality from anybody speaking badly of the Companions of the Prophet as for his pro-*bidun* position.

111. Deputy of Da'iyya in 1992.

112. Dr. Sami N. Khalifa al-Khaldi is a political scientist teaching at the Arab Open University and author of the book *Ahzab al islamiyya al siyasiyya fil Kuwait: al shi'a, al ikhwan, al salaf* [Political Islamist Parties in Kuwait: Shiites, Muslim Brothers and Salafis] (Kuwait: Dar al naba' lil-nashar wa al tawzi', 1999). Dr. Salah al-Fadli was teaching in the Department of Philosophy of Kuwait University (KU) at the time of writing.

113. Dr. Sajid al-'Abdali, Mustafa al-Musawi, Fahd Rashid al-Mutairi, Hamad Naif al-'Anazi and Dr. Hasan Jawhar.
114. Interview, Kuwait, 26 April 2008.
115. Independent Islamist elected in 2008 only in the fourth constituency.
116. 'Mutairi more concerned to give Bedouns civil and human rights', *Arab Times*, 24 August 2008.
117. 'Islamist MP tables draft bill on granting Bedouns their "rights"', *Arab Times*, 20 July 2008.
118. 'Panel backs Bedoon rights'. *Kuwait Times*, 27 November 2007. Both MPs are from the Salafi Movement in Kuwait.
119. 'Government may pull nationality of 82 persons if records found shady', *Arab Times*, 7 November 2008.
120. 'Islamist MP tables draft bill'. Ahmad al-Mulaifi was, like Hasan Jawhar, deputy of Hawalli from 1996 till 2006 with the exception of 1999. He won the 2008 and December 2012 elections in the third constituency.
121. 'Al-Najjar: yajib 'adam tajahul al taqarir al dawlia 'ayn al Kuwait' [Al-Najjar: international reports on Kuwait should not be ignored], *Al-Qabas*, 9 April 2006.
122. 'Duwailah proposes "green card" for Bedoon, expats'. *Kuwait Times*, 23 September 2008. Like Husain al-Mutairi, he is an independent elected once in the fourth constituency in 2008.
123. Gary P. Freeman and David K. Hill, 'Disaggregating immigration policy: the politics of skilled labor recruitment in the US', in Michael P. Smith and Adrian Favell (eds), *The Human Face of Global Mobility: International Highly Skilled Migration in Europe, North America and the Asia-Pacific* (New Brunswick, NJ: Transaction Publishers, 2006), pp. 103–130.
124. Interview, Kuwait National Assembly, 17 July 2007.
125. Interview, Kuwait, 8 June 2008.
126. 'Draft bill calls on granting Bedouns their basic rights', *Arab Times*, 8 August 2008.
127. 'Yawm al shahid al bidun' [Day of the *Bidun* martyr], Kuwait Society for Human Rights (KSHR), *Bidun* Popular Committee, Kuwait Bar Association (KBA), 12 February 2007.
128. 'Dirasat hulul qadiyyat al bidun fi itar al mafahim al madaniyya wa tajarub al duwal al mujawara'. The following is based on an article published in *Al-Qabas* and posted online at http://www.kuwaitibedoons.com on 2 December 2006; transmitted to me by the author, Kuwait, 7 January 2007.
129. This is a bone of contention between Islamists: Shiites – Jawhar being a prominent example – are usually far more favourable to the rights of women than Sunnis, especially traditional Salafis.
130. 'Dr. Faris al-Waqian: al bidun juz' min al nasikh al Kuwaiti wa la-hum ishamat tarikhiyya kubra' [Dr. Faris al-Waqian: the *Biduns* are part of the

Kuwaiti social fabric; their historic contribution is considerable], *Haraka* 57/5, 26 February 2007.

131. 'Government to submit "solution" to Bedoons issue', *Kuwait Times*, 29 April 2007.

132. This section is based on research first into a file entitled 'Human rights in Kuwait' kept at the Institute of Arab and Islamic Studies, Arab World Documentation Unit, Library and Information Service, University of Exeter, and secondly, into the United Nations Human Rights Committee website, treaty bodies database, document with a special focus on the CCPR as of 1996, when Kuwait became a state-party. Available at http://www.ohchr.org (accessed 6 June 2017).

133. Amnesty International, *Iraq/Occupied Kuwait, Human Rights Violation since 2 August 1990*, December 1991.

134. Some *biduns* too received reparations for the war: 'Bedoons Get Compensation', *Kuwait Times*, 17 October 2005, '14,000 '*Bidun*' Benefit from 10 Million Dinars of Reparation', *Al-Siyasa*, 28 February 2006.

135. Chase, Brian, 'The problem of statelessness: the Gulf War, Palestinian evacuees and United States immigration policy', *Georgetown Immigration Law Journal*, 6 (1992), pp. 567–89, p. 570.

136. AI, 'Kuwait cases of "disappearance", incommunicado detention, torture, extrajudicial execution under martial law', October 1992. Available at https://www.amnesty.org/en/documents/mde17/002/1992/en/ (accessed 6 June 2017).

137. Human Rights Watch (HRW), *The Bedoons of Kuwait: 'Citizens without Citizenship'* (New York: Human Rights Watch, 1995).

138. See, for instance, the strong opposition to the 1980 amendment to the Nationality Law by the College of Law and Shari'a (Dr. Badria al-'Awadi), the open column 'The Bidun cancer' (by Musa'ad al-'Ajmi) and its reply 'Enough of this silence' (by Hasan al-'Anazi) in *Al-Qabas*, 19 and 13 November 1985 or the press statements by Dr. Ahmad al-Khatib in *Al-Tali'a*, 'We criticize the discrimination in the world … while we practice it against our people and the sons of our nation', 21 June 1986 (following the extension to 30 years of the period before which a naturalised person can vote).

139. 'Abd al-Aziz al-'Adsani demands a review of all nationality files: only 4 per cent of the *biduns* qualify for citizenship', *Al-Watan*, 5 September 1994.

140. 'UNHCR to report on "stateless" persons', *Arab Times*, 12 July 2007.

141. See United Nations Commission on Human Rights, 'Implementation of the programme of action for the third decade to combat racism and racial discrimination', Mission to Kuwait, 14 January 1997.

142. *Dishdasha* and *ghutra* are the white gown and headwear worn by Kuwaitis.

143. *Shmagh* is the red checked headwear worn throughout the year in Saudi Arabia and only in winter in Kuwait.

144. Maureen Lynch and Michael Scott, 'Statelessness: international blind spot linked to global concerns', report from Refugees International, 2 September 2009, p. 1.
145. Maureen Lynch and Patrick Barbieri, 'Kuwait: state of exclusion', report from Refugees International, 25 July 2007, p. 2.
146. 'Kuwait: council sets plan to solve Bedoun issue: stateless divided into three categories', *Arab Times*, 14 February 2010.
147. Claire Beaugrand, 'The return of the Bahraini exiles (2001–2006): the impact of the ostracization experience on the opposition's restructuring', paper delivered at 'Mapping Middle Eastern and North African Diasporas', British Society for Middle Eastern Studies Annual Conference, Leeds, July 2008.
148. Electronic correspondence, 14 August 2008.
149. Conversation with a *bidun* whose application for asylum was rejected in the UK, Ashford, Kent, December 2004.
150. Document handed over to the author, Kuwait, 15 December 2005.
151. When it was invaded on 2 August 1990 parliamentary life in Kuwait was going through a deep crisis: the members of the National Assembly dissolved in 1986 were hatching plans within the private framework of their *diwaniyya* and calling for the application of the constitution and new general elections. On 22 April 1990, Sheikh Jabir al-Ahmad, under pressure, issued a decree for the creation of a 'National Council', consisting of 50 elected and 25 appointed members, which compared poorly with the 50 elected members of the National Assembly as stated in the 1962 constitution.
152. 'Sheikh Jaber blasted over naturalisations', *Kuwait Times*, 7 January 2008.

CHAPTER 6   *SANS-PAPIERS* MOBILISATION IN AN OIL MONARCHY

1. Dr. Abd al-Hakim al-Fadli, member of a youth *bidun* movement called Al Muwatinun or Citizens. Most of the material in this chapter is drawn from a fieldwork trip to Kuwait in April 2014.
2. The name of the mosque refers to the Imam al-Sha'bi, from the early times of Islam.
3. Dominic Evans, '30 wounded in Kuwait protest on Friday', Reuters, 19 February 2011. Available at http://www.reuters.com/article/2011/02/19/us-kuwait-protest-casualties-idUSTRE71I0VS20110219 (accessed 6 June 2017).
4. In an article published in *Al-Siyasa* on 24 August 1997, the president of the Popular Committee in solidarity with the *bidun* denounced the decision of the KOC to evict the *biduns* from their houses in the absence of Parliament. 'Al-Qallaf: sharikat naft al Kuwait qarrarat tarad 'al bidun' min masakin-ha fi ghyiab majlis al Umma'. [Al-Qallaf: the Kuwait Oil Company decided to expel the *biduns* from its houses in the absence of parliament].

5. Interview, Ahmadi, 22 April 2014.

6. Interview, 17 April 2014.

7. Interview with a *bidun* activist, Kuwait, 19 April 2014.

8. Campaigning under the motto *Sakhr al watan* – Cry of the nation – or *katatib al bidun* – *biduns'* schools.

9. Johanna Siméant, *La Cause des sans-papiers* (Paris: Presses de Sciences-Po, 1998), p. 25.

10. Marie Brokstad Lund-Johansen, 'Fighting for citizenship in Kuwait', Masters degree dissertation, University of Oslo (2014), pp. 35–40.

11. In an article dated 3 September 1997 in *Al-Qabas* the head of the Public Authority for Housing Welfare (PAHW) stated that there was 'no intention to demolish the popular housing in Sulaibiyya and Tayma' ('la niyya li-hadm al buyut al sha'abiyya fil Sulaibiyya wa Tayma').

12. Interview, Kuwait, 29 April 2014.

13. Ibid., Kuwait, 27 April 2014.

14. Whose file is with the Martyrs' Desk (*maktab al shahid*) depended directly on the Emiri Diwan. See http://www.da.gov.kw/ara/martyrsbureau/martyrs-bureau.php (accessed 6 June 2017).

15. See http://www.bedoon.org/en/ (accessed 30 May 2016).

16. Interview with a member, Kuwait, 27 April 2014.

17. Interview, Kuwait, 27 April 2014.

18. Interview with a member, Kuwait, 17 April 2014.

19. Phone interview, London, 22 January 2014.

20. Ibid.

21. Interview with a *bidun* activist, member of *Muwatinun*, Jahra, 22 April 2014.

22. Interview, Kuwait, 27 April 2014.

23. Interview, 27 April 2014.

24. Engin F. Isin and Kim Rygiel, 'Abject spaces: frontiers, zones and camps', in Elizabeth Dauphinee and Cristina Masters (eds), *The Logics of Biopower and the War on Terror: Living, Dying, Surviving* (Basingstoke: Palgrave Macmillan, 2007), pp. 181–203, p. 183; Claire Beaugrand, 'Urban margins in Kuwait and Bahrain: decay, dispossession and politicization', *City* 18/6 (2014), pp. 735–45.

25. Interview with a *bidun* member of the G29, 19 April 2014.

26. Interviews with a member of the Kuwaiti *biduns'* Committee (*Lajna*) and *Muwatinun*, Kuwait, 17 and 25 April 2014.

27. Interview, Kuwait, 29 April 2014.

28. Interview, Ahmadi, 22 April 2014.

29. Interview, Kuwait, 25 April 2014.

30. Interview, Kuwait, 29 April 2014.

31. Sheikha al-Muhareb, one of the founders, for instance stated that she was involved in university elections, and later, while working at the hospital, lobbied for health reform. Interview, Kuwait, 16 April 2014.

32. See https://www.facebook.com/Group29q8/info?tab=page_info (accessed 30 May 2016).
33. Brokstad Lund-Johansen, 'Fighting for citizenship in Kuwait', p. 15.
34. Interview with a *bidun* member of G29, Kuwait, 19 April 2014.
35. Interview, Kuwait 16 April 2014.
36. Interview with Sheikha al-Muhareb, Group 29, Kuwait, 16 April 2014.
37. Interview with a G29 member, Kuwait, 16 April 2014.
38. Interview, Kuwait, 18 April 2014.
39. Ibid.
40. Siméant, *La Cause des sans-papiers*, p. 64: 'De fait, l'intérêt du modèle de la frustration relative appliqué à notre objet est de montrer que ce ne sont pas forcément les personnes les plus démunies de ressources, et donc les plus susceptibles a priori d'avoir accumulé des griefs, qui se mobilisent. Au contraire, la frustration peut être due à une augmentation des attentes sans que ces dernières ne soient satisfaites' (translation mine).
41. This is also true for activists who got involved in G29 but as a low-profile member: 'I am the only one who completed my studies among 11 children. I went to public school because my dad was in the police. In 1991, I was put in a low-level private school but since I took 93 per cent so I was admitted to study Computer Sciences in Bahrain University. It took me two years to get the travel permit. I obtained our bachelor in 2000: my *bidun* flatmate ranked first, I was third. In 2008, I resumed my studies when the Maastricht School of Management opened in Kuwait and took an MA in Business Strategy and Social Computing Strategy. I want to do a PhD now.' Interview, Kuwait, 14 April 2014.
42. Interview, Kuwait, 18 April 2014.
43. Brokstad Lund-Johansen, 'Fighting for citizenship in Kuwait', p. 81.
44. Interview, Kuwait, 18 April 2014.
45. Correspondence, 15 January 2014.
46. Dr. Abd al-Hakim al-Fadli was arrested and detained in the early stages of the protest in February 2011 as he was suspected of being the initiator of a Facebook call to demonstrate.
47. Correspondence, 3 March 2014.
48. See Bedoon Rights website. Available at http://www.bedoonrights.org/2014/03/27/statement-from-the-families-of-bedoon-detainees/ (accessed 6 June 2017).
49. Abd al-Hakim al-Fadli mentioned striking for 47 days.
50. Interview, Kuwait, 16 April 2014.
51. Muhammad al-Sharhan, 'Al-Jarrah to *Al-Jarida*: *biduns* to the Comoros islands', *Al-Jarida*. Available at http://m.aljarida.com/pages/news_more/2012693535 (accessed 9 July 2015).
52. The leaflet of the Central System, for instance, shows a picture of Tawakul Karman, the icon of the Yemeni revolution, co-recipient of the 2011 Nobel Prize for Peace, meeting with Salih al-Fadala.

53. Engin F. Isin and Greg M. Nielsen, 'Introduction' in Engin F. Isin and Greg M. Nielsen (eds), *Acts of Citizenship* (Chicago, IL: University of Chicago Press, 2008), p. 2.

54. Article 44 of the 1962 Constitution states that: 'Public meetings, processions and gatherings shall be permitted in accordance with the conditions and manner specified by law, provided that their purpose and means are peaceful and not contrary to morals.'

55. For want of the exact judgment, this information is based on two interviews that brought it to my attention: interview with Group 29, 16 April 2014 and with a Kuwaiti lawyer, Kuwait, 28 April 2014.

56. Siméant, *La Cause des sans-papiers*, p. 279.

57. In October 2012, for instance, the protest led to at least 25 arrests. See Amnesty International, 'Urgent action: Bidun arrested after peaceful protests', 9 October 2012. Available at http://www.amnestyusa.org/sites/default/files/uaa30712.pdf (accessed 9 July 2015). Amnesty International further states: 'The Kuwait Criminal Court this week reportedly postponed until 19 May 2013 the trial of 33 Bidun for participating in "unauthorised demonstrations" in December 2012'; 'Kuwait: small step forward for Bidun rights as 4,000 "foreigners" granted citizenship', 21 March 2013. Available at https://www.amnesty.org/en/latest/news/2013/03/kuwait-small-step-forward-for-bidun-rights-as-4000-foreigners-granted-citizenship/ (accessed 6 June 2017).

58. 'Under Article 2 of the decree establishing the Central System, this agency may take all executive measures to resolve the status of this class. In turn, the agency is in constant, active contact with all government bodies, agencies, public institutions, and competent security bodies, which provide the Central System with the data and information it needs, derived from these bodies' records and official files. These files indicate the true nationality of the person claiming to belong to this class'; Government of Kuwait's letter, 'Report on the Human Rights Watch Report and response to its questions and inquiries', 6, further to the 13 June 2011 Human Rights Watch publication, 'Prisoners of the past: Kuwaiti bidun and the burden of statelessness', 13 June 2011, p. 41. Available at http://www.hrw.org/sites/default/files/reports/kuwait0611WebInside.pdf (accessed 9 July 2015).

59. This included, in May 2010, journalist Muhammad Abd al-Qadir al-Jasim but also opposition activists who stormed Parliament in November 2011.

60. Interview, Kuwait, April 18, 2014.

61. Skype interview, 15 January 2014.

62. Ibid., 15 January 2014.

63. Skype interview, 15 January 2014.

64. Kristian Coates Ulrichsen, 'Politics and opposition in Kuwait: continuity and change', *Journal of Arabian Studies* 4/2 (2014) pp. 214–30; Mary A. Tétreault, 'Looking for revolution in Kuwait' *MERIP Reports* 281 (November 2012).

65. The opposition was first made up of anti-corruption youth movements, joined by parliamentary opponents to the prime minister, Sheikh Nasir al-Muhammad, who resigned in November 2011 further to the storming of parliament. After the Emiri decree reducing the number of candidates chosen by the voters from four to one, the opposition crystallised on this electoral reform and boycotted the December 2012 and July 2013 elections. In April 2014, the 'opposition' made of the Hadam, the Democratic and Civil Movement (former youth movement with religious leaning), the Popular Action Bloc, a tribal-populist parliamentary group created in the 1990s and turned into a Movement of Popular Action (Hashd), the political arm of the Muslim Brothers, the Islamic Constitutional Movement (ICM or Hadas), part of the Salafis of the *Hizb al Umma* and a leftist group (the Progressive Current), presented their National Project of Reform. The islamists (ICM and Salafis) ended their boycott before the elections held on 26 November 2016.

66. Interview with Tariq al-Mutairi, head of the Civil and Democratic Movement, one of the signatories to the National Reform project. This project proposed 36 constitutional amendments that would proclaim the sovereignty of the nation as source of all the powers and establish a full parliamentary regime whereby the elected government (*hukuma muntakhaba*) would be drawn from the elected majority in Parliament.

67. Abdullah AlKhonaini, 'Kuwaitis Debate Power over Citizenship', *The Arab Gulf Institute in Washington*, 17 May 2017. Available at http://www. agsiw.org/kuwaitis-debate-power-citizenship/ (accessed 12 June 2017).

68. Habib Toumi, 'Proposal to grant citizenship to Kuwait's stateless rejected', *Gulf News*, 11 April 2017. Available at http://gulfnews.com/ news/gulf/kuwait/proposal-to-grant-citizenship-to-kuwait-s-stateless-rejected-1.2009882 (accessed 12 June 2017).

69. For a full discussion of the requirements to obtain certificates, health and education rights, see Human Rights Committee, CCPR, 103rd session, Geneva, 17 October–4 November 2011, 'Consideration of reports submitted by states parties under article 40 of the Covenant – Kuwait, Addendum, Replies from the Government of Kuwait to the list of issues (CCPR/C/KWT/Q/2) to be taken up in connection with the consideration of the second periodic report of Kuwait (CCPR/C/KWT/2)', 29 July 2011, pp. 7–9; Government of Kuwait, 'Report on the Human Rights Watch report and response to its questions and inquiries', further to the 13 June 2011 Human Rights Watch, 'Prisoners of the past, Kuwaiti Bidun and the burden of statelessness'. Available at http://www.hrw.org/sites/default/ files/reports/Response%20of%20the%20Kuwaiti%20Government%20to %20HRW_0.pdf (accessed 6 June 2017).

70. 'Kuwait: council sets plan to solve Bedoun issue: stateless divided into three categories', *Arab Times*, 14 February 2010.

71. '80,000 of 110,000 Bedouns have no hope of getting Kuwaiti citizenship – they must correct their status: Maj-Gen Sheikh Mazen', *Arab Times*, 6 April 2016. Available at http://www.arabtimesonline.com/news/80000-110000-bedouns-no-hope-getting-kuwaiti-citizenship-must-correct-status-maj-gen-sheikh-mazen/ (accessed 12 June 2017).

72. '8,378 among illegal residents amended their status: CSRSIR', *Arab Times*, 26 May 2017. Available at http://www.arabtimesonline.com/news/8378-among-illegal-residents-amended-status-csrsir/ (accessed 12 June 2017).

73. United Nations High Commissioner for Refugees (UNHCR), 'Nationality and reduction of statelessness: international, regional and national perspectives', special issue of *Refugee Survey Quarterly* 25/3 (2006), p. 6; 'Citizenship law amendment backed', *Gulf Daily News*, 13 January 2014. Available at http://www.unhcr.org/cgi-bin/texis/vtx/refdaily?pass=52fc6fbd5&id=52d4d9dc5 (accessed 6 June 2017).

74. A Kuwaiti lawyer specialising in *bidun* cases estimated those who were not registered at maybe 10,000, to which should be added those who obtained forged passports in the 2000s and as such exited the registration system. Interview, 28 April 2014.

75. The conditions of the arrest of the *bidun* blogger Ahmed Abdul Khaleq on 22 May 2012, as he was summoned to regularise his legal status and accept a Comorian passport in exchange for his current ID, illustrated the same administrative ascribing of identity as the Kuwaiti *bidun* suffered when they were obliged to carry identity documents stating 'illegal resident'. See Human Rights Watch, 'UAE: free blogger activist', 28 May 2012. Available at www.hrw.org/news/2012/05/28/uae-free-blogger-activist (accessed 12 March 2015).

76. In April 2012, Salih Fadala toured the GCC countries, in particular the UAE and Saudi Arabia, and 'exchanged views over illegal residents'; Kuwait News Agency (KUNA), 'Kuwaiti official in charge of illegal residents arrives in Dubai', 3 April 2012. Available at http://www.kuna.net.kw/ArticlePrintPage.aspx?id=2231582&language = en (accessed 12 March 2015).

77. Habib Toumi 'Kuwait denies Comoros citizenship agreement', *Gulf News*, 20 June 2016. Available at http://gulfnews.com/news/gulf/kuwait/kuwait-denies-comoros-citizenship-agreement-1.1849101 (accessed 12 June 2017).

78. The departure of President Sambi as well as the disgracing of the project engineer, Bashar Kiwan. See Atossa Araxia Abrahamian *The Cosmopolites: The Coming of the Global Citizen* (New York: Columbia Global Reports, 2015).

79. The term 'economic citizenship' is in fact a misnomer, as citizenship implies a certain bond to a political community. The more correct word would be 'nationality' (the one used in Arabic, *jinisyya*), which tends sometimes to be equated with official documents, identification or passports.

80. Atossa Araxia Abrahamian, 'Special report: passports … for a price', *Reuters*, 12 February 2012. Available at http://www.reuters.com/article/ 2012/02/12/us-passport-idUSTRE81B05A20120212 (accessed 26 November 2014). Since 1984, St Kitts has offered so-called 'citizenship by investment' for a price of $250,000 (a cash donation for the pension of retired sugar workers) or $400,000 to buy approved real estate, while the Dominican Republic set the price at $75,000; Atossa Araxia Abrahamian, 'Passports for sale', *Dissent Magazine* (Fall 2014). Available at http://www.dissentmagazine.org/article/passports-for-sale (accessed 12 March 2015).

81. Austria requires an investment of at least US$10 million to grant citizenship.

82. Cypriot nationality is granted in return for mixed investments (€2 million) and a donation to a state fund (€0.5 million), direct investment or bank deposits of at least €5 million, a combination of the three, or three-year-long business activities in Cyprus, with the amount paid to the state fund, or in business services in the country reaching €500,000 annually. Special provision is made for those whose deposits with the Bank of Cyprus and the Popular Bank were harmed during the financial crisis of March 2013. In any case, the 'applicant must hold a permanent privately-owned residence in the Republic of Cyprus, the market value of which must be at least €500,000'. Information taken from now disabled Cypriot Ministry of the Interior link at www.moi.gov.cy/moi/crmd/crmd.nsf/All/ 0DFC69BD46FBCB89C2257BF800238148?OpenDocument&highlight= investment (accessed 20 December 2013).

83. *Comores-Droit*, 'La gestion opaque des fonds de la citoyenneté économique', 20 August 2013 (translation mine). Available at http:// www.comoresdroit.centerblog.net/1353-la-gestion-opaque-des-fonds-de- la-citoyennete-economique (accessed 6 January 2014).

84. See the KPMG document at the end of the article:, Peter Salisbury, 'Inside the $100 million scheme to send the Middle East's most unwanted people to Africa', *Vice News*, 19 November 2015. Available at https://news. vice.com/article/inside-the-100-million-scheme-to-send-the-middle- easts-most-unwanted-people-to-africa (accessed 5 December 2015).

85. See the debates surrounding the stripping of nationality for those with dual nationality involved in terrorist actions in France; *Le Monde*, 'Déchéance de la nationalité: attention, danger!', 2 December 2015. Available at http://mobile.lemonde.fr/idees/article/2015/12/02/ decheance-de-nationalite-attention-danger_4822246_3232.html (accessed 5 December 2015).

86. See new forms of selective migration policies: from Australia and the UK, countries that pioneered point-based migration policies, it even reached Saudi Arabia, which is famous for applying stringent rules for granting citizenship. In 2005, the Kingdom amended its Nationality Law and

naturalisation process, giving priority, on the basis of points, to the applicants holding doctorates in medicine, engineering and other sciences (13 and 10 points respectively out of the 23 required to qualify for the first stage of the process). 'Naif calls for study on providing citizenship to undocumented Saudis', *Arab News*, 9 April 2008. Ten points are also given for a ten-year continuous stay or family relations, and eight for a Masters degree.

87. Nicolas Jounin, *Chantier interdit au public. Enquête parmi les travailleurs du bâtiment* (Paris: La Découverte, 2008).

CONCLUSION

1. Embodied, in the Palestinian case, by the novel of Ghasan Kanafani, *Rijal fil shams*, (Beirut: Mu'asasat al abhath al 'arabiyya, 1963).
2. As I was finishing this book, I met by chance a British academic who had taught English in military institutions in Kuwait before the Iraqi invasion, recalling that the *biduns*, rather poor students, were incentivised to take English courses as part of the requirements to obtain nationality.
3. Further investigation is still needed to study the phenomenon of Shiite to Sunni conversions as well as trajectories of radicalisation in the 1990s–2000s under the work of religious charities in order to take the full measure of the phenomenon.
4. Anh N. Longva, 'Nationalism in pre-modern guise: the discourse on *hadar* and *badu* in Kuwait', *International Journal of Middle East Studies* 38/2 (2006), pp. 171–87, p. 184.

Select Bibliography

Ababsa, Miriam, Baudouin Dupret and Eric Denis (eds), *Popular Housing and Urban Land Tenure in the Middle East* (Cairo: American University in Cairo Press, 2012).

Abdel Aziz, Mays, 'Rethinking FDI's and development: the case of Kuwaiti investments in Jordan', Masters degree dissertation, Paris School of International Affairs, Paris (2014).

Abdul-Aziz, Moudi M., *King Abdul-Aziz and the Kuwait Conference, 1923–24* (London: Echoes, 1993).

Abrahamian, Atossa A., *The Cosmopolites: The Coming of the Global Citizen* (New York: Columbia Global Reports, 2015).

Abu Hakima, Ahmad M., *The Modern History of Kuwait, 1750–1965* (London: Luzac, 1983).

——, *Histoire moderne du Koweït, 1750–1965* (Unknown, 1992).

Alawadi, Abdulhadi M., 'Low- and middle-income housing in Kuwait', *Habitat International* 4/3 (1979), pp. 339–44.

Alessa, Shamlan Y., *The Manpower Problem in Kuwait* (London: Kegan Paul International, 1981).

Alghanim, Salwa, *The Reign of Mubarak Al-Sabah: Shaikh of Kuwait 1896–1915* (London: I.B.Tauris, 1998).

Alhajeri, Abdullah, 'Citizenship and political participation in the state of Kuwait: the case of National Assembly (1963–1996)', PhD thesis, Durham University (2004). Available at http://etheses.dur.ac.uk/1261/ (accessed 6 June 2017).

——, "The Bedoun': Kuwaitis without an Identity' *Middle Eastern Studies* 51/1 (2015), pp. 17–27.

Ali, Youssef, 'Statelessness and citizenship rights in the Middle East: the case of Kuwait', *DOMES: Digest of Middle East Studies* 15/1 (Spring 2006), pp. 62–76.

Alissa, Reem I.R., 'Building for oil: corporate colonialism, nationalism and urban modernity in Ahmadi, 1946–1992', PhD thesis, University of California, Berkeley (2012).

Al-Anezi, Rashid H., 'A study of the role of nationality in international law with special reference to the law and practice of Kuwait', PhD thesis, University of Cambridge, Cambridge (1989).

——, *Al bidun fil Kuwait [The Biduns in Kuwait]* (Kuwait: Dar al Qurtas, 1994).

——, *Al jinsiyya al kuwaitiyya [The Kuwaiti nationality]* 4th edn (Kuwait City: Kuwait University, 2005).

Altorki, Soraya, 'The concept and practice of citizenship in Saudi Arabia', in Suad Joseph (ed.), *Gender and citizenship in the Middle East* (Syracuse, NY: Syracuse University Press, 2000), pp. 215–36.

Alzubairi, Fatemah, 'Kuwait and Bahrain's anti-terrorism laws in comparative and international perspective', Masters degree dissertation, University of Toronto (2011).

Anonymous, 'The monthly record', *The Geographical Journal* 40/3 (1912), pp. 330–9.

Anonymous, 'Ard bila 'adala: qadiyyat al duktur Abdullah Fahd al-Nafisi. Lajnat al difa' 'ayn al huriat' [Land without Justice: the case of Dr. Abdullah Fahd al-Nafisi. Committee for the Defence of Liberties], booklet, unknown publisher (1979).

Anscombe, Frederick, 'An anational society: Eastern Arabia in the Ottoman period', in Madawi Al-Rasheed (ed.), *Transnational Connections and the Arab Gulf* (New York: Routledge, 2004), pp. 21–38.

Arendt, Hannah, *The Origins of Totalitarianism* [1968] (London: Harvest Book, Harcourt Inc., 2004).

Ashford, Douglas E., 'L'Etat Providence à travers l'étude comparative des institutions', *Revue Française de science politique* 39/3 (June 1989), pp. 276–95.

Ashkenazi, Touvia, 'The 'Anazah tribes', *Southwestern Journal of Anthropology* 4/2 (Summer 1948), pp. 222–39.

Asmar, Marwan R., 'The state and politics of migrant labour in Kuwait', PhD thesis, University of Leeds, Leeds (1990).

Assiri, Abdul-Reda, *Kuwait's Foreign Policy: City-State in World Politics* (Boulder, CO: Westview, 1990).

—— *The Government and Politics of Kuwait: Principles and Practices* (Kuwait: Al-Watan Printing Press, 1996).

Azoulay, Rivka and Claire Beaugrand, 'Limits of political clientelism: elites' struggles in Kuwait fragmenting politics', *Arabian Humanities* 4 (2015). Available at http://cy.revues.org/2827 (accessed 6 June 2017).

Balibar, Étienne, Monique Chemillier-Gendreau, Jacqueline Costa-Lascoux and Emmanuel Terray, *Sans-papiers: l'archaïsme fatal* (Paris: La Découverte, 1999).

Baram, Amatzia, 'Neo-tribalism in Iraq: Saddam Hussein's tribal policies 1991–96', *International Journal of Middle East Studies* 29/1 (February 1997), pp. 1–31.

Barbero, Iker, 'Expanding acts of citizenship: the struggles of Sinpapeles migrants', *Social and Legal Studies* 21/4 (2012), pp. 529–47.

Barron, Pierre, Anne Bory, Lucie Tourette, Sébastier Chauvin and Nicolas Jounin, *On bosse ici, on reste ici. La grève des sans-papiers: une aventure inédite* (Paris: La Découverte, 2011).

Beaugrand, Claire, 'Émergence de la "nationalité" et institutionnalisation des clivages sociaux au Koweït et au Bahreïn', *Chroniques yéménites* 14 (2007), pp. 89–107.

—— 'The return of the Bahraini exiles (2001–2006): the impact of the ostracization experience on the opposition's restructuring', paper delivered at 'Mapping Middle Eastern and North African Diasporas', British Society for Middle Eastern Studies Annual Conference, Leeds, July 2008.

—— 'Statelessness and transnationalism in Northern Arabia: *biduns* and state building in Kuwait, 1959–2009', PhD thesis, London School of Economics and Political Science (2011).

—— 'Urban margins in Kuwait and Bahrain: decay, dispossession and politicization', *City* 18/6 (2014), pp. 735–45.

—— 'Deconstructing minorities/majorities in parliamentary Gulf States (Kuwait and Bahrain)', *British Journal of Middle Eastern Studies* 43/2 (2016), pp. 234–49.

Beblawi, Hazem and Giacomo Luciani, *The Rentier State* (London: Croom Helm, 1987).

Birks, John S. and Clive A. Sinclair, *International Migration and Development in the Arab Region* (Geneva: International Labour Office, 1980).

—— Ian J. Seccombe and Clive A. Sinclair, 'Migrant workers in the Arab Gulf: the impact of declining oil revenues', *International Migration Review* 20/4 (1986), pp. 799–814.

Bloch, Alice and Sonia McKay, *Living on the Margins: Undocumented Migrants in a Global City* (Bristol: Policy Press, 2016).

Boghardt, Lori P., *Kuwait amid War, Peace and Revolution: 1979–1991 and New Challenges* (Basingstoke: Palgrave Macmillan, 2006).

Brokstad Lund-Johansen, Marie, 'Fighting for citizenship in Kuwait', Masters degree dissertation, University of Oslo (2014).

Brubaker, Rogers, *Citizenship and Nationhood in France and Germany* (Cambridge, MA: Harvard University Press, 1992).

Buchanan, Colin and Partners, *Studies for National Physical Plan for the State of Kuwait and Master Plan for the Urban Area, Second Report: The Short Term Plan* (Kuwait: Kuwait Municipality, 1971).

Bulut, Esra, '"Friends, Balkans, statesmen lend us your ears": the trans-state and state in links between Turkey and the Balkans', *Ethnopolitics* 5/3 (2006), pp. 309–26.

Butenschøn, Nils A., Uri Davis and Manuel S. Hassassian (eds), *Citizenship and the State in the Middle East: Approaches and Applications* (Syracuse, NY: Syracuse University Press, 2000).

Carens, Joseph H., 'The dispossessed? Democracy and irregular migration', paper presented at the annual meeting of the American Political Science Association, Chicago, 30 August 2007.

—— 'The rights of irregular migrants', *Ethics and International Affairs* 22 (2008), pp. 163–86.

Carey, Jane Perry C., 'Some aspects of statelessness since World War I', *The American Political Science Review* 40/1 (February 1946), pp. 113–23.

Castles, Stephen, 'Guestworkers in Europe; a resurrection?', *International Migration Review* 40/4 (Winter 2006), pp. 741–66.

Castles, Stephen and Mark J. Miller, *The Age of Migration: International Population Movements in the Modern World*, 2nd edn (Basingstoke: Macmillan, 1998).

Celine, K., 'Kuwait living on its nerves', *MERIP Reports* 130 (February 1985), pp. 10–2.

Central System to Resolve Illegal Residents' Status, Department of Public Relations and Media, *Illegal Residents: Facts and Data* (2013).

Chase, Brian, 'The problem of statelessness: the Gulf War, Palestinian evacuees and United States immigration policy', *Georgetown Immigration Law Journal* 6 (1992), pp. 567–89.

Chatty, Dawn, *From Camel to Truck: The Bedouin in the Modern World* (New York: Vantage Press, 1986).

—— (ed.), *Nomadic Societies in the Middle East and North Africa: Entering the 21st Century* (Leiden: Brill, 2006).

Coates Ulrichsen, Kristian, 'Politics and opposition in Kuwait: continuity and change', *Journal of Arabian Studies* 4/2 (2014) pp. 214–30.

Cole, Donald P. and Soraya Altorki, 'Production and trade in North Central Arabia: change and development in 'Unayzah', in Martha Mundy and Basim Musallam (eds), *The Transformation of Nomadic Society in the Arab East* (New York: Cambridge University Press, 2000), pp. 145–59.

Cordesman, Anthony H. and Khalid R. Al-Rodhan, *The Gulf Military Forces in an Era of Asymmetric War: Kuwait* (Washington, DC: for Strategic and International Studies, 2006).

Crystal, Jill, *Oil and Politics in the Gulf: Rulers and Merchants in Kuwait and Qatar* (Cambridge: Cambridge University Press, 1990).

—— *Kuwait: The Transformation of an Oil State* (Boulder, CO: Westview Press, 1992).

—— 'Authoritarianism and its adversaries in the Arab world', *World Politics* 46/2 (January 1994), pp. 262–89.

—— 'Civil society in the Arabian Gulf', in Augustus R. Norton (ed.), *Civil Society in the Middle East*, vol. 2 (Leiden: E.J. Brill, 1996), pp. 259–86.

—— 'Public order and authority: policing Kuwait', in Paul Dresch and James Piscatori (eds), *Monarchies and Nations: Globalisation and Identity in the Arab States of the Gulf* (London: I.B.Tauris, 2005), pp. 158–81.

Davidson, Christopher, *After the Sheikhs: The Coming Collapse of the Gulf Monarchies* (London: Hurst & Co., 2012).

Dazi-Heni, Fatiha, 'La diwaniyya: entre changement social et recompositions politiques au Koweït au cours de la décennie 1981–1992', PhD thesis, Institut d'Etudes Politiques, Paris (1992).

Al-Dekhayel, Abdulkarim, *Kuwait: Oil, State and Political Legitimation* (London: Ithaca Press, 1999).

Delanty, Gerard, *Citizenship in a Global Age: Society, Culture, Politics* (Buckingham: Open University Press, 2002).

Derrida, Jacques, *Marges de la philosophie* (Paris: Éditions de Minuit, 1972).

Dickson, Harold R.P., *The Arab of the Desert: A Glimpse into Badawin Life in Kuwait and Saudi Arabia* (London: George Allen & Unwin Ltd, 1949).

Dickson, Violet, *Forty Years in Kuwait* (London: Allen and Unwin, 1971).

Dresch, Paul, *Tribes, Government and History in Yemen* (Oxford: Clarendon Press, 1989).

—— 'Foreign matter: the place of strangers in Gulf society', in John W. Fox, Nada Mourtada-Sabbah and Mohammed al-Mutawa (eds), *Globalization and the Gulf* (London: Routledge, 2006), pp. 200–22.

Ebrahim, Mohammed H.S., 'Problems of nomad settlement in the Middle East with special reference to Saudi Arabia and the Haradh project', PhD thesis, Cornell University (1981).

Eldemerdash, Nadia, 'Being and Belonging in Kuwait: Expatriates, Stateless Peoples, and the Politics of Citizenship', *Anthropology of the Middle East*, 10/2 (winter 2015), pp. 83–100.

Al-Fahed, Mohammed, 'An historical analysis of police in Kuwait: prospects for the future', PhD thesis, University of Exeter, Exeter (1989).

Fandy, Mamoun, *Saudi Arabia and the Politics of Dissent* (London: Palgrave Macmillan, 1999).

Fahrmeir, Andreas, *Citizenship: The Rise and Fall of a Modern Concept* (New Haven, CT: Yale University Press, 2007).

Fernea, Robert A., 'State and tribe in Southern Iraq: the struggle for hegemony before the 1958 revolution', in Robert A. Fernea and William R. Louis (eds), *The Iraqi Revolution of 1958: the Old Social Classes Revisited* (London: I.B.Tauris, 1991), pp. 142–53.

Finnie, David H., *Shifting Lines in the Sand: Kuwait's Elusive Frontier with Iraq* (Cambridge, MA: Harvard University Press, 1992).

Freeman, Gary P. and David K. Hill, 'Disaggregating immigration policy: the politics of skilled labor recruitment in the US', in Michael P. Smith and Adrian Favell (eds), *The Human Face of Global Mobility: International Highly Skilled Migration in Europe, North America and the Asia-Pacific* (New Brunswick, NJ: Transaction Publishers, 2006), pp. 103–29.

Fuccaro, Nelida, 'Ethnicity, state formation, and conscription in postcolonial Iraq: the case of the Yazidi Kurds of Jabal Sinjar', *International Journal of Middle East Studies* 29/4 (1997), pp. 559–80.

Fuller, Graham E. and Rend R. Francke, *The Arab Shi'a: The Forgotten Muslims* (New York: Palgrave, 1999).

Gellner, Ernest, *Nations and Nationalism* (Oxford: Blackwell, 1983).

Ghabra, Shafeeq, 'Palestinians in Kuwait: the family and the politics of survival', *Journal of Palestine Studies*, 17/2 (Winter 1988), pp. 62–83.

—— 'Kuwait and the dynamics of socio-economic change', *Middle East Journal* 51/3 (Summer 1997), pp. 358–72.

Glubb, John. B., *Arabian Adventures: Ten Years of Joyful Service* (London: Cassell, 1978).

Al-Haddad, Mohammad S., 'The effect of detribalization and sedentarisation on the socio-economic structure of the tribes of the Arabian Peninsula: Ajman tribes as a case study', PhD thesis, University of Kansas (1981).

Halliday, Fred, *Arabia without Sultans* (London: Saqi Books, 1974).

—— *Nation and Religion in the Middle East* (London: Saqi Books, 2000).

—— *The Middle East in International Relations: Power, Politics and Ideology* (Cambridge: Cambridge University Press, 2005).

Al-Hatim, Musa G., *Tarikh al shurta fil Kuwait* [*History of the Police in Kuwait*] (Kuwait: Dar al Qurtas, 1999).

Herb, Michael, 'A nation of bureaucrats: political participation and economic diversification in Kuwait and the United Arab Emirates.', *International Journal of Middle East Studies* 41/3 (August 2009), pp. 375–95.

—— *The Wages of Oil: Parliaments and Economic Development in Kuwait and the UAE* (Ithaca, NY: Cornell University Press, 2014).

Hertog, Steffen, 'Arab Gulf states: an assessment of nationalisation policies', GLMM Research Paper, pp. 1–29 (2014).

Herzog, Ben, *Revoking Citizenship: Expatriation in America from the Colonial Era to the War on Terror* (New York: New York University Press, 2015).

Heydemann, Steven, 'Social pacts and the persistence of authoritarianism in the Middle East', in Oliver Schlumberger (ed.), *Debating Arab Authoritarianism: Dynamics and Durability in Nondemocratic Regimes* (Stanford, CA: Stanford University Press, 2007), pp. 21–38.

Hill, Allan, 'The population of Kuwait', *Geography* 54/1 (January 1969), pp. 84–8.

Human Rights Committee, CCPR, 103rd session, Geneva, 17 October– 4 November 2011, 'Consideration of reports submitted by States parties under article 40 of the Covenant – Kuwait, Addendum, Replies from the Government of Kuwait to the list of issues (CCPR/C/KWT/Q/2) to be taken up in connection with the consideration of the second periodic report of Kuwait (CCPR/C/KWT/2)', 29 July 2011.

Human Rights Watch (HRW), *The Bedoons of Kuwait: 'Citizens without Citizenship'* (New York: Human Rights Watch, 1995).

——, 'Prisoners of the past: Kuwaiti bidun and the burden of statelessness', 13 June 2011. With the reply of Government of Kuwait, 'Report on the Human Rights Watch report and response to its questions and inquiries', further to the 13 June 2011 Human Rights Watch, 'Prisoners of the Past, Kuwaiti Bidun and the Burden of Statelessness'.

——, *Kuwait: Promises Betrayed: Denial of Rights of Bidun, Women, and Freedom of Expression* (New York: Human Rights Watch, 2000).

Hutchings, Kimberley and Roland Dannreuther (eds), *Cosmopolitan Citizenship* (New York: St Martin's Press, 1998).

Hutt, Michael, *Unbecoming Citizens: Culture, Nationhood, and the Flight of Refugees from Bhutan* (Oxford: Oxford University Press, 2006).

Ibn Huthlayn, Sultan bin Kalid, *Tarikh qabilat al 'Ajman: dirasat watha'iqiyya [History of the Ajman tribe: Documentary Study]* (Kuwait: Manshurat zat al salasil, 1998).

Ingham, Bruce, 'Notes on the dialect of the Dhafir of north-eastern Arabia', *Bulletin of the School of Oriental and African Studies* 45/2 (1982), pp. 245–59.

——, *Bedouin of Northern Arabia: Traditions of the Al-Dhafir* (London: Kegan Paul International, 1986).

International Crisis Group (ICG), 'Bahrain's sectarian challenge', Middle East/ North Africa Report No. 40, 6 May 2005.

——, 'The Shiite question in Saudi Arabia', Middle East/North Africa Report No. 45, 19 September 2005.

International Institute for Strategic Studies (IISS), *The Military Balance* (London: Routledge, 1974–1987; 2003; 2006).

Isin, Engin F., *Citizens Without Frontiers* (London: Bloomsbury, 2012).

—— and Kim Rygiel, 'Abject spaces: frontiers, zones and camps', in Elizabeth Dauphinee and Cristina Masters (eds), *The Logics of Biopower and the War on Terror: Living, Dying, Surviving* (Basingstoke: Palgrave Macmillan, 2007), pp. 181–203.

—— and Greg M. Nielsen (eds), *Acts of Citizenship* (London: Zed Books, 2008).

Ismael, Jacqueline S., *Kuwait, Social Change in Historical Perspective* (Syracuse, NY: Syracuse University Press, 1982).

Jabar, Faleh A., 'Shaykhs and ideologues: detribalization and retribalization in Iraq, 1968–1998', *Middle East Report* 215 (Summer, 2000).

——, 'Sheikhs and ideologues: deconstruction and reconstruction of tribes under patrimonial totalitarianism in Iraq, 1968–1998', in Faleh A. Jabar and Hosham Dawod (eds), *Tribes and Power: Nationalism and Ethnicity in the Middle East* (London: Saqi Books, 2003), pp. 69–109.

Jamal, Abdulmohsen Y., 'Political opposition in Kuwait', PhD thesis, University of Sunderland (2003).

Jarman, Robert L., *Sabah al-Salim Al-Sabah, Amir of Kuwait 1965–77: A Political Biography* (London: London Centre of Arab Studies, 2002).

Joffé, George, 'Concepts of sovereignty in the Gulf Region', in Richard Schofield (ed.), *Territorial Foundations of the Gulf States* (London: UCL Press, 1994), pp. 78–93.

Joseph, Suad (ed.), *Gender and Citizenship in the Middle East* (Syracuse, NY: Syracuse University Press, 2000).

Jounin, Nicolas, *Chantier interdit au public. Enquête parmi les travailleurs du bâtiment* (Paris: La Découverte, 2008).

Joyce, Miriam, *Ruling Sheikhs and Her Majesty's Government, 1960–69* (London: Frank Cass, 2003).

Kanafani, Ghasan, *Rijal fil shams* (Beirut: Mu'asasat al abhath al 'arabiyya, 1963).

Kamrava, Mehran, 'The semi-formal sector and the Turkish political economy', *British Journal of Middle Eastern Studies* 31/1 (2004), pp. 63–87.

Kapiszewski, Andrzej, *Nationals and Expatriates: Population and Labour Dilemmas of the Gulf Cooperation Council States* (Reading: Ithaca Press, 2001).

—— 'Non-indigenous citizens and "stateless" residents in the Gulf monarchies', *Krakowskie Studia Miedzynarodowe* 2/6 (2005), pp. 61–78.

Al-Khaldi, Sami N. Khalifa, *Ahzab al islamiyya al siyasiyya fil Kuwait: al shi'a, al ikhwan, al salaf [Political Islamist Parties in Kuwait: Shiites, Muslim Brothers and Salafis]* (Kuwait: Dar al naba' lil nashar wa al tawzi', 1999).

—— 'Al "bidun" fil Kuwait ... bayn al huquq al madaniyya wa al tajnis' [The *biduns* in Kuwait ... between civil rights and naturalisation], unpublished manuscript (2007).

Khalaf, Sulayman N., 'Gulf societies and the image of unlimited good', *Dialectical Anthropology* 17/1 (March 1992), pp. 53–84.

Al-Khatib, Ahmad, *Al Kuwait: min al imara ilal dawla [Kuwait: from an Emirate to a State]* (Casablanca: Al markaz al thaqafi al 'arabi, 2007).

Al-Khonaini, Abdullah, 'Kuwaitis Debate Power over Citizenship', *The Arab Gulf Institute in Washington*, 17 May 2017. Available at http://www.agsiw. org/kuwaitis-debate-power-citizenship/ (accessed 12 June 2017).

Khoury, Philip S. and Joseph Kostiner (eds), *Tribes and State Formation in the Middle East* (Berkeley, CA: University of California Press, 1990).

Khuri, Fuad I., *Tribe and State in Bahrain: the Transformation of Social and Political Authority in an Arab State* (Chicago, IL: University of Chicago Press, 1980).

—— *Tents and Pyramids: Games and Ideologies in Arab Culture from Backgammon to Autocratic Rule* (London: Saqi Books, 1990).

—— *An Invitation to Laughter: A Lebanese Anthropologist in the Arab World* (Chicago, IL: University of Chicago Press, 2007).

Kiefe, Robert, *La nationalité des personnes dans l'Empire Britannique* (Paris: Rousseau & Cie, 1926).

Koopmans, Ruud, Paul Statham, Marco Guigni and Florence Passy, *Contested Citizenship Immigration and Cultural Diversity in Europe* (Minneapolis, MN: University of Minnesota Press, 2005).

Kostiner, Joseph, *The Making of Saudi Arabia, 1916–1936: From Chieftaincy to Monarchical State* (New York: Oxford University Press, 1993).

Kurpershoek, Marcek, *Arabia of the Bedouins*, trans. Paul Vincent (London: Saqi Books, 2001).

Lahoud-Tatar, Carine, *Islam et politique au Koweït* (Paris: Presses Universitaires de France, 2011).

Lawson, Fred H., 'Class and state in Kuwait', *MERIP Reports*, No. 132, 'The future of the Gulf' (May 1985), pp. 16–21.

Le Renard, Amélie, *Femmes et espaces publics en Arabie Saoudite* (Paris: Dalloz, 2011).

Linklater, Andrew, 'Cosmopolitan citizenship', in Kimberley Hutchings and Roland Dannreuther (eds), *Cosmopolitan Citizenship* (New York: St Martin's Press, 1998), pp. 35–59.

Lloyd, Martin, *The Passport: The History of Man's Most Travelled Document* (Stroud: Sutton Publishing Ltd, 2005).

Longva, Anh N. *Walls Built on Sand: Migration, Exclusion, and Society in Kuwait* (Boulder, CO: Westview Press, 1997).

—— 'Citizenship in the Gulf States: conceptualization and practice', in Nils A. Butenschøn, Uri Davis and Manuel S. Hassassian (eds), *Citizenship and the State in the Middle East: Approaches and Applications* (Syracuse, NY: Syracuse University Press, 2000), pp. 179–97.

—— 'Neither autocracy nor democracy but ethnocracy: citizens, expatriates and the socio-political system in Kuwait', in Paul Dresch and James Piscatori (eds), *Monarchies and Nations: Globalisation and Identity in the Arab States of the Gulf* (London: I.B.Tauris, 2005), pp. 114–35.

—— 'Nationalism in pre-modern guise: the discourse on *hadhar* and *badu* in Kuwait', *International Journal of Middle East Studies* 38/2 (2006), pp. 171–87.

Lori, Noora, 'Unsettling state: non-citizens, state power and citizenship in the United Arab Emirates', PhD thesis, Johns Hopkins University (2013).

Louër, Laurence, 'The political impact of labor migration in Bahrain', *City & Society* 20/1 (2008), pp. 32–53.

—— *Transnational Shia Politics: Religious and Political Networks in the Gulf* (London: Hurst & Co., 2008).

Luciani, Giacomo (ed.), *The Arab State* (London: Routledge, 1990).

—— 'Linking economic and political reform in the Middle East: the role of the bourgeoisie', in Oliver Schlumberger (ed.), *Debating Arab Authoritarianism: Dynamics and Durability in Nondemocratic Regimes* (Stanford, CA: Stanford University Press, 2007), pp. 161–76.

Mahdavi, Pardis, *Gridlock: Labor, Migration, and Human Trafficking in Dubai* (Stanford, CA: Stanford University Press, 2011).

Maisel, Sebastian, 'The Construction of Virtual Identities: Online Tribalism in Saudi Arabia and Beyond' in Sherin Hafez and Susan Slyomovics (eds) *Anthropology of the Middle East and North Africa: Into the New Millennium* (Bloomington: Indiana University Press, 2013), pp. 285–300.

Maktabi, Rania, 'The Gulf Crisis (1990–1991) and the Kuwaiti regime: legitimacy and stability in a rentier state', PhD thesis, Department of Political Science, University of Oslo (1992).

—— 'The politics of citizenship in Kuwait – membership and participation in a rentier state', paper presented at the 13th Annual National Political Science Conference, Hurdalsjoen, Oslo, 5–7 January 2005.

Al-Mansur, Abd al-Aziz. M., *Dirasat fi tarikh al Kuwait, al Kuwait wa 'ilaqat- ha bi 'Arabistan wa al Basra bayn 'am 1896–1915* [*Studies in Kuwait's History: Kuwait's Relationships with Arabistan and Basra between 1896 and 1915*] (unknown: Matba'a Labib, 1970).

Mantu, Sandra, *Contingent Citizenship: the Law and Practice of Citizenship Deprivation in International, European and National Perspectives* (Leiden: Brill, 2015).

Marshall, Thomas H., *Citizenship and Social Class and Other Essays* (Cambridge: Cambridge University Press, 1950).

Matthiesen, Toby, *The Other Saudis: Shiism, Dissent and Sectarianism* (Cambridge: Cambridge University Press, 2014).

McNevin, Anne, 'Political belonging in a neoliberal era: the struggle of the sans-papiers', *Citizenship Studies* 10/2 (2006), pp. 135–51.

—— 'Undocumented citizens? Shifting grounds of citizenship in Los Angeles', in Peter Nyers and Kim Rygiel (eds), *Citizenship, Migrant Activism and the Politics of Movement* (New York: Routledge, 2011), pp. 165–83.

Al-Mdaires, Falah A., *Islamic Extremism in Kuwait: From the Muslim Brotherhood to al-Qaeda and Other Islamist Political Groups* (London: Routledge, 2010).

Ménoret, Pascal, *Joyriding in Riyadh: Oil, Urbanism, and Road Revolt* (Cambridge: Cambridge University Press, 2014).

Miller, David, 'Bounded citizenship', in Kimberley Hutchings and Roland Dannreuther (eds), *Cosmopolitan Citizenship* (New York: St Martin's Press, 1998), pp. 60–82.

—— *Citizenship and National Identity* (Malden, MA; Oxford: Polity Press, 2000).

Moghadam, Amin, 'De l'Iran imaginé aux nouveaux foyers de l'Iran: pratiques et espaces transnationaux des Iraniens à Dubaï', *Arabian Humanities* 2 (2013). Available at http://cy.revues.org/2556 (accessed 29 November 2015).

Mohammed, Nadeya S.A., *Population and Development of the Arab Gulf States: the Case of Bahrain, Oman and Kuwait* (Aldershot: Ashgate, 2003).

Al-Moosa, Abdulrasoul A., 'Bedouin shanty settlements in Kuwait: a study in social geography', unpublished PhD thesis, SOAS, University of London (1976).

—— and Keith McLachlan, *Immigrant Labour in Kuwait* (London: Croom Helm, 1985).

Al-Mubaylish, Khalid, *Al 'awa'il al kuwaitiyya fil ahia' wa al qura al qadima* [*The Kuwaiti Families in the Old Neighbourhoods and Villages*] (Kuwait: Sharikat al siyasi lil nashr wa al tawzi', 2007).

Mueller, John H., *Koweit, Cadillac et Coca-Cola* (Paris: Robert Laffont, 1963).

Al-Mughni, Haya and Mary A. Tétreault, 'Citizenship, gender, and the politics of quasi-states', in Suad Joseph (ed.), *Gender and Citizenship in the Middle East* (Syracuse, NY: Syracuse University Press (2000), pp. 237–60.

Müller, C. Victor, *En Syrie avec les Bédouins. Les tribus du désert* (Paris: Ernest Leroux, 1931).

Al-Mutairi, Hakim, 'tabi'un la muwatinun' [Subjects not citizens]. Available at http://www.ommah.net (accessed 19 July 2005; no longer available).

Almutairi, Talal, 'Police-Community Relationship in Kuwait: Public Relations Perspective', PhD thesis, University of Stirling (2013).

Al-Nafisi, Abdullah F., *Kuwait: al ra'i al akhar* [*Kuwait: the Other Perspective*] (London: Ta-ha Advertising, 1987).

Al-Najjar, Ghanim, 'Challenges of security sector governance in Kuwait', Working Paper 142, Geneva Center for Democratic Control of Armed Forces (2004).

—— 'Qadiyya In'idam al jinsiyya fil Kuwait' [The issue of lacking nationality in Kuwait], unpublished manuscript (2005).

Nakash, Yitzhak, 'The conversion of Iraq's tribes to Shiism', *International Journal of Middle East Studies* 26/3 (1994), pp. 443–63.

Al-Nakib, Farah, 'The lost "two-thirds": Kuwait's territorial decline between 1913 and 1922', *Journal of Arabian Studies* 2/1 (2012), pp. 19–37.

—— 'Revisiting *hadhar* and *badu* in Kuwait: citizenship, housing and the construction of a dichotomy', *International Journal of Middle East Studies* 46/1 (2014), pp. 5–30.

—— *Kuwait Transformed: a History of Oil and Urban Life* (Stanford, CA: Stanford University Press, 2016).

Al-Nakib, Mai, '"The people are missing": Palestinians in Kuwait', *Deleuze Studies* 8/1 (2014), pp. 23–44.

Al-Naqeeb, Khaldoun H., *Society and State in the Gulf and Arab Peninsula: A Different Perspective*, trans. L.M. Kenny, amended Ibrahim Hayan (London: Routledge, 1990).

Al-Naqeeb, Sula, 'The question of citizenship and integration in Kuwait: looking at the Bidoun as a case study', MA thesis, School of Oriental and African Studies, London (2006).

Neumann, Peter R., 'Foreign fighter total in Syria/Iraq now exceeds 20,000; surpasses Afghanistan conflict in the 1980s', International Centre for the Study of Radicalisation and Political Violence, Department of War Studies, King's College, 26 January 2015. Available at http://icsr.info/2015/01/foreign-fighter-total-syriairaq-now-exceeds-20000-surpasses-afghanistan-conflict-1980s/ (accessed 6 June 2017).

Ngai, Mae M., *Impossible Subjects. Illegal Aliens and the making of Modern America* (Princeton, NJ: Princeton University Press, 2004).

—— 'No human being is illegal', *Women's Studies Quarterly* 34/3 and 4 (Fall–Winter, 2006), pp. 291–5.

Noiriel, Gérard, 'Du "patronage" au "paternalisme": la restructuration des formes de domination de la main-d'oeuvre ouvrière dans l'industrie métallurgique française', *Le Mouvement Social* 144 (1988), pp. 17–35.

—— *État, nation et immigration: vers une histoire du pouvoir* (Paris: Editions Belin, 2001).

—— *Réfugiés et sans-papiers: la République face au droit d'asile, XIXe–XXe siècle* (Paris: Hachette Littératures, 2006).

—— *A quoi sert 'l'identité nationale'?* (Marseille: Agone, 2007).

Nyers, Peter, 'The regularization of non-status immigrants in Canada: limits and prospects', *Canadian Review of Social Policy* 55 (2005), pp. 109–14.

Pall, Zoltan, 'Kuwaiti Salafism and its growing influence in the Levant', *Carnegie Endowment for International Peace*, 7 May 2014. Available at http://carnegieendowment.org/2014/05/07/kuwaiti-salafism-and-its-growing-influence-in-levant-pub-55514 (accessed 6 June 2017).

Panaspornprasit, Chookiat, *US–Kuwaiti Relations, 1961–1992: An Uneasy Relationship* (London: Routledge, 2005).

Partrick, Neil, 'Kuwait's foreign policy (1961–1977)', PhD thesis, London School of Economics and Political Science (2006).

Peterson, John E., 'The nature of succession in the Gulf', *Middle East Journal* 55/4 (2001), pp. 580–601.

Pratt, Martin and Janet A. Brown (eds), *Borderlands under Stress* (London: Kluwer Law International, 2000).

Al-Radihan, Khaled O., 'Nomadic sedentarisation with special reference to the Shararat of Northern Saudi Arabia', PhD thesis, University of Wales, Swansea (2001).

Ragazzi, Francesco, 'Post-territorial citizenship', in Sonika Gupta and Sudarsan Padmanabhan (eds), *Politics and Cosmopolitanism in a Global Age* (New Delhi: Routledge India, 2015), pp. 489–97.

Raswan, Carl R., 'Tribal areas and migration lines of the North Arabian Bedouins', *Geographical Review* 20/3 (1930), pp. 494–502.

Al-Rasheed, Madawi, *Politics in an Arabian Oasis: The Rashidis of Saudi Arabia* (London: I.B.Tauris, 1991).

—— 'Durable and Non-Durable Dynasties: The Rashidis and Sa'udis in Central Arabia' *British Journal of Middle Eastern Studies, 19/2* (1992), pp. 144–158.

—— 'Tribal Confederations and Emirates in Central Arabia' in Faleh A. Jabar & Hosham Dawod (eds), *Tribes and Power: Nationalism and Ethnicity in the Middle East* (London: Saqi Books, 2003), pp. 214–233.

—— (Ed.). *Kingdom without Borders: Saudi Political, Religious and Media Frontiers* (London: Hurst & Co., 2008).

—— and Robert Vitalis, *Counter-narratives: History, Contemporary Society, and Politics in Saudi Arabia and Yemen* (London: Palgrave Macmillan, 2004).

Al-Rawdan, Abd 'Awan, *Mawusu'at 'asha'ir al 'Iraq: tarikh, ansab, rijalat, ma'thir [Encyclopaedia of Iraq's Tribes: History, Genealogy, Men and Deeds]*, 2nd edn (Amman: Al Ahlia lil-nashr wa al tawzi', 2008).

Refugees International, 'Kuwait: state of exclusion', report by Maureen Lynch and Patrick Barbieri, 25 July 2007.

—— 'Statelessness: international blind spot linked to global concerns', report by Maureen Lynch, 2 September 2009.

Rodriguez, Robin M., *Migrants for Export: How the Philippine State Brokers Labor to the World* (Minneapolis, MN: University of Minnesota Press, 2010).

Ruhs, Martin and Philip Martin, 'Numbers vs. rights: trade-offs and guest worker programs', *International Migration Review* 42/1 (Spring 2008), pp. 249–65.

Rumaihi, Muhammad G., *Beyond Oil: Unity and Development in the Gulf* (London: Saqi Books, 1986).

Rush, Alan de Lacy, *Al-Sabah: History and Genealogy of Kuwait's Ruling Family, 1752–1987* (London: Ithaca, 1987).

Russell, Sharon S., 'International migration and political turmoil in the Middle East', *Population and Development Review* 18/4 (December 1992), pp. 719–27.

Al-Sabah, Su'ad M., *Saqr al khalij: Abdullah Mubarak Al-Sabah [The Falcon of the Gulf: Abdullah Mubarak Al-Sabah]*, 4th edn (Kuwait: Dar Su'ad Al-Sabah lil nashr wa al tawzi', 2000).

Sagher, Mostafa A., 'The impact of economic activities on the social and political structures of Kuwait (1896–1946)', PhD thesis, University of Durham (2004). Available at http://etheses.dur.ac.uk/1266/ (accessed 6 June 2017).

Al-Sa'ydan, Hamad M. *Al mawusu'a al kuwaitiyya al mukhtasara, [Small Encyclopaedia of Kuwait]*, vol. 2 (Kuwait: KFAS, 1992-3).

Salamé, Ghassan, '"Strong" and "weak" states: a qualified return to the *muqaddimah*', in Giacomo Luciani (ed.), *The Arab State* (London: Routledge, 1990), pp. 29–64.

Salih, Kamal Osman, 'The 1938 Kuwait Legislative Council', *Middle Eastern Studies* 28/1 (Jan. 1992), pp. 66 –100.

Schofield, Richard, *Kuwait and Iraq: Historical Claims and Territorial Disputes* (London: Royal Institute of International Affairs, 1991).

Scott, James C., *Seeing Like a State: How Certain Schemes to Improve the Human Condition Have Failed* (New Haven, CT: Yale University Press, 1998).

—— *The Art of Not Being Governed: an Anarchist History of Upland Southeast Asia* (New Haven, CT: Yale University Press, 2009).

Seale, Patrick, *The Struggle for Syria: a Study of Post-War Arab Politics 1945–1958* (London: I.B.Tauris, 1986).

Segal, Eran, 'Rulers and merchants in pre-oil Kuwait: the significance of palm dates', *British Journal of Middle Eastern Studies* 41/2 (2014), pp. 167–82.

Selvik, Kjetil, 'Elite rivalry in a semi-democracy: the Kuwaiti press scene', *Middle Eastern Studies* 47/3 (2011), pp. 477–96.

Shah, Nasra M., 'Kuwait revised labor laws: implications for national and foreign workers', *Asian and Pacific Migration Journal* 20/3–4 (2011), pp. 339–63.

—— 'Second generation non- nationals in Kuwait: Achievements, aspirations and plans', research paper, Kuwait Programme on Development, Governance and Globalisation in the Gulf States 32 (2013).

Siméant, Johanna, *La Cause des sans-papiers* (Paris: Presses de Sciences-Po, 1998).

Smith, Simon C., *Kuwait, 1950–1965: Britain, the Al-Sabah and Oil* (Oxford: Oxford University Press, 2000).

Tapper, Richard (ed.), *The Conflict of Tribe and State in Iran and Afghanistan* (London: Croom Helm, 1983).

Terray, Emmanuel, 'Le travail des étrangers en situation irrégulière ou la délocalisation sur place', in Étienne Balibar, Monique Chemillier-Gendreau, Jacqueline Costa-Lascoux and Emmanuel Terray (eds), *Sans-papiers: l'archaïsme fatal* (Paris: La Découverte, 1999), pp. 9–34.

Tétreault, Mary Ann, *Stories of Democracy: Politics and Society in Contemporary Kuwait* (New York: Columbia University Press, 2000).

—— 'Looking for revolution in Kuwait' *MERIP Reports* 281 (November 2012).

—— and Haya Al-Mughni, 'Modernization and its discontents: state and gender in Kuwait', *Middle East Journal* 49/3 (1995), pp. 403–17.

Torpey, John C., *The Invention of the Passport: Surveillance, Citizenship, and the State* (Cambridge: Cambridge University Press, 2000).

Toth, Anthony B., 'Tribes and tribulations: Bedouin losses in the Saudi and Iraqi Struggles over Kuwait's frontiers, 1921–1943', *British Journal of Middle Eastern Studies* 32/2 (2005), pp. 145–67.

Tripp, Charles, *A History of Iraq* (Cambridge: Cambridge University Press, 2007).

United Nations Commission on Human Rights, 'Implementation of the programme of action for the third decade to combat racism and racial discrimination', Mission to Kuwait, 14 January 1997.

United Nations High Commissioner for Refugees (UNHCR), 'Nationality and reduction of statelessness: international, regional and national perspectives', special issue of *Refugee Survey Quarterly* 25/3 (2006).

Villiers, Alan J., *Sons of Sinbad* (New York: Charles Scribner's Sons, 1940).

Vink, Maarten P., Arjan H. Schakel, David Reichel, Gerard-René de Groot and Ngo Chun Luk, 'The international diffusion of expatriate dual citizenship', paper presented at the 22nd International Conference of Europeanists, Paris, France, 8–10 July 2015.

Visser, Reidar, *Basra, the Failed Gulf State. Separatism and Nationalism in Southern Iraq* (Münster: LIT Verlag/Transaction Publishers, 2005).

Vora, Neha, *Impossible Citizens: Dubai's Indian Diaspora* (Durham, NC: Duke University Press, 2013).

Whitley, Andrew, 'Minorities and the stateless in Persian Gulf politics', *Survival* 35/4 (1993), pp. 28–50.

Wilkinson, John C., *Arabia's Frontiers: the Story of Britain's Boundary Drawing in the Desert* (London: I.B.Tauris, 1991).

—— 'Nomadic territory as a factor in defining Arabia's boundaries', in Martha Mundy and Basim Musallam (eds), *The Transformation of Nomadic Society in the Arab East* (New York: Cambridge University Press, 2000), pp. 44–62.

Williamson, John F., 'The political history of the Shammar Jarba tribe of al Jazirat 1800–1958', PhD thesis, Indiana University (1975).

World Health Organisation (WHO), *Weekly Epidemiological Record* (Geneva: World Health Organisation, 1967).

Zahlan, Rosemarie S., *The Origins of the Arab United Emirates: A Political and Social History of the Trucial States* (London: Macmillan, 1978).

—— 'King Abd al-Aziz's changing relationship with the Gulf States during the 1930s', in Timothy Niblock (ed.), *State, Society and Economy in Saudi Arabia* (London: Croom Helm (1982)), pp. 58–74.

Zdanowski, Jerzy, *Slavery in the Gulf in the First Half of the 20th Century: A Study Based on Records from the British Archives* (Warsaw: Askon, 2008).

Zolo, Danilo, *Cosmopolis: Prospects for World Government* (Cambridge: Polity, 1997).

Zubaida, Sami, 'Community, class and minorities in Iraqi politics', in Robert A. Fernea and William R. Louis (eds), *The Iraqi Revolution of 1958: The Old Social Classes Revisited* (London: I.B.Tauris, 1991), pp. 197–210.

—— 'Cosmopolitan citizenship in the Middle East', *Open Democracy*, 20 July 2010. Available at https://www.opendemocracy.net/sami-zubaida/cosmopolitan-citizenship-in-middle-east (accessed 6 June 2017).

NEWSPAPERS (INCLUDING *PRINT* ARCHIVES), NEWS OUTLETS, WEBSITES CITED

Newspapers and news agencies

Agence France Presse (France), https://www.afp.com/en/home

Al-Anba' (Kuwait), http://www.alanba.com.kw

Arab News (Saudi Arabia), http://www.arabnews.com

Arab Times (Kuwait), http://www.arabtimesonline.com

Al-Dustur (Jordan), http://www.addustour.com

BBC (UK), http://www.bbc.com/

Gulf News (UAE), http://gulfnews.com

Haraka (Kuwait), print magazine

Al-Jarida (Kuwait), http://m.aljarida.com

Al-Khalij (UAE), http://alkhaleej.ae

Khaleej Times (UAE) http://www.khaleejtimes.com

Kuwait News Agency (KUNA) (Kuwait), http://www.kuna.net.kw

Kuwait Times (Kuwait), http://news.kuwaittimes.net

Al-Masri al Yawm (Egypt), http://www.almasryalyoum.com

Le Monde (France), http://lemonde.fr

Al-Nahar (Kuwait), http://www.annaharkw.com

Al-'Arabi al jadid (UK), http://www.alaraby.co.uk

The Peninsula (Qatar), https://www.thepeninsulaqatar.com

Al-Qabas (Kuwait), http://alqabas.com

Al-Ra'i (Kuwait), http://www.alraimedia.com

Al-Ra'i al 'Amm (Kuwait), print version. Stopped in 2006.

Reuters (UK), http://www.reuters.com

Al-Shahid (Kuwait), http://alshahed.net

Al-Siyasa (Kuwait), http://al-seyassah.com
Al-Tali'a (Kuwait), http://altaleea.com
Al-Wasat (Kuwait), http://www.alwasat.com.kw
Al-Watan (Kuwait), http://alwatan.kuwait.tt

Other news outlets and blogs

Comores-Droit (Comoros Islands), http://www.comoresdroit.centerblog.net
Dissent Magazine (US), http://www.dissentmagazine.org
Vice News (US), http://news.vice.com
WikiLeaks, www.wikileaks.org

International organisation, academic and official websites

Amnesty International, https://www.amnesty.org
Central Statistical Bureau, Ministry of Planning, State of Kuwait, https://www.csb.gov.kw
Al-Diwan al-Amiri, State of Kuwait, http://www.da.gov.kw/eng/index.php
Human Rights Watch, http://hrw.org
Kuwait National Assembly, http://www.kna.kw/clt/index.asp
Kuwait Politics Database, http://www2.gsu.edu/~polmfh/database/database.htm
United Nations Conference on Trade and Development, http://unctad.org
United Nations Statistics Division (UNSD), UNdata, http://data.un.org/
World Bank, www.data.worldbank.org/

Index